Dr Hannah Durkin is a historian specialis... [in]
African diasporic art and culture. She hol[ds]...
from the University of Nottingham and a...
nalism from Leeds Trinity University. She has taught at Nottingham and
Newcastle universities, and recently served as a Guest Researcher at
Linnaeus University in Sweden. She is an advisor to the History Museum
of Mobile, which is working to memorialise the *Clotilda* survivors, and
was the keynote speaker at Africatown's 2021 Spirit of Our Ancestors
Festival founded by the Clotilda Descendants Association.

'Gripping . . . a remarkably wide-ranging book taking in everything from
science to soft drinks to show how slavery's insidious hand wormed its
way into the very fabric of American life' **The Times**

'Hannah Durkin lets the enslaved speak for themselves, and they tell a
story not only of unimaginable suffering but also of courage and survival'
Wall Street Journal

'A fascinating work of popular history' **Washington Post**

'Devastating and visceral . . . Durkin's exhaustive, exhilarating research
has created something new – something personal, emotional, almost
tangible – from the history of this collective trauma' **Literary Review**

'[*Survivors*] is without a doubt the best book ever written about that
voyage and its afterlives' **TLS**

'A very powerful piece of historical writing because it is both thorough
and reflective but also because it also provides us with a mirror to our
own times' **Aspects of History**

'Absorbing and affecting . . . Sheds new light on the experiences of female
survivors of the slave trade . . . The author captures the complexities of
the survivors' experiences' **Christian Science Monitor**

SURVIVORS

The Lost Stories of the Last Captives
of the Atlantic Slave Trade

HANNAH DURKIN

WILLIAM COLLINS

William Collins
An imprint of HarperCollins*Publishers*
1 London Bridge Street
London SE1 9GF

WilliamCollinsBooks.com

HarperCollins*Publishers*
Macken House
39/40 Mayor Street Upper
Dublin 1
D01 C9W8, Ireland

First published in Great Britain in 2024 by William Collins
This William Collins paperback edition published in 2025

1

ISBN 978-0-00-844658-1

Typeset in Perpetua MT Std by Jouve (UK), Milton Keynes

Printed and bound in Great Britain by CPI Group (UK) Ltd, Croydon

For the 110 and the 12.5 million

Contents

Maps

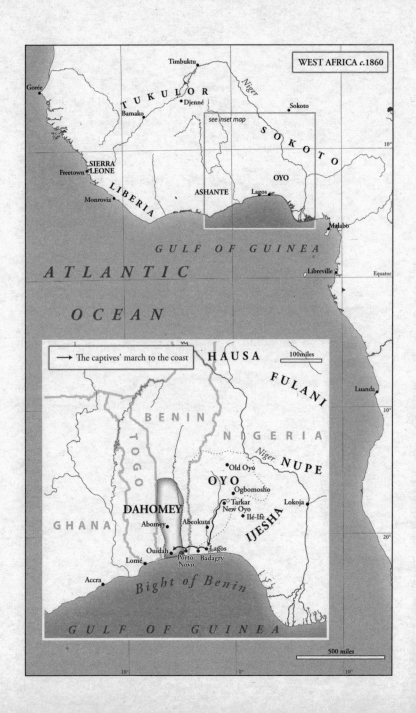

WEST AFRICA *c.*1860

Gorée

TUKULOR

Timbuktu

Niger

Djenné

Bamako

Sokoto

see inset map

SOKOTO

SIERRA
LEONE

Freetown

LIBERIA

OYO

Monrovia

ASHANTE

Lagos

Malabo

GULF OF GUINEA

ATLANTIC

Libreville

Equator

OCEAN

→ The captives' march to the coast

100miles

HAUSA

FULANI

BENIN

Luanda

TOGO

NIGERIA

NUPE

Niger

GHANA

Old Oyo

OYO

Ogbomosho

Lokoja

Tarkar
New Oyo

Ilé-Ifè

DAHOMEY

Abomey

Abeokuta

IJESHA

Ouidah

Lagos

Lomé

Porto-
Novo

Badagry

Accra

Bight of Benin

GULF OF GUINEA

500 miles

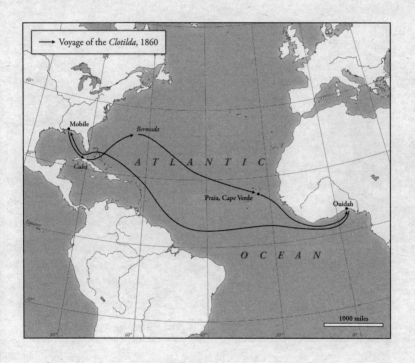

Voyage of the *Clotilda*, 1860

Mobile

Bermuda

Cuba

A T L A N T I C

Praia, Cape Verde

Ouidah

O C E A N

1000 miles

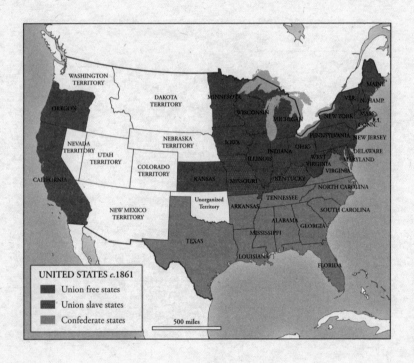

WASHINGTON
TERRITORY

OREGON

NEVADA
TERRITORY

UTAH
TERRITORY

CALIFORNIA

NEW MEXICO
TERRITORY

DAKOTA
TERRITORY

NEBRASKA
TERRITORY

COLORADO
TERRITORY

KANSAS

MINNESOTA

WISCONSIN

MICHIGAN

IOWA

ILLINOIS

INDIANA

MISSOURI

KENTUCKY

OHIO

WEST
VIRGINIA

VIRGINIA

MAINE

VER. N.HAMP.

NEW YORK MASS.
CONN. R.I.

PENNSYLVANIA
NEW JERSEY

DELAWARE
MARYLAND

NORTH CAROLINA

Unorganized
Territory

ARKANSAS

TEXAS

LOUISIANA

TENNESSEE

ALABAMA

MISSISSIPPI

SOUTH CAROLINA

GEORGIA

FLORIDA

UNITED STATES *c.*1861

Union free states

Union slave states

Confederate states

500 miles

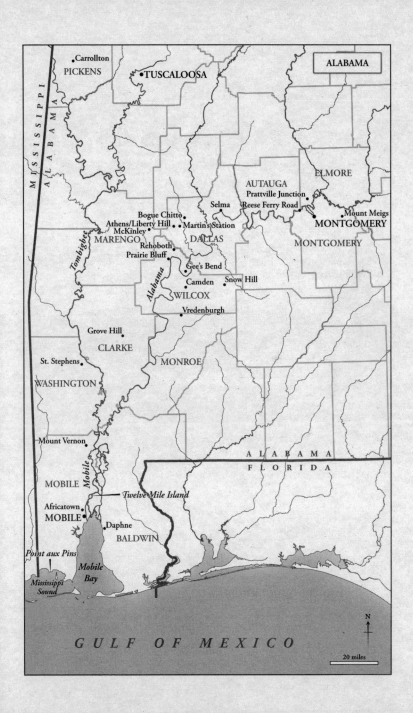

The *Clotilda* Africans

<u>Drowned at Sea</u>
Unnamed 16-year-old girl   (*c.*1844–*c.*26 May 1860)
Unnamed 14-year-old (?)
   girl   (*c.*1846–June/July 1860)
Unnamed Tarkar man   (*c.*1840–June/July 1860)
Unnamed Tarkar boy
   (cousin of Matilda McCrear)   (*c.*1850–June/July 1860)
Unnamed Tarkar boy   (*c.*1850–June/July 1860)
Unnamed young person   (*c.*1845–June/July 1860)
Unnamed young person   (*c.*1845–June/July 1860)

<u>Pickens County</u>
Miller   (*c.*1848–*c.*August 1860)
Sawnee   (*c.*1850–????)

<u>Baldwin County</u>
Judy Holland   (*c.*1830s–188? or 189?)
Mary Langman   (*c.*1842–188? or 189?)
Lucy Dick   (*c.*1830s–1 April 1897)
Malinda Evans   (*c.*1850–191?)
Napoleon Bonaparte   (*c.*1850–14 August 1918)
Amey Greenwood/Phillips   (*c.*1842–2 May 1923)

<u>Mobile County</u>
'Ecotah'   (*c.*1840s–December 1860)
'Bully'   (*c.*1849–186?)

Archie (Osia?) Thomas	(*c*.1840−186?)
Polly Shade	(*c*.1840−187?)
John 'Africa'[1]	(*c*.1840−187?)
Uriba/Areba (Yoruba?)/Nellie Riggins/Lillie Nichol	(*c*.1845−1883)
Peter Johnson	(*c*.1834−188? or 189?)
Bose/Rose/Rosallie (Bose/Abosede?) Allen	(*c*.1841−*c*.1891)
Jabez/Jaybee Shade	(*c*.1830s−189?)
Maggie/'America' Lewis	(*c*.1845−189?)
Josephine Lee	(*c*.1848−189?)
Gumpa/Peter Lee	(*c*.1840−11 September 1902)
Inez/Innie/Annie Keeby	(*c*.1850−25 July 1906)
Abila/Abile/Celia Lewis	(*c*.1845−14 November 1908)
Adisa Wiggfore/Bruntson	(*c*.1845−190?)
Samuel Johnson	(*c*.1840s−190?)
Anthony/Tony Thomas	(*c*.1840−13 January 1910)
Sampson Martin	(*c*.1850−191?)
Shamba Donizer/Wigfall	(*c*.1844−18 May 1912)
Orsey (Osia?)/Charles/ Charlie Lewis	(*c*.1840−29 November 1912)
Kanko/Lottie Dennison	(*c*.1847−16 April 1917)
Zuma/Juma/Juna/Kazooma/ Saner/Zinnia/Zimmer/ Zooma/Zunia 'Africa'/ Leveston/Livingston	(*c*.1845−*c*.1918 or 1919)
Omolabi/Katie Cooper	(*c*.1850−10 October 1919)
Abaché/Abacky/Abasha/ Absha/Clara Aunspaugh/ Turner	(*c*.1845−23 October 1919)
Polee/Pollee (Kupollee?) Allen	(*c*.1841−19 August 1922)
Alice/Allie Amstead/Williams (Parloro?)	(*c*.1855−19 November 1922)
Osia/Ossa Keeby/Oluwale	(*c*.1841−22 February 1923)

Kossula/Kazoola/Gossolaw/
   Cusolu/Consouloa/Cudjo
   Lewis   (*c*.1841−26 July 1935)[2]

<u>Washington County</u>
Appy/Abbie Royle   (*c*.1850−190?)

<u>Dallas/Marengo/Wilcox counties</u>
Cransy Creagher   (*c*.1840−May 1870)
Guy Crear   (*c*.1830s−187?)
Mahala King/Dansby   (*c*.1830s−187?)
May Haywood   (*c*.1846−187?)
Peggy Crear   (*c*.1840−187?)
York Bryant   (*c*.1830s−187?)
Gracie Crear   (*c* 1830−December 1879)
Pinkney Claiborne   (*c*.1830s−188? or 189?)
Pat Bradley   (*c*.1846−188? or 189?)
Cuffy/Cuffee Smith   (*c*.1830s−188? or 189?)
Jinnie/Jenny Smith   (*c*.1830s−188? or 189?)
Martha Martin   (*c*.1830s−188? or 189?)
Lucy Hunt   (*c*.1846−188? or 189?)
Ossa Hunt/Allen   (*c*.1845−189?)
Rachel Taylor   (*c*.1840s−190?)
Cresia Dansby   (*c*.1840−190?)
Hester Thompson   (*c*.1830s−190?)
Angus Cheney   (*c*.1840−190?)
Peter Johnson   (*c*.1830s−190?)
Peter Johnson[3]   (*c*.1848−188? or 189?)
Caroline Winters/Perkins   (*c*.1835−*c*.191?)
Yawith/William Smith   (*c*.1830s−12 October 1918)
Penelope/Penny Britton   (*c*.1830s−192?)
Sally Walker   (*c*.1850−192?)
Quilla Hutchinson/Clanton/
   Wheeler   (*c*.1848−9 June 1922)

Survivors

Alice Burns	(*c*.1850–19 June 1925)
Alex/Aleck Burns	(*c*.1840–29 April 1927)
Nathanael/Nathanial Brown	(*c*.1855–29 July 1930)
Dinah Jenkins/Miller	(*c*.1847–31 July 1933)
Redoshi/Sally Smith	(*c*.1848–13 December 1936)
Matilda McCrear	(*c*.1858–13 January 1940)

Autauga/Elmore/Montgomery counties

Liza 'Africa'	(*c*.1830s–187?)
Charlotte Knight	(*c*.1842–187?)
Joseph Porter	(*c*.1830s–188? or 189?)
Isaac Porter	(*c*.1830s–188? or 189?)
'Beast'/Bease/Beasey/Beasly Porter (Abdoul?)	(*c*.1830s–189?)
Reuben Given/Givens	(*c*.1848–189?)
Unsey/Unsie/Unsy/Euncie/Onecy/Owncey Sallie/Blair	(*c*.1843–190?)
Martha Porter	(*c*.1839–190?)
William/Willis 'Africa'/Sea/Seay	(*c*.1830s–29 June 1904)
Dinah/Bettie 'Africa'/Sea/Seay	(*c*.1840–1906)
Nannie Smith	(*c*.1856–22 April 1910)
Komo/Robert Jones	(*c*.1845–191?)
Tamer/Toma (Fatima?) Rose/Moor	(*c*.1845–191?)
Ella/Victoria Duncan	(*c*.1848–6 November 1918)
Sarah 'Africa'/Jones	(*c*.1830s–3 October 1920?)
Bougier/Bougia/Bulga/Bulger/Bulja 'Africa'/Moor/More	(*c*.1837–27 June 1930)

A Note on the Spelling of Names

Many of the *Clotilda* survivors were compelled to adopt European names in the United States. A few of them managed to retain their African names throughout their lives, and some of the others shared their original names with interviewers. Where possible, this book refers to the *Clotilda* survivors by their African names, or at least the closest possible approximation of their African names as transcribed by nineteenth- and twentieth-century writers. The text uses Osia Keeby's own spelling of his name, as documented by an early twentieth-century minister. A few other names (e.g. Adisa, Oluwale) are identifiable Yoruba names, but where a name remains open to interpretation (e.g. Zuma), the text uses historical spellings. Abaché and Kanko are spelled as they were transcribed by *Clotilda* artist and historian Emma Langdon Roche, but the text uses Zora Neale Hurston's 'Kossula' for the man also known as Cudjo Lewis rather than Roche's 'Kazoola' as there is no 'z' in the Yoruba alphabet. The names Redoshi and Yawith come from Alston Fitts's 1989 book *Selma: Queen City of the Blackbelt* and are unlikely to closely match the couple's real names. But as that is the only known record of their names, this text reproduces those spellings. The name Bougier is spelled as it was transcribed by a 1920s *Montgomery Advertiser* journalist who, despite preferring to nickname the woman 'ol' Bulja', stated that was her 'real African name'.[4]

1

Kidnap

The male and female warriors who stole the liberty and destroyed the town of those trafficked to the United States on the slave ship *Clotilda* launched their assault before dawn. The townsfolk were taken by surprise and had no time to defend themselves against the Fon warriors from the Kingdom of Dahomey, a regional power located in present-day Benin. Some of the town's farmers, keen to complete their labours before they grew hot on that day in mid-April 1860, had already left its parameters to plant their corn, groundnut and melon crops when the army struck. The warriors killed them all to ensure no one could warn their neighbours of an impending attack.[1]

Even at the end of his life, a medium-sized, balding man with a small goatee beard and a missing fingertip named Kossula, who became known in the United States as Cudjo Lewis, hugged his body in a self-protective gesture and rocked from side to side when recollecting the horrors of his kidnap. Warriors armed with machetes, axes, clubs and flintlock muskets smashed the gates. Shaven-headed women in brown-belted cotton tunics, knee-length shorts and white cotton skullcaps attacked the town first. Male soldiers formed a second line of attack that caught those who sought to flee.[2]

Tall, round-faced Abaché was woken by the sound of shouts and gunfire. The 15-year-old girl jumped out of bed and tried to run away but was quickly captured. '[W]hen we all asleep, they come and take us,' a small, slender-framed 12-year-old named Redoshi recalled at the end of her life. 'I ran, but they caught me. I fought, but they beat me. I didn't know what they was saying, but it wasn't good.'[3]

Alerted to the sounds of gunfire and screams, Kossula tried to flee into the woods. But there was no escape. The enemy had surrounded the town. After trying to bolt through its gates, Kossula slipped quietly into a neighbour's house and buried himself beneath a pile of rags. But women warriors soon wrenched him from his hiding place and took him hostage. Kossula wept at the memory. 'Oh, oh! I runnee this way to that gate, but they there. I runnee to another one, but they there, too. All eight gates they there. Them women, they very strong. I nineteen years old, but they too strong for me. They take me and tie me. I don't know where my people at. I never see them no more.'[4]

Those who were not captured were cut down by giant blades and shot with guns, and then decapitated. Kossula was forced to watch the brutal slaughter of his townsfolk. 'I see de people gittee kill so fast! De old ones dey try run 'way from de house but dey dead by de door, and de women soldiers got dey head. Oh, Lor!' he recalled, weeping and hugging his arms to his chest at the memory. Kossula begged in vain to be released to his mother and to be allowed to search for his family. 'I beg dem, please lemme go back to my mama, but dey don't pay whut I say no tenshun.'[5]

Many men and women died, and everyone else was taken prisoner. Two-year-old Matilda was kidnapped with her mother Gracie and four older siblings, but her father Osie and Kossula's parents Oluwale and Ny-fond-lo-loo were almost certainly among the dead. The town's ruler was brought before the King of Dahomey and beheaded with a giant, black-handled razor when he refused to leave the land of his ancestors as a prisoner. The ruler chose immediate death over enslavement.[6]

The *Clotilda* captives' hometown, Tarkar, was wiped off the face of the earth by Fon warriors that mid-April morning. It does not appear on any map. But Kossula placed it in the heart of Yorubaland, the cultural home of the Yoruba people that comprises present-day southwest Nigeria and extends into Benin and Togo. Two years before his death in 1935, Kossula told a Yoruba-speaking missionary that his home was about seventy-five miles from Abeokuta, the capital of Ogun State in southwest Nigeria and a metropolis whose population of 110,000 rivalled that of Chicago, then the United States' ninth biggest city. He also said that he traveled 'many times' to Ogbomosho, a city of 70,000 people in neighbouring Oyo State, and told *Harper's Monthly Magazine* that he and his wife Abile were from 'Whinney'. Historian Natalie S. Robertson has identified 'Whinney' as Owinni (Owini Hill), an elevation three miles northeast of the city of Oyo ('New Oyo') on the Oyo-Ogbomosho Road, a major trade route east of the Ogun River linking Oyo with Ogbomosho. Owini Hill is about sixty-five miles in a straight line from Abeokuta.[7]

The survivors of the *Clotilda* would always remember their lost homeland as a paradise. Bananas introduced long ago by eastern traders, pineapples recently imported from the west and enormous melons were so abundant in the forest around their town that the air was thick with the aroma. 'Know how we find de fruits? By de smell,' Kossula explained of the fruit-hunting game he played as a child. Polee Allen, a man whose round face was punctuated by deep-set, expressive eyes and whose hair and goatee beard stayed dark even into old age, told the same story of material abundance to his children. 'He would always tell us how the climate was so much warmer in Africa and the soil was so much better. He always said he wanted to go back so bad,' Polee's daughter Clara Eva Bell Allen Jones recalled. 'You know, I never seen my daddy ever eat a banana or an orange. I think maybe it made him homesick.'[8]

Kossula and Polee emphasized the 'superior quality' of their homes. The residents of Tarkar lived in eight-foot-tall round houses made from clay bricks 18 inches thick, with waterproof roofs constructed from palm poles bound together with cord and overlaid with earth and multiple layers of grass. Palm oil-fueled iron and earthenware lamps gave light to the windowless dwellings, whose walls were typically painted black or red. The bricks were impervious to fire, and a burnt-up roof could easily be rebuilt. The houses were built in circular formation so their inhabitants could more easily defend themselves against attack, a practice known as agbo-ile ('flock of houses'), although the town's chief source of protection was its eight manned gates.[9]

Abaché, who was kidnapped alongside her sister Uriba, described in a soft, slow voice and expressive physical gestures the peaceful home life she enjoyed as a child. Her townsfolk were highly successful farmers whose labours were aided by an incredibly fertile landscape. Abaché described how the men tilled the ground to plant yams and rice, and how the women traded harmoniously with other ethnic groups.[10]

'I lived in clean village; I was much happy. My people weave cloth from grass, bathe in sunshine and river, no fights, no beatings, no killings. We live together like one family,' Redoshi stressed of the childhood that brutally ended when she was 12 years old. As fellow child captive Kanko, a small, light-skinned woman with a facial mark on her right cheek, explained to her children and grandchildren, the standard of living was high in her hometown.[11]

Like other African societies, Tarkar was not beholden to capitalistic notions of land ownership that regarded land as a commodity. The town's ruler, whose name was recorded variously as 'Adbaku', 'Ibaku' and 'Akabana', and who Redoshi remembered as a 'good man', was the custodian of the land in his territory, which was communally owned and split between kinship groups and handed down the generations; each family had access to its own portion of land, which could not be sold.[12]

The planting season began in February. The town's menfolk cleared weeds from the rust-coloured earth with cutlasses, knives and axes. They used short-handled hoes and billhooks to prepare the ground for sowing; the earth was bountiful and there was no need for fertilizer or ploughs. They planted yams in February, and then corn, groundnuts and melons in April and May. After the

August harvest, they planted new crops of corn, beans and ground-nuts in September.[13]

Yams were a major crop in Oyo State, and Tarkar's yams grew so big – two feet long and six inches wide according to one regional eyewitness account – that no one could eat a single yam in one sitting. '[W]e go way, we come back, push, dig de dirt – great beeg yam like keg, nail keg. We cut off vine with little piece of yam and cover it up again. Another beeg yam. Whole family couldn't eat at one time. For seven years don't need no new seed, it keep making yams,' Kossula explained.[14]

Yams were eaten in manifold ways. Their starchy white flesh could be turned into elubo (yam flour), added to stews, roasted, or boiled and crushed with a pestle and mortar to make iyan (pounded yam). The townsfolk extracted palm oil and beer from the fruit of palm trees and wove cloth from its leaves. The women owned and raised cows, pigs, chickens, goats and sheep for a profit, which they kept in the inner court of their households to protect them from predators. 'Nobody ever go hungry. Nobody ever go cold,' Kossula declared of his homeland at the end of his life. Children like Polee learned a craft from their parent and became proficient in that skill by the age of 16. He and other male *Clotilda* survivors exiled to Mobile were so good at woodwork that they handmade toys for their children and built and sold their own furniture.[15]

Many women, such as the young, energetic Bougier, managed motherhood with trading responsibilities. The small, round-faced, dark-skinned woman had just become a mother for the third time in the spring of 1860, and she bound her baby in a sling on her back and balanced her wares on her head when heading to and from the vast market in Ogbomosho. As one nineteenth-century observer noted, selling crops at market was the 'peculiar privilege' of Yoruba-speaking women, whose trading activities meant they had inde-pendent incomes. Palm oil was their dominant item of trade.[16] Market trading was so important to Bougier's sense of self that she determinedly carried on the practice after her liberation from slavery. The long-lived woman traded twice a week in the heart of Alabama until she was physically unable to do so.

The items Bougier encountered for sale at Ogbomosho were far more luxurious than the foraged berries, plums and medicinal plants that were her only available wares in exile, however. A US missionary who went to Ogbomosho in the late 1850s likened the experience to visiting any 'Anglo-Saxon city'.[17] Products from around the world could be sourced at the marketplace, which was neatly divided into relevant sections according to the produce and merchandise for sale, and which attracted thousands of people at a time.

According to Kanko, the small, light-skinned girl with a facial mark on her right cheek, business was conducted with shillings, a silver coin linked to the British Empire that was used throughout present-day Nigeria. Cowries, porcelain-like seashells that served as religious objects among the Yoruba, were also exchanged as currency, and traders could be trusted to shop unsupervised and leave money for an item at the place of purchase for the seller to collect later. Stealing was so rare that possessions could be safely left in the open air. 'Suppose I had left my purse in town in the public square,' Kossula told an interviewer in the early twentieth century. 'To-day I have not the time to go for it – nor to-morrow – am I worried? No, for I know when I go I will find it where I left it. Could you do that in America?' Crimes were tried in open court, and the punishment for murder was execution by sword, regardless of the criminal's wealth and social status. As Polee explained of an offender's powerlessness to buy their way out of punishment, 'Money don't plea you there.'[18]

There were enslaved people in Tarkar, including criminals, people forced temporarily into bondage to pay off debts and people seized in warfare with other ethnic groups. Many were of northern, particularly Hausa, origin. But their experiences of bondage were vastly different from the chattel slavery practised in the Americas, which was centred on intense labour, reduced people to commodities that could be shipped around the world, and defined people in racialized terms so their enslaved status could be passed onto their children. Enslaved people in West Africa included soldiers and administrators, and social mobility was possible. Kossula's grandfather was an officer of and regular companion to his town's king who owned a large compound managed by several wives and enslaved labourers. Yet his idle threat to sell the son of a captive labourer to a Portuguese slave trader for tobacco when he disturbed him while sleeping highlights how much more greatly feared was sale overseas than enslavement at home.[19]

When Kossula was nearly 15, he was thrilled to receive military training like his older brothers. The teenager spent whole nights in the woods being taught how to track and hunt deer, buffalo, elephants, lions and leopards, how to stalk silently through the forest and conceal himself, how to leave a trail for others to follow and how to make camp. Kossula learned how to shoot arrows and throw spears, and how to beat the drum that accompanied the town's war song. Kossula spent five years learning military skills that he understood were solely for defensive purposes. The community's economy was centred around agriculture, and the king had no plans to make war, but his people needed to be ready to defend their town against attack.[20]

While the boys learned to hunt and fight, little Kanko was taken by her mother Conco to gather medicinal plants and to learn the curative properties of the world around her. Although there were professional medical practitioners known as onisegun in Yoruba-speaking societies, herbal knowledge was a collective enterprise. After a day spent gathering curative herbs, Kanko resisted her mother's call to go home and hid behind what she thought were beautiful large leaves for treating headaches. When she fetched Conco to point them out, the leaves came alive: the pair were face-to-face with a giant snake. Kanko's horrified mother grabbed her child sharply by the hand when she saw the danger. Kanko felt her feet leave the earth as Conco pulled her to safety. Hunters sought out the snake, but it had disappeared.[21]

Conco could not protect her daughter from all the dangers of her environment, however. Nearly seventy years after Kanko's death, her granddaughter Mable Dennison attempted to document the circumstances of her kidnap. Even though Kanko was ripped from her homeland while still a child, she understood that slave traffickers deliberately stoked inter- and intra-ethnic divisions to create prisoners of war who could be shipped and sold overseas. As Mable explained, 'she had learned that once these slave ships arrived on the African coast, there was little trouble in procuring a cargo of slaves for it had long been a part of the traders' policy to instigate tribes against each other and in this manner keep the markets stocked . . . there had been numerous wars with foreign countries as well as in the surrounding nations and also between tribes within her country. It seemed as though some kind of war would go on for years.'[22]

Mable suggested that Kanko was from the 'town' of Dahomey, and that she was kidnapped by slave traders while performing an errand for her mother at a local store. It's likely that Kanko was from the same Yoruba-speaking town as Kossula. Like Polee, who never discussed the circumstances of his capture, Kanko probably concocted a tale of isolated kidnap because the destruction of her hometown and murder of her family were too harrowing to recall. Kanko also told her descendants that she and Kossula were cousins, indicating that they grew up together in Tarkar, and, as Mable remembered, 'there was a close relationship in their ways and customs.'[23]

The mid-nineteenth century was a particularly dangerous time for Yoruba speakers such as Kanko and Kossula. 'Yoruba' was historically an umbrella term applied by missionaries who began arriving in the region after 1840 to different ethnic groups that shared the language and culture of the Oyo Empire of present-day western Nigeria and eastern Benin. The empire's origins stretched back to the twelfth century and centred on the city-state of Oyo ('Old Oyo'), which was about one hundred miles north of New Oyo and Tarkar. Its highly organized and commanding cavalry enabled it to capture surrounding territories and expand from a minor state to the most powerful empire in present-day southwest Nigeria by the end of the sixteenth century.

While they were connected by common myths of origin and even shared a spiritual capital in the ancient city of Ilé-Ifè, 50 miles southeast of Old Oyo in neighbouring Osun State, each Yoruba group represented a largely autonomous city-state with its own industries and trade networks and its own oba (king), who ruled a capital town and its surrounding territories. For hundreds of years, the communities lived in relative peace with each other until invasions from Oyo's Muslim Fulani neighbours to the north, the rise of Dahomey and conflicts between the empire's alaafin (emperor) and his advisers combined with popular resistance to an increasingly authoritarian aristocracy undermined its stability from the 1780s onwards. Yoruba-speaking territories lost vital trade routes and were plunged into competition and civil warfare for the next eight decades, and Yoruba-speaking captives became victims of the transatlantic slave trade.

The gradual disintegration of the Oyo Empire, followed by its total collapse in the 1830s, changed the balance of power in the region. Dahomey's capital Abomey was no longer vulnerable to assault by Oyo, and Yoruba-speaking communities east, northeast and southeast of Abomey that previously were shielded by their association with Oyo were now open to attack by newly empowered Dahomey. Dahomey's king, Ghezo, recognized the southeastern region around Abeokuta – a city recently founded by the Egba people, Yoruba-speaking refugees fleeing the collapse of Oyo – would be easiest to attack. Annual battles between Dahomey and the Egba soon turned into a major ongoing conflict.

The transatlantic slave trade fanned the flames of war. European hunger for African labour between the sixteenth and nineteenth centuries to power its newly established economies in the American hemisphere created a tragically self-perpetuating cycle of self-destruction on the African continent.[24] This trade in human life fuelled demographic breakdown and social instability, which in turn created military states compelled to engage in warfare instead of agriculture and trade prisoners for weapons to protect against their own people's transatlantic enslavement by foreigners.

An estimated 10.7 million Africans were displaced to the Americas between the turn of the sixteenth and the late nineteenth centuries, an additional 15 per cent – about 1.8 million people – died on the Atlantic voyage, and perhaps as many as six million more people died in slave raids, on the journey to the West African coast, and in the barracoons (slave pens) that held them prisoner before they could be shipped across the ocean. An African person enslaved in the Americas had a life expectancy of around seven years.[25]

In 1803, Denmark became the first nation to end its slave trade. The British Empire abolished the practice in its territories four years later, and the United States banned its trade on 1 January 1808 and declared it piracy in 1820. But illegal trade continued over the following decades. After being compelled to abolish its trade in 1814 by Britain, which had dominated the trade in the decades before 1807 but now led the campaign to end it, the Netherlands signed a treaty to comprehensively outlaw the practice in 1818. France, which had outlawed slavery altogether in 1794 before reinstating it under Napoleon Bonaparte in 1802, reimposed a trading ban the same year as the Netherlands. Spain promised to end its trade in 1820, newly independent Brazil finally legislated against the traffic in 1831, and Portugal formally abolished the trade five years later.[26]

However, the bans were poorly enforced and even ignored and more than one million people continued to be trafficked to Brazil and the Spanish island of Cuba even after 1836. More than 25 per cent of all the transatlantic slave trade's victims, around 3.2 million people, were forced onto slave ships after the 1808 ban. Nearly 38 per cent (1.8 million) of all Africans displaced to Brazil arrived after that date, and almost 71 per cent (552,000) of all Africans displaced to Cuba arrived after 1820.[27]

Dahomey's imperial growth and engagement in this trade was probably precipitated by a desire to protect its own citizens against the threat of transatlantic enslavement. As King Ghezo's grandfather King Kpengla reportedly told a Yorkshire-born enslaver and slave trader in the 1780s, 'You, Englishmen ... are surrounded by the ocean . . . whilst we Dahomans, being placed on a large continent, and hemmed in amidst a variety of other people . . . are obliged by the sharpness of our swords, to defend ourselves from their incursions, and punish the depredations they make on us . . . Your countrymen, therefore, who alledge [sic] that we go to war for the purpose of supplying your ships with slaves, are grossly mistaken.'[28]

Nor was the Dahomey Empire the only military threat to the children and young people that ended up on the *Clotilda*. Although the Africans repeatedly referred to their captors as Dahomey warriors, so intense was the warfare between former members of the Oyo Empire, whose own growth had been fuelled by slave trading, that the *Clotilda* shipmates could just as easily have been kidnapped and sold by other Yoruba speakers.[29]

Except for a Fon nobleman named Gumpa, all 110 captives who were imprisoned on the *Clotilda* were almost certainly captured in the same slave raid. Kossula admitted as much to the writer Zora Neale Hurston in the late 1920s. He referred repeatedly to his shipmates as 'my countrymen' and 'de folks of my country' and recalled being sold alongside his townsfolk in a single slave pen before his displacement across the Atlantic: 'each nation in a barracoon by itself.' Hurston understood why captives were segregated: different ethnic groups might fight, and ethnicities were assumed by slave traders to have specific temperaments and therefore different values.[30]

Not all the captives were Yoruba speakers though. Kossula, Polee and another *Clotilda* survivor named Osia Keeby explained that 'some people' were Fulani, Hausa (who Yoruba speakers knew as Gambari), Ijesha and Nupe (who Yoruba speakers knew as Takpa), ethnic groups from territories surrounding the former Oyo Empire who had the tremendous misfortune to be visiting the town at the time of the raid.[31]

The British Royal Navy's increasingly aggressive policing of the illegal slave trade in Brazilian waters forced the South American nation finally to enforce effective anti-slave trade legislation in September 1850. Two years later, the British government compelled King Ghezo to sign a treaty accepting the abolition of the trade, and he suspended the military attacks that had provided traffickers with captives.[32] But the trade in palm oil that the British government hoped would replace Dahomey's trade in human beings was nowhere near as lucrative for King Ghezo, especially as the crop's price began to decline in the middle of the decade. A coincidental French project to purchase so-called 'free emigrants', African youths intended to serve as indentured labourers in the Caribbean, and a revival of the Cuban slave trade at the end of the decade, led to renewed demands for kidnapped souls. In 1857, King Ghezo resumed the trade in human beings.

Ghezo died in November 1858 while attempting to conquer Abeokuta, and his son and successor, Badohou, who took the royal name Glele, inherited the throne. Glele sought to avenge his father's defeat at Abeokuta and declared publicly that he would carry on his slave raids. Glele was reported in mid-April 1860 to be in Abeokuta with a force of 30,000, although the army abandoned its assault and 'subsequently retired, after having destroyed a town, whose population was no doubt enslaved or slaughtered'. But there were no obstacles west of the Ogun River that would have prevented him from advancing north and launching another assault in the direction of New Oyo.[33]

Kossula had just had his teeth filed to sharp edges in the style of his kinship group in mid-April 1860. He had endured only one initiation into adulthood: he had begun to learn the secret of the Oro (the bullroarer), an oath-bound fraternal society dedicated to the Yoruba orisha (spirit) Oro, whose 'voice', created by spinning a stick on a string, is forbidden to women's ears. The 19-year-old was still considered a child within his community, although he had begun to signal an interest in girls by going to market to admire the sound of their bracelets. He became so enamoured with one girl's beauty that his family started negotiations for him to marry her when he was older.[34]

Kossula was at the market when he witnessed three messengers from Dahomey approach his townsfolk with a request to speak with their king. 'For many days they come to Tarkar. Tell him Dahomeys good friend. We till fields and believe bad folks,' child captive Redoshi recalled. The ruler agreed to meet them, and they set out Glele's demands: the town must give him half its crops, or he would make war on them. Tarkar's ruler fiercely refused such an outrageous demand. The town's eight gates were heavily fortified, and he was confident the Dahomey Empire was too far away to pose a military threat. He did not know Glele and his army had camped nearby. Kossula claimed a banished member of his town betrayed them to Dahomey by telling its warriors military secrets that would allow them to enter the town's gates and overcome its guards. The next day, the army launched an attack.[35]

So sudden was the Dahomeyan army's assault on Tarkar that Abaché estimated it took just half an hour to kill and imprison everyone in the town, which was then set alight. On 6 March 1860, about six weeks before the *Clotilda* Africans' kidnap, Jamaican-born traveller Robert Campbell was journeying to Abeokuta from New Oyo. He was about five hours out from New Oyo when he stumbled on the tragic aftermath of a village caught up in intra-ethnic violence between Oyo loyalists and the separatist kingdom of Ijaye. Campbell was shaken by how swiftly and totally an entire community could be destroyed in warfare: 'We crossed the Ogun [River] and suddenly encountered one of the saddest spectacles in Africa, a village only a few days before full of life and activity, now entirely depopulated, its inhabitants captured as slaves, itself in ruins and ashes.'[36]

Abaché, Kossula, Redoshi and their fellow adult and child survivors were forced into iron collars and chained together in random groups of twelve in preparation for the roughly 250-mile march to the sea.[37] To their horror, the decapitated heads of their kinsfolk were gathered up by their captors and carried as trophies.

The sun was just beginning to rise as the long march through the woodlands began. The prisoners were made to walk in single file along beaten paths throughout the heat of the day. Kossula could still recall the agony of the journey nearly seventy years later. 'All day dey make us walk. De sun so hot!' The teenager was too sick with shock and grief to think about food, but his thirst became so overwhelming that he never forgot the relief of finally receiving water. King Glele and his Dahomeyan noblemen were carried from the scene in hammocks, which also served as their beds. The captives were forced to make do with the hard earth, which afforded no protection against the leopards and other large predators that howled unseen all around them, and which were only kept at bay by the party's fires. 'I thinkee too 'bout my folks and I cry. All night I cry,' Kossula remembered.[38]

The prisoners woke at dawn and were given food before a second long day's march began. Late in the afternoon, the procession stopped at a town with a red flag. A translator was sent to fetch the town's king, whose conversation with King Glele prompted its inhabitants to switch the red flag for a white flag and fetch yams and corn, which the Dahomey warriors ate on the spot. As Kossula later explained, a red flag meant the town was prepared to fight Dahomey, a white flag meant the town would pay its ransom demand and a black flag meant the town was without an adult king and was to be left alone according to the Dahomey Empire's moral code. The army continued to stop at towns demanding their crops throughout the rest of the day.[39]

To Kossula's horror, the heads that had been collected as trophies began to rot on that second day. 'Oh, Lor', I *wish* dey bury dem! I doan lak see my people head in de soldier hands; and de smell makee me so sick!' The warriors paused the march and made camp at the end of that day. But they did not bury the heads; instead, they lit a fire, placed the heads on poles and smoked them. 'Oh Lor', Lor', Lor'! We got to set dere and see de heads of our people smokin' on de stick,' Kossula recalled in horror.[40] The party camped for nine days before the journey to the coast resumed.

In the early twentieth century, Kossula sketched a map showing the captives' march to Ouidah. The African man traced the journey more than fifty years after his kidnap, but he confidently claimed that any of his townsfolk would recognize the route.

First, the prisoners were marched down to the coast. Then they were marched west through three slave ports: Lagos, an independent maritime city-state prior to its annexation by the British in 1862, which Yoruba speakers knew as Eko; the neutral trading zone of Badagry; and finally, Porto-Novo, which was on the edge of the Dahomey Empire, and which the Yoruba knew as Ajachè.[41]

Finally, two weeks after they were torn away from their burning hometown and the bodies of their relatives, the captives reached Ouidah. The prisoners, still chained together by the neck and still forced to bear witness to their dead loved ones' heads, were marched through customs and into the city, where there awaited them the novel sight of a vast blue ocean and a terrifyingly unknown future.[42]

2

The Conspiracy

On a bitterly cold Monday night in January 1856, a 33-year-old salesman from Lowell, Massachusetts, with high cheekbones, a carefully trimmed chin beard and a head of receding wavy hair boarded the white-painted two-storey steamboat the *William Jones, Jr.* as it left Alabama's port city of Mobile for its capital, Montgomery. Clear glass bottles filled with mild opiates clinked in the salesman's luggage as poorly clad enslaved youths hoisted the cargo onto the 200-foot-long, nearly 400-ton vessel. Frederick Ayer was halfway through a tour through northern Texas, southern Louisiana, southern Alabama and southern Georgia to distribute his brother James Cook Ayer's 'Cherry Pectoral' medicine, which claimed to cure fatal childhood diseases such as influenza, whooping cough and tuberculosis.[1]

That January was the coldest month in Alabama since the state's admission to the Union in 1819. The temperature dropped as low as twenty degrees Fahrenheit, or minus seven degrees Celsius. Roads were blocked, trains and newspaper deliveries halted, and the weight of the ice toppled telegraph wires and snapped branches of trees throughout the state. The cold spell lasted from late December until February.[2] Shirtless enslaved labourers were forced to battle through the freezing weather as they collected and fed firewood into the *William Jones*'s furnaces to power its journey up the Mobile and Alabama rivers. Ayer and his fellow passengers, who included

Southern enslavers and other Northern businessmen, hid from the cold and darkness in the steamboat's forecabin and began a conversation.

Growing fears in the South that its chief labour source was coming under threat meant the discussion soon turned to slavery, and to the possibility of trafficking more African captives despite an 1808 federal law banning the importation of slaves to the country and an 1820 law declaring the trade piracy. Ayer's business trip brought him into contact with the South's slavery-based economy for the first time. The future father-in-law of Second World War general George S. Patton even stayed at the residence of a Louisiana enslaver, who took him on a night-time deer hunt guided by a captive bearing a pine-knot torch, although the hunt was cut short when the enslaver accidentally shot one of his mules in the darkness. Ayer could not help sharing his judgement on the long-term future of slavery, which was legal only in the nation's fifteen most southerly states, declaring that it could not last: 'with the supply by importation from Africa cut off, and any further spread in the Territories denied, the thing was doomed.'[3]

But Alabama had built its economy on slavery. Of the approximately 965,000 people living in the state on the eve of the Civil War, about 435,000 — just under half — were enslaved. They comprised a large proportion of the approximately one million enslaved people displaced from the Upper South to labour in the Deep South's rapidly expanding cotton economy between 1820 and 1860, labour that would quickly transform cotton from a minor crop in the western hemisphere to the nineteenth-century world's chief commodity. Slavery-produced cotton was shipped down the Alabama, Tombigbee and Mobile rivers to be sold in Mobile by the same steamboats that were now ferrying Frederick Ayer's cure-all north. Much of this 'white gold' was then sold to Northern ports, to Havana, and across the Atlantic to Le Havre and Marseilles in France, but most importantly to Liverpool in England, by then the world's largest producer of cotton cloth, which bought between 85 and 90 per cent of each year's crop. The million bales of cotton shipped to Mobile in 1860 represented almost a fifth of the United States' output. By that year, the value of cotton exports reached $192 million (equivalent to $700 billion today) and accounted for nearly 60 per cent of the nation's merchandise exports.[4]

A Louisiana enslaver named Matthews, perhaps the same man who shot the unfortunate mule, joined the conversation. He asserted that a shipment of African captives could be landed on the US coast despite the slave trade ban and was backed by several of the Northern businessmen. A heated debate followed before Matthews wagered $100 (equivalent to $3,700 today) that Africans could be smuggled to the United States. More bets were placed before the Maine-born steamboat's captain Timothy Meaher, a round-faced man in his mid-forties with grey eyes, long dark hair and muttonchop whiskers, added a significant sum of his own to support his claim that a trans-atlantic smuggling operation was 'not impossible'.[5]

The businessmen on board the *William Jones* that day perhaps included Robert R. Snow. Frederick Ayer and Robert Snow's itiner-aries overlapped – they arrived at the same New Orleans hotel on the same day – and the icy weather meant there were very few steamboat journeys back north that January. Snow was from a family of New York shipping agents originally from Thomaston in Maine, about thirty miles east of Timothy Meaher's Whitefield birthplace. Meaher was the same age as Snow's half-brother and agency head Ambrose Snow, who was arrested off the coast of Texas early in the Civil War for blockade running on the *Royal Yacht*, a schooner whose Massachusetts-born captain Thomas B. Chubb was known for trick-ing African American sailors into slavery and who in 1857 fled custody to escape a charge of human trafficking.[6]

Snow's presence in the South that winter, and the broader readiness of the Northern businessmen to support Matthews, highlights what Meaher and those businessmen surely knew when they placed their bets: the slave trade had never stopped. Despite the 1808 ban, New York was a hub of slave-trading activity in the 1850s. Dozens of slave ships bound for Africa were sent from Lower Manhattan each year. US-built slave ships also left Baltimore, Boston, Providence, Salem and other New England ports, and somewhere between fifteen and twenty-eight vessels either owned or outfitted in New Orleans were identified as slavers or caught trafficking people in the years 1857 and 1858 alone.[7]

Few of the captives were landed on US soil, though. Instead, they were taken to Cuba, which by the middle of the century was the last major human trafficking market in the Americas. Nearly 500 illegal journeys carrying almost 200,000 people were conducted as part of this US–Africa–Cuba trade between 1853 and 1867. Nearly 90 per cent of the slave ships were US-built: vessels registered in the United States and able to fly its flag provided human traffickers with significant protection. US-built ships also carried more than half a million, or two-thirds, of the Africans who were displaced to Brazil and Cuba in the 1830s and 1840s. The British Royal Navy's West Africa Squadron, which played a major role in catching traffickers, was reluctant to antagonize its former military enemy by stopping and searching US-registered ships, and the US naval patrol was far too small to meaningfully police the trade.[8]

President James Buchanan finally expanded the US's anti-slavery patrol in the autumn of 1859, and the US Navy caught twenty slave ships between 1859 and 1860, more than double the number it captured between 1851 and 1858. But it was Abraham Lincoln's administration that finally helped bring the trade to a close. An 1862 treaty gave the US and British navies reciprocal rights to search each other's ships and condemn anything that might be linked to the trade. Special courts presided over by both a British and US judge were set up in New York, Sierra Leone and the Cape of Good Hope to convict and jail slave traders. In 1862, Captain Nathaniel Gordon of the slave ship *Erie* was hanged in New York for his crime, becoming the only person to be executed under the United States 1820 piracy law. The Emancipation Proclamation and Thirteenth Amendment to the US Constitution outlawed slavery altogether. The heightened policing of traffickers and Spain's growing international isolation as a slavery-based empire finally brought an end to the slave trade to Cuba.[9]

The year 1867 is widely accepted in the English-speaking world as the one in which the transatlantic slave trade ended. But there is compelling evidence that trafficking continued into the next decade, and with US involvement. Two slave ships were widely reported in the US press to have landed in Cuba in June 1872, weeks after a British politician, referring to the suspicions of that nation's Madrid ambassador, stated in Parliament that he 'did not attach implicit credit to the assurances of the Spanish Government that there had been no importation of slaves into Cuba of late years'. When Welsh-born explorer Sir Henry Morton Stanley visited Ouidah in December 1873, he also learned that two slave ships had landed in Cuba a year earlier. The first was a Spanish bark that flew the Portuguese flag; 200 captives aged from 10 to 40 were trapped on board. The second was believed to be a US ship and was reported to have as many as 630 prisoners packed in its hold. Stanley confronted the alleged seller, a man named 'Desoza', almost certainly Francisco Félix de Souza, aka 'Chico', son and namesake of the notorious Brazilian slave trader Francisco Félix de Souza, who King Ghezo appointed as his chief trading agent in Ouidah. Chico denied all knowledge of the sales. But Stanley claimed to have seen 300 trafficking victims locked in a barracoon at Ouidah and to have encountered a community of would-be traffickers at the port, including US-born men who worshipped Captain Gordon as a martyr. Cuban historian Juan Perez de la Riva also found evidence in his homeland's newspapers of a slave landing at the western province of Pinar del Río in 1873, and an African woman named María la Conguita asserted in 1907 that she was trafficked to that island in 1878. British historian Hugh Thomas referred to María's case only to conclude she was mistaken about the date of her arrival, but he also speculated that the *Clotilda* voyage 'may have been a hoax'.[10]

The confidence of Meaher's bet revealed what he also knew: a schooner capable of smuggling scores of kidnapped Africans had just been built by enslaved labourers at his neighbour William

Foster's shipyard on Telegraph Road, a long dirt road that ran north of Mobile, parallel to the Mobile River. Foster was a long-faced man in his mid-thirties with piercing eyes and unkempt facial hair that framed a long, broken nose. He arrived in Mobile in 1844 or 1845 from the eastern Canadian province of Novia Scotia. Novia Scotia was then one of the provinces of British North America, and Foster cherished his British status throughout his life. He considered himself a 'loyal Englishman' even after he became a naturalized American and remembered well the coronation of Queen Victoria in 1838. His new schooner, which he named *Clotilda*, undertook its maiden voyage to Havana, Cuba, on 27 October 1855, returning to Mobile just days before the salesman Frederick Ayer boarded the *William Jones*. The *Clotilda*'s construction just prior to the bet suggests that Meaher and Foster may already have been considering a transatlantic trafficking operation. The two-masted, 120-ton schooner stood eighty-six feet long and measured twenty-three feet at its widest point. The *Clotilda*'s almost seven-foot-deep hold was unusually large for a Gulf schooner; the vessel was built not for the local fishing trade, but for carrying lumber, sugar, cotton and other large cargo long distances.[11]

For the next four years, the *Clotilda* travelled back and forth numerous times between Mobile, New Orleans, Texas, Mexico and Cuba with shipments of sugar, salt, cotton, meat, animal hides, whisky and lumber. The schooner may even have trafficked people during this period. All the ports it visited between 1855 and 1859 had trading connections with Cuba and were also sites where captives were shipped as part of the United States' internal trade in human beings. In January 1857, the vessel arrived in New Orleans with a suspiciously unspecified cargo and was assigned to a local firm with links to the trade. Members of the same firm were unindicted participants in the voyage of the brig *Echo* that sought to traffic more than 300 people from West Central Africa to northern Cuba in August 1858.[12]

Regardless of the *Clotilda*'s history, one of its last voyages proved deadly in a cruel foreshadowing of the vessel's later role in snuffing out the lives and futures of captive children and young people. On 23 October 1859, the schooner accidentally ran over a paddle boat that was fishing on the Mobile River. As the two vessels collided, the white occupant of the paddle boat managed to latch onto the *Clotilda*'s anchor chain. But the other occupant, an enslaved passenger named Alfred, was thrown into the river and drowned.[13]

Meaher recognized the *Clotilda* and its owner as ideally suited for a transatlantic trafficking operation and approached major enslavers in Alabama, who agreed to buy most of the Africans he planned to kidnap, and who allegedly each subscribed $1,000 (equivalent to $37,000 in 2023) to pay for the voyage.[14] Many of the conspiracists were among the richest and most powerful men in their respective counties and, in some cases, their state. Some held high political office. The participants included brothers, business partners and neighbours. Yet in many ways their identities were starkly different. The illegal voyage united Presbyterians with Catholics, surgeons and lawyers with steamboat builders, members of old US families with foreign-born men, Northerners with Southerners, and, perhaps most strikingly, men who campaigned to keep Alabama in the Union in 1860 with men who led the state's push to secede and, ultimately, to civil war. What united the group, and what drew them to partake in human trafficking, was a shared determination to perpetuate slavery.

Timothy Meaher took charge of the conspiracy and spent months planning the crime with his brothers James Millay Meaher and Patrick Burns Meaher. The siblings were the three surviving sons of James Meagher, an engineer who emigrated, first to Newfoundland and then to Maine, from Rathcash/Ráth Chaise in Co. Kilkenny, Ireland, at the turn of the nineteenth century, supposedly to avoid conscription into the British Army during the Napoleonic Wars. Their mother was Susan Flanders Millay, whose own mother Abigail Eastman could trace her ancestry back to the seventeenth-century Massachusetts Bay Colony. Ironically, the Meahers shared a common ancestor in Massachusetts Bay settler Roger Eastman with Max Eastman, a leading Greenwich Village socialist editor and patron of the Harlem Renaissance, an interwar explosion of African American art and culture. Greenwich Village celebrity poet Edna St. Vincent Millay was the brothers' first cousin twice removed.[15]

The Meaher brothers relocated from Maine to Mobile at different times between 1836 and 1850 with the aim of making a fortune in the lumber and shipping industries. The sawmill Timothy Meaher built near Chickasabogue Creek, just north of Mobile, in 1847 was reportedly one of the largest in the South at that time. Shipbuilding developed as an industry in Mobile in the years prior to the *Clotilda*'s voyage. The city's abundant magnolia and live oak trees made it an ideal location for the construction of ships such as the *Clotilda*. Oldest brother James managed the finances of the brothers' steamboat and sawmill businesses, while Timothy and Burns captained boats on the Alabama and Tombigbee rivers. Burns was the youngest and tallest of the three at six feet three inches in height and also carried a knife wound inflicted on him in self-defence by his steamboat clerk 18 months prior to the *Clotilda* bet. The deep, misshapen scar ran the length of his shoulder to his elbow.[16]

Frederick Ayer lived for another 62 years but may never have known of his part in the *Clotilda* conspiracy, or even that the voyage took place. There is no record that he placed a bet, he left the South four years before the plan was executed, and his brother James stood unsuccessfully for US Congress on a Republican ticket in 1874. But Ayer remembered his Southern trip as a 'most interesting winter's experience', and the one man who bought his medicine in Montgomery that winter was local surgeon and pharmacist Dr. Benjamin Rush Jones, who would go on to claim approximately fifteen of the *Clotilda* captives.[17]

Dr. Jones's role in the conspiracy places the trafficking voyage at the heart of a much wider effort to legalize the transatlantic slave trade on the eve of the Civil War. Jones and his fellow *Clotilda* enslaver Alexander ('Alex') Frederick Given were closely acquainted with leading secessionist and former US senator William Lowndes Yancey, who owned a plantation near Jones, east of Montgomery. In February 1854, Jones founded with Yancey the Alabama Bible

Society at the Alabama State Capitol in Montgomery. In July 1855, Jones and Given were two of the five trustees who incorporated Montgomery's First Presbyterian Church six blocks from the state capitol. Yancey was appointed one of the church's ruling elders. On New Year's Eve 1855, Jones, Given and Yancey gathered to attend the Montgomery County Convention of the Democratic and Anti-Know Nothing Party.[18] A week later, around the same time the *Clotilda* bet was placed, Yancey headed the Alabama state convention and persuaded it to readopt his 'Alabama Platform', which demanded federal action to protect slavery in new US territories.

Compact. Hard to pick out in a crowd. 'Ill-painted features.' Physical descriptions of William Lowndes Yancey, a square-faced man in his early forties with light brown hair and grey eyes, were not kind. But the writers knew his standout feature was his voice. Yancey, 'the orator of secession', was US slavery's most zealous apologist, a man who could speak for hours in defence of an economic system based on bondage. As the 'prince' of the Fire-Eaters, a group of pro-slavery extremists who urged the South's secession from the Union as early as 1850, he was, according to an obituarist, 'more, perhaps, than any other person instrumental in producing the separation of the Southern from the Northern States'. In April 1860, as the *Clotilda* was sailing to the West African coast, Yancey led a walkout of Southern Democrats at the Democratic National Convention in Charleston, South Carolina, when delegates voted against a version of his 'Alabama Platform'. The rebels rallied behind their own candidate in the 1860 presidential election, split-ting the Democratic vote and paving the way for the presidency of Abraham Lincoln, whose Republican Party was founded in the North in 1854 to oppose the expansion of slavery to new territo-ries.[19] Although it is not clear exactly what Yancey knew of the *Clotilda* conspiracy, the plot was a realization of a slavery expansion-ist ideology, framed around human trafficking, that he spent much of the decade championing.

Newspaper editor and lawyer Leonidas William Spratt, a second cousin of former US President James Knox Polk, played a key role in bringing Southern calls to reopen the US slave trade into the mainstream. In 1853, Spratt bought Charleston newspaper the *Southern Standard* to advocate for transatlantic trafficking. Dubbed the 'philosopher of the African slave trade' by pro-abolition newspaper editor Horace Greeley, Spratt argued that 'inequality was necessary to man's progress', and that the South's 'aristocrat[ic]' race-based class structure offered the best hope for the future of humankind. Less than a year before the *Clotilda*'s transatlantic voyage, he successfully defended in the federal court in Charleston the crew of the slave ship *Echo*.[20]

But it was the 1854 Kansas–Nebraska Act that made the question of slavery expansion a central concern of the nation's politics. The act allowed settlers in the new states of Nebraska and Kansas to decide whether slavery should be allowed in those states. Migrants rushed to the states to sway the vote, which fuelled a violent conflict known as 'Bleeding Kansas'. Slave trade advocates argued that the South's economy was at threat; unlike the North, which produced 90 per cent of the nation's manufacturing output, and which was growing in industrial strength thanks to European migrants, the South, they claimed, was being starved of cheap foreign agricultural labour that would increase the region's productivity. Pro-slave trade campaigners hoped to increase the affordability of enslaved people by importing captives directly from Africa. New enslaved workers were also central to Southerners' territorial ambitions in a rapidly expanding US nation. Environmental factors drove the push for new land and, by extension, new captives to work it. Land exhaustion – cotton so depleted soil of its fertility that it could only be grown in the same spot a few years in a row – meant the long-term survival of the region's cotton economy was unsustainable without territorial expansion.[21] More captives in the South also meant increased political representation: although enslaved people had no voting rights, they were counted as three-fifths of a person for tax and representation purposes.

The North's perceived economic advantages over the South and the need for enslaved labourers to fill new territories were also the rallying cries of James Dunwoody Brownson De Bow, editor of Southern nationalist magazine *De Bow's Review*, who in August 1856 began using his publication to call publicly for the reopening of the transatlantic slave trade. '*We must have Africans*,' De Bow wrote to Virginian enslaver and fellow Fire-Eater Edmund Ruffin.[22]

In May 1858, more than 500 Southern political leaders gathered to attend the Southern Commercial Convention in Montgomery. Southern Commercial Conventions were annual gatherings to promote economic growth in the South that became increasingly politically extreme in the 1850s. Yancey and *Clotilda* conspiracist Alex Given were among the session's 28 Montgomery delegates. Leonidas Spratt produced a report at the event calling for the reopening of the US slave trade, and Yancey acted as the report's leading spokesperson. Yancey ensured the slave trade dominated the convention. In a three-day speech – the longest of his life – he argued that debating human trafficking would not alienate Northern Democrats, and that, if it did, he was in favour of disunion. Yancey tried to find a constitutional justification for human trafficking by pointing out that the US Constitution never specified the slave trade's abolition and so never granted US Congress the power to end it. Thus, the 1808 slave trade ban and 1820 law declaring the slave trade piracy were violations of the spirit of the Constitution and were 'unjust and an insult to the South'. He suggested that federal anti-slave trade laws should be repealed so each state could decide for itself whether to continue human trafficking.[23]

Yancey asked his audience, 'If slavery is right *per se*, if it is right to raise slaves for sale, does it not appear that it is right to import them?' If it was legal to enslave Africans, why was it illegal to traffic them? He denied he was calling for the trade's reopening but argued that enslaved labourers were too expensive in the Deep South states of Alabama, Georgia, Louisiana, Mississippi, South Carolina and Texas, which were forced to import them from the Upper Southern states of Delaware, Kentucky, Maryland, North Carolina, Tennessee and Virginia. And, he suggested, if more white people in the South could afford enslaved labour, there would be more white people with enslaved labourers to settle new territories and strengthen the slavery-based economy, and more class unity among white people to support Southern expansion. The delegates then debated and tabled Spratt's slave trade reopening resolution, which he took home to South Carolina to try to push through its legislature.[24]

Six months later, the *Clotilda* conspirators invested their support in a Nashville-born mercenary who promised to expand slavery into new territories and revive the slave trade. His ambition would be short-lived. William Walker, a blond-haired, grey-eyed doctor and lawyer who stood just over five feet tall and weighed little more than 100 pounds, had launched military invasions of Mexico in 1853 and Nicaragua in 1855, where he installed himself briefly as president and issued a decree to reinstate slavery before his overthrow by other Central American governments. The reopening of the transatlantic slave trade was central to Walker's expansionist endeavour, which attracted widespread Southern support. He even predicted in *De Bow's Review* that there would be no more British opposition to reviving the slave trade, which he dismissed as misguided sanctimoniousness. 'The frenzy of the British public against the slave trade has exhausted itself,' he declared. When Walker launched a new invasion of Nicaragua in December 1858, Timothy Meaher and William Foster donated to his campaign the *Susan*, a schooner in which they had a shared interest, although the vessel's crew were fortunate to be towed back to Mobile by the Royal Navy when it ran aground off Honduras. Walker was executed by the government of Honduras in September 1860.[25]

At the 1859 Southern Commercial Convention in Vicksburg, Mississippi, James De Bow introduced a resolution calling for a reopening of the slave trade and recommending a repeal of the national laws banning it that was supported by a majority of 44 votes to 19. Delegates also overwhelmingly passed a resolution calling for the Gulf of Mexico, Cuba and Central America to form a US South-dominated slavery-based empire. Nevertheless, most delegates felt it was inadvisable to attempt to reopen the trade while the South remained in the Union, prompting De Bow to establish at the convention an 'African Labor Supply Association' whose purpose was 'to promote the supply of African labor'; Yancey was named in absentia as an officer. He accepted the role publicly, declaring in a letter sent to the *Montgomery Advertiser*, "'I must confess that the inclination of my mind is in favor of a regulated and limited supply of African Slave labor." Limited, at least, until the inevitable conquest of Latin America as far south as William Walker's Nicaragua, when "the cause of civilization will demand as large drafts upon Africa for slaves as that continent can supply".[26]

Nine months later, the *Clotilda* began its transatlantic voyage.

Alabama's enslaved labourers were still racing to harvest the previous year's vast, waterlogged cotton crops when the *Clotilda* anchored at Timothy Meaher's shipyard ahead of its final, fateful journey in late February 1860. The two-masted, 120-ton *Clotilda* made for an arresting sight on the water. Northerly winds whipped giant canvas sails that the ship's masts and spars had recently been expanded to hold, drawing attention to its newly enhanced size and speed, and making it seem impatient to set sail on its voyage across the Atlantic. Workers at the shipyard loaded the schooner's nearly seven-foot-deep hold with almost 350 barrels of assorted meat, flour, bread, rice, sugar, vinegary water and rum. They then added piles of freshly cut wood to hide the provisions and make it look as if the schooner was doing a benign trade in lumber to St. Thomas in the Danish West Indies (now the US Virgin Islands), a journey for which the vessel was soon cleared by port authorities. When the schooner reached West Africa and was safely out of sight of US authorities, the lumber planks could then be used to construct stacked platforms below deck on which its captives would be forced to lie.[27]

William Foster had promised his future brother-in-law William Vanderslice that he could take part in the voyage, but the 21-year-old was out of the county as the ship prepared to set sail. In the end, those appointed as the *Clotilda*'s eleven-man crew included three Mobilians, Joseph Deflow, James Small and William Copeland,

and Bostonian James Welch. The mates were John M. Simonton from Portland in Maine, and James S. Smith of Boston. All were dark-haired, heavily tanned and physically imposing young men. Unlike Foster, none knew when they began the journey that they had signed up for an arduous, dangerous and illegal human trafficking voyage.[28]

The surgeon Rush Jones happened to be in Mobile and New Orleans February with his wife Frances Amelia Taliaferro Jones and their son and five daughters. Officially, the family were on a 'pleasure excursion'; the trip coincided with Mardi Gras. But the timing of their visit meant Jones had opportunities to view the *Clotilda* before it set sail and perhaps help prepare its illegal voyage. The Jones family even had a connection to Walter Smith, one of the Mobile Bay customs officials paid to catch smugglers such as Foster; the Jones's son married one of Walter Smith's twin daughters during the Civil War. Jones returned to Montgomery just before the ship set sail and held a dinner party that trumpeted his commitment to slavery expansion. The guests included a pale-eyed, bald 37-year-old named Birkett Davenport Fry. Fry had fought alongside mercenary William Walker in his unsuccessful effort to turn Nicaragua into a slave state, and his 'glowing description of the country, its climate, timber, soil and productions' suggested to at least one fellow guest that he was ready to resume his colonial campaign.[29]

On Sunday 4 March, William Foster boarded the *Clotilda* by the early morning light and smuggled a sack of gold inside the cabin's bulkhead. He then fetched its crew, who piloted the vessel out of Mobile Bay and into the Gulf of Mexico. The schooner initially met good weather and reached Cuba in three and a half days. But the winds soon strengthened, and the vessel was caught in a gale north of Bermuda. It lasted nine days, tore off half the steering wheel, tipped much of the deck's contents into the sea and damaged the main sail's boom. As dawn rose on a final day of heavy winds, a Portuguese anti-slavery patrol spotted the vessel and pursued it for as long as there was daylight, a full 10 hours. The *Clotilda*'s foresail was ripped to shreds as the vessel escaped into the darkness. An exhilarated Foster later judged the chase 'the most exciting race I ever saw'.[30]

After six weeks at sea, the battered schooner finally reached the African continent. On 16 April, the crew prepared to dock at Fogo in Cape Verde before the *Clotilda* was sighted by another Portuguese anti-slavery patrol and forced to move on to Praia, the next island in the archipelago. Foster's crew had been furious to find they were participants in a perilous and exhausting human trafficking expedition and mutinied when they reached land, threatening to expose the operation. But Foster's offer of double wages persuaded them to repair the damaged vessel and continue their journey without incident; it was probably at that stage that the series of low-lying platforms on which the captives would be confined were laid in the hold. The Portuguese officials and United States consul at Praia then cleared the schooner for trade without question when the captain presented shawls and ornaments to their wives. On 22 April, the *Clotilda* sailed for the African mainland, but not before colliding with and taking off the spar, sail and main boom of another anti-slavery patrol. Foster waited for the stricken vessel to intercept his schooner with gunfire, but no shots came and a strong breeze soon carried the schooner to the safety of West Africa's yellow sandy coast.[31] The would-be human trafficker was now ready to carry out his crime.

3

The Coast

No sooner had the captives arrived in Ouidah than their Dahomeyan kidnappers forced them into a large circular prison with a thatched roof and tall bamboo walls. Strong hands grasped Redoshi, the slender 12-year-old, and pulled her to a wooden stake, where she was lashed by the wrists to prevent her escaping. In the dark space, helpless, she heard a chorus of wails all around her. The noises told her she was in one of a series of barracoons, or slave pens. As many as three thousand other prisoners were trapped in other enclosures only feet away.[1] Some had been there many days.

The barracoons into which Redoshi and her fellow captives were thrown at the beginning of May 1860 were located at the back of Ouidah's slave market, a space enclosed on three sides by bamboo poles set about ten feet apart that supported a roof made of palm leaves. Outside, a dozen women warriors bearing swords and spears guarded the space. The market was a vast area in the centre of town that came alive with trading activity for a few hours each morning as white men gathered to inspect the prisoners and local women sold their wares. It contained a pavilion identified by one nineteenth-century observer as Glele's council chamber, from whose roof, perched atop bamboo poles, flew the king's red and blue cotton battle flags.[2]

The Dahomeyan guards eventually released the captives from their stakes, and families, friends and newly orphaned children huddled together in the dark, poorly ventilated space for the next three weeks. For some of the captives, the fetid barracoon, which was designed to incarcerate hundreds of people, would prove to be cruel preparation for the slave ship's hold. The stench of urine was overwhelming, a section of the prison wall serving as a toilet. One contemporary eyewitness described the barracoons at Ouidah as a site of 'filth, disease and famine'. While the precise mortality rates of these places are unknown, they are likely to have been high. The captives had arrived during the wet season and rain, occasionally punctuated by thunderclaps, beat down on the thatched roof one day in every three. Yet the barracoon remained agonizingly hot throughout the prisoners' incarceration and sweat soaked the cotton clothes they had been wearing since their kidnap. The temperature around Ouidah hovered around 75 to 85 degrees Fahrenheit (24 to 30 degrees Celsius) throughout the month of May.[3] In the barracoon only the nights were tolerable.

After its capital Abomey, 60 miles to the north, Ouidah was the Dahomey Empire's largest settlement and its chief commercial centre. Located two and a half miles north of the Atlantic Ocean and separated from the sea by a lagoon running parallel to the coast, the bustling town was about two miles wide and half a mile from north to south. It contained a few brick buildings. But most of its roughly twelve to fifteen thousand inhabitants and traders occupied houses built of clay with roofs of woven palm matting. The buildings were spaced far enough apart to prevent the spread of fires during the November to January dry season, when coastal temperatures often exceeded 85 degrees Fahrenheit.

The size and energy of their new environment – or at least what they could see, hear and smell of it behind their prison walls – must have been striking to the young captives. Ouidah was a key Dahomey administrative centre, a military garrison town, a major fishing port and a site of salt production. Most importantly, though, Ouidah was a major European trading centre. At its heart was the 14-acre marketplace of Zobe, where tradeswomen, some with babies cradled in their arms, sold a vast array of manufactured goods and fresh produce from raised market stalls. Fish recently caught in the adjoining lagoon, slices of hot pork sprinkled with chillies and served on plantain leaves, and goat-skin cushions together with the pins, needles and scissors required to make them could all be bought from Ouidah with either cowrie shells or coins.[4] But by far the most profitable business throughout much of the town's history was its trade in human beings.

Ouidah was the second most important slave port in the whole of Africa, behind only Luanda in Angola. The port was located above the Bight of Benin, a 400-mile stretch of water off the west coast of Africa running from Cape St. Paul in what is now Ghana to the Nun outlet of the Niger River. The region bore the European nickname 'Slave Coast' for the vast numbers of people that were forcibly displaced from there between the mid-seventeenth and mid-nineteenth centuries. Almost two million people, around one in six of all enslaved people sent to the Americas, are estimated to have been transported from the Bight of Benin. Around a million of them are thought to have been sent directly from Ouidah.[5]

Upon their arrival at the town and their incarceration in a barracoon, Redoshi and her fellow captives' hopes of evading their kidnappers and returning home ended. Mahommah Gardo Baquaqua, a young Muslim man who was displaced from Djougou in northwest Benin and held at Ouidah 15 years before the *Clotilda* captives, described his despair on reaching Dahomey and realizing that escape was now impossible. Baquaqua grieved most of all for his beloved mother: 'my heart felt sad and weary within me, as I thought of my home, my mother! whom I loved most tenderly, and the thought of never more beholding her, added very much to my perplexities. I felt sad and lonely . . . and my heart sank within me, when I thought of the "old folks at home".'[6]

Nineteen-year-old Kossula, too, was tortured by uncertainty at his parents' fate, unsure whether they were even alive. During their weeks of incarceration in the barracoon, he and his fellow captives periodically called across to the neighbouring prisons in vain attempts to locate their lost loved ones. But each attempt was met with disappointment, serving only to confirm to Kossula that 'each nation [was] in a barracoon by itself'.[7] All his captive townsfolk were in Kossula's prison. His parents, it dawned on him, were not in Ouidah.

Captives who were displaced to Cuba found that the barracoons stalked them across the Atlantic. As a child, Esteban Montejo, whose father Nazario was trafficked from Oyo in the mid-nineteenth century, was locked up every night with 200 other prisoners in a Villa Clara barracoon until he found sanctuary in the mountains, where he survived as a cimarrón (escaped slave) until abolition finally reached that island in 1886. Even well into the 1960s, he could still describe the agonizing nights of his childhood. For Montejo, the barracoon was an 'oven' whose toilet comprised a corner of the prison wall, and whose suffocating stenches were inevitably followed by sickness. 'And there was no modern ventilation there,' he said. 'Just a hole in the wall or a small barred window. The result was that the place swarmed with fleas and ticks, which made the inmates ill with infections and evil spells, for those ticks were witches.'[8]

Montejo was equally disturbed by the brutal hostility of his child-hood prison. Aside from the insects that were a constant torment, the barracoon was a soulless space evacuated of natural life. As he remembered, 'There were no trees either outside or inside the barracoons, just empty solitary spaces. The Negroes could never get used to this . . . Africa was full of trees, god-trees, banyans, cedars.'[9] Montejo's memory gives clues as to how Kossula and his fellow townsfolk must have felt in their prison. The unnaturalness of the barracoon must have been especially disturbing for young Africans thrown into such a prison for the first time, and who can only have encountered it as a terrifyingly godless space that compounded their sense of spiritual abandonment and hopelessness. There were no signifiers of home, no ancestors to guide them and nothing to affirm their identities as Fulani, Hausa, Ijesha, Nupe or Yoruba.

As the hours turned into days, Redoshi and her fellow captives began to adjust to their prison environment. As their immediate fears of death and separation dissipated, they found ways to resist their grim circumstances. Most of the captives were children, and they made up games, charging their barren environment with youthful energy and pleasure that it was not designed for, and they even climbed up the bamboo walls of their prison to gain a sense of their surroundings. 'We not so sad now, and we all young folks so we play game and clam up de side de barracoon so we see whut goin' on outside,' Kossula later told Zora Neale Hurston.[10]

From the top of the barracoon's wall, Kossula caught glimpses of large floating objects in the sea. But he could not make sense of what he was seeing; a large, whitewashed house, probably the old Portuguese fort just east of the Zobe market that in recent years had been under the command of major slave-trading family the De Souzas, obscured his view.[11] Kossula could not have known it at the time, but his limited vision meant no one was coming to his rescue. Anti-slavery cruisers were a constant presence on the coast, but Ouidah's slave market and barracoons were well hidden. The British Royal Navy stepped up its policing of the transatlantic slave trade after finally ending slavery in its own overseas territories in 1838, which meant the purchase and transportation of human beings could no longer be carried out in the open. Instead, captives were held in the cramped barracoons for weeks or even months before a buyer was ready to purchase them, and their ship was ready to sail away with them. Once sold, the prisoners were then spirited quickly to the sea.

With his outlook obscured, Kossula's attention shifted instead to a chilling sight on the ground below. There were white men wearing linen suits and carrying parasols and fat cigars, and they bore sinister expressions on their sunburned faces. Kossula had never seen white men before and may not have recognized them as slave dealers, but their presence outside his prison can only have been a bad omen for the 19-year-old, who had grown up with stories of these mysterious beings, who were known in his town as oyibo or oyinbo (men with their skin stripped off).[12]

As the hours in the barracoon turned into days and the days into weeks, Kossula and his fellow prisoners' youthfulness began to fade.

Their captors, keen to turn a profit from them, were reluctant to spend money on their welfare, which meant they were forced to subsist on a sparse daily diet of maize, cassava and rice. They were released from their prison into an adjoining yard just twice a day to exercise to maintain their strength ahead of their sale.[13] Those brief ventures outdoors were their only opportunities to stretch their limbs and to inhale fresh, clean air. By the end of their confinement, they had all begun to lose their physical strength. The weakest among them lacked the energy to do anything but lie on the ground and moan in despair.

On 15 May 1860, two weeks after Kossula and his fellow captives were forced into the barracoon, the *Clotilda* reached the West African coast. There was no harbour for Captain William Foster to sail to, and the heavy surf meant large vessels could not get close to shore. The surf before him broke in three places, forming a series of endless waves so dangerous that men dared not fish in the water. Instead, the schooner had to anchor one and a half miles offshore and wait for rescue by the coast's specialist canoeists, who rode in state-of-the-art boats that could rise above the waves, and who knew how to manoeuvre their vessels across the treacherous surf at high speeds. So skilled was their occupation that such men had to be hired from hundreds of miles away to ferry goods and people between the ships and the land. Even then, canoes capsized on a practically daily basis, dragging their unfortunate passengers into the shark-infested waters.[14]

The *Clotilda* was soon met by 20 of King Glele's boatmen, who recognized Foster as a man who had come to do business, and who expertly guided him across the perilous waters to land. Three strong men then carried him by hammock, first across the lagoon that ran parallel to the coast, and then two miles further north to Ouidah, where, as a trader with goods to offer the Dahomey kingdom, he spent the night in what he later described as 'splendid accommodations'.[15]

Foster breakfasted the following morning with a guide, who took him to the court of Akodé, the king's nephew, where he found the prince being waited on by fifty officials. Akodé bore the title Chodaton, meaning 'the king owns everything', and was the assistant to the Yovogan, or 'Chief of the white men', the man in charge of liaising with white traders. After selecting from the whisky, palm wine, cachaça from Brazil and other fine drinks presented to prospective slave traders in Ouidah, Foster explained to the prince that he wanted to buy captives and that he had $9,000 in gold as well as fine cloth and alcohol to trade. The prince subsequently sent him away, leaving Foster to endure an agonizing eight-day wait for a transaction to be agreed, and fearing capture during that time by either the king or an anti-slavery cruiser.[16]

Foster distracted himself by touring the town and visiting the shrine to Dangbe, the guardian snake spirit of the coastal kingdom of Whydah that was inherited by the Dahomeyans when they conquered the kingdom and its chief port, Ouidah, in 1727. Located behind a grove of fig trees in Ouidah's main square was a round, whitewashed, clay temple about fifteen feet in size and with three entrances. Clinging to the inside of its thatched roof and the top of its 10-foot-high walls were dark brown and cream ball pythons of about three and a half feet in length. The large but placid creatures were invited to wrap themselves around the bodies of Dangbe's male and female priests, who bowed down before them. To Foster, the snakes were merely 'repulsive things', their sacred significance lost on him.[17] Tellingly, it was his only admission of disgust at what he saw in Ouidah.

Foster claimed that he 'went to see the King of Dahomey' during his eight-day wait, presumably at his palace at Abomey. King Glele was a tall, lean, broad-shouldered man of around forty attired in silk, with a stately bearing, closely shaven hair but for two small tufts decorated with beads, long fingernails and a heavily pockmarked face; he smoked tobacco through a silver pipe.[18] Foster then returned to Ouidah, and Akodé agreed to accept his cargo of gold, cloth and rum in return for 125 enslaved people.

It had now been three weeks since the captives had arrived, and their incarceration was becoming increasingly unbearable. They appealed to their kidnappers' humanity and promised to meet King Glele's original demand that they give him half their town's crops. But their pleas fell on deaf ears. Instead, their captors tormented them with violence and the sight of their dead loved ones. Kossula recalled, 'Our women weep and beg to go home. Our men beg to go home and promise to give de yams. Dahomey's men kick us and beat us and show us the heads of our fadders and mudders. Then come de white man.'[19]

Into the barracoon stepped William Foster. Alongside him were Akodé and a German man who acted as translator.[20] Kossula had spent days watching white men from the top of his prison. Suddenly two were standing mere feet from him. The presence of the translator gave Kossula little doubt about Foster's purpose. Worse still, the business dealer was granting him complete discretion to buy whosoever he chose.

Ahead of a captive's sale, slave traders would do their best to hide the prisoners' suffering and make them appear healthy. Palm oil is likely to have been rubbed on their skin to make it alive, and the women and girls may also have been dressed in attractive clothing. Not that this had any effect on Foster, who later described the captives as being 'in a state of nudity'.[21] He may have sought to play up the apparently 'uncivilized' state of his captives to justify their transatlantic displacement and enslavement.

Kossula and his fellow captives were forced to stand in circles of 10, divided by sex. They then endured a humiliating physical examination at Foster's hands as he walked into each circle and sought to pick out the healthiest among them. To Kossula, the inspection seemed endless. His mouth was pried open and his teeth inspected to assess his age and general health; his bare skin was examined for depth of muscle tone and for signs of skin disease; despite his youth, his genitals were probably also inspected for signs of venereal disease. 'Den de white man lookee and lookee,' Kossula would later recall of the inspection. 'He lookee hard at de skin and de feet and de legs and in de mouth.'[22] Whenever Foster selected a prisoner, he pointed at them; they would then be taken to a corner of the barracoon. A satisfactory examination meant a place on the *Clotilda*.

Sometimes Foster selected family groups, but he took no care to keep families together. The woman who would be known in the United States as Gracie stood out to him, for she had six children, including a 2-year-old girl later known as Matilda and three older daughters who would soon be physically capable of producing children of their own. But Foster had no use for Gracie's two sons, who were made to stand in a different ring from their mother. He opted not to buy them.

A few metres away from Gracie stood the small, dark-skinned young woman named Bougier, who had a baby only a few months old and two other young children.[23] But the effort of keeping an infant of no immediate economic value alive on a confined slave ship held no appeal for Foster. Therefore he selected only the mother. Gracie and Bougier, who were already grieving for lost husbands, were now confronted with their worst nightmare: the imminent loss of their children. A tall, broad-shouldered, light-skinned and round-faced young man named Yawith was also faced with separation from his children across the ocean. Yet each parent was helpless to protect their offspring, and Bougier, Gracie and Yawith's family units would be forever severed by the Atlantic. For Bougier, who would go on to be one of the longest lived and most visible of all the *Clotilda*'s trafficking victims, the devastating loss of her children would haunt her for the next 70 years.

As William Foster finished making his selections, 125 children and young people stood weeping and despairing in a corner of the barracoon. They could not begin to conceive of what fate would have in store for them, but the broken circles that still held their loved ones were stark signs of their imminent separation. In order to maximize his profits, Foster had selected captives with many years of labour and fertility ahead of them. Most of those he purchased were children and teenagers.[24] Some, like Kossula, were already grieving for their parents. Others would never see them again.

Akodé picked out three of Foster's captives and offered to have them branded with a hot iron, but the slave ship captain refused. Foster had no use for branding and no desire to signpost the captives' origins or ownership. They already bore telltale facial and bodily markings that to federal officers back home would have been irrefutable evidence of the crime that would soon land them in Mobile. Facial marks are historical beauty symbols among the Nupe and Yoruba whose patterns, specific to town and kinship groups, paid tribute to lost ancestors and could help reunite family members separated by warfare or enslavement by signifying precisely where a lost person originated. Historian Emma Langdon Roche noted that the Mobile *Clotilda* survivors had three horizontal marks on their cheeks, a style of mark known as Abaja that was predominant among Yoruba speakers living under the influence of the Oyo Empire.[25]

Knowing that malnutrition and possible death faced the captives on their journey across the Atlantic, the Dahomeyan guards presented them with a big feast. Baked yams, goat meat and fish from the lagoon were among the dishes laid out before them. The food was a cruel reminder to the prisoners that they were being sent far away from their loved ones. As Kossula recalled, 'de people of Dahomey come bring us lot of grub for us to eatee 'cause dey say we goin' leave dere'. After eating, the Africans started weeping. They did not yet know what would happen to them, but they were aware that their departure was imminent, and that they would probably never see parents, children, siblings, cousins and close friends again. As Kossula stressed to Zora Neale Hurston almost seventy years later, it was a night of intolerable misery that he could never forget. 'Den we cry, we sad 'cause we doan want to leave the rest of our people in de barracoon. We all lonesome for our home. We doan know whut goin' become of us, we doan want to be put apart from one 'nother,' he told her.[26]

The following morning, shortly before dawn, the Africans' irreversible voyage across the Atlantic – the so-called Middle Passage – began.[27] Those captives who had managed to sleep through their last night in their homeland were shaken awake and pulled apart from their loved ones. Chains connecting groups of up to eight people were forced around the boys' and men's necks and fastened with padlocks; the girls and women were tied together by neck ropes. Only the very youngest were not restrained. Two-year-old Matilda was too young to walk unaided and remained in her mother Gracie's tight embrace. The prisoners were then marched in the semi-darkness for around an hour to the sea.

In single file, chained and roped, the captives walked for 2 miles across sand and then crossed a marshy expanse 1,000 yards long and filled with water four and a half feet deep. The lagoon was surrounded by giant palmyra trees, which meant the ship was largely hidden from view until the captives reached its edge. But Kossula paid anxious attention to the sights around him and noticed the outline of many ships in the sea. He saw William Foster standing before him as he was marched around the whitewashed house that may have been the old Portuguese fort and watched as the white man communicated in a strange tongue with Akodé via the German interpreter. When he saw the captives, Foster broke off his conversation with Akodé and climbed into a hammock borne by strong men who carried him safely across the lagoon. The Africans were forced to follow Foster's journey from town to sea on foot. 'We walk behind and wade de water. It come up to de neck and Cudjo think once he goin' drown,' Kossula recalled.[28] For Kossula's younger, smaller companions, whose heads were dragged beneath the surface by their chains and by those to whom they were tied, the experience was even more terrifying. They thrashed around in the murky water until they reached the safety of the shore.

The African prisoners were given little time for relief. As he emerged from the lagoon, Kossula found himself on a narrow strip of land before the sea. Kru oarsmen from Liberia with vertical blue-black stripes tattooed on their foreheads surrounded the dripping wet captives in their canoes. Kossula later cursed the oarsmen who snatched him from the African coast as 'Many-costs', a term of derision that meant their work was so poor that it cost many times the labour of a single good man.[29] As they stood exhausted and afraid on the yellow sand, the prisoners saw the vast expanse of blue before them. The *Clotilda* stood one and a half miles away, a small floating object of canvas and wood silhouetted against the horizon.

The schooner's white sails were cast in shadow, but the water, which stretched away seemingly without end, glistened in the dawn light. The young Africans, who like Nigerian-born Middle Passage survivor Ukawsaw Gronniosaw had probably heard rumours about magical 'houses with wings to them [that could] walk upon the water', must have been shocked finally to see one of those mythical vessels. Kossula never forgot the sight of the slave ship in the water. Decades later, he picked up a small piece of chopped wood in his left hand and waved it in the air to show how the schooner had bobbed about in the water as it lay at anchor off the African coast, his right fist clenching tight at the memory.[30]

Even at the end of her life, bereft mother Bougier lacked the English to convey the enormity of the strange object looming before her and could only describe it as a 'biggee ship'. But other slave trade survivors gave a sense of how she must have felt. Olaudah Equiano stressed his 'astonishment' at both the sight of the ship that was about to transport him across the Atlantic and the vast expanse of ocean before him. Thinking the ship was a sacred object of the white man's religion where he and his fellow captives would be murdered, Mahommah Gardo Baquaqua was overwhelmed by fear and despair. 'At length, when we reached the beach, and stood on the sand, oh! how I wished that the sand would open and swallow me up. My wretchedness I cannot describe.'[31]

When asked at the end of her life why she ended up on the *Clotilda*, child captive Redoshi underscored her powerlessness to resist her trafficking. 'I couldn't help myself. Africa is my home. White man took it from us. They made animals out of us.' Redoshi was among many Middle Passage survivors who described their exile as a form of human theft.[32] Tragically, she lamented not just that she had been stolen from home, but that home had been stolen from her.

William Foster had his crew throw overboard the cargo that he had agreed to trade for the captives. The Africans watched 20 barrels of rum and eight cases of calico cloth in watertight casks tumble from the ship into the sea, where they were quickly collected and brought to shore by the Kru oarsmen. 'De boats take something to de ships and fetch something way from de ships. Dey comin' and goin' all de time,' Kossula remembered.[33]

Then it was time for the captives to be boarded. First, they watched Foster as he stepped into a canoe and was piloted across the one and a half mile stretch of water separating the ship from the land. Then it was their turn to board the canoes in small groups. In the tempestuous rainy season, the surf beat most ferociously along the coast, and the southeasterly sea breeze was beginning to gather strength. The captives were forced to listen to what one witness described as the 'dull booming roar' of the water as they waited to be taken across the sea. Mahommah Gardo Baquaqua watched dozens of enslaved people on the boat ahead of him drown in the tumultuous sea on his short journey to the slave ship that would spirit him from Ouidah to Brazil. Only one particularly strong captive man was able to right the canoe and save himself.[34] The *Clotilda* captives were much luckier: none of their boats capsized.

As they were about to board the schooner, their captors stripped the prisoners of their clothes and almost certainly shaved them. Kossula never forgot the shock of his enforced nakedness. 'When we ready to leave de Kroo boat and go in de ship, de Many-costs snatch our country cloth off us. We try save our clothes, we ain used to be without no clothes on. But dey snatch all off us. Dey say, "You get plenty clothes where you goin'".' Nearly seventy years later, tears sprang to his eyes and his voice cracked when he shared the memory of it. 'Oh Lor', I so shame! We come in de 'Merica soil naked and de people say we naked savage. Dey say we doan wear no clothes. Dey doan know de Many-costs snatch our clothes 'way from us.'[35]

To the identity of a Yoruban youth such as Kossula, dress was everything. Clothing, hairstyles and body adornments indicated one's place in society, as underscored by the Yoruba saying 'iri ni si ni isonilojo' (one's appearance determines the degree of respect one receives). That made the removal of his hair and clothing particularly devastating; without the signifiers of his personhood, Kossula felt his Yoruba identity being stripped away. Abaché, the tall, round-faced woman who was kidnapped at 15, asserted pride in her appearance throughout her life in the United States; her centre-parted hair was always neatly combed. She also engaged until her death in Yoruba skin-beautifying practices, using face powder in place of the traditional plant- and mineral-based cosmetics she had known as a child.[36]

Among the captives forced onto the *Clotilda* was Gumpa, a small, slender-framed young Fon man. Like Kossula, Gumpa was probably no more than 19 or 20 years old, although the intricate body markings covering his stomach indicated that he was already an initiate in the aesthetics of Vodun, the religion of Dahomey. His sale was highly unusual; rarely did a Dahomey leader force a member of his own ethnic group into slavery. The kingdom's general rule was that their subjects should only be placed in bondage for committing a clearly defined and serious crime, and those it enslaved were mostly foreigners who had been kidnapped during an ambush or defeated in warfare. So how did one of King Glele's subjects end up in transatlantic exile? Redoshi remembered more than seventy years later being shaken by the sight of a Fon man when she was forced up the *Clotilda*'s rope ladder. She assumed he'd been helping to transport the captives before becoming trapped when the ship departed suddenly. 'Some Dahomey, he get on ship too. They never see ship before and big man on ship sail off with them too,' she told a journalist.[37]

It's true that the *Clotilda* left Ouidah in a hurry. Yet Emma Langdon Roche documented a more likely explanation for Gumpa's presence on the ship when, a decade after his death, she interviewed those *Clotilda* survivors who knew and lived with him. To promote good relations with the human trafficker, Akodé invited William

Foster to take into captivity a Dahomeyan subject he deemed to be of 'superior wisdom and exalted taste'. According to the historian, Gumpa was one of Akodé's cousins, and Foster chose a close relative of the prince in order to flatter him. Gumpa certainly understood that he had been given away by his kingdom. He latched onto oft-repeated words to convey to interviewers, with his limited English, the cruel logic of his circumstances: 'My people sold me and your people bought me.'[38]

A small 13-year-old girl known in the United States as Dinah Miller described being dazzled by red objects as she was piloted towards the slave ship. Her enslavers had noticed that the child captives, who were as young as 2 years old, were unusually drawn to the colour red. 'Then they decked the ship up with red lights and red bow ribbons 'cause they understood that the Africans loved the color red so much, and then the Africans got on there,' her great-granddaughter Arlonzia Pettway recalled. A small boy called Sawnee remembered being handed 'strands of bright colored beads', which were among the trinkets that William Foster packed onto the slave ship. Bougier went even further, describing 'a magic lantern show, music and good things to eat' as tactics used to lure the African children onto the schooner.[39]

Why might the young Africans have been so entranced? Red held visual power for West Africans prior to colonialism to an extent that is hard for contemporary eyes to comprehend. Not only did red hold spiritual significance in the Africans' homeland, but it was also unusual to encounter it in the natural world. In Benin and Lagos, according to one early seventeenth-century German merchant, red items and brass were prized above gold and silver. Cotton cloth was also highly prized as a commodity in West Africa. The region's longstanding familiarity with luxury Indian textiles and its own homegrown cotton industry made the cloth an important form of currency for Europeans and Americans buying human captives on the continent, including those now being forced onto the *Clotilda*.[40]

After 75 of the captives had been dragged on board and into the ship's hold, a loud and, to the Africans, incomprehensible cry came from up above them. 'Sail ho.'[41] A lookout in the ship's crow's nest had spotted an anti-slavery patrol 10 miles away. Foster scanned the waters and saw two steamboats bearing black and white distress flags speeding towards them. His illegal kidnapping operation had been rumbled. Panic ensued among the *Clotilda*'s crew. They were so sure the ship would be captured that they stopped boarding the Africans and tried to flee. But they were helpless against the heavy surf, which only the Kru oarsmen could navigate safely, and returned to imprisoning their human cargo as quickly as possible on a stream of canoes moving to and from the boat.

At that stage, Kossula was in one of two canoes that were crossing the one and a half mile stretch of water between the shore and the slave ship. Agonizingly for an African youth who spent the rest of his life grieving for his homeland, Kossula was almost one of those left behind. 'I in de last boat go out. Dey almost leaves me on de shore.' But the teenager, who had just endured the loss of his parents and most of his community, could not bear to lose sight of his friend and fellow 19-year-old Osia Keeby, a youth five and a half feet tall who later sported a carefully trimmed moustache on his round face and whose haunted eyes in old age gave stark expression to the horrors of his early life experiences, on his mysterious journey across the water. '[W]hen I see my friend Keebie in de boat I want go wid him,' he recalled. 'So I holler and dey turn round and takes me.'[42]

Those 35 captives still on the water, who included Kossula and Osia Keeby, were hurried onto the ship. With the anti-slavery patrol in sight, there was no time to board the final boat of 15 captives, who were still on the beach. As the *Clotilda* quickly set sail, it immediately found itself in a race with an anti-slavery patrol made up of two British steamboats, which got closer and closer and shifted position in their effort to intercept the slave ship. But the wind was in Foster's favour and the slave ship began to pull away.[43] After four hours at sea, the *Clotilda* had left both Ouidah and any chance of immediate rescue for the Africans far behind.

4

The Sea

The *Clotilda* survivors could never hope to forget the horrors of the Middle Passage, but they adopted different ways of responding to the searing traumas and aching losses that stalked them throughout their lives. Polee, the round-faced man with expressive eyes who kept his dark hair and goatee beard into old age, worked to shield his 15 children from the pain he endured as a 19-year-old. 'Papa was so sweet,' his daughter Clara Eva Bell Allen Jones remembered shortly before her death in the 1990s. 'He didn't tell us nothing bad, because we would have cried.' Instead, Polee talked constantly of his Yoruba homeland and how much he longed to take Eva and her siblings there: 'His whole heart's desire was to take us back to Africa with him.' When Emma Langdon Roche visited him in the final decade of his life, Polee sought stoically to bury his trauma. His interviewer was not fooled. She saw the haunted look in his eyes.[1]

By contrast, Dinah, the small 13-year-old who described seeing dazzling red objects on the *Clotilda*, recounted the injustices of her experiences daily right up to her death in 1933. She forced her descendants to gather around her and beat them if they did not pay attention, so determined was she that they should neither forget what she had endured nor the land from which she came.[2] But not even Dinah's daily re-enactments of her agonies could begin to impart the vicious loss of innocence the child endured when she arrived on the *Clotilda*. Once on board the ship, the young girl's confusion was swiftly replaced by the brutal realization that she was trapped. Those vibrant red colours that she remembered as having lured her onto the schooner were drowned out by an unyielding darkness as she was forced into the hold.

The captives' arrival on the *Clotilda* on 24 May 1860 brought both mortal terror and existential dread. Their imprisonment marked the beginning of a permanent estrangement from their homelands and heritages. Bereft of their freedom and of all but the body adornments that defined their ethnic identities, and ripped from almost everything and everyone that had given their lives logic, they were left in a crowded, sightless and ever-moving space. Kossula reported being chained to the floor of the hold. It's likely that only the young men were shackled, although 15-year-old Abaché, 12-year-old Redoshi and a dark-skinned 15-year-old girl with three deep marks running from the top of her nose to her cheeks named Zuma indicated that the women and some of the children might have been chained, too.[3] Regardless of how many were restrained, all were horribly confined in a space measuring no more than seven feet in height.

Thus began the shipmates' irreversible journey. For the next 13 days, the Africans were locked in the pitch-black and poorly venti-lated hold normally used to carry sugar, lumber and cotton, and found themselves wallowing in their own vomit and excrement. Most of them had never seen the sea before, let alone travelled on it. The water seemed to stretch away endlessly, raising in the young Africans countless questions but offering up none of its mysteries. Where did it lead? Did it lead anywhere at all?[4]

The shipmates' fears that they would never see land again were exacerbated by their hellish surroundings. The deafening sound of the waves beating against the boat, punctuated by the screams and groans of their fellow prisoners, left them in constant terror that the ship would keel over. Kossula expressed his suffering many decades later:'Oh Lor! I so skeered on de sea! De water, you unner-stand me, it make so much noise! It growl lak de thousand beastes in de bush. De wind got so much voice on de water. Oh Lor'!

Sometime de ship way up in de sky. Sometime it way down in de bottom of de sea. Dey say de sea was calm. Cudjo doan know, seem lak it move all de time.'5

Most of the shipmates were younger than 20. The Atlantic voyage must have been especially petrifying for those many child captives, some of whom — like Matilda and another little girl named Nannie — were as young as two and four years old. Few were accompanied by their parents on the voyage. Some did not even have extended family members to comfort them. One 14- or 15-year-old girl named Uriba was so terrified that she wept for days. Her shipmates tried in vain to reassure her despite their own agonies. Even 40 years later, Abaché, the girl with the centre parting, who was understood by Uriba's descendants to be Uriba's sister, was unable to recall the Middle Passage experience without crying. For those uninitiated young Africans, the transatlantic journey was the most perverse rite of passage into adulthood. There would be no banquets with wine and roast meat such as Kossula received when he learned the secret of the Oro, no kinfolk to mark their journey. Two-year-old Matilda's solitary facial mark, which spread from the bridge of her nose and then branched in two directions down her left cheek, would serve as a permanent reminder of the father she never knew and the West African childhood that was arrested almost as soon as it began. Her 10-year-old sister Sally's face bore the same 'crow-foot' pattern as well as four additional marks, marks Matilda would also have received if she had been allowed to grow up in Tarkar. Redoshi's crow-foot marks stood out on her high, wrinkled cheeks in the days before her death as the last visual evidence of her long-lost childhood.6

For those who were mothers, the journey was no less traumatic. Bougier's unused milk and the incessant cries of distressed children were torturous reminders that she was miles away from and powerless to return to her own three children. Gracie, who managed to hold onto her four daughters but was separated from her two sons, was forced to endure the young girls' fear and pain without being able to console them. Helpless to rescue them from the hell in which they found themselves or to protect herself, let alone her children, from the horrors of their journey, Gracie could only cling tightly to them as they whimpered in the darkness, their soft cries a cruel reminder of their lost brothers' voices.

The shipmates' agonies were exacerbated by extreme physical immobility and torturous claustrophobia. The slave ship's hold was six feet eleven inches deep, unusually large for a Gulf schooner, and Emma Langdon Roche noted that the Africans could at least stand up. 'The hole [sic] of the *Clotilde* [sic] was deep enough to permit of the men of lesser stature to stand erect,' she reported. However, recent archaeological investigations suggest the captives were confined to stacked platforms measuring no more than six feet long and one and a half feet wide. The section of the hold in which the 110 captives were confined was just twenty-three feet long and, accounting for the curve in the hull, ranged from eighteen to twenty-three feet wide.[7]

Foster's failure to board 15 of his prisoners before an anti-slavery patrol gave chase ensured the *Clotilda* was at least less crowded than the *Wanderer*, the penultimate slave ship to dock on US soil, which landed at Jekyll Island, Georgia, in November 1858. The prisoners of that vessel, mostly Congolese boys aged between 13 and 18, were packed so tightly together that they must have felt as if they had been buried alive. Forced to lie spoon fashion and each apportioned a space merely twelve inches wide, eighteen inches high and less than five feet in length, the youths' floating prison quickly became a human oven, so intense was the combined heat of so many closely packed bodies. By the time the foul-smelling, cockroach-infested ship reached Georgia, some 79 of the 487 ship-mates had died of suffocation and sickness. Astoundingly, at least one captive gave birth – to a baby girl named Clementine – in the *Wanderer*'s inferno.[8]

But the slightly less packed conditions on board the *Clotilda* were of little consolation to its captives, who were still 110 souls locked together in an extremely confined and deadly space. Despite the blistering heat, water was strictly rationed to about half a cup twice a day, which meant that relief from dehydration was a constant obsession. The liquid was stagnant and foul-tasting; vinegar had been added to it in the belief that it would prevent scurvy. The small daily ration of salt pork and crackers did little to sate the group's hunger but did increase their raging thirst. Kossula never forgot the agonizing physical deprivations he endured on the *Clotilda*: 'Dey doan give us much to eat. We so thirst! Dey give us a little bit of water twice a day. Oh Lor', Lor', we so thirst!'[9]

As the days wore on, the sickening stench of sweat mixed with bodily evacuations became increasingly unbearable. Twelve-year-old Redoshi remembered the smell being intense 'enough to kill you'. Though 2-year-old Matilda had no memory of the slave ship, she knew from her mother Gracie that it was 'evil smelling'. For the first 13 days, there was no relief. Poor ventilation combined with the June sun and the heat of closely packed bodies meant the captives were left struggling for breath amid the heavy, toxic air. With no knowledge of when they would ever see daylight again, those first days on the ship must have seemed an eternity. On average, a slave ship would typically be out of sight of land after eight days, by which point the captives would normally be brought on deck. But the *Clotilda* shipmates' confinement in the darkness was painfully extended. On 4 June, the captives' twelfth day at sea, the ship finally passed Cape Palmas, a headland on the southeastern edge of Liberia which was both the *Clotilda*'s last sight of the African continent and a settlement for repatriated ex-bondspeople. A boat on anti-slavery patrol then spotted the schooner, and Foster feared he would be arrested for people smuggling. While he was saved by a heavy squall that carried the *Clotilda* away, he chose not to release the shipmates from the hold until the following day, when he felt sure they would not be seen.[10]

Redoshi felt so sick during that time that she thought she would die, even wishing for death to alleviate her suffering.[11] And the chances of death at sea were in fact perilously high. A host of pathogens, appalling sanitation and the captives' weakened immune systems made the slave ship incredibly dangerous for human habitation. The most common killer was dysentery, which cruelly depleted fluid from bodies wracked by dehydration. Deadly infectious diseases such as influenza, malaria, measles and smallpox were also common, all of them thriving in the cramped, unsanitary quarters. Flesh rubbed raw by iron restraints and sores caused by lying continually on hard wood planks could easily become infected. Scurvy was a constant threat after months at sea. Torturous skin and eye conditions could also have deadly consequences.

To survive these physical and psychological horrors, the captives strove to hold onto reminders of their African identities during their Atlantic voyage. In Tarkar, traditions were valued and respected. Children learned parables from their mothers and other community elders. The stories were framed metaphorically around the animals that lived in the surrounding savanna and forest and were intended to teach children how to be good citizens. Kossula loved listening to his elders and held onto the stories for the rest of his life. 'Cudjo like very much to listen,' he explained. For shipmates such as Kossula and Kanko, the small, light-skinned child who remembered paying for goods back home with shillings and who bore a facial mark on her right cheek, parables would later serve as vital psychological links with their homeland, and they devised their own stories to help them process the many traumas they endured in the United States.[12]

To their enduring shame, the *Clotilda* shipmates were, as we have seen, forced to travel across the Atlantic naked. But Dinah told her great-granddaughter Arlonzia that she managed to save from Africa a small piece of raffia cloth, which she called 'African grass pattern or something like that'. For Dinah and her descendants, that piece of cloth was her one physical connection with home. As late as the 1890s, one shipmate still wore on each wrist bracelets that she made or received, perhaps as a symbol of betrothal, as a young girl in West Africa. Bracelets were an important source of currency in West Africa during the transatlantic slave trade. Perhaps the girl hoped she could use the items to survive financially in the United States, or even buy her freedom 6,000 miles away from home. But there, the hand-crafted objects would have no monetary significance. Whether or not Polee retained a bracelet of cowrie shells that marked him as a servant, or devotee, of the orishas is unclear. But for the rest of his life, he wore hoop earrings that served as enduring symbols of his Yoruban faith.[13]

Like other Yoruba speakers, Polee and his fellow townsfolk believed in a single creator god named Oluwa and expected their actions on earth to be judged in heaven. They also believed in a pantheon of spirits, or orishas, each with its own dedicated priest, shrine and associated symbol. Orishas were intermediaries between worshippers and their god that were ritually invoked for advice or to praise. Some orishas, such as the iron spirit Ogun and sea spirit Yemoja, were believed to have accompanied God at the time of creation. Others, such as the thunder spirit Shango, were revered ancestors, for the Yoruba believe that while the soul ascends to heaven, the spirit remains on earth. Other orishas were associated with specific places, such as hills, rivers and forests. The earrings that Polee wore throughout his life indicate that he was a servant of the orishas and had already completed many months of religious devotion before he arrived in Alabama. 'Polee' was probably a diminutive of his initiation name, Kupollee.[14]

Lacking physical objects from home to hold onto, Zuma, the dark-skinned 15-year-old with prominent facial markings, and another girl in her late teens named Amey, clung instead to lullabies. More than forty years after the *Clotilda*'s voyage, Zuma readily recited her song, which her mother used to sing to her, to a visitor. She never forgot the words of the song. By that stage of her life, Zuma had finally come to accept that she would never see her mother again, but she continued to hope that somehow news of her survival and ultimate transition to freedom had reached her.[15]

After 13 days at sea, the *Clotilda* encountered northeast trade winds that would carry the vessel at a rate of 12 to 14 miles, or about 9.5 to 11 knots, per hour across the Atlantic for the next three and a half weeks. With all sight of Cape Palmas – and West Africa – left behind, the hatch was finally raised and the *Clotilda* captives were pulled from the hold. They rapidly shielded their faces from the sudden glare of the sun, which must have felt like pokers to the eyes after nearly two weeks in constant darkness. Salty sea spray whipped their unprotected bodies and cut into flesh rubbed raw by shackles and the wooden planks on which they were forced to lie, but the fresh, clean air meant they could finally breathe freely. They tried to stand, but their legs failed them, their muscles having atrophied during their confinement. Their captors led them in small groups on painful walks around the deck until finally the feeling and some of the strength in their limbs returned. Kossula described the gruelling experience to Zora Neale Hurston. 'We so weak we ain able to walk ourselves, so de crew take each one and walk 'round de deck till we git so we kin walk ourselves.' Kossula's shackles were left on as he learned to walk again, rendering the 'therapy' even more torturous and making it impossible for him to walk without stumbling.[16]

As they were led around the boat, the shipmates looked keenly all around them, desperately seeking to gain a sense of their bearings. Kossula craned his neck in every direction, hoping for some sign of an end to their journey. 'We lookee and lookee and lookee and lookee and we doan see nothin' but water. Where we come from we doan know. Where we goin, we doan know.' Kossula's spatial confusion was echoed by Bougier. The grieving mother tried to make sense of her surroundings, but later recalled that she 'can't see nothin', just endless water'.[17] There were miles of ocean all around. No land was in sight. Nor was any end to their ordeal.

The words of their pale-skinned tormentors, distorted and incomprehensible, held no clues as to the captives' fate beyond an expectation that it would be marked by violence. The men's rough voices were rarely directed at the shipmates anyway, except for when a captive was slow to follow their physical gesticulations, which, to the shipmates, were equally crude and cryptic. Child captive Redoshi remembered physical force as her captors' main means of communication, especially towards those who indicated that they might try to end their misery by jumping overboard. 'White men, yes, many white men with whip and stick keep us from going off boat.'[18]

The shipmates' total ignorance of what was going to happen, and their captors' readiness to use violence against them, infused them with tremendous fear. A 15-year-old girl named Abile, the future wife of Kossula, expected to be eaten by the pale-faced men who held her prisoner when the ship reached land.[19] Abile assumed that her maturing body was the reason for her kidnappers' interest in her and in a cruel sense she was right. Her buyers were looking for young girls with many fertile years ahead of them who would be capable of enriching them with lots of enslaved children. Yet Abile's fear was also a logical consequence of the ways in which she and her shipmates were mistreated. The forced nakedness. The intrusive physical examinations. The occasional exercise on deck to reawaken their muscles. To Abile, it was clear her captors were interested in them only as objects, not as people.

Fears of white cannibalism were widespread throughout West Africa during the era of the transatlantic slave trade. In his 1789 memoir, abolitionist Olaudah Equiano reflected on his abject terror of being eaten, first when he was placed on a slave ship to Barbados, then when he was sold on the ship, and finally when he was sent back across the Atlantic to England. Equiano's contemporary Ottobah Cugoano also expected to be eaten when he first saw the white men who would spirit him from Cape Coast in modern-day Ghana to Grenada.[20]

In fact, Abile had every reason to fear being eaten. Yet her would-be predators were not the white men who held her captive, but, rather, the sharks whose silver fins flashed in the waters around her. Sharks and other species of fish latched onto slave ships from their arrival on the West African coast and they were known to follow the boats across the Atlantic. Kossula remembered being tortured throughout the *Clotilda*'s journey by the possibility that the ship would tip over and the shipmates would become shark food.[21] The predators were attracted by the bodily waste and other refuse that was thrown over the sides of the ships. To sharks, slave ship detritus represented reliable sources of sustenance. The creatures seemed instinctively to know that, where bodily waste fell, bodies were likely to follow. Lengthy journeys and already unsanitary conditions, frequently exacerbated by intense heat, meant that cadavers were not stored on ships. Instead, to be thrown to the sharks was the fate of all those who died on board as well as all those who hoped, by jumping overboard to their deaths, to return to Africa.

If the captives spent nearly the first third of their journey trapped in the ship's hold, then they at least appear to have been granted more time than average above deck for the final 32 days of the voyage. '[W]e spend some time layin' down in de ship till we tired, but many days we on de deck,' recalled Kossula. After the thirteenth day, the captives had relative freedom to move about on deck. They were divided into gangs. One group at a time was allowed to ascend to the deck, while their shipmates below took on the miserable task of cleaning out the waste in which they had been forced to lie. The occasional arrival of wet weather whenever the captives were out on deck brought unimaginable relief for Kossula and his shipmates, for it meant they could at least drink the rainwater they caught in their mouths and hands.[22]

However, the shipmates' mobility was swiftly curtailed whenever Foster thought the ship's illegal activities might be uncovered. According to Redoshi, 'Cap'n, he put glass to eye and look all day. When he see danger come, he drive us below. But we go on deck when danger gone.' The Africans watched Foster hold his telescope against his long nose constantly, so fearful was he of being caught at every stage of the voyage. The US Navy had just increased from five to thirteen vessels its Home Squadron, which was charged with catching ships smuggling Africans across the Atlantic. The new vessels included four steamships that were situated in the Gulf of Mexico. On the twentieth day of the Africans' captivity, Foster ascended the *Clotilda*'s mast, gazed for some time into the distance and then hurried back down to the deck. He had sighted another ship that he feared might arrest him. In response, the crew was ordered to lower the sails and drop the anchor. The shipmates were forced below deck and made to wait there until nightfall.[23] Any time back inside the hold, especially after being granted limited freedom on deck, must have seemed nightmarish to the captives.

As their ordeal continued for a seemingly interminable period, the Africans were forced to measure their voyage in time rather than space. Totally unfamiliar with the motions of a ship, they had no way of knowing how far they had travelled and just how far from home they were. Uncertainty was cruelly unscored by incessant repetition. Apart from the changes in the weather and their captors' behaviour, one day was exactly like the next for most of the voyage, with no sign that their journey would ever end. While the moon's cycles told them how long they had spent on deck, they told them neither how far they were from home nor where they were going. Time, for the shipmates, came to a standstill. Kossula repeatedly suggested that the 44-day Atlantic passage had lasted 70 days or more. Redoshi went even further, speculating that she might have been on the boat for a year.[24]

A man and probably at least three children died during the *Clotida*'s voyage, joining the approximately 1.8 million – or 15 per cent – of Africans who died on the Middle Passage voyage. Redoshi remembered a young girl who was terribly sick on board the ship and witnessed first-hand the captors' disposal of the child's body. One night, when they thought the other captives were asleep, crew members crept into the hold with torches. They wrapped the girl in muslin cloth, gathered up her small form and carried her up the ladder and out of the hold. Redoshi followed them onto the deck to see what they were doing. She then watched in horror as they dropped the child into the sea. 'They no tell us what [they] do, but I know she dead.' Redoshi watched one of her townsfolk suffer the same watery fate after falling ill. 'Bimeby, man Tarkar, he go same way.' Gracie also told her daughter Matilda when the child was old enough to comprehend the brutal circumstances of the pair's arrival in the United States that she saw the bodies of two Yoruba boys who died from illnesses thrown out to sea. One of the children was Gracie's nephew and Matilda's cousin.[25]

Three, or possibly four, other shipmates very probably died at sea or within days or even hours of their arrival in the United States. According to an anonymous handwritten note, a 16-year-old girl perished just two days or so into the voyage, presumably from shock and terror. That cannot have been the girl whose sea burial Redoshi witnessed, as her death occurred before the Africans were allowed out of the hold. A journalist who interviewed Kossula immediately after the death of Osia Keeby in February 1923 learned from the grieving man that 'eight of these unfortunates died', while US marshal Cade Madison Godbold reported shortly after the *Clotilda*'s landing that he had located 103 trafficked Africans. Cade's assertion was supported by a *Montgomery Mail* article published less than a week after the *Clotilda*'s landing that stated 103 captives were brought ashore. That figure, which suggests seven captives died at sea, is likely to be quite accurate as its author gave other strikingly precise details about the schooner's arrival: the captives were taken 12 miles above Mobile (the schooner was scuttled at Twelve Mile Island, whose name marks its distance from the port of Mobile) and moved to Alabama's 'Cane district' (the Africans were hidden amid a maze of canebrakes at Mount Vernon). Later that month, federal proceedings were initiated against conspirators John Milton Dabney and Burns Meaher for trafficking 103 Africans.[26]

For a West African, death at sea was particularly horrifying. There was no opportunity for funeral rites, no sacred burial ground and no objects that they could take with them to sustain them in the afterlife. When Kossula's grandfather became ill and died at home in Africa, his body was wrapped in the finest cloths his loved ones could afford and buried deep beneath the clay floor of his property to ensure his continual spiritual attachment, as an ancestor, to his family. Kossula explained the custom to Zora Neale Hurston: 'We say in de Affica soil, "We live wid you while you alive, how come we cain live wid you after you die?" So, you know dey bury a man in his house.'[27] But there was no clear route to the ancestral realm in the middle of the ocean. Instead, the captives were consigned to oblivion.

It is unclear from Matilda and Redoshi's accounts if the children and man were already dead when they were cast into the water. If William Foster thought their illnesses could spread to the other captives or even to the crew, he might not have waited until they had stopped breathing before getting rid of them, for it was not unusual for slave ship captains to dispose of still-living captives. A harrowing story that Kossula supposedly gave to an Alabama journalist in 1925, and which the journalist reported four months after the African man's death in 1935, suggested that the *Clotilda*'s captain had been only too ready to dispose of his prisoners when they jeopardized his own precarious situation at sea. According to Kossula's posthumously documented account, at one stage of the voyage, fearful that the ship would be boarded by an anti-slave trade cruiser policing the Atlantic Ocean, all the captives were forced on deck and shackled to the anchor chain. If the cruiser had caught up with the *Clotilda*, the ship's anchor would have been released, plunging the helpless shipmates into the ocean.[28]

Whenever the captives were allowed above deck, they continued to scrutinize their surroundings, seeking to understand their ocean environment and when their journey might possibly end. Unable to measure the distance they had travelled, they began to interpret their surroundings in colours. Kossula and his friends remembered the surface of the sea turning from blue to green as they moved closer to land, a change reflected by the rise in plant life as they travelled nearer to the shore. The Africans also described passing through water the colour of blood.[29] They may have encountered a red tide, a harmful bloom of algae that causes the sea surface to turn red and can poison the air around it. Red tides are typically engendered by powerful storms and are common around Florida each summer. Equally, the Africans' description of lurid red water may have been a coded reference to the disposal of their shipmates in the shark-infested ocean.

On the evening of 30 June, after 37 days at sea, the schooner sailed by Great Abaco, an island in the Bahamas. The sun was setting and Kossula and his shipmates gazed in amazement at the beam of light that shone from the island's red and white lighthouse tower. The sight of land for the first time in six weeks brought them breathless hope that they would finally be released from their maritime prison. To their dismay, however, the *Clotilda* did not stop, although it did dramatically change direction to avoid hitting a shipwreck. Spotting it just in time in the falling light, the lookout yelled out 'hard-a-starboard'.[30] Before the shipmates knew what was happening, the *Clotilda* lurched suddenly to the right and the schooner continued onward, having missed the wreck by just ten feet.

The next day, the *Clotilda* entered the Gulf of Mexico and passed by Dry Tortugas, a group of islets inhabited by turtles and seabirds 70 miles west of Key West, Florida. The ship was then spotted by two anti-slave trade patrols that were stalking the waters north of Cuba. But it drew no attention from them, for its crew had removed the square sail yards and foretopmast that marked the *Clotilda* as an ocean-going vessel. There was nothing to indicate to the patrollers that more than 100 young African people were trapped on board. Foster and his accomplices made it safely to US waters with their prisoners.

The *Clotilda* carried on steadily towards Alabama's port city of Mobile, eventually anchoring off the Point aux Pins peninsula on the eastern edge of Grand Bay in the Mississippi Sound on Saturday 7 July 1860. As they approached land, the Africans were sent back below deck to wait and wonder in their pitch-black prison. Finally, their captors handed them tree branches, thick with green leaves, to tell them that land was near. Kossula understood immediately what that meant: after more than six weeks at sea, their ordeal was almost at an end.[31] Soon they would find out what was waiting for them on land.

5

Arrival

In the early hours of Sunday 8 July 1860 the Africans heard fierce shouting from the white men holding them prisoner. Unbeknown to the captives, William Foster's human smuggling operation was not going to plan, and the schooner's crew were mutinying out of fear he would abandon them. The captain had promised the men they would be met at Point aux Pins by his co-conspirators, who would immediately pay them and rid them of their incriminating human 'cargo'. They were then to sail the *Clotilda* across the Gulf to Tampico in eastern Mexico, where they were to register the schooner with a new name to hide its crime before sailing it back to US waters.[1] But lookouts posted to spot the *Clotilda* had failed to do so and there was no one at Point aux Pins to meet the ship, leaving them at risk of being spotted – and their crime exposed – at any minute. So fearful were the crew that Foster would take the captives without paying them and leave them to their fate that they threatened to kill him. That left him with only one option: to spirit the schooner and its prisoners up Mobile Bay.

Hoping that the removal of its rigging, spars and sails would fool onlookers that the *Clotilda* was a local trading vessel rather than a transatlantic sailing ship, Foster went off to find a steamboat that could tow it up the Spanish River, a secluded eight-mile stretch of water surrounded by marshes and bayous at the north of Mobile Bay. Foster climbed down the *Clotilda*'s rope ladder and boarded a small boat rowed by four of his sailors. As the party reached the mouth of the bay, shots rang out, fired by men on land who were suspicious of this mysterious man on the water. Foster waved a white handkerchief, which reassured the aggressors that he posed no threat. In his desperation to hide his crime, he offered the outlandish sum of $25 (around $900 in today's money) for a horse, wagon and enslaved driver to transport him 30 miles north to Mobile.[2]

It was not yet daybreak when the *Clotilda*'s captain reached the house of his friend William Henry Toomer on Telegraph Road, a seven-mile stretch of highway running north from the city of Mobile; he woke the South Carolina-born steamboat captain to tell him of the schooner's successful landing. Toomer leapt out of bed and jumped on a horse to share the news with Timothy Meaher, who lived five miles up the road in a two-storey, south-facing house perched on top of a red clay hill. Meaher was already awake and smoking on the upper deck of his balcony with his heels resting on its railings when he heard hooves on the hard clay road and saw his fellow captain pull up at his gate red-faced, breathless and waving one arm in the air. Meaher's enslaved house servant, a man in his mid-thirties named Noah Hart, witnessed the commotion. Noah had been unaware of the slave ship conspiracy until then, but he deduced what was happening when William Toomer panted out in a breathless whisper, "the n——s have come!"[3] Meaher ran to his stable, ordered Noah to saddle up his horse and then raced back down Telegraph Road into the city with William Toomer.

Timothy Meaher had been due the following afternoon to captain his 135-passenger steamboat the *Roger B. Taney* on its weekly journey from Mobile to Montgomery, but he put his second mate in temporary charge of the vessel and promised to catch up with it later that day.[4] He gave the mate strict instructions to wait for him before allowing supper to be served on the *Taney* so that he would have an alibi. Meaher tasked his younger brother Burns with piloting his steamboat the *Czar* to the Spanish River, where he told him to lie in wait.

The Meahers then arranged for a third steamboat to tow the

Clotilda up Mobile Bay. Four and a half years earlier, the *William Jones, Jr.* was where the *Clotilda* bet was placed. Now the vessel would help conceal its captives. The steamer's pilot James 'Captain' Hollingsworth was worshipping in St. John's Episcopal Church that Sunday. Timothy Meaher's other brother James rushed to the two-storey wooden structure on Dearborn Street in downtown Mobile. Accompanying him was Burns Meaher's enslaved steamboat pilot James Dennison, a Charleston-born 20-year-old of mixed African American and Muscogee (Creek) heritage who wore two five-inch plaits in his otherwise straight black hair. Despite his youth, he already had an outstanding knowledge of the local rivers and water-ways that were vital to the Meahers' smuggling operation. James Meaher made his enslaved pilot wait outside the church while he went inside. Then, he found Hollingsworth at his pew and told him that a perishable cargo needed towing upriver from Point aux Pins, with no questions asked.[5] The two of them hurried out of the church together and made their way to Mobile Bay, and Hollingsworth quickly piloted the steamer down the bay in search of the *Clotilda* with William Foster, brothers Timothy and James Meaher, and James Dennison.

Foster still had no money for his crew and when he returned with the *William Jones* they mutinied again, refusing to let him take command of the schooner. Foster was forced to travel back into Mobile from Mobile Bay with the steamboat to fetch money to pay his men. His fellow conspirators and the *Clotilda*'s crew were deeply afraid that the federal authorities would catch up with them in the meantime, and the shipmates were ordered to stay silent. Though the English words were strange to them, the threatened violence in their captors' voices and gestures was clear.

As the *Clotilda* waited to be tugged up Mobile Bay, the shipmates were forced to lie for hours in the dark, foul-smelling hold. Their suffocating agony was made worse by the extreme heat that coincided with the final days of their transatlantic voyage and the first days of their arrival in Alabama. In Cahaba, a town 150 miles upriver, the mercury barely dropped below 95 degrees Fahrenheit (35 degrees

Celsius) from 29 June to 11 July. No white settler could remember such perishing temperatures, and Mobile recorded 58 deaths in one week, many directly attributable to the heat.[6] That evening, the blaring sun lingered in the sky until eight o'clock, as if keen to spotlight the crime that had brought the shipmates there. But their captors waited for darkness and for the return of William Foster and his money, so they could journey up the bay in secrecy.

Eventually, night fell. Foster returned with $8,000 and five additional men, and the *William Jones* began to tow the *Clotilda* up the 24-mile-wide bay. 'When it night de ship move agin,' recalled Kossula. 'Cudjo didn't know den whut dey do, but dey tell me dey towed the ship up de Spanish Creek to Twelve-Mile Island.'[7] The steamboat ran at about ten miles, or eight knots, per hour, which meant the journey just to the mouth of the bay took an excruciating three hours. Every movement of the schooner was read by the Africans as a potential sign of danger, and they were deeply alarmed by the constant blasts of hot steam that rose noisily out of the steamboat's high-pressure boiler through its tall metal steam whistles. They assumed a swarm of bees had latched themselves onto the ship.

As it reached the mouth of Mobile Bay, the steamboat veered right up the Spanish River for eight miles instead of going straight up the Mobile River, which would have taken the *Clotilda* through the city of Mobile and past the customs at Magazine Point, where its crime was certain to be exposed. The steamboat then re-entered the Mobile River when the two rivers rejoined each other north of the city. As the *Clotilda* passed Mobile from a distance, the clock on the old Spanish tower struck eleven times, and the watchman called out: 'Eleven o'clock and all's well.'[8] Such words would have seemed callous to the shipmates if they had understood them.

Even in the decades after the Africans' emancipation, the clandestine nature of the *Clotilda*'s voyage and its status as an enduring secret meant that many of them never learned the full details of their journey. The mysteries of their kidnapping added to their experience of transatlantic dislocation as an incomprehensible trauma. Even at the end of her life, Redoshi did not know the name of the schooner that smuggled her to the United States. In answer to a journalist's question, 'What was the name of the boat?', she replied, 'Me no know. Can't read and nobody said.' She only knew the first name of her kidnapper, who she called 'Wa-Yam' because English was still a strange language to her, and her tongue could never manage to shape the double 'L' and 'I' in the middle of his name.[9]

In the early hours of the morning, the captives reached Twelve Mile Island, a roughly one-mile square island about 12 miles above the Port of Mobile. Emma Langdon Roche termed the site 'a lonely, weird place by night' when she visited it five decades later.[10] There, the shipmates found a massive steamboat, the *Czar*, capable of transporting 150 passengers lying in wait. Burns Meaher had followed his brother's instructions to bring the *Czar* to meet him. The *Clotilda* and *Czar* were positioned side-by-side just south of the island behind a bend on the Spanish River. The *William Jones*, having completed its task, left the schooner and returned to Mobile. Then, torches were extinguished, and the captors crept into the *Clotilda*'s hold under cover of darkness. They removed the prisoners from the hold and gave them some clothes to cover their bodies. Though these clothes amounted to nothing more than a few sparse rags, the captives' relief was unimaginable. It was their first access to clothing for nearly seven weeks.

The captors then wordlessly drove the prisoners into the hold of the *Czar*. Kossula and the other captives were too sick, emaciated and dehydrated to resist being forced from one boat's hold to another, or to do anything other than listen in terror as the hatches above them were fastened down and their new prison began to move. Their captors were deeply afraid, too, but for different reasons. They could be executed for their crimes, and they knew the schooner might have been sighted as it was towed up the river. Emma Langdon Roche reported that the plot to kidnap Africans was so open a secret locally that Timothy Meaher understood he was under government surveillance even before the *Clotilda*'s arrival. Conversely, Irish journalist Sir William Howard Russell learned when speaking with Meaher and another conspirator in May 1861 that local officials deliberately turned a blind eye to the vessel's arrival. 'Oddly enough, the sheriff was not about at the time, the United States Marshal was away,' he noted. The traffickers were also determined to hold onto their prisoners, who were each worth at least $1,000.[11]

After the captives were disembarked, the *Clotilda* was scuttled and set alight in the marshy bayou next to Twelve Mile Island. Kossula understood what that meant: 'dey skeered de gov'ment goin' rest dem for fetchin' us 'way from Affica soil.' Foster added seven cords of fatwood to speed up the destruction of the boat and his crime. But the concealment was only partially successful, for the glow from the burning wreck could be seen for miles around, and the *Clotilda*'s charred hull was still visible at low tide more than sixty years later.[12]

For the much of the next day, the Africans were locked in the *Czar*'s hold as it journeyed 37 miles further up the winding Mobile River. The captives spent hours in the sweltering darkness before the steamboat came to a halt near Mount Vernon in the far north of Mobile County. Relieved at last to escape the claustrophobic, stifling hold, the shipmates now found they were prisoners on the plantation of John Milton Dabney, where they were guarded by some of the Meahers' trusted conspirators. Dabney was a Virginia-born enslaver and merchant who relocated to Alabama in the 1840s. His wife Elizabeth was the great-granddaughter of US founding father Patrick Henry, whose 'Give me liberty, or give me death!' speech calling for militiamen to take arms against the British at the Second Virginia Convention in March 1775 helped shape the course of the American Revolution.[13]

The Africans were trapped in a nearly three-thousand-acre maze of endless canebrakes, swamps and forests of ash trees, white oaks and giant bald cypress trees bearing nests of grey Spanish moss so long and thick they almost touched the ground. The *Clotilda*'s sails were crafted into a tent, which served as the survivors' only shelter and provided little protection against the snakes and mosquitoes as the group lay hidden among the canebrakes. Kossula remembered that the captives were bitten so badly by mosquitoes 'dey 'bout to eat us up'.[14]

After transplanting the Africans on the Dabney plantation, William Foster, the Meahers and the *Clotilda*'s crew returned to the *Czar* and travelled slightly further upriver, to the point where the Mobile branched off to form the Tombigbee and Alabama rivers. The group then waited for the *Roger B. Taney* to appear on its evening journey. But the *Clotilda*'s crew were angry. The $8,000 that Foster had brought from Mobile meant they would receive only their originally agreed salary of around $700 each. They would not see the double wages that Foster had been forced to promise them when they reached Africa and found they were part of an illegal trafficking voyage. The men mutinied one final time. Foster was worried his kidnapping venture was still in danger and used threats of extreme violence to put down the mutiny. He took a pistol in each hand and fired both weapons before ordering the men to 'hit the grit and never be seen in Southern waters again'.[15]

At 9.00 p.m., the *Taney* appeared. The *Clotilda*'s crew were quickly smuggled aboard and locked inside the upper deck of the steamer with cards and whisky to keep them occupied, and Timothy Meaher also quietly boarded the vessel. When supper was served 30 minutes later, Meaher took his seat at the head of the dinner table, pretending to have been on the steamboat all evening. He now had a compelling alibi: scores of witnesses could confirm he had been on the *Taney* as usual that day. Still, his absence had been noticed and his fellow diners queried his whereabouts. He gave no direct answer to their questions. He confined the *Clotilda*'s crew until the steamboat reached Montgomery, when he sneaked them onto a mail train to New York.

Despite his supper performance, news of the *Clotilda*'s landing spread quickly. According to William Foster 40 years later, it was known about in Mobile the next day. Henry Romeyn thought the enslaved steamboat workers coopted into transferring the Africans from the schooner to the *Czar* shared the information. Conversely,

S. H. M. Byers understood that witnesses reported seeing a mysterious boat standing on the coast and that Timothy Meaher had even sighted a US government vessel as he was hurrying to reach the *Clotilda* and its captives. Regardless of how the information leaked out, the schooner's trafficking voyage immediately made the national news. On 10 July, newspapers in Kentucky, Louisiana, Mississippi, New York State, Ohio, Tennessee and Wisconsin reported that the 'schooner *Clotilda*' had landed between 103 and 124 Africans in Mobile Bay the previous day and that the group had then been taken upriver by steamboat. Newspapers throughout the nation repeated the information the next day. New York-based *Harper's Weekly*, the best-selling illustrated newspaper in the country, reported twice on the *Clotilda*'s landing that month, and the news travelled internationally on 18 July when Cuban newspaper *Diario de la Marina* referenced the schooner, and again on 23 July, when the *Liverpool Mercury* and London *Standard* repeated the story.[16]

The *Mobile Register*'s editor John Forsyth was almost certainly aware of the *Clotilda*'s crime. On 12 July, three days after the schooner was scuttled and burned, he called in his newspaper for what he termed the 'odious' anti-slave trade statutes to be repealed. Asserting that reopening the slave trade was a decision for the South alone, Forsyth claimed to speak for the entire region when he declared that 'we chafe with a scarcely repressible impatience under the degrading reflection which these Slave-trade statutes cast upon our institutions and our people', even as he acknowledged that 'the mind of the South is *as yet* unprepared' for the slave trade's reopening and time needed to be spent 'developing and elucidating the question'. Two days later, the *Mobile Register* commented directly on the *Clotilda*'s arrival, declared that the 'sons of Africa' were now 'safe' from '*deportation*' and that 'whoever conducted this affair has our congratulations on his or their success.' In a 23 July article partially reprinted in the *New York Times*, the *Mobile Mercury* at first feigned ignorance of the schooner. 'Who has seen the Clotilde [sic]? Was she burned and nobody saw a vessel on fire in the bay?' But then it acknowledged, 'We have an idea that her rigging and *all portable things of value* were saved.'[17]

The act of piracy that brought the Africans to the United States, and even the name of the ship that had trafficked them, were now public knowledge, and the Mobile Custom House was forced to investigate reports a schooner had slipped up the Mobile River without paying custom duties. On 12 July, Mobile customs officer Thaddeus Sandford wrote to US Secretary of the Treasury Howell Cobb informing him of the schooner's arrival and followed up with a telegram the next day reporting that he had telegraphed the New Orleans customs office to help investigate. Around the same time, acting district attorney Lewis S. Lude sent a letter to the US Attorney General in Washington DC 'relative to the recent importation of negroes in Alabama'.[18]

Timothy Meaher and his co-conspirators moved the captives around repeatedly and divided them into smaller groups in order to escape detection. The shipmates correctly deduced they were being hidden from someone working against their captors. But the canebrake that ran rampant on John Dabney's land and the endless trees behind them made it easy to conceal the Africans. It also added to the shipmates' feelings of disorientation and despair. Vast thickets of cane that were much taller than they were grew all around them in every direction. Once again, their vision was obscured by a hostile landscape where everything in front of them looked the same. The *Clotilda* survivors' grief was overwhelming. How could they ever hope to find their way home amid such a maze of trees and bamboo?

The captives had spent the past two months with very little food, water, sunlight or fresh air. There was little flesh left to cover the bones beneath their discoloured skin, which was ridden with open sores, and their eyes protruded alarmingly above their hollow cheekbones. Captain Edmund Gardiner Fishbourne, a British seaman who was involved in the suppression of the slave trade off the coast of Sierra Leone in the 1830s and 1840s, was so appalled by the skeletal physique of slave ship survivors that he likened them to 'paper-jointed men', and despaired that it took three whole months to nurse them back to health.[19]

The Africans continued to suffer physically on their arrival in the United States as they were so poorly fed. Redoshi remembered initially being 'tied . . . out to eat grass' as if she were an animal before finally being fed ground corn mixed with water. The shipmates' bodies were wracked by intestinal and skin diseases and probably also scurvy. If they were anything like the *Wanderer* survivors who demolished raw the ears of corn that had still to be picked from a Georgian field in the winter of 1858, then they ravenously filled their empty bodies with anything that passed for food.[20]

For the next 11 days, the Meahers moved the captives around the swamp to conceal them from federal authorities, which only added to their confusion and anguish. 'They take us up river and hide us in dogwoods. Wagons come and move us about from place to place,' Redoshi recalled.[21] They were forced to communicate in whispers, because their captors were afraid that their Yoruba language might be overheard and give their crime away.

On 18 July, 10 days after the *Clotilda*'s arrival, Thaddeus Sandford wrote to Howell Cobb that US marshal Cade Madison Godbold had in fact found more than 100 captives at the Dabney plantation, and that while he did not locate the *Clotilda*, he 'gained information that appears to be conclusive that she had been scuttled and sunk somewhere up the river'. Timothy Meaher claimed years later to have been arrested around that time, but his alibi – that he had never missed a journey on the *Taney* in the past year and was onboard it the day the *Clotilda* was burned and the Africans were smuggled upriver – meant he was immediately released on bond and free to continue concealing the captives and arranging their sale. His whereabouts when the *Clotilda* was towed up Mobile Bay appear not to have come under scrutiny. Moreover, he was supposedly charged only with 'personally' importing the Africans, a charge that would not have stuck as he remained in Alabama throughout the *Clotilda*'s voyage.[22]

Godbold wanted permission from the courts to seize the captives, but US District Judge William Giles Jones was suspiciously unreachable and acting district attorney Lewis S. Lude insisted, according to Cobb, that 'there is "no warrant in the statutes authorizing a process for taking possession of the negroes" in the absence of a Judge'. Local authorities were still waiting for a response from the US attorney general in Washington DC, Lude's letter in fact reaching him that same day. Sandford and Godbold nevertheless expressed determination to recover the captives. Sandford was concerned that the *Clotilda* Africans would be sold 'and so distributed and mingled with our slave population that they can never be identified', and reported that Godbold was 'much chagrined at this aspect of the case and proposed if I would stand by him to take the negroes at once into his possession'.[23]

Government officials did at least hire a steamboat, the *Eclipse*, after the captives were located. But Timothy Meaher made sure he was stationed with the *Taney* at Montgomery as the government vessel waited to leave the city, and he paid one of his employees to incapacitate its crew. 'The *Eclipse* is going after the negroes this evening. Take this and fix the crew with liquor,' Meaher instructed the man. He then set off down the Alabama River on the *Taney* to the Dabney plantation. It was not the first time the two steamboats had raced each other: Meaher had crashed into the *Eclipse* while showing off the *Taney* on its maiden voyage from Mobile to Montgomery three years earlier.[24] But this time there would be a clear winner. When the government officials sobered up the next day, Meaher and the *Taney* were miles away. The vessel spent the next week looking in vain for the captives.

When Meaher finally reached Mount Vernon on 20 July, he forced the Africans into the *Taney*'s hold. He then turned the boat around, but instead of returning up the Alabama River he turned left up the Tombigbee to his brother Burns's plantation 50 miles upriver in Grove Hill, Clarke County. Once again, Timothy Meaher called on the expertise of young James Dennison to help him conceal the *Taney* from the authorities. As Burns Meaher's enslaved steamboat pilot, James was forced to spend most of his days on the Tombigbee

River, and he expertly navigated its many sharp bends and the countless pieces of driftwood on the water that could sink the boat. When the federal officers arrived at the Dabney plantation many hours later, they found an abandoned camp but no Africans. They spent the next 10 days searching the canebrakes in vain for the captives. A rumour that a second slave ship had landed at Mullet Point on the eastern edge of Mobile Bay was spread to confuse their search still further.[25]

Those early days on Burns Meaher's plantation were torturous for the captives, who felt totally alienated by their unrecognizable, hostile environment. They were given no proper shelter and were forced to spend their nights under a wagon shed. When the sun rose each day, they were shooed onto wagons like farm animals and hidden in a swamp, where they passed the day before being driven back to the plantation at night. Their loneliness, uncertainty and fear, combined with the endless waiting and brutal treatment by their captors, made their grief overwhelming.

As the days passed, enslavers arrived one at a time to buy the Africans. The sales took place over a week and the drip feed of departures prolonged the shipmates' agony.[26] Every day, they were forced to repeat the trauma of separation and loss. On each occasion, the captives were made to stand in two long rows divided by sex while their would-be purchaser walked between them in a crude and degrading ritual that must have revived memories of the barracoon. They were subjected yet again, and this time repeatedly, to intimate physical examinations to judge their perceived value as enslaved property. These intrusions were once more a reminder that their captors viewed them as objects, not people, and Abile continued to fear for some time afterwards that she would be eaten by those rough pale-faced men.

At the end of the humiliating ordeal, some of the shipmates were forced to stand to one side and wait. The enslaver then waved his arm around them before bringing it to his chest, gesturing that he had decided to purchase them and that they must go with him. Those left behind knew only that their friends and relatives were being taken away from them. Their gradual under-standing that the separations were permanent filled them with dread for the next one.[27]

Selma banker and former Alabama state legislator Washington McMurray Smith, a large-framed, stern-faced 46-year-old with small, piercing eyes and receding curly hair, picked out two Africans from each row and purchased them as 'married' couples who, he hoped, would soon enrich him with enslaved children. Redoshi was one of the two female captives that Smith selected. Yawith, the tall, broad-shouldered, light-skinned and round-faced young man who had been separated from his children in the barracoon, was now her 'husband'. Redoshi was just a child and completely unprepared for a sexual partnership. She described her shock and despair at the arrangement 70 years later to civil rights leader Amelia Boynton Robinson. 'I was twelve years old and he was a man from another tribe who had a family in Africa.' Yawith was equally devastated, but for different reasons: attachment to a new wife was another sign he would never again see his family back home. So inappropriate was Redoshi and Yawith's partnership that they struggled to communi-cate with each other. 'I couldn't understand his talk and he couldn't understand me,' Redoshi recalled.[28]

Redoshi may already have been informally betrothed in Tarkar, but she would not have been expected to marry before the age of 20 and she would have been at liberty to reject her parents' chosen suitor. If she agreed to wed, she may not have been her husband's only bride. Tarkar was a polygamous society, with each man – including Kossula's father – having up to three wives. Polygamy was practised because large families were associated with higher social status, and women's economic contribution to the family was believed to outweigh the cost of their upkeep. Polygamy under-scored a wife's subservience to her husband, but it also afforded her a striking degree of economic and social independence for a nineteenth-century woman. Shared child and household care meant women had extensive freedom to travel and make their own money.[29]

Marriage and parenthood also failed to protect 2-year-old Matilda's mother Gracie from being paired arbitrarily to a fellow *Clotilda* survivor. The couple were sold to Memorable Walker Creagh, a tall 51-year-old with dark eyes and grey hair, who chose their bondage names Gracie and Guy to cement their pairing. Like Washington Smith, Creagh had been a Marengo County state legislator. He also happened to be one of the biggest enslavers in Wilcox County. What made things even more devastating for Gracie was that while Creagh also decided to purchase Matilda and her 10-year-old sister Sally, their two older sisters were not among the approximately twenty *Clotilda* Africans that he claimed that day.[30]

Thirteen-year-old Dinah, the child who remembered seeing dazzling red objects on the *Clotilda*, was forced to watch as her mother and brother were sold away from her and disappeared from her sight. 'She was separated from all of them right there and never seen them again,' her great-granddaughter Arlonzia explained. Dinah claimed she was the last person to be sold and that she was bought for just a dime because she was so small. 'This white man bought her, and she said she cost a dime. He paid a dime for her,' Arlonzia emphasized.[31] It is highly unlikely that a *Clotilda* survivor was sold for as small an amount as Dinah remembered, especially as they were worth at least $1,000 each to their captors. The dime may instead have been a token transaction between William Foster and the Meahers, for Dinah recalled being among 25 Africans who were first put to work in Mobile Bay, which suggests Timothy Meaher initially held on to her. Regardless of its accuracy, Dinah's dime story helped convey to her descendants the shock the *Clotilda* survivors felt to find their humanity so callously disregarded, and their lives reduced to mere monetary value. Dinah's size underscored the cruelty of her separation and her captors' broader disregard for enslaved children. Dinah was deemed too young for physical labour and yet still considered old enough to be ripped away from her family.

Those shipmates who had no family members left to lose were also devastated. The Africans formed a powerful bond on the

Clotilda and aided each other's survival on the transatlantic voyage. Adolescent captives helped to comfort even younger shipmates and supported them through their fear, pain and agonizing isolation. Now many of their friends were gone. The community they had forged on board the slave ship was being torn apart. In many cases, they would never see each other again.

The experience was almost too much for Kossula to describe even 70 years later. 'We very sorry to be parted from one 'nother,' he told Zora Neale Hurston. 'We cry for home. We took away from our people. We seventy days cross de water from de Affica soil, and now dey part us from one 'nother. Derefore we cry. We cain help but cry.' The sales were particularly traumatic because they reignited memories of the many losses the shipmates had endured over the past three months. 'Our grief so heavy look lak we cain stand it. I think maybe I die in my sleep when I dream about my mama. Oh Lor'!' Kossula recalled. The group sang a lament before their part-ing whose words included 'Iona se wu', which translates in English as 'no danger on the road'.[32] Powerless to protect each other from their respective fates, they instead offered one another spiritual protection on their journeys.

The *Clotilda* captives were scattered. Two boys were sent to Pickens County, near the border with Mississippi. Other captives found themselves on cotton plantations in Dallas, Marengo, Montgomery and Wilcox counties, all of them bordering or close to the Alabama River. A group of young girls and women – Amey, Judy, Lucy, Malinda and Mary – and a boy named Napoleon Bonaparte ended up in Baldwin County, on land overlooking Mobile Bay. Others remained in Clarke and Mobile counties. Colonel Thomas Buford, a Mobile-based enslaver and client of John Dabney whose Kentucky family claimed descent from Lady Margaret Beaufort, mother of King Henry VII and grandmother of King Henry VIII of England, bought four captives. William Foster received between eight and sixteen captives, including Abile. Kossula was one of about eight captives who were enslaved to James Meaher. Burns Meaher's plantation became the prison of Kanko, the small, light-skinned child with a distinctive crow-foot marking on her right cheek, and several other Africans. Timothy Meaher held on to the other shipmates, at least until they had recovered some of their strength and he could sell them on for a bigger profit.[33]

Timothy Meaher discarded the children and young people that he, Burns and William Foster claimed as their captives in a swamp less than a mile from his estate before returning home. His young wife Mary had received no news from him and rushed up to him, sobbing, for reassurance. 'It is all right?' she asked. 'We've done fooled 'em now,' he replied, throwing back his head and laughing; 'they're chasin' n——s the other side o' Montgomery, while the whole passel of 'em is dumped in a cane-brake about a mile from here.'[34] After supper, he decided it was time for the captives to eat and instructed his house servant Noah to supply them with pork and hoecake, a type of cornmeal flat cake.

When Noah located the shipmates that evening, he was confronted by what he later described as a 'terrible sight': the Africans were emaciated, disoriented and deeply afraid. Noah was also shocked to see the shipmates so poorly dressed. The few clothes they had been given when they were removed from the Clotilda were merely 'rags an' pieces er corn-sack an' skins tied round dey bodies'.[35] The materials hung off their slight frames. All the new sights and sounds that surrounded the Africans in their new environment filled them with terror, but they were too weak and too emotionally attached to their shipmates to do anything except wander around the swamp in confusion and fear, dreading whatever fate next had in store for them. Their starved bodies could not tolerate the food that Noah brought, so he spent the next four days trying to make them eat before they were moved to Timothy Meaher's plantation.

Noah could not understand the Africans and struggled to communicate with them, but he was struck by the beauty of their accents, which he later described as 'all quick an' soft an' smooth', and by the dignified way they carried themselves despite their emaciated states.[36] For the Africans, the rage they felt at their circumstances was made worse by its inexpressibility. Their anger unnerved Noah, who recalled that while they were never violent, they somehow seemed fierce.

Fifteen-year-old Abile suffered especially. She later confided to Foster's wife Adelaide that 'Albine [sic] not eat when she first come to America, because Albine know she fat an' did not want white people to eat her.'[37] The Atlantic voyage had robbed Abile of all her body fat, but her mistreatment like an animal for two months meant her fear of imminent destruction and consumption by her kidnappers had not faded.

Meanwhile, the hunt for the captives continued. On 27 July, US District Attorney Augustus Julian Requier shared with US District Judge William Giles Jones an affidavit from Cade Godbold stating that 103 Africans had been trafficked to the United States and that 40 of them were on John Dabney's plantation. The judge ordered them to be seized, and Dabney and Burns Meaher, who was accused of trafficking 'twenty five men, & twenty five women, twenty five boys, & twenty five girls', both received court summons. The following day, the government in Washington DC issued a writ of habeas corpus demanding the Africans' seizure, the *Eclipse* having now spent 10 fruitless days hunting for the captives. But they had already been sold and moved on. On 7 August, Requier reported to the judge that William Foster had failed to declare the *Clotilda* to customs, although a charge of piracy was never raised against him. In December, Burns Meaher and John Dabney were finally summoned before the Southern District Court of Alabama to answer smuggling charges, and William Foster appeared in court twice that month charged with customs law violations for failing to declare the *Clotilda*'s arrival and for withholding its passenger and crew lists.[38]

The conspirators had little to fear. Judge Jones had recently struck down the prosecution of a *Wanderer* survivor's enslaver. In his ruling, he acknowledged that the African slave trade 'had long been an extensive and lawful branch of the foreign commerce of our country'. The *William Jones, Jr.*, where the trafficking bet was placed and which towed the *Clotilda* up Mobile Bay, was probably named after him. On 20 December, Cade Godbold informed the court that 'the within named negroes [are] not found in my district'. Burns Meaher and John Dabney's cases were thrown out three weeks later; supposedly, there was no evidence of any Africans in the State of Alabama. Timothy Meaher was also reportedly brought before the court, but his alibi that he had never missed a steamboat journey throughout the *Clotilda*'s voyage was supported by witnesses and his case was dismissed. William Foster's customs case was held over on 7 January because witnesses, including Burns and Timothy Meaher, and James Dennison, failed to appear and then the Civil War began. Judge Jones resigned from his federal position and became a district judge for the Confederacy. Augustus Requier became a district attorney for the Confederacy and one of its leading poets. The customs case was never closed, and Foster, the Meahers and the shipmates' other captors escaped punishment for their crimes.[39] The Africans were secure in the custody of their enslavers. No one was coming to save them.

6

The River

It was late July 1860, and the heat was stifling. Kossula was one of eight shipmates who found themselves on James Meaher's 420-acre plantation in northern Mobile County. Meaher was unsure how to put his uncomprehending, emaciated and grief-stricken young captives to work. Nor was there much corn to shuck, most of his crop having burned up in the record-breaking summer heat. Upon his arrival, Kossula was given no proper shelter but was instead consigned to the dark and dusty gap beneath the brick piers that held up Meaher's house, where he was forced to shiver in rags through the increasingly cold Alabama nights when the summer ended and the temperature began to drop. Eventually, Kossula was sent to work in the fields, where he was stunned to see soil that gave up its bounties so readily in Yorubaland farmed so intensively in Alabama. 'We astonish to see de mule behind de plow to pull,' he recalled. To his dismay, Kossula discovered that the Africans were made to 'workee so hard' in the fields. Unlike back home, where his townswomen managed their households and sold their wares, women and girls were made to take on the arduous field labour, too. 'In night time we cry,' Kossula remembered. 'We say we born and raised to be free people and now we slave. We doan know why we be bring 'way from our country to work lak dis.'[1]

Kanko and the other captives who were sent to James Meaher's brother Burns's 450-acre plantation in Grove Hill, Clarke County were treated even more poorly than Kossula. They were immediately put to work in the cotton fields, where they were required to labour from sunrise until nightfall, before tracing their way back to bed by torchlight and repeating the ordeal the next day. They were whipped repeatedly whenever they failed to show deference — 'Yes, Sir', 'Thank you, Sir' and 'Please, Mistress' — to their enslavers. That happened often, as the shipmates could barely speak English. Only after one of their American-born fellow captives began taking them aside at night secretly to teach them the language did the violence stop. The group received just one pair of leather shoes each during their five years of enslavement. After assaulting their feet from constant use, their shoes soon disintegrated, leaving them with no protection against frostbite or the hard, hostile earth.[2]

Timothy Meaher's wife Mary had shirts, trousers, dresses and petticoats made for the Africans on his estate. She handed the items to her house servant Noah Hart, instructing him to 'make them heathens dress like folks'.[3] Unlike the fine red ribbons that supposedly helped to entrance the youngest *Clotilda* survivors onto the slave ship, the clothing provided by Mary was of coarse cheap material, a sad reminder of the schooner's false promise of wealth. But the Africans, who had endured weeks of nakedness at sea, were nevertheless grateful for substantial clothing. They retreated to change into the fabrics.

In the nineteenth century, a young, unmarried Yoruban woman's clothing consisted of a tobi, an apron-like undergarment secured with strong cord at the waist, two wrappers or lengths of cloth fixed above the breast and at the waist, and a matching gele (headscarf). The girls and women dressed accordingly. Using the sleeves as ties, they wrapped the dresses around their waists; some of them also tried fastening the petticoats around their necks. The male captives, used to fitted garments, pulled the shirt sleeves over their legs. Noah ridiculed them and burst into laughter at the memory more than thirty years later; from his Eurocentric perspective, the African 'savages' did not know how to wear clothes. Humiliated, the shipmates soon learned to wear them like Americans. Most of the girls and women imprisoned by the Meahers were later forced to fashion their own dresses from old flour and feed sacks. The material had to be washed with soap handmade from lye mixed with pork fat, then boiled, and finally dyed with sumac blossom, elderberries, or onion skins; the colours had to be set with urine.[4]

Despite their dire circumstances, however, the Africans met the violence of their new world with outrage and took brave steps to protect each other. When an overseer on Burns Meaher's plantation tried to whip one of the captives, perhaps for the simple reason that she could not comprehend his instructions, her shipmates quickly disarmed him and turned the whip on him. Kossula described the event as it was told to him by his companions: 'One man try whippee one my country women and dey all jump on him and take de whip way from him and lashee *him* wid it.' The Africans successfully cowed their companion's tormenter. 'He doan never try whip Affican women no mo',' Kossula recalled.[5] Despite the tremendous risks involved, the shipmates had fought successfully to shield those they saw as their most vulnerable companions from some of the violence of Burns Meaher's plantation.

Another young girl was saved from brutal treatment in Timothy Meaher's household when her fellow Africans again came to her rescue. Meaher's young wife Mary took a shine to the beauty of Uriba, the 14- or 15-year-old child who had wept throughout the *Clotilda*'s voyage. Mary sent Uriba (who her enslavers knew as 'Areba') to clean her house and help raise her children and sent another young African girl to work in her kitchen. Mary asked her cook, Polly, to instruct Uriba how to dust and sweep, but the child's futile attempts to decipher Polly's English instructions failed to satisfy the cook, who beat her over the head. Uriba was deeply distressed and cried. Noah, who was working in the house at the time, likened her agonized sobs to the sound of a wildcat. The other Africans on the plantation were alerted to Uriba's suffering and came running, armed with farming tools and looks of fury and roaring at the top of their lungs to avenge their shipmate. The Africans hammered on Timothy Meaher's door and Polly fled upstairs, afraid of what she termed the 'heathens'. Mary finally opened the door, terrified by the sight of the Africans, but trying not to show they had the upper hand. Despite the language barrier, Noah managed to persuade the group to leave without entering the house. But they succeeded in protecting Uriba, for Polly soon left her job. Uriba eventually learned English from her enslaver's children.[6]

A teenage shipmate named Amey who was enslaved on John Greenwood's plantation in neighbouring Baldwin County was not so fortunate. According to her grandson Percy Phillip Marino, Amey's enslaver was a 'good man' and she even learned to speak French from his business partner and neighbour Reuben D'Olive. But Greenwood hired out Amey to unidentified enslavers in another state who beat her. He retrieved Amey when he learned of the abuse, but the scars on her legs never healed. After returning to Baldwin County, Amey gave birth to a daughter named Caroline Marino and a son, Robert J. Marino. The children's father was Benito Julian Moreno, a New Orleans-based commission merchant of Spanish descent who was living on the Greenwood estate for much of 1862 and again at the time of his death from tuberculosis on 1 June 1865. Benito Moreno was the son of Don Francisco Moreno, the Spanish vice-consul in Pensacola, Florida, and the brother-in-law of Stephen Mallory, whose role as secretary of state for the Navy made him the fourth highest-ranking member of the Confederacy. Before the Civil War, Benito's brother Fernando Joaquin Moreno was the US marshal for the Florida Keys. Fernando oversaw the confinement in a depot at Key West of 1,432 Africans rescued from the *Wildfire*, *William* and *Bogota*, three illegal slave ships intercepted by the US Navy near the Cuban coast in April and May 1860, just weeks before the *Clotilda*'s arrival in Mobile. The *Wildfire*, *William* and *Bogota* Africans were so ill from their transatlantic voyage and conditions were so crowded at Key West that 294 of them died there; the rest were relocated to Liberia. A slave trade sympathizer in the *Montgomery Mail* reported that five would-be human traffickers had tried but failed to smuggle some of the Key West Africans into their custody just a day before the *Clotilda*'s landing at Point aux Pins.[7]

Not all the Africans who were enslaved to the Meahers ended up working the land. Some of the men and boys were sent to fell pine and cypress trees and chop and haul wood at James and Timothy Meaher's shipyard and lumber mill on Telegraph Road, a stone's throw from where the charred remains of the *Clotilda* lay. Kanko spent much of her enslavement as a domestic servant at Burns Meaher's residence, where she was made to cook, clean and cultivate the garden. Another African girl was imprisoned in the Mobile household of William Waldo Ingalls. Like the Meahers, Ingalls was originally from Maine and was a partner in Timothy Meaher's sawmill business. His teenage wife Frances, an Irish Famine survivor who married into the family two years after the *Clotilda*'s arrival, praised the young woman as an 'excellent servant' and described those who laboured in the sawmills for both Timothy Meaher and her husband as 'excellent workers'.[8] The girl and Kanko had to be especially good at their jobs. Their proximity to their enslavers meant they were under constant surveillance, and any mistakes in their work were likely to be met with whippings and beatings.

Kossula's time on James Meaher's plantation proved to be short-lived, for he was among a group of *Clotilda* survivors who were sent back onto Timothy Meaher's steamboat the *Roger B. Taney*. But this time, the Africans were not being taken anywhere. Instead, Kossula and his shipmates were expected to work and live on the steamboat on its week-long journeys along the Alabama and Mobile rivers between Montgomery and Mobile. Their labour was overseen by their hostage taker, Timothy Meaher, who captained the 301-ton cotton carrier. Still traumatized by the terrifying 44-day sea voyage that had killed around seven of their party and tested the survivors to their physical and psychological limits, bondage on the constantly twisting 363-mile river system that connected Alabama's capital to its seaport must have felt like a return to hell for Kossula and his companions. The murky and constantly rising waterway, which coursed up and down southern Alabama like a snake, was now their home.

Steamboats' high-pressure engines fuelled trade, travel and

communication in the South in the early decades of the nineteenth century and made possible the rise of the region's cotton kingdom. The vessels' speed and ability to travel upriver at about ten miles, or eight knots, per hour meant that cotton and other goods could be transported quickly between river landings and urban areas for the first time, fuelling the growth of major trading centres such as Mobile. With vast, three-tiered decks designed for passenger travel, their ability to transport people long distances accelerated the massive demographic upheaval that occurred in the region. Native Americans were driven off the land on steamboats as profit-hungry white men used the vessels to venture into and stake a claim to the region's fertile soil, dragging their thousands of bondspeople with them as they did so.

Steamboats were also highly segregated vessels that captured in microcosm the racialized social structure that had cemented itself in the slavery-era South. For the rich white passengers who strolled around their upper decks, steamers were opulent symbols of wealth and prestige. Their grand and expensively decorated rooms offered a variety of leisure activities, including card games and dancing. Alcohol flowed freely in their grand saloons, and rich food was served in their dining rooms. Black people were barred from booking cabin passage and were consigned to the main deck, where the cotton bales and other freight were stored, and where the mostly enslaved workforce laboured to collect and stoke the steam engines with firewood to power the boat.

Kossula was one of roughly a dozen *Clotilda* survivors who were made to work on the five steamboats that the Meaher brothers ran on the 363-mile stretch of waterway between Mobile and Montgomery County. He would never forget the exploitative treatment he endured on the Alabama River, which was characterized by incessant hard work and the constant threat of violence and even death. Forced to haul wood on the river at night, the Africans, some of whom were young boys, risked falling into the river and drowning in the darkness. As a 1930s writer remarked of the deep, yellow, vegetation-strewn river's dangers, 'No one plays in the Alabama.'[9]

The River

The wood that fuelled the steamboats' journeys was stored in wood yards along the riverbanks. The *Taney*'s boiler was always hungry, which meant that Kossula had to work quickly. 'It burnee de wood an' it usee so muchee wood!' he recalled. Kossula was expected to jump onto the marshy bluff to gather as much firewood as he could carry whenever the boat reached a landing point. Enslaved deck crews could be expected to pile as many as 20 to 40 cords of wood on deck at each landing and were required to feed moving vessels' boiler with logs every 15 minutes. The teenager was given only a pair of loose-fitting pantaloons to wear even in mid-winter when the average temperature was 48 degrees Fahrenheit (9 degrees Celsius), leaving him unprotected against both the changing elements and the piles of wood that he was expected to collect with each journey up and down the bank, which rubbed painfully against his bare arms and chest.[10]

Kossula braved the constant pain, lack of protection from the wind and rain and the giant red paddle wheel that threatened to suck him underwater every time he jumped back onto the boat because he dreaded the distressing crack of the overseer's whip on his unprotected back. The Africans learned their job quickly despite not speaking English because every perceived shortcoming was met by a whipping. 'He cutee you wid de whip if you ain' run fast 'nough to please him. If you doan git a big load, he hitee you too', the still-traumatized Kossula remembered at the end of his life. But the river's precipitously steep banks were equally as frightening. At certain points on the waterway, the bluffs reached up to one hundred and fifty or even two hundred feet in height. Mammoth wooden cotton slides lurched down from them at 45-degree angles. So high were the banks that the shipmates sometimes had to toss down their woodpiles and climb after them; it could take two or three throws before the wood arrived at the river's edge.[11]

The Africans also had to load and unload freight, including sugar, flour, fertilizer and, most importantly, cotton. Cotton loading was especially dangerous. An emphasis on quick profits ensured that the enslaved workers were required to load the cotton quickly, even working at night by torchlight. Kossula soon found the intense labour changed him physically. The brutal injuries to his hands and arms included a severed fingertip, and his upper body became a knot of muscles that stretched and strained constantly. Out of necessity, he developed a new-found dexterity that enabled him to meet the rhythms of the steamboat and the freight waiting to be loaded. Cotton bales weighing up to six hundred pounds were sent shooting down the wooden slides on the banks. There they were quickly met by two enslaved men who, with perfect timing, sank heavy hooks deep into each bag of cotton and worked to slow it down before it smacked into a third man who then added a third hook to help lift and stow away the mass of white gold. Slips, baggage breakages and occasional failures to secure the hooks meant that all three men were frequently thrown into the water. Such accidents were repeated many times. Timothy Meaher calculated that his boats alone landed 1.7 million bales of cotton at Mobile to be shipped to New England and Europe during his 24-year career as a steamboat owner.[12]

Death in the river was a constant peril for the Africans as there was no railing on a steamboat's main deck. Kossula understood just how easily a fatality could occur, especially after dark: 'in de night time if you doan watchee close you fall overboard and drown yo'self.' But Kossula and his fellow Africans faced many other deadly hazards on the Taney. The cotton onboard was highly flammable, as was the boat itself. Collisions with other vessels were frequent, large pieces of driftwood and partially submerged tree trunks if not spotted on time could punch holes in and sink boats, and the steamer's boiler, operating constantly at high pressure, had the potential to explode. In late July 1860, days after the Africans arrived in Alabama, the Taney almost sank after hitting a snag at Black's Bluff in Wilcox County. The vessel took in water so quickly that newspapers predicted it would be lost. Kossula remembered having to battle against time to prevent a similar sinking. 'De boat leak and we pumpee so hard!' he told Zora Neale Hurston.[13]

The Taney's main deck, which was typically overloaded with cargo and pine wood, was both workplace and rest place to the Africans. Their beds were burlap sacks on the hard floor. The incessant rush of water through the paddle, the creak of wood, the screaming engine and the regular sound of the steam whistle accompanied them through the night. The torturous sleeping arrangements left the group constantly exhausted despite the ever-present dangers of their work, which heightened their risk of slipping and drowning in the river. 'Oh Lor'! I so tired. No sleepee,' Kossula recalled.[14]

Each week on the boat, Kossula longed desperately for Sunday, for it was the Africans' only day of respite from the steamboat. Sunday was the one day of the week in which Kossula did not fear immediate death or the loss of a loved one in the river. It was also the only day in which the Africans could come together to dance – something that was central to their sense of identity. To create music, they constructed a wooden drum wrapped in goatskin like the instruments they had known in their homeland. Dance was the one means by which the lost shipmates could communicate with home. These sacred movement practices allowed kidnapped Africans to foster psychological connections with and seek spiritual advice from lost ancestors on the other side of the ocean. It was the one way in which they could reclaim their bodies and assert their autonomy amid their bondage. As Kossula remembered, 'we dance lak in de Afficky soil'.[15]

But the ritual and cultural significances of the shipmates' dances were lost on their fellow bondspeople, who laughed at them and spoke to them only to accuse them of being savages. Kossula and his fellow Africans found that any expressions of their heritage were used against them as proof of their apparent cultural inferiority. They learned to adjust to their new environment by downplaying their Yoruban and Fon identities. 'Free George' was among a tiny handful of free Black people in Alabama, his freedom having recently been bought by his wife, who laboured for a wage as a cook. He warned the group that it was wrong to dance on a Sunday. In the Christian land of their enslavers, their sacred expressions were deemed heretical. Made to feel ashamed of their behaviour, they soon stopped dancing together and their Sundays became less joyful.[16]

Although linguistic and cultural differences prevented them from forming relationships with their fellow bondspeople, Kossula and his shipmates nevertheless bore witness to the suffering of the poorly clad women and even children who were forced to load the cotton slides along the Alabama River.[17] Poignantly, many of their fellow captives were now labouring in misery near those landing points. Twelve-year-old Redoshi, her 'husband' Yawith, and two other paired shipmates named Jinnie and Cuffee were living 15 miles west of Selma. Two-year-old Matilda and her mother Gracie and sister Sally were at Prairie Bluff, a Wilcox County landing point set high above the river. Thirteen-year-old Dinah was a few miles south of the river at Snow Hill. Childless mother Bougier was among a group of Africans who were confined on plantations near Montgomery; other shipmates were labouring in the heart of the capital. The Africans were all trapped in their respective prisons, unaware of each other's location.

One night in December 1860, the month that US marshal for the Southern District of Alabama Cade Madison Godbold assured the district court the *Clotilda* Africans could not be found, the worst happened. As the *Taney* was travelling between Montgomery and Selma, one of the Africans slipped from the steamer and fell into the pitch-black, vegetation-thick water. Torches were lit and the boat was turned around in a futile search for the missing young man. His shipmates were thrown into a state of panic and despair. Knowing that following their friend into the river meant almost certain death, they could only scour the surface of the water as the torch-light struck it in the hope of spying their lost companion. But the river level was especially high that winter, and their eyes met only darkness. One of the Africans stood on the steamer's bow and called and called.'*Eh*-cotah! Eco-*tah*!' He refused to believe that his friend was gone. His voice was so full of despair that a student who witnessed the scene could still describe the young man's anguished cry 52 years later.[18]

After an hour, the search was abandoned. The boat continued its journey to Selma and Kossula and the small band of remaining Africans were forced to resume their exhausting labour while coming to terms with yet another devastating loss. Their friend and probable relative, with whom they had withstood kidnap, six and a half weeks-long transatlantic incarceration, enslavement and separation, had disappeared from their lives with brutal suddenness. Kossula and his fellow Africans were shattered, but they had no time to mourn before they were put back to work. Nor could they accord their friend the Yoruba death rites that could ease him into the afterlife, let alone hope that his spirit could find his way home to Africa. Instead, they were forced to travel past the site of his death twice a week, knowing that his brutal fate could just as quickly and easily be their own.

In the same week the *Clotilda* shipmates lost their friend in the Alabama River, the *Taney*'s white passengers held a symbolic joint vote on secession from the North with the *St. Nicholas*, a steamboat that had concealed nearly forty *Wanderer* survivors in and around Montgomery nearly two years earlier. Unbeknownst to the grieving Africans, their enslavers were readying up for war to prolong their bondage. Abraham Lincoln, whose Republican Party was established to oppose slavery expansion, had just been elected the new US president. *Clotilda* conspiracists Rush Jones's and Alex Given's close acquaintance William Lowndes Yancey, who led the walkout of Southern Democrats at the 1860 Democratic National Convention that split the party and paved the way for Lincoln's presidency, was on board the *St. Nicholas* to oversee the vote. Both counts were almost unanimously in favour of secession.[19]

Timothy Meaher was certainly not one of the two men on the *Taney* who voted for cooperation with the North, for his slave trading venture had just made him very rich. The 1860 drought wiped out half of Alabama's cotton, forcing even the state's wealthiest men to tighten their belts. But Meaher profited so heavily from the *Clotilda* conspiracy that he was able to build a new steamboat, on which Kossula and his companions were soon put to work. On the

Alabama River, the size and ostentatiousness of steamboats increased in the years up to the Civil War as the Meahers and their competitors sought to outdo each other, and wealthy travellers demanded furnishings that matched their lifestyles. In 1856, the *St. Nicholas* set the template for luxurious river travel, boasting intricately decorated doors and walls and rosewood furniture.[20] The new vessel that Timothy Meaher had built at his shipyard in the autumn of 1860 would be the biggest and most ostentatious steamer of all. He named the boat the *Southern Republic* to assert his allegiance to the radical voices in the South whose agitation for secession from the Union would soon lead the nation to war.

The *Republic* was launched on 7 January 1861. A double-cabin vessel commanded by Timothy Meaher, the side wheeler was the largest steamboat ever to travel on the Alabama River. Gleaming red and gold in the Alabama sun and bearing a Confederate flag fashioned by its owners, the boat was more than 250 feet long, 40 feet wide, and could house more than 200 passengers in its upper and lower cabins. So ostentatious were its furnishings, which included a luminous saloon stretching 100 feet by 30 feet and a tinted glass skylight, that one Montgomery newspaper likened it to an 'Aladdin's palace'. A calliope perched on the steamboat's metal roof converted steam from the vessel's propulsion boilers into shrill music through its vast whistle pipes. This organ-like instrument, whose keyboard was commanded by a drunken Frenchman, blasted out 'Dixie', a tune rooted in blackface minstrelsy that became the Confederacy's unofficial anthem, and drew sizeable crowds at every landing. Thanks to the Africans' incessant labours on the boat, the vessel was soon ferrying nearly 600 bales of cotton down the river to Mobile each week.[21]

For the Africans, the new steamer was even more frightening than the *Taney*. The three-storey structure was tested to the limit around the constantly winding Alabama River and left little room for other vessels at the waterway's narrowest points. Dublin-born London *Times* reporter Sir William Howard Russell, who rode on the *Republic* at the start of the Civil War, described the steamer's frequent and perilous exertions as it sought to dock on the river as 'like an elephant turning at bay' and suggested that it was as befitting of its location as a 'whale in a canal'. Another observer described the boat as 'more like some fabled marine monster than a vessel meant for speed and comfort'.[22]

None of that deterred Timothy Meaher from engaging the vessel in races with other steamboats, a highly dangerous practice as it was during such contests that a vessel's boiler was most likely to explode. A night-time race between the *Republic* and rival steamboat the *Senator* in April 1861, the month that Confederate forces fired on Fort Sumter in Charleston, South Carolina, and war was formally declared, was memorialized by one journalist who witnessed it as a metaphor for Confederate confidence in the region's military might and the promise of future victories.[23] It had been just under a year since Kossula and his fellow captives were forced aboard the *Clotilda*. Yet here they were again, beholden to the unpredictable behaviours of a lurching, creaking boat. This time, though, they were required to power its journey. Expected to work at breakneck speed to protect their enslaver's pride, they tossed one pine beam after another into the fires and repeatedly stoked the roaring flames for miles until finally the *Republic* inched away from its rival.

Perhaps inevitably for a boat whose name heralded secession, the *Republic* played its part in the Civil War by circulating pro-slavery propaganda and ferrying food donations for Confederate soldiers up and down the Alabama River. When war was officially declared in April 1861, the *Republic* was among the vessels that mobilized the troops. The sight of soldiers embarking on the steamer to tremendous fanfare was deeply disconcerting to Kossula and his fellow Africans, who were still barely able to speak English and who watched the 'white folks runnee up and down' without at first knowing what was going on. Even without understanding that the defence of slavery was the cause of their fight, the young white soldiers' boisterous joviality, accompanied as ever by the *Republic*'s exuberant 'Dixie' wail alongside roaring cannons and ringing bells on the Mobile docks where they were waved on their journey by family and friends, was in stark contrast to the African youngsters' miserable entrapment on the steamer.[24]

Over time, the shipmates learned from their fellow bondspeople that the North was fighting a war with the South to end slavery. Kossula was overjoyed by the news. Daring to hope that they would soon be freed, the Africans waited for their liberation. They followed Timothy Meaher's order to '[r]un to the swamp' whenever Confederate officers tried to commandeer enslaved labourers to fortify Mobile's defences. Knowing that the North had blockaded the South's food imports on account of the war, they fought off starvation as they waited, for their enslavers had very little food to give them. The African men and boys old enough to have received the military training that was a crucial component of their adolescence back home drew on that training to bravely hunt the ferocious wild hogs on James Meaher's land. The women and girls grew what they could around their cabins and experimented with burned rice to make coffee, which they flavoured with molasses. Kossula never forgot the nasty taste of the viscous, gritty liquid. But, apart from the sound of a gunfight, the Africans encountered no first-hand signs of warfare over the next four years. President Lincoln's Emancipation Proclamation theoretically freed all bondspeople in the breakaway states on 1 January 1863, but the federal order went unrecognized behind Confederate lines. By that point, the shipmates had been enslaved for nearly two and a half years. It would be almost the same period before there was any sign of liberation. To the Africans, it seemed that no one was coming to rescue them and all eventually gave up hope, bitterly concluding the fight was over something else.[25] In the meantime, Kossula continued to labour on the Meahers' steamboats.

The crowds that flocked to see the *Republic* and the many soldiers and travellers that journeyed on the vessel were signs of just how visible Kossula and his fellow *Clotilda* survivors were on Alabama's waterways during the war. Their presence on the steamboats meant they were effectively hidden in plain sight, for the vessels were the main method of transportation in the state before the advancement of the railroad. Yet they seem to have been widely mistaken for *Wanderer* survivors, a confusion that Timothy Meaher, their captor and captain, may have sought to play up. The student who saw one of them drown was told they were *Wanderer* 'Congoes'.[26] As they were unable to speak English, the young Africans were powerless to correct that falsehood. Their true identities and the conspiracy that brought them to Alabama were easily obscured to outsiders.

That did not stop Timothy Meaher from boldly flaunting his captives before Sir William Howard Russell, the London *Times* reporter who travelled on the *Republic* at the start of the war. Leering at the journalist, who noted that 'a good many of the hands' on the boat were African, he picked out a boy of about twelve years of age with prominent body markings, whom he nicknamed Bully. Meaher made the boy claim to come from South Carolina. When Russell questioned him about signs of Bully's West African identity, Meaher joked that the boy's mother had created his facial marks to tell him apart from other children, attributed his chest markings to smallpox, and suggested he had filed his own teeth. Meaher also protested Bully's seemingly good physical health as evidence of his happiness. The boy was caught in a blatant masquerade with his enslaver and the scene must have looked to Russell exactly as it was: a man aged nearly fifty tormenting a barely comprehending child. Eventually, Meaher ended his charade, confessing that the boy had been stolen from Africa and admitting to resentment at the activities of the Underground Railroad, a secretive network of people and safe houses that helped people in bondage escape north to freedom. 'We're obleeged to let 'em in some times to keep up the balance agin the n—s you run into Canaydy,' he told the journalist of his trafficking activities.[27]

Meaher made his captives dance on the lower deck at night to show just how 'happy they were' to the foreign journalist.[28] In scenes such as this, Yoruba and other West African dance traditions culturally significant to the young Africans and their ancestors, and which had enriched Kossula's Sundays at the start of his enslavement, were stripped of their meaning and reconfigured, in their enslaver's imagination, as trivial entertainment.

The forced dancing must have felt like a return to the deck of the *Clotilda* for Kossula and his shipmates. Compelled to jump awkwardly amid firewood and barrels on a moving steamboat to the alien screech of a violin and the penetrating twangs of a banjo, and at risk of repeating their friend's deathly fate in the river if they overbalanced, the Africans made no attempt to hide their misery. Having failed to achieve a sufficiently convincing performance of merriment for his Irish passenger, Meaher plied his captives with rum to make them move with more energy and enthusiasm, increasing their risk of falling overboard. 'Yes, sir, jist look at them, how they're enjoying it; they're the happiest people on the face of the airth,' he declared.[29] The journalist wasn't fooled.

Kossula never forgot the trauma of his enslavement on the Alabama River and its ever-present dangers. At the beginning of June 1861, just a few weeks after the *Times* journalist watched the Africans' forced dance on the *Republic*, the shipmates heard an almighty bang. A flue had exploded on the boat. The steamer suffered little damage, but a child was killed and others onboard were badly injured. Such incidents left Kossula and his companions in a constant state of terror throughout their time on the steamboats. In the final years of his life, Kossula could still visualize and recall in geographical order many of the landing points on the river journey, none of which he had visited since 1865. His relief at being released from such horrors even sixty or so years later was palpable. 'Oh, Lor'! I 'preciate they free me.'[30]

Like Kossula and Bully, shoeless Kanko found herself bound to the river during her enslavement, but her relationship to Alabama's waterways was more complex than that of her shipmates. Only two months into the war, Kanko was forced by her captors into a marriage ceremony with James Dennison, the Charleston-born youth who was enslaved to Burns Meaher and who had helped conceal the *Clotilda* captives when they arrived in the United States. James was an expert pilot who ferried steamboats laden with cotton and other supplies, including turpentine, meat, molasses, flour and rum, down the Tombigbee River to Mobile. On the return journey, his boats were stacked with sacks of groceries and fertilizer, as well as whisky and fresh fruit. He knew well how to navigate the winding river and to look out for fallen trees and other detritus that might sink his craft.

Not only was Kanko enslaved on American soil, but she was now bound to an American man. According to her granddaughter Mable, Kanko was unhappy with the marriage arrangement and refused to sleep with her husband. Since the pair had not been married according to Yoruba practices, Kanko did not view the wedding as legitimate. Nor was Kanko, who was perhaps as young as 12 or 13, necessarily ready to become a wife.[31] Over time, Kanko eventually gave in to her husband's desires and gave birth to a son, Willie, in the first year or two of her enslavement. Home, and the possibility of her return, stretched ever further away.

Yet James, too, was hungry for liberty, and it would not be long before Kanko embarked on a daring river race of her own. When the Union Army captured Mobile's outer defences at the Battle of Mobile Bay in August 1864, James decided to lead his fellow captives in a bid for freedom by stealing away on one of the Meahers' steamers. His plan was to sail it down the Tombigbee River south of Grove Hill to the mouth of the Mobile River.

As James and Kanko prepared to depart, they were alarmed to find that one of their fellow bondsmen had betrayed them. With no time to lose, they could only gather some of James's family members and close friends before the window of opportunity for escape closed. They had to board the steamboat quickly. It was Kanko's first time on the water since she had been taken to Burns Meaher's plantation. But she swallowed her fears despite her dark memories of the *Clotilda* and climbed onto the boat with the others, her little boy clutched tightly in her arms.

The Meahers soon learned of the group's escape and chased them on horseback along the side of the river, but just when it looked as if they might catch up with them their pursuers hit a water barrier and had to stop. The small group had shaken off their pursuers at Twelve Mile Island, the same spot where the *Clotilda* had been scuttled and burned. After four years in captivity, Kanko's flight to freedom must have been intoxicating, the banks of the Mobile River momentarily changed from its resemblance in the summer of 1860. She may even have dared to hope it was the start of a long journey home. The thought that she was leading her small son to freedom must have made her journey all the sweeter. Tragically, however, the group's taste of liberty did not last. Their captors alerted other enslavers that they had escaped, and a posse of white men was waiting for them when they arrived at Mobile. Kanko, James and the others were returned to Burns Meaher's plantation, where the standard punishment for running away was 39 lashes each.[32]

It would not be long before the Africans were liberated, though. Kanko was two months pregnant with a second son, Gerry, when Confederate troops were called to evacuate Mobile on 10 April 1865 and she and James heard from their fellow bondspeople that they were free. The violence, exhaustion and physical deprivations that Kanko and her shipmates had helped each other endure for five years on Burns Meaher's plantation were finally over. James Dennison joined the Union Army, enrolling for three years in Company K of the 47th Infantry regiment of the Colored Troops. Dressed in navy blue and armed with a sword and gun, he expected to spend the coming months fighting his former enslavers, only to discover that the conflict was already over. Instead, he spent the next year attending to military stock and battling ill health caused by the wet, swampy conditions of the Red River near Baton Rouge before being discharged. Temporarily without her partner, the still-shoeless Kanko picked up Willie and headed 80 miles south with the other remaining Africans on Burns Meaher's plantation. Together, they boarded a rudimentary flatboat and endured its knotty week-long journey down the Tombigbee and Mobile rivers to reunite with Kossula and the other Mobile shipmates.[33]

Mobile Bay, the site of Kossula's arrival on US soil, would become the site of his freedom. Two days after Kanko was liberated and while she was still making her way south, Kossula was working on the Alabama and Mobile rivers. The news arrived as he and his fellow Africans were waiting to journey upriver as usual. There was no sign of their enslaver that day. Instead a group of blue-coated Union soldiers arrived at the bay and helped themselves to handfuls of the red and purple mulberries which hung from the trees around them. When the soldiers saw the Africans staring at them from the deck of one of Timothy Meaher's steamboats, they told them to leave the vessel, for they were now free.

Kossula and the other Africans were overjoyed, but waited patiently to share the news with another group of shipmates who were still stuck on a steamboat travelling south from Montgomery. Then they gathered up their few belongings and contemplated their next step. Their liberation from the Meahers meant they were now homeless and were forced to seek refuge in the temporary barracks of a railway section house. But as Kossula told Zora Neale Hurston 62 years later, he was too elated to worry yet where he slept or what might happen next. 'Cudjo doan keer – he a free man den.'[34]

7

The Black Belt

As 12-year-old Redoshi was driven by wagon to her new prison in the summer of 1860, her shipmates prayed that she would encounter no danger. Redoshi's community of *Clotilda* survivors had shrunk from more than a hundred persons to around thirty. The small band included Gracie, a distraught mother clutching two little girls, 10-year-old Sally and 2-year-old Matilda, who were all that were left of her family. It also included Yawith, the young man who Redoshi was now expected to call her husband. As the party reached a track on the edge of the woods on Burns Meaher's plantation, Redoshi was distressed to find herself at a new stretch of waterway: the Alabama River. The route back to her shipmates was about to become untraceable. One of the Meahers' steamboats, most likely the *Czar*, stood before her. Rough hands removed her from the wagon and drove her back into its stifling hold. Redoshi would see the hatch slammed shut and hear its padlock securely fastened, before the steamboat once again began to stir on the water.

After around five hours in the suffocating darkness, the steamboat came to a halt on the cusp of a sharp bend in the river. Redoshi struggled out of the hold into the blazing sunlight. The shipmates had reached the edge of Prairie Bluff in Wilcox County, a crumbling town 130 miles northeast of Mobile. A vast expanse of water and row upon row of elm trees stood before them; the town was high above the river and just above its widest section. The captives were dragged up the steep, rugged embankment towards a large wooden building perched on top of the hillside and from which a crooked wooden slide descended precipitously. Although they did not know it, they had reached a key storage and delivery point of Alabama's slavery-driven cotton economy.

Prairie Bluff was founded in 1815, shortly after the 1814 Treaty of Fort Jackson forced the Muscogee (Creek) peoples to cede most of central Alabama to the United States. Today, only the remains of its cemetery survive, but in the 1830s it was second only to Claiborne in neighbouring Monroe County as the Alabama River's biggest and most commercially important settlement. Prairie Bluff's success owed *everything* to its slavery-based cotton industry: as many as 16,000 bales of the fibre were loaded from there in just one season. According to one late nineteenth-century journalist, it was once the largest trading point in the country. Numerous bars, billiard tables, ten-pin bowling alleys and even a racetrack were set up to indulge those made suddenly rich by the trade. There was also a gin factory, two wagon factories, a blacksmith, tailor and shoe and sweet shops. But there was no church. Instead, a Masonic Lodge was established by Thomas Bivin Creagh (pronounced Crear), a South Carolina-born son of Irish immigrants who was perhaps the first Grand Master Mason in Alabama. While a wave of fatal diseases in the late 1830s meant the town was no longer such a hub of activity by the time Redoshi and her fellow *Clotilda* survivors were displaced there, it was still extremely wealthy. Thomas Creagh's son Memorable Walker Creagh tallied up 704 cotton bales on his Prairie Bluff plantation in June 1860, making him the richest enslaver in western Wilcox County.[1]

Shattered both physically and emotionally, the Africans reached the top of the riverbank only to find themselves divided up again. The kidnappers and their purchasers knew they could exchange the captives at Prairie Bluff in secrecy, for it was 100 miles north of Mount Vernon – where Timothy Meaher had hurried his captives into the *Taney*'s hold – and set below vast acres of anonymous woods, swamps and cotton fields. Prairie Bluff was a space where the marked faces and foreign voices of trafficked children and young people were well hidden from federal authorities. Four decades later, Matilda and her sister Sally and Redoshi and her husband Yawith told Presbyterian missionaries who arrived in the area to establish schools about the horror of those final separations. 'If the oaks and elms that skirt the river had tongues what tales they could tell! Parents and children were separated ruthlessly, all the cruel inventions of the awful institution [of slavery] were here in startling evidence.'[2]

Gracie's despair at the unknown fate of her lost children mingled with dread at what might happen to her remaining daughters Matilda and Sally as the shipmates were forcibly separated at Prairie Bluff. Memorable Creagh was now her enslaver. The physically imposing grey-haired man ultimately opted to keep the mother and her youngest daughters together as a family, but he also made it clear to Gracie that fellow *Clotilda* survivor Guy was to be her new 'husband'. Creagh claimed about two-thirds of the approximately thirty captives on the riverbank. He sent Gracie and her family, as well as seven little girls and young women, to join the 166 other prisoners on his 3,500-acre Prairie Bluff plantation.[3]

Memorable Creagh's land stretched into neighbouring Marengo County, and he transplanted at least nine more *Clotilda* captives to his property near McKinley, about twelve miles northwest of his Prairie Bluff estate. The young group spent their first torturous days in McKinley wracked by grief and in a state of extreme starvation. Their bodies struggled to digest the coarsely ground cornmeal that their captor provided, but they were still so hungry that they scoured the land for anything that passed for food.[4]

An 11-year-old girl named Quilla and two teenage captives named Ossa and Lucy were forced into the hands of William H. Hunt, who owned land adjacent to Creagh's Prairie Bluff estate in an area named Rehoboth. William Hunt was in his early forties and, like Creagh, originally from South Carolina, although unlike his neighbour he had only recently settled in Alabama. Hunt hired out his services as a plantation overseer to major enslavers such as

Creagh, although he had his own farm and declared $41,025 in wealth (equivalent to $1.5 million today) on the 1860 census. Hunt had already enslaved twenty-seven people before he bought the three shipmates, although twelve of his captives were even younger than Quilla.[5] He used his own land for livestock; his work contracts meant his new child prisoners would be forced to labour, under his watchful eye, on the major cotton plantations of western Wilcox County.

Beyond the Alabama River, a seemingly endless array of drying up cotton plants stuck up from countless fields of sticky black soil. Though Quilla could not have known it at the time, here was the Southern slavery system at its most brutally efficient, and she was just one among many thousands of captives who had been forcibly displaced into it. Quilla and her shipmates had landed in the heart of the Black Belt (also known as the Canebrake, Cotton Belt and Prairie Belt), a region named after the dark, fossiliferous, incredibly nutrient-rich soil that stretched approximately 4,600 square miles across central and southern Alabama and swept west into eastern Mississippi. Here was where cotton grew best. Throughout the early nineteenth century, enslaved adults and children were displaced from Virginia, the Carolinas, Maryland, Delaware, Kentucky and Tennessee to work the soil. The crops they were forced at the crack of a whip to pick made the Black Belt one of the wealthiest regions in the United States. More than a fifth of the nation's cotton was grown in Alabama; most of it was cultivated in the Black Belt.[6] Powerful enslaver families such as the Creaghs arrived early from the Upper South to claim the land, and the wealth their captives' labour generated gave the region an exaggerated influence on the state's politics.

While Quilla and Gracie were on separate estates, they and their shipmates landed in the Black Belt at the start of harvest time, which began in late August and continued until the end of the year and sometimes beyond. As soon as they were strong enough to work, they were sent to the fields to separate the cotton fibre from the boll and remove detritus that might spoil its quality, before placing it in a large, cumbersome sack. Their fingers were frequently cut by the prickly bolls, but the captives still had to pick up to one hundred pounds of cotton per day, and then to feed what they collected through a gin to remove the seeds and allow the lint to be baled. They could be expected to gin, card, spin and reel cotton into the night.[7] When the harvest was over, they had to hoe down and burn the cotton stalks, clear ditches to prevent the crops from flooding and fell trees to create new cotton fields. The young and inexperienced Africans struggled to keep up with all the labour, which left them vulnerable to frequent whippings.

A life of incessant labour and violence in the Black Belt also awaited Redoshi, Yawith and two other captives named Jinnie and Cuffee, who were separated from their shipmates at Prairie Bluff, and were displaced 25 miles northeast to Dallas County. The group's bumpy journey by wagon along dirt roads to their new destination took around two hours; their physical agony, grief and fear was made worse by the sun's incessant glare. As she passed through fields and forests en route to her mysterious prison, Redoshi witnessed acres of burned-up corn and hundreds of dead trees. They had all dried up in the record-breaking summer temperatures, which in the final full week of July stood stubbornly at 93 to 95 degrees Fahrenheit (34 to 35 degrees Celsius).[8] The sight of their bare branches was a bad omen indeed.

Eventually, Redoshi and her companions arrived at an 1,800-acre plantation in Bogue Chitto (pronounced locally *Boga Chitta*). The land, which consisted mostly of dense forest, belonged to Black Belt enslaver Washington Smith. Bogue Chitto was a township 15 miles west of Selma, a major city on the Alabama River and the capital of Dallas County, a 1,000-square-mile stretch of highly fertile land. Alabama's cotton production was the highest of all in Dallas County. The size of the county's crop doubled between 1840 and 1850; it had doubled again by 1860. In that year alone, the region produced 63,410 bales of cotton, more than anywhere else in Alabama. Thousands of enslaved people were displaced every year to Selma to be inspected and sold in its three-storey wooden auction house. The building lay on Water Avenue, immediately north of the Alabama River and just metres away from the future site of the Edmund Pettus Bridge, a key landmark in the civil rights movement struggle. The year before the *Clotilda* set sail, 25,760 people were enslaved in Dallas County. Slave trading began on 1 September and carried on until spring.[9]

Redoshi's enslaver, Washington Smith, was a Kentucky-born lawyer and banker in his mid-forties and one of the state's wealthiest men. He moved to Alabama in the early 1840s, initially settling in Dayton and then Linden in Marengo County, where he served on the state legislature five years before Memorable Creagh, before moving to Mobile and then to Selma. By 1860, Smith was president of the recently founded Bank of Selma and a major cotton broker who exported vast quantities of the fibre to Northern ports and to Britain. Each summer, he crossed the Atlantic to do business in Liverpool, which had been Britain's largest slave-trading port from about 1740 until the UK abolished its trade in 1807 and which was now Europe's chief importer of slavery-grown cotton. Alongside his Bogue Chitto estate, Washington Smith owned a large plantation in Mobile and a turpentine distillery near Citronelle, just west of Mount Vernon. By 1857, his profits from cotton were so vast that he commissioned a Greek Revival mansion to be built in the heart of Selma as his family home. The Lapsley Street property, which was built by enslaved labourers and lay six blocks north of the Alabama River, was made of burned red bricks handcrafted on the premises and white Doric columns that glistened in the sun.[10]

Despite Washington Smith being so deeply invested in slavery to the degree that he was prepared to buy enslaved children directly from Africa, he was a pro-Union man on the eve of the Civil War. In the 1860 presidential election, Smith stood as the Dallas County candidate for the short-lived Constitutional Union Party (CUP), a third party made up of members of the now defunct Whig and Know-Nothing parties who were opposed to secession and wanted to defuse slavery as a political flashpoint. On 21 August 1860, a few weeks after purchasing Redoshi and her fellow shipmates, Smith gave a speech at Dallas County Courthouse in Selma at which he sought to defend the CUP as a pro-slavery party. For him, there was no contradiction between his pro-Union and pro-slavery stances; his banking and business operations depended on the smooth flow of slavery-produced goods and finances between those states and nations that allowed slavery in their territories and those that did not. In fact, the German-born brothers Emanuel and Mayer Lehman had recently set up a bank that provided loans to cotton farmers along the Alabama River. When war was declared in April 1861, Manhattan-based Emanuel wrote 'All is finished' on his business documents; he assumed the Lehman Brothers would not survive the conflict.[11]

When war became inevitable, Washington Smith switched allegiance to the secessionists and became a leading figure of the Confederacy. In August 1861, a year after Redoshi was displaced to his plantation, he was elected for two years to the Alabama Confederate Legislature. He later served as an aide to Alabama's Confederate governor Thomas Hill Watts, and his bank was a depository of the Treasury Department of the Confederacy. Smith financed an entire company of soldiers to prove his loyalty to secession, with Company G of the 44th Alabama Infantry Regiment marching under the banner of the 'Wash Smith Guards'. He also campaigned unsuccessfully with fellow lawyers John Whitfield Lapsley and his wife's cousin William McKendree Byrd to make Selma the Confederacy's capital when it became clear that Montgomery lacked the resources to sustain that position. Richmond in Virginia was selected instead, but Selma became the site of the Confederacy's arsenal after the Union Army captured New Orleans in May 1862.[12]

Redoshi's arrival at Washington Smith's plantation was a profound culture shock for her. The young girl, who was renamed Sally by her enslaver and whose new 'husband' Yawith was renamed William, should have been under the care of her family in West Africa.

Instead, a lonely cabin hidden by pine, poplar, ash and oak trees and built with little thought for its occupants' needs was now her home. Even more devastatingly, she was required to share it with a grown man whose language and cultural habits she did not understand.

The slave cabin to which Redoshi was displaced upended everything the little girl knew about home and community. Back home, her family's compound was surrounded by many similar communities within a fortified Yoruba town. Beyond its walls were palm trees, wild fruit and carefully cultivated fields of yams, beans and rice. But in place of the round, clay-brick, thatched-roof house of her childhood was a plain, square, wooden box. The cabin in which she was now forced to live stood alone amid parched grass. The small shack was hidden in isolated woodland and was one of a tiny handful of slave cabins scattered around Smith's plantation.[13] A few planks of wood supported by wooden beams served as a porch. A tiny chimney poking up from the centre of the roof was the cabin's only other adornment.

Two doors that were barely large enough for Yawith to squeeze through opened into the cabin's single room. The hut's two tiny windows were shuttered, making the space extremely dark even in bright sunlight. In the summertime, the cabin became unbearably hot and stuffy; in the winter, it was extremely cold. Sleep for Redoshi was a torturous experience. At best, her bed was a plank of wood raised like a shelf from the ground, if not the hard earth that comprised the cabin's floor. Like other captives transplanted to the Black Belt, she was probably forced to make her own bedding from cornhusks. That afforded the two Africans little protection against the wind, which whistled through the gaps in the wooden walls throughout the night.[14]

As soon as they regained their physical strength, the two pairs of captives, Redoshi and Yawith, and Jinnie and Cuffee, were made to labour on Washington Smith's plantation. When not at work in their enslaver's Selma mansion, they were forced to chop down and haul away trees on his land to create corn and cotton fields that they would then be expected to cultivate and harvest. 'Me and Billy

[Yawith] work in fields some time, around house some time,' Redoshi remembered.[15]

Redoshi's daily labours in Washington Smith's mansion brought the child into regular contact with her captor, his wife Susan, their five young children, and perhaps also with leading figures of the Confederacy such as Governor Watts. The kitchen was in the mansion's backyard, next to the domestic slave quarters; food and drink had to be carried up a breezeway adjoining the two buildings. Beyond the large hallway and its gleaming, pine-red floor were two twenty-foot-square rooms filled with expensive rosewood furniture brought back by Washington Smith from Paris. A long, wide staircase faced the front door and led up to four large bedrooms. Each room contained a four-poster bed whose mahogany and rosewood canopies stretched up to the sixteen-foot-high ceiling.[16] Redoshi was probably made to dust the rooms, scrub their wooden floors and polish the bedposts. She may have been required to wash and clothe Susan and her children there. Other likely tasks included cleaning out the dirty bedpans and stripping, laundering and ironing the bedsheets.

If Redoshi's enslavers' spacious, well-adorned mansion was a world apart from her own tiny, bare cabin, the difference between the rich delicacies she served them and the bland food that formed the basis of her new diet was equally stark. Redoshi was shocked by the sparseness, simplicity and monotony of the food available to her as an enslaved girl in the Black Belt. Gone were the abundant oranges, mangos, coconuts, cassava, butter and yams of her childhood. 'We feed on molasses, mush, and water,' she recalled of the coarse cornmeal and refined sugarcane she subsisted on when she arrived in the United States.[17]

Isom Moseley was born into slavery in Bogue Chitto three years before Redoshi was transplanted there. His oral narrative sheds vital light on Redoshi's experience of slavery. He detailed the meanness of her diet, the labour required to produce it, and the humiliating way she may have been forced to consume it. Moseley outlined the day-to-day lives of men and women in Bogue Chitto. Theirs was a meagre existence in which they made their own molasses, shoes and soap. Molasses was produced by boiling sugarcane in large kettles over a furnace; the resulting thick treacle was allowed to cool before being poured into troughs that were then covered with planks of wood. Lizzie Major, whose great-grandfather Bill Campbell was a neighbour of Quilla around the time of her captivity, made a similar claim when recalling Campbell and his wife Emma's experiences: 'They used to tell us about slavery time, hard life at that time. They ate out of a trough like a hog. They knock off work and bring them to the trough, pour the food in the trough. Everybody went to the trough, got down like a animal and eat with they hand out of the trough.'[18]

Beyond the meagre diet, Redoshi also described an environment of extreme physical abuse much like that on Burns Meaher's plantation, where the shipmates were beaten whenever they failed to comprehend an overseer's command. 'The slave masters and overseers beat us for every little thing when we didn't understand American talk. Overseer bad master, want to beat all the time,' the woman remembered. Redoshi and Yawith quickly learned to navigate their own language barriers and developed a loving relationship shaped by survival. The young man shielded his child bride as much as possible from the hardships of their new environment, and the pair's love endured until his death nearly sixty years later. 'My husband, he good man, wise man,' Redoshi emphasized at the end of her own life.[19]

Despite Redoshi's extreme youth, her partnership with Yawith was designed to enrich Washington Smith's plantation with enslaved children. Her enslaver's twisted scheme worked. Though Jinnie and Cuffee remained childless, Redoshi and Yawith's forced intimacy soon led to pregnancy. A daughter named Lethe was born within two years of the couple's arrival in Alabama; two other children died in infancy. Another *Clotilda* captive named Alice was probably even younger than Redoshi when Memorable Creagh paired her with a youth named Alex and sent the couple to McKinley in Marengo County. Yet she soon gave birth to Maria, the first of 13 children born between 1861 and 1895. Gracie too fell pregnant to Guy. Their son John was born during their enslavement, and their daughter Mary arrived a year or so after their emancipation.[20]

When Dinah landed in the Black Belt shortly after her fellow shipmates, forced intimacy with strange men defined the horrors of her experiences. The 13-year-old, who remembered being sold for a dime because she was so small, spent her first weeks of bondage at a plantation in Mobile where, according to her great-granddaughter Arlonzia in one of two interviews with art historian William Arnett in August 2000 and February 2001, 'there wasn't nobody else farming that land but the Cherokee Indians'.[21] She did not spend long in Mobile, though, and was soon sold and sent to the swamps of Snow Hill 30 miles east of Prairie Bluff in eastern Wilcox County. An enslaved girl bought for so little in West Africa was too profitable for a man as money-minded as Timothy Meaher to hold onto.

In Snow Hill, Dinah was horrified to find that not only would she be forced to work in the cotton fields despite her small size, but that she would also be sharing a cabin with 'four big healthy mens, two Indians and two whites.' Despite being a child, Dinah was raped frequently. 'The plantation owner wanted big men to work as slaves, so my great-grandmother was bred like they breed hogs and cows,' Arlonzia recalled in a 2002 newspaper interview.[22] Dinah was caught in a system of abuse that was designed to maximize the plantation's profits, where women and girls were confined with men until they became pregnant. When that happened, another unlucky soul was sent to the cabin to replace them.

Dinah's experience aligned with a documented pattern of child abuse in that section of the Black Belt. After she gave birth to her first child, Dinah was sent 20 miles southwest to Vredenburgh to cook and clean for her enslaver's wife. There were no settlers in Vredenburgh until around 1910, when Illinois-born Peter Vredenburgh set up a sawmill among the pine trees.[23] But just a short distance away was Dry Fork Plantation, otherwise known as James Asbury Tait

House, a home of one of Wilcox County's largest-enslaving and most politically powerful families.

Nicknamed the 'Patron of Alabama' for his central role in founding the state, James Tait's father Charles was a US senator from Georgia. Together with his son, Charles Tait established a plantation in Wilcox County that dominated the area; he owned extensive property on both sides of the Alabama River. The estate was extremely profitable for three key reasons: its proximity to the river made it easy to ship goods and people to and from the estate; its enslaved workforce was made to work extremely hard, with the average worker required to pick up to 120 pounds of cotton a day at the height of the harvesting season; and, most disturbingly, Charles Tait forced enslaved girl children to have sex. Devoting what he termed 'a full share of attention to this end of the business', he bought numerous young girls on the cusp of puberty, readily paying as much as $50 more for them than for boys the same age, a figure equivalent to $1,500 extra today. Fifty-eight enslaved children were born on Tait's property between 1819 and 1834.[24]

Dinah was afforded little time to care for her baby before she was forced to hand her to a grown woman to nurse and sent back to labour in the cotton fields. Cotton's strangeness, and the highly specialized knowledge and stamina that were required to plant and pick it at speed, were unimaginably stressful and terrifying for the child-mother, whose agonies were exacerbated by her worry for her baby. January and February were spent clearing the field and ploughing the soil before planting began in March and April. Enslaved women and girls guided horse-drawn ploughs to create ridges in the soil that the captives would then be expected to shape by hand into little mounds; once drilled, the cotton seed would then also be planted by hand. Cotton plants began to burst through the soil in late May and typically grew to about four or five feet. For the next few months, enslaved labourers were made to continually thin and weed the crop in the baking heat, taking care to cut back weeds within half an inch of the plants without damaging them. When the cotton shoots were small, the weeding had to be done by hand, forcing the labourers to stoop constantly. When they switched to hoes, the wooden handles blistered their hands. The captives' labour was made especially difficult by the uncooperative Black Belt soil, which baked dry in summer and turned to sticky mud in winter.

The English naturalist Philip Henry Gosse was a tutor for eight months in 1838 for Reuben Saffold, a former chief justice of Alabama and the owner of Belvoir Plantation, near Pleasant Hill, 15 miles north of Snow Hill. Gosse identified the Black Belt plantation as a hellish environment, in which landowners 'of the highest standing' secretly used torture devices to control their captives. He could not bring himself to list the specific cruelties that enslavers applied, but he made clear that a whipping was likely for those whose cotton count fell short. Given the vast quantities of cotton that enslaved labourers were required to pick each day, the count was often short. The overseer, or 'boss man', rode through the fields three or four times a day to judge the efficiency of Dinah and her fellow prisoners' work. If a performance was deemed unsatisfactory, brutal violence was meted out. Punishments of 50 or even 100 lashes delivered with a thick cow-hide whip were typical during cotton-picking time. One man could never keep up with the arduous labour and was whipped every day, and Dinah was forced to watch the blood pour down his back.[25]

Many enslaved labourers fled simply to escape a whipping; others fled for want of food, which typically consisted of eight dry quarts of cornmeal and three and a half pounds of meat per week, sometimes supplemented with molasses and fruit in the summer and autumn. Dinah's meals consisted simply of cornbread and boiled peas, which she had to rush to eat or risk not eating at all. Arlonzia recalled, 'They give them about ten to twelve minutes to get to the food and to eat and get back to work. If they didn't eat it in that time, they didn't get no more food for the day.'[26]

Other forms of slavery-based violence in Wilcox County were even more extreme. An enslaved man was shot and killed by overseer James S. Jobe for resisting a whipping on a plantation near Prairie Bluff the year before the *Clotilda*'s arrival. So many enslaved people were hanged by ropes from a particular tree on the summit of a hill just outside the town of Camden that the spot was nicknamed 'Hangman's Hill'. The victims perhaps included a man known to history only as George, who was tried in Camden in April 1858 for killing an overseer. Even 40 years later, the people living in the community still shuddered when discussing the site.[27]

Back in Prairie Bluff, Gracie's two small daughters narrowly escaped the worst of the Black Belt's violence when they made a daring attempt to flee their prison within a year of their displacement to Alabama. The older child, Sally, by now 11 years old, saw an opportunity to sneak away from her cabin and hide in the swampy woods nearly. Matilda was only 3 years old and would have been a burden to her sister, but Sally had already lost four siblings and was determined not to lose another. She clung tightly onto the toddler, ensuring that she remained by her side throughout their bid for freedom.

The timing of Matilda and Sally's flight suggests it was precipitated by a visit to Memorable Creagh and William Hunt's plantations by two members of the Underground Railroad. A young bondsman recruited by the men on their planned journey north to freedom went around his neighbours' cabins imploring them to join him. Though the young man was arrested, the following night the corn house, fodder house and stables of Hunt's neighbouring plantation suspiciously caught fire. The enslaver's 12 mules were killed, and his $41,000 estate suffered at least $4,000 worth of damage.[28]

Matilda and Sally did not get far. Late January was dark and cold, and the earth was sodden with rain. As young children in a foreign land, the pair had almost no chance of permanent escape. They managed to hide for several hours in the swamp near the slave quarters before William Hunt's dogs hunted them down. As Philip Henry Gosse noted of the challenges the little girls faced, 'the chance of a poor wretch's escape, through a thousand miles of hostile country, without funds, without friends, without knowledge of geography, - every white man he sees his enemy, ipso facto, and his colour betraying him to all, - is small indeed'. As one man who did make it north observed, 'Escape from Alabama is almost impossible, - if a man escapes, it is by the skin of his teeth.' In October 1863 one of Washington Smith's captives, a young man named George, tried to run away. He was quickly lodged in Clarke County jail.[29]

A runaway who could not climb a tree quickly enough to evade the bloodhounds faced a violent death. A youth named Bill Pickens fled to the woods to escape a whipping for breaking his enslaver's order never to leave his southern Alabama plantation. A slave patrol soon set its dogs on him, and he was forced to run up a tree to save his life. 'De dogs is terrible,' Pickens recalled 50 years later. 'When dey's after yer dere ain't nothin' to do but climb a tree or dey tear yer all to pieces.'[30]

While the hunts brought unimaginable terror to those running away, they served as sporting activities to many of those who sought to catch them. Slave patrols roamed the countryside opportunistically at night, and often attacked groups of enslaved people before checking if they had travel passes. The legal punishment for being caught without a pass in Alabama was 39 lashes, but patrols paid little heed to the law and whipped their captives hundreds of times.[31]

The first shipmates to successfully break free from their enslaver were those on William Hunt's estate. On 9 July 1864, four years to the day after Quilla disembarked the *Clotilda*, Hunt died unexpectedly. He was only 45 and had been appointed just three weeks earlier as justice of the peace for Wilcox County, a role that gave the child kidnapper responsibility for overseeing criminal cases in a court of law. The death of her enslaver must have brought unimaginable relief to the now 15-year-old Quilla, but whatever hopes of freedom her enslaver's death raised in her, Quilla's immediate circumstances did not change. She remained bonded to his widow Siloma, and her status as chattel was compounded five months later when Siloma had her husband's estate, including his captives, valued to pay off his debts. Teenager labourers Quilla and Ossa were priced at $3,000 each, equivalent to $58,000 each in 2023. Their 17-year-old shipmate Lucy and her six-month-old son were valued together at $3,000. They were among 31 enslaved people listed in William Hunt's estate file. Their names appeared immediately above a list of mules that Hunt bought to replace those killed in the stable fire. In fact, some of the mules were valued more highly than Siloma's youngest and oldest captives, and they bore similar one-word names. Both groups included an 'Eliza'.[32]

The three African youths on Hunt's estate were valued as property nearly two years after President Abraham Lincoln's 1863 Emancipation Proclamation, which changed the legal status of bondspeople in the Confederacy from enslaved to free. But the secessionists refused to recognize Lincoln's executive order, and the group had no idea that their bondage had legally ended. Nevertheless, the Union Army was making increasing inroads into Confederate territory and Alabamian enslavers feared they would be forced to liberate their prisoners. Memorable Creagh's neighbour Thomas W. Price anticipated the Confederacy's imminent defeat in 1864 and negotiated the sale of a woman and her six children to the *Clotilda* enslaver. But by the time Quilla and her shipmates were valued, Mobile Bay and Atlanta had fallen under Union control and even Creagh realized it would soon no longer be possible to enslave people. Siloma Hunt sold her livestock and farming equipment, but she could not sell the teenage Africans, who remained trapped on her plantation. Quilla fell pregnant for the first time to an unknown American man about a month later.[33]

Another *Clotilda* enslaver would also soon be dead. Two child shipmates, Sawnee and Miller, were displaced on their arrival in Alabama to a 1,300-acre cotton plantation on the bank of the Tombigbee River in southern Pickens County. The estate was nearly a hundred miles northwest of Prairie Bluff and only a few miles away from the Mississippi border. Sawnee and Miller's enslaver was LaFayette Mordecai Minor, whose late father Henry Minor was one of Alabama's earliest settlers and briefly one of its Supreme Court justices. Miller was in such poor health when he landed in Pickens County that he died of a fever soon after his arrival. According to LaFayette Minor's niece Mary Friend, the enslaver used Sawnee's unruly displays of grief as an excuse to confine him to the bedroom of his big brown mansion. To the child's unimaginable horror, he was forced to sleep alongside his enslaver for next three years.[34]

LaFayette Minor spent the first half of the war storing cotton on his land to raise money for the secessionists. But in July 1863 he was conscripted for three years of soldier duty with Company I, 7th Alabama Cavalry. On 23 July 1864, two weeks after William Hunt's death and almost exactly four years after he bought Miller and Sawnee, Minor was captured by the Union Army. The now Sergeant Minor was one of three prisoners held on a plantation near Pollard, a town on the Alabama–Florida border. The 82nd Regiment US Colored Infantry and six companies of the 86th Regiment US Colored Infantry were part of the advance that led to Minor's capture. Many of the African American soldiers involved in the raid, which reported no casualties on the Union side, were former bondsmen.[35]

LaFayette Minor's capture and subsequent death some months later in a cold Northern prison signalled that the federal forces were winning; slavery was nearly over. In the spring of 1865, Union soldiers finally reached central Alabama. In the first week of April, United States troops led by General John Thomas Croxton marched on the north of the state. The troops destroyed sections of the University of Alabama in Tuscaloosa, LaFayette Minor's alma mater and the source of some of his captives. Croxton's brigade then turned to Pickens County and burned down the courthouse at Carrollton.[36] When they reached Minor's plantation, they were met by an ecstatic Sawnee, by now in his mid-teens, who immediately volunteered to join them.

Sawnee was one of at least four Middle Passage survivors who served in the Union Army. Unlike the others, Sawnee was imprisoned throughout the war; he only managed to join the conflict at its end. But he probably saw significant action. Sawnee disappears from the historical record after his liberation, but General Croxton's brigade's journey through Alabama makes it possible to map the African teen-ager's movements in the last weeks of the war. The troops survived a rearguard attack near Romulus, 30 miles east of Carrollton, and then ventured north and east through the state, capturing prisoners and artillery and destroying railroad bridges and depots, an iron works, a military training camp and cotton mills. On 23 April, Sawnee participated in the easy overthrow of Confederate General Benjamin Jefferson Hill and his troops at Munford's Station, 40 miles from Georgia's border. The Battle of Munford was the last Civil War battle to take place east of the Mississippi; its casualties were the last to die in open combat.[37]

As Sawnee marched with Croxton's brigade on Pickens County, General James Harrison Wilson led his Union troops to Selma, where they quickly overcame the eight-feet-tall parapets and up to fifteen-feet-wide ditches that enslaved labourers had been forced to build to defend the town's arsenal. The Confederates burned 25,000 bales of cotton in anticipation of the army's arrival on 2 April 1865, and Washington Smith rushed to hide the Bank of Selma's gold in one of his mansion's white Doric columns. Confederate general Nathan Bedford Forrest, who with his brothers Aaron and William trafficked and sold 37 *Wanderer* survivors at their slave trading business in Tennessee, and who oversaw a massacre of surrendering African American troops at the Battle of Fort Pillow in April 1864, led the city's defence. But the future first grand wizard of the Ku Klux Klan could not hold back the Union forces. It proved to be a largely bloodless takeover. Colonel of the Dallas Militia William Townsend Minter, whose late brother Anthony Morgan Minter and sister Mary K. 'Polly' Gardner enslaved three Africans in nearby Burnsville, was one of the very few men to die in the Battle of Selma.[38]

While the Union soldiers destroyed Selma's state arsenal, muni-tions works and nitre plant, they never found the Bank of Selma's gold. According to a 1979 *Montgomery Advertiser* article, General Wilson spared Washington Smith's property from destruction because both men were 32nd Degree Masons, the top level of the

Scottish Rite sub-group of Freemasonry. Instead, the ground floor of the building was used as a hospital and headquarters for Union soldiers. When they left, Smith was hailed locally as a hero for safeguarding the secessionists' money.[39]

Newly freed people in Selma crowded around the Union Army in joy at its victory and those who met the physical criteria enlisted in the army. On 7 April, the chosen young men and boys gathered in the city to be organized into three regiments. Nearly five thousand men and boys in Alabama, including Sawnee, emancipated themselves by joining the federal troops. More than five hundred people enlisted under General Wilson on a single day in April 1865.[40]

After a week in Selma, the Union Army left the city and marched 50 miles east to Montgomery, proudly joined by their freshly liberated recruits. The soldiers never came near Prairie Bluff, McKinley, Bogue Chitto or Snow Hill. From her isolated cabin in the woods 15 miles west of Selma, Redoshi did not hear the military men who brought liberation and elation to the city's enslaved community. She did not watch the racialized power structure that held her in bondage fall. In fact, the army's message of emancipation may not even have reached her. Her neighbour Isom Moseley was eight years old when the war ended and too young to meaningfully comprehend the shift from slavery to freedom. But his elders told him later that it was 'a year before the folks knowed that they was free'. As for Washington Smith's false clemency claim that 'much the large portion' of his estate was 'reduced to ashes and swept away by the United States soldiers', the federal government certainly never scrutinized it.[41] Smith and Memorable Creagh were both pardoned by the end of the summer and allowed to keep their estates. There would be no material change in Redoshi, Quilla, Gracie or Dinah's circumstances in the months and years ahead. Their lives were set to carry on as before.

8

The Capital

Bougier's faint hope that she might somehow find her way back across the Atlantic to her three small children turned to despair as she was separated from her shipmates on Burns Meaher's plantation. Bougier was among at least 16 captives who were sold to enslavers in Montgomery. That meant a days' long journey across the state in the dark, suffocating hold of one of the Meahers' steamboats. The summer's searing heat had dried out the Alabama River, which sank to a record low in late July 1860.[1] For more than two hundred looping miles of the river, the boat in which Bougier was confined journeyed at a snail's pace along its rocky bed. A shipmate named Sarah tried in vain to comfort her four-year-old daughter Nannie as the steamboat lurched backwards and forwards up the river. The tiny child's inconsolable cries must have been a constant torment to Bougier.

Eventually, the steamboat docked in the north of the city. Bougier and her fellow captives were pulled out of the hold at a wide bend in the river and forced up the tall embankment under cover of night. They were then hoisted onto a wagon that drove them along Montgomery's wide dirt road streets, countless gas lamps casting the urban surroundings in a pale light. Trees that would have been recognizable in the daytime as maple, magnolia, pecan, pine and oak lined rows of rigidly laid out walkways. As she passed through the city, Bougier caught sight of the Alabama State Capitol, which loomed up on a hill less than a mile east of the waterfront. Even in the darkness, the Greek Revival-style building was incomprehensively grander than anything the young woman had ever seen before. A marble staircase led up to the white three-storey structure, which was framed by six Corinthian columns and topped by a rust-coloured wood and cast-iron dome.

Montgomery in the mid-nineteenth century was a major cotton distribution and communication centre, its central location in the state making it the epicentre of its market economy. Key foodstuffs such as meat and corn were stored in the city, and more than a million cotton bales were loaded onto steamboats from its wharf in the autumn of 1860. Montgomery was also Alabama's largest slave market; 164 slave dealers paid licences to sell or trade people in the city between 1838 and 1860.[2] Half its population of around nine thousand people were enslaved, and slave pens were situated in the heart of the city. The horrors of US slavery were immediately apparent to the *Clotilda* shipmates.

One of the most chilling sights for the young Africans were the many bondspeople of mixed African and European heritage. Sir William Howard Russell of the London *Times* was so struck by the 'considerable number' of mixed heritage enslaved people in Civil War-era Montgomery that he quickly saw through 'the statements made to me by some of my friends, that the planters affect the character of *parent* in their moral relations merely with the negro race'. Seven *Wanderer* survivors, including six children, were horrified by the sight of mixed heritage enslaved people when they were trafficked to Tennessee in May 1859 by future Confederate general and first grand wizard of the Ku Klux Klan Nathan Bedford Forrest. As the *Memphis Appeal* coldly noted, 'the mixture of white does not please their eye'.[3] Such men and women served as living evidence of slavery's sexual violence, and signalled to even its youngest captives that there was little hope of escape. Enslaved Africans had been in the United States for decades. America had become their home.

The streets between the Alabama River and the capitol formed Montgomery's business district. At its centre, half a mile directly west of the capitol via Market Street, was an artesian well enclosed by a large iron fence, where slave auctions were frequently held. During his visit nine months after the *Clotilda* shipmates' arrival in the city, William Russell watched the plight of two young people who were put up for sale near the well. A short, broad-shouldered man in his mid-twenties wore coarse worn clothing and a grief-stricken expression as he met his uncertain fate. A young girl named Sally, who wore shreds of leather for shoes and a threadbare bonnet, held her life's possessions in a small bundle clutched tightly in her hand, and Russell noted the misery in her eyes. A group of white men in long black coats and tall hats inspected but did not buy her despite the competitive price the sweaty, corpulent auctioneer offered, which doomed her to repeat the ordeal the next day. Russell was disturbed by the normalization of the captives' trauma. Their psychological pain was potent, yet their agonies were met with indifference by their would-be buyers, who chewed tobacco, whittled sticks and spat carelessly onto the dusty ground.[4]

Montgomery's population of just under nine thousand was more than fifty per cent smaller than Ouidah and an eighth of the size of Ogbomosho, but Alabama's capital was also much more compact than the West African town- and cityscapes that Bougier knew. The sight of strange white brick buildings with hard, slanted roofs crowded together in rows was deeply disconcerting to the young woman. As the inhabitants of Tarkar well understood, closely packed houses were a fire hazard, and she saw how easily the whole city could go up in flames. Unlike Bougier's fortified hometown, Montgomery's edges met the open air. But there was no sanctuary for miles around and no hope of escape for the young woman even if she had the strength to try. Slave patrols roamed the city at night to catch any enslaved person bold enough to break curfew, which was marked by a 9.00 p.m. bell. As William Russell noted, 'There is something suspicious in the constant never-ending statement that "we are not afraid of our slaves." The curfew and the night patrol in the streets, the prisons and watch-houses, and the police regulations, prove that strict supervision, at all events, is needed and necessary.'[5]

Nineteen months before the *Clotilda* survivors' arrival, 38 *Wanderer* survivors were sent to Montgomery. South Carolina-born surgeon Dr. Benjamin Rush Jones relinquished his interest in his Perry Street drug store, a short distance east of the waterfront, the very week of their arrival. Their treatment as exotic spectacles in front of leering crowds only seemed to cement his commitment to the *Clotilda* plot, and he bought about fifteen of the Africans when they arrived in Alabama, which raised his tally of mostly child and teenage captives to an even 100.[6] Bougier and four-year-old Nannie and her mother Sarah were among Rush's prisoners. Their new captor must have seemed like an otherworldly creature. Rush's long nose framed a markedly long, smooth face. Only thick, dark eyebrows interrupted the strange paleness of his skin, which glowed in the moonlight.

Jones was a wealthy man who could easily afford his more-than-eighth share of the *Clotilda* shipmates. He had recently expanded to 1,500 acres the size of his Prairie Place estate, which lay eight miles east of Montgomery in the village of Mount Meigs. The land was so ripe for cotton growing that Jones was prepared to pay $27.50 (equivalent to $1,000 in 2023) per acre. So fertile and well positioned was his estate that a visitor to his land on the eve of the *Clotilda*'s voyage described it as the 'garden spot' of Alabama and concluded the surgeon's wealth could only grow. Jones was joined by his younger brother and fellow surgeon Bartlett Constantine Jones, who transferred to the region from their mother Eliza Jane Dunlap Jones's cotton plantation in nearby Lowndes County. Constantine Jones bought $42,800 worth of land (equivalent to nearly $1.6 million in 2023) northwest of his brother on what was known as the Line Creek and Mount Meigs Road (now Ware's Ferry Road), where he enslaved 57 people.[7]

Other *Clotilda* survivors who fell into Rush Jones's hands included a 12-year-old girl named Victoria. According to Jones's youngest daughter Susie Jones Waller, Victoria was a West African princess. In reality, the facial and body markings in which she took great pride suggest she was already a servant of the orishas. But Victoria's regal-sounding name, which had only recently been popularized in the English-speaking world by Britain's queen, was probably a racist joke. The name's hard consonants were difficult for a Yoruba speaker to pronounce, and she became known to her family as Ella. Ella was sent to live with Jones, his wife Frances Amelia, and their son and five daughters on their Montgomery property, where she was forced to prepare the family's food. Ella's work was closely supervised by her female enslaver, who she was made to call 'Miss Em'. The Jones's daughter Susie gave unwitting insight into the exacting nature of her mother's management of the child's work when she asserted that Ella 'developed into a very fine cook'.[8] The other Africans were sent to labour on the Jones's Mount Meigs plantation.

Another *Clotilda* captive, a small, slender-framed boy named Reuben, remained in Montgomery, where he was sent to join the six adults and four children enslaved to Alexander 'Alex' Frederick Given. Given was a 40-year-old Irish-born cotton merchant who owned a grocer's shop halfway down Commerce Street, a 400-metre-long walkway that linked the waterfront to the well. Given had made a fortune from Alabama's cotton trade since his arrival from County Tyrone in Ulster 20 years earlier. The week before the *Clotilda* captives were sold on Burns Meaher's plantation, the combined value of Given's real estate and personal estate was over $113,000 (equivalent to nearly $4.2 million in 2023), which meant he could easily afford the Meahers' $1,000 asking price for a *Clotilda* survivor.[9] Reuben's sale perhaps stemmed from a personal arrangement between Given and Jones, who were so close that when Given's fourth son was born 18 months after the *Clotilda*'s landing, he christened him Rush Jones.

The Africans enslaved to Given and Jones may have included some of the shipmates whom William Foster claimed as his payment for human trafficking. As a proud subject of Queen Victoria, the *Clotilda*'s captain probably came up with the child captive's American name, and his presence in central Alabama two months after the *Clotilda*'s landing points up connections to the crime's Montgomery participants. On 6 September, Foster married his landlord's 20-year-old daughter Adelaide at the city's Exchange Hotel, which Given managed after the war, and the couple honeymooned at Talladega Springs, a favourite holiday haunt of Jones and his family. The three hundred-by-one hundred-feet-wide Exchange Hotel lay on the corners of Montgomery and Commerce streets, next to the well, from which it sourced its water, and was just two blocks west and one block north of Ella's new prison. The Greek Revival building was directly opposite the capitol on the other side of Market Street, the site of three of the city's four slave depots. The four-storey brick structure was the grandest hotel in the city. Balconies and plate-glass-panelled bar and billiards rooms provided guests with spaces of relaxation, and oysters, champagne and lobster salad were served by enslaved waiters in the dining room. When the first capitol burned down in December 1849, the Exchange Hotel became the temporary home of Alabama's legislature and the official gathering place of the state's politicians thereafter. When Alabama seceded from the Union, the hotel became the first official headquarters of the Confederacy.[10]

The claustrophobic terror of Ella and Reuben's entrapment in Montgomery was made worse by their proximity to the city's increasingly fiery politics. Although they could not understand what was going on around them, the young Africans' closeness to the Exchange Hotel and capitol placed them at the epicentre of the secessionist movement on the eve of the Civil War. The Jones's property, on the corner of Adams and Lawrence avenues, was just four blocks west of the capitol. As Rush Jones's middle daughter Virginia 'Jennie' Jones Vass recalled, 'My home was . . . just back of our courthouse, and being centrally located, everything of excitement or importance seemed to pass.'[11] Ella's prison even became a site where secession was debated, as future leaders of the Confederacy visited the household in the weeks and days before the conflict. Guests who frequented the Jones's drawing room included William Lowndes Yancey, the 'orator of secession' and drafter of Alabama's Ordinance of Secession, whose law office was just one block north on the corners of Washington Avenue and Perry Street and who, like Given and Jones, was a leader of Montgomery's First Presbyterian Church. They also included future Confederate attorney general and Montgomery governor Thomas Hill Watts, whose aides during the conflict included Redoshi's enslaver Washington Smith. As a cook in the household, Ella almost certainly prepared and perhaps even served the guests' food.

Reuben also watched his enslaver prepare for war. On 10 November 1860, four days after Abraham Lincoln, whose Republican Party promised not to interfere with slavery in the South but only to halt its expansion westwards, was elected president, Alex Given was named as one of fifteen vice-presidents of a mass meeting that called for immediate secession from what its leaders termed the 'Abolition party'. Alabama governor Andrew Barry Moore spoke first at the crowded gathering at Estelle Hall on the corner of Market and Perry streets, one block east of the well. The governor stressed that secession was now unavoidable, and that Alabama should join the other Southern states in forming a separate confederacy. Yancey went further, promising that secession would be peaceful yet advocating war in a speech that likened Southern enslavers to the outnumbered Spartan warriors of ancient Greece: 'rather than live on subject to a government that . . . places me in a position of inequality, of inferiority to the Northern free negro . . . I would *in the cause of my State gather around me some brave spirits who, however few in number, would find a grave which the world would recognize, my countrymen, as a modern Thermopylae.*' His words were met with rapturous applause. Seven days later, a meeting was held at the Capitol to select delegates to a state convention on 7 January whose purpose was to consider secession. Yancey and Thomas Watts were chosen.[12]

Ella and Reuben were not the only African children trapped in the heart of the Confederacy on the eve of the Civil War. When Northern journalist Thomas Low Nichols visited Montgomery in spring 1860, he found one of the child *Wanderer* survivors still imprisoned in the city, and he marvelled at the boy's rapid command of English and Southern manners. The African youth, who his enslaver renamed

Jackson Smith, had quickly grasped the skills he needed to survive violence and enslavement alone on the wrong side of the Atlantic. Nichols coldly – and falsely – suggested that the threat of a return to Africa was the only discipline the child needed.[13]

Jackson was 13 years old when he was transplanted from Congo to Montgomery. He was sold twice. His first enslaver was South Carolina-born John Miles Smith, a 41-year-old plantation owner and Commerce Street furniture dealer whose cool stare and grizzled muttonchops must have been terrifying to the young boy. His second enslaver was a Maryland-born banker and railroad investor in his early forties named Josiah Morris, whose First National Bank was across the road from John Smith's furniture shop. So heavily did Josiah Morris's bank profit from Montgomery's slavery-based economy that he singlehandedly bankrolled the 4,150 acres of land on which Birmingham was founded and is also rumoured to have given the post-war industrial city its name. He was regarded as Alabama's richest man at the time of his sudden death from a stroke in 1891.[14]

Jackson was sent to navigate the vast machinery that filled the pro-secession *Montgomery Advertiser*'s pressroom perhaps within weeks or even days of his arrival in the state capital. The *Advertiser* was located at 12 North Perry Street, one block east and a few feet north of the well, and about two hundred metres east as the crow flies from Smith's furniture shop and Morris's bank. Jackson's labours perhaps stemmed from or engendered a racist joke that appeared in another Alabama newspaper, the *Cahaba Gazette*, a month after the *Wanderer* shipmates arrived in Montgomery: 'A few more [Africans] must be imported to bring down the price, when we will get one and make a pressman of him. A wild African working a press would be something new in the history of the country.'[15] The small boy found himself charged with printing the pro-slavery propaganda that had precipitated his imprisonment on the wrong side of the world.

After President Lincoln's election, the secessionist mood became increasingly oppressive and terrifying for the four million enslaved

Kossula, *c.*1912.

Emma Langdon Roche's portraits of Abaché (top) and Polee (bottom), *c.*1912.

Daily life in nineteenth-century Oyo.

A map drawn by Kossula tracing the route of the captives' forced march to Ouidah. 'Eko' is Lagos, 'Budigree' is Badagry and 'Adaché' is Porto-Novo.

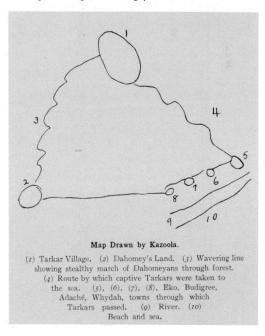

Map Drawn by Kazoola.

(*1*) Tarkar Village. (*2*) Dahomey's Land. (*3*) Wavering line showing stealthy march of Dahomeyans through forest. (*4*) Route by which captive Tarkars were taken to the sea. (*5*), (*6*), (*7*), (*8*), Eko, Budigree, Adaché, Whydah, towns through which Tarkars passed. (*9*) River. (*10*) Beach and sea.

Chief *Clotilda* conspiracist Timothy Meaher in 1886.

Clotilda captain William Foster in 1890.

The wreck of the
*Clotilda, c.*1912.

Matilda,
*c.*1920s or 1930s.

Jefferson Davis being sworn in as President of the Confederacy
outside Montgomery's Capitol Building, 18 February 1861.

Gumpa, the leader of
African Town, *c.*1890s.

Emma Langdon Roche's portrait
of Osia Keeby, *c.*1912.

African Town judge Charlie in 1912.

persons across the Southern states. Armed soldiers began drilling in the centre of Montgomery in December 1860. A few blocks away, Yancey and other Alabama Secession Convention delegates gathered at the capitol and voted to secede from the Union and form a slavery-based Southern republic. Secessionist feelings were by no means unanimous, though. Yancey was burned in effigy in Athens, the county seat of Limestone County in northern Alabama. Even in the Black Belt, the *Selma State Sentinel* published a scathing critique of 'this creature, Bill Yancey', noting that he had killed his wife's uncle in a street brawl and abandoned the Democratic Party in 1848 and 1852 and split it in 1860. The vote ultimately passed by a majority of 61 to 39. Alabama became the fourth state after South Carolina, Mississippi and Florida to secede from the Union. When secession was declared in the city on 11 January, thunderous cheers followed the raising of the new state's flag from the capitol's dome. It featured a cotton plant surrounded by a rattlesnake above the Latin words 'noli me tangere' (Touch Me Not). Cannon fire, church bells that rang for hours and firecrackers also announced the news, and Rush Jones's former drug store was one of the buildings illuminated in celebration. The warlike noises continued into the night.[16]

Montgomery was named the capital of the Confederacy, which brought with it the ominous presence of hundreds more pro-slavery men. On 9 February, a constitutional convention at the capitol building chose Mississippi senator Jefferson Davis as the breakaway states' president. Ella, Reuben and Jackson watched processions of soldiers parade in the streets in preparation for Davis's arrival. Around 10.00 p.m. on 16 February, Davis stepped off a train to the sound of cheers, and yet more church bells and cannon fire, and was met by Yancey and other local dignitaries, who joined him in a four-horse coach that was greeted by fireworks as it travelled through the city. The procession stopped at the Exchange Hotel, where local dignitaries showed Davis to his room.

Rush and Amelia Jones and their children were given leading roles in the Confederate president's inauguration. Thousands of visitors gathered at Montgomery for the event on the bright morning of

18 February. An ornate carriage drawn by four grey horses and driven by an enslaved coachman stopped at the hotel and Jefferson Davis stepped into it. A brass band played 'Dixie' and martial music, and military companies, including newly recruited soldiers such as Jones's son, Benjamin Rush Jr., led the presidential procession the half-mile up Market Street to the capitol. The presidential party and other carriages bearing local officials, including Rush, Amelia and their daughters, followed behind. Up to eight thousand people cheered the procession from the street, windows and rooftops. Their cries were amplified by cannon fire, and steamboat, shop and foundry whistles. When Davis walked into the capitol, the band struck up 'La Marseillaise', the French national anthem. As the capitol's huge black clock tower struck 1.00 p.m., Davis took the oath of office outside the building, and Yancey declared to the audience on the grass below and the balconies above, 'the man and the hour have met'.[17]

Unbeknown to the shipmates, the events taking place around them unwittingly helped to make them the US slave trade's last recorded victims. Secession postponed for political expediency's sake the resolution passed at the 1859 Southern Commercial Convention to overturn the slave trade ban and brought an end to the 'African Labor Supply Association' of which William Lowndes Yancey was an officer. The secessionists' constitution, which was written into law and signed at the capitol in February of that year, instead ruled that 'the importation of negroes of the African race . . . is hereby forbidden', and the following month Jefferson Davis vetoed a slave trade bill that sought to reduce the crime of human trafficking from piracy to a 'misdemeanor'. The ban was not intended to be permanent, but the separatists knew that reopening the slave trade risked alienating Upper Southern states such as Virginia, where the slave trade had few supporters, and potential overseas allies that the fledgling, soon-to-be war-gripped Confederacy desperately needed. It was believed that a breakaway Southern republic that positioned itself as pro-cotton, but anti-slave trade, might gain diplomatic recognition from Britain and France, which had been the chief customers of the region's cotton crops before the war. It was also feared that Britain would join the war on the Union's side if the Confederacy sought to reopen the slave trade. Just one day after vetoing the bill, Jefferson Davis appointed Yancey as head of a diplomatic mission to Britain and France that sought to secure existing US treaties with the two European empires by persuading them of the Southern Republic's legitimacy.[18] Davis, too, would soon leave Montgomery, which he deemed too small and inadequately resourced a national capital. In late May, just over a month after war was formally declared, Virginia's capital Richmond became the Confederacy's new base.

Unlike Ella, Bougier did not witness the raucous birth of a pro-slavery republic. But the Mount Meigs plantation on which she found herself brought its own agonies. When she arrived, the cotton was almost ready to be harvested. Vast crops of red apples, golden pears, pink peaches and purple grapes that filled her enslaver's orchards and gardens, and from which his captives brewed his widely regarded wines and peach brandy, also needed picking. So abundant with fruit was Rush Jones's plantation that he could not identify all the pear varieties.[19] As a young woman enslaved in Montgomery County, Bougier's own likely diet was corn and a pound of pork a day, possibly supplemented, if she had time to spare, by raising her own poultry.

Bougier and a teenage shipmate named Unsey fell pregnant to unknown men within weeks of their arrival in Montgomery. Although it is unclear if they were subjected to regimented sexual violence like their shipmate Dinah in Snow Hill, the birth of their daughters Amanda and Hattie so soon after their displacement to the United States underscored their vulnerability to abuse. Nor did pregnancy and motherhood afford them any respite from their unremunerated labour. While the men hoed, women such as Bougier were responsible for driving the strange mules and directing the ploughs that had not been needed for an abundant harvest back home. Violence was a constant threat; the overseer rode from field to field with a whip. Enslaved labourers in Mount Meigs worked into the night, picking out balls of cotton by candlelight.[20]

The labour expected even of young girls such as Unsey was unimaginably arduous. Martha Bradley was enslaved as a child to Rush Jones's neighbour and friend Dr. Charles S. Lucas, who made her haul big logs by hand to clear the land for cotton growing. Thick leather straps were attached to the little girl's arms and then fastened around a freshly felled tree. Martha tottered again and again with her load to the log pile, her body bent double as the rough bark rubbed against her skin. One wet morning, Martha decided she could no longer bear the physical agonies of her labour and refused to work. The overseer caught up with her and began whipping her. Horrified by the pain and too young to realize that his violence was authorized within the plantation system, Martha fought back. 'I jumped on him and bit and kicked him 'til he lemme go. I didn't know no better then.'[21] Martha was silent about the punishment she received for her act of resistance, but her story made clear she learned a hard lesson about the authorized violence of a Mount Meigs plantation.

Jones's youngest daughter Susie claimed that the shipmates of another *Clotilda* captive named Liza would not let her work in the fields because she was a West African queen.[22] Susie's account is unreliable; she was only a year old when the *Clotilda* shipmates arrived in Alabama. Even if Liza's friends endeavoured to protect her, a captive young woman bought to enrich her enslaver would not have been able to escape the arduous labour of Jones's plantation. Yet, like the defensive actions other shipmates took to protect young girls from the violence of Timothy Meaher's cook and Burns Meaher's overseer, Susie's account suggests her father's captives resisted what they saw as the especially unnatural torments endured by their female friends and relatives, who would not have been expected to labour in the fields back home.

Such protective gestures were stunningly brave, for Mount Meigs on the eve of the Civil War was a community terrorized by spectacles of extreme violence. Jones himself was probably a participant in the August 1854 lynching of an enslaved man named Gilbert who killed in self-defence his enslaver Dr. Alfred McDonald, who like Jones was a South Carolina-born, Philadelphia-trained Mount Meigs physician. McDonald shot at Gilbert when he refused to submit to a whipping, but Gilbert wrestled the gun away as he pulled the trigger. McDonald tried to hunt him down, but Gilbert beat him to death with a thick piece of white oak as the enslaver mounted his horse. The following day, the white community of Mount Meigs – 60 to 70 people in total – arrested Gilbert, chained him to a pine tree and burned him to death. His murderers followed their act with a chilling warning in the *Montgomery Advertiser*: 'From some cause or other, there is a spirit of insubordination in our slave population that is constantly leading to the commission of the most diabolical crimes, and which call for prompt and summary *examples*.' The political leaders of nearby Macon and Tallassee, among them Rush Jones's fellow Montgomery surgeon James Gillah Freeny, voted to endorse the killing.[23]

Mid-century Montgomery was the scene of other kinds of physical horror. Those shipmates imprisoned by Rush Jones found themselves at the epicentre of a medical revolution whose advancements depended on the bodies and labour of enslaved girls and women. Jones was the brother-in-law, and former schoolmate, business partner and neighbour of Dr. J. Marion Sims, a president of the American Medical Association and one of the most celebrated surgeons of the nineteenth century. Sims had even been trained in medicine by Jones's uncle, Dr. Churchill Jones. Sims's groundbreaking repairs to devastating childbirth injuries earned him the moniker 'the father of modern gynaecology'. He developed his techniques by performing countless experimental surgeries on enslaved women and teenage girls in Montgomery in an era before pain relief was widely offered. Sims's career and the medical advances he developed were made possible – and driven – by a Southern plantation system that held hundreds of thousands of young women in bondage, which assaulted their bodies by subjecting them early and frequently to childbirth for their enslavers' profit, and which demanded they be 'fixed' when they could no longer give birth.

There is no evidence that Rush Jones operated on his own captives; by the time the *Clotilda* shipmates landed in Montgomery, he wasn't even practising medicine, having closed his surgery when he sold his drug business. But he aided and bore witness to Sims's operations, and he shared his brother-in-law's desire to extract medical knowledge from his prisoners, including and perhaps especially his African captives. Just before the Civil War, another of Jones's brothers-in-law, fellow surgeon Dr. George Wilkins McDade, learned – via the advocate of Gilbert's lynching James Freeny – that an enslaved man called Lawson had adopted a Muscogee (Creek) method of treating syphilis patients using the plant *Stillingia sylvatica*. Lawson's herbal remedy was held to be so effective that Jones and other large enslavers in and around Montgomery each identified among their bondsmen a specialist doctor whose job was to protect their fellow captives from syphilis and other deadly diseases that threatened their enslavers' income. They were 'medical men of the highest intelligence', according to Marion Sims. Jones had a particularly deep appreciation for such folk remedies and the skills of their practitioners. In an article for the *British Medical Journal*, Sims noted that 'Dr. Rush Jones . . . has really had a larger experience with McDade's anti-syphilitic fluid extract than any one else'. Jones selected one of his *Clotilda* captives, a man named Abdoul, as his plantation doctor, hoping to capitalize on his prisoner's West African medical knowledge. He was not disappointed. Perhaps Abdoul had been an onisegun (doctor) before his kidnap; perhaps he simply drew on the shared herbal knowledge of his community. Whatever the case, Abdoul was 'said to have wrought some wonderful cures', according to Jones's daughter Susie.[24]

On 27 July 1863 William Lowndes Yancey, whose mission to secure diplomatic recognition of the Confederacy in Europe had ended in failure eighteen months earlier, died two weeks before his forty-ninth birthday on his cotton plantation on Mount Meigs Road. The chronic nephritis that had plagued him since the mid-1850s finally destroyed his kidneys. The *Montgomery Advertiser* was effusive in its praise of a man it hailed as the secessionist movement's 'ablest and truest supporter in the councils of the Government'. But Yancey's death received few other write-ups in Alabama's newspapers and the feeling among the white population of his adopted city, now suffering the economic and psychological effects of prolonged conflict and with the war's direction turning increasingly against them, was not kind. Montgomery teacher Sarah G. Follansbee was surprised by the level of ire directed at the dead man on the morning of his funeral. She even heard two people lament that he hadn't passed before drawing the nation into war. The pastor of First Presbyterian Church, Reverend Dr. George Petrie, failed to pay tribute to Yancey at his sparsely attended service, prompting his widow to quit the church that her husband had used as a platform for promoting slavery, the slave trade and secession.[25] In December, Thomas Watts, formerly the Confederacy's attorney general but now a critic of Jefferson Davis's administration, was sworn in at the capitol as the state's governor, with Redoshi's enslaver Washington Smith serving as his aide.

In early April 1865, the Union Army marched from Selma towards Montgomery. *Wanderer* survivor Jackson and Alex Given's captive Reuben were probably among the enslaved labourers who were coerced into barricading the state capital in a vain attempt to hold off the soldiers. General Daniel Weisiger Adams, who was among the defeated troops at the Battle of Selma, and *Clotilda* enslaver Thomas Buford's first cousin Brigadier General Abraham Buford took charge of the city's defence. But they found few military recruits and were forced to conscript them, and Montgomery's wealthy white citizens began to abandon the city in anticipation of an invasion. Knowing that its troops were badly outnumbered, the Confederacy's military leaders decided ultimately to mount no defence against the federal forces. Adams was instructed to evacuate his troops and Buford was sent to harry the Union soldiers as they moved east to Columbus, Georgia.[26]

On 10 April, Montgomery's military burned all the city's cotton to prevent the Union Army from claiming it, despite residents' protests that the resulting fires could destroy Alabama's capital. Buford's soldiers set fire to between 80 and 85,000 bales in total, worth about $40 million (equivalent to nearly $750 million in 2023). Sixty thousand bushels of corn were added to the pyres. As the residents had forecast and the Africans could have predicted, smoke and flames spread through the city, including toward the Jones household, which was only half a mile from the waterfront. As the blaze tore up the sky, Rush Jones fetched captives from his Mount Meigs plantation to save his house. Bougier and other *Clotilda* shipmates may have been among the terrorized captives forced onto Jones's roof armed only with wet blankets to remove the flying embers of cotton and timber before they destroyed his property.[27] Volunteer African American firefighters also raced to put out fires as they burned out of control. Eventually, an easterly wind blew away the flames and prevented the Jones house and the rest of the city from becoming an inferno. The Confederate Army abandoned Montgomery the next day.

In the early hours of 12 April, the Union Army, headed by Generals James Harrison Wilson and Edward Moody McCook and whose members included United States Colored Troops and recently freed men from Selma, reached the city and took a stand at the capitol, from whose rust-coloured dome the US flag was raised. The stars and stripes were also unfurled above the Exchange Hotel, where Wilson set up headquarters. Ella, Reuben and Jackson joined long rows of newly liberated men and women who gazed in joyful amazement at the Union soldiers as they marched through the dusty streets. The army could see there was no war left to fight in the city, and it stayed in Montgomery for only two days, but not before burning the files of the *Montgomery Advertiser*. Jackson's imprisoners' documents were piled in the street and set on fire. When Union general Frederick Steele passed through the city with a unit of African American soldiers, the newspaper, which was being printed on a makeshift press, was suppressed, and not allowed to print again until July.[28]

African American men and boys clamoured to join the soldiers. There were so many volunteers that they were made to race each other for a place in the Union Army. Teacher Sarah Follansbee witnessed what seemed like 'thousands upon thousands' of former bondsmen leave the city with their liberators. Black men and women, newly freed from the surrounding plantations, rushed to meet the army, and hoped to follow it on its journey east too. Bougier and her fellow shipmates perhaps were among them. But they were sent home before it moved on to Columbus, Georgia, a route that took it in the direction of the Jones plantation.[29]

Like Redoshi's captor Washington Smith, Bougier's enslavers rushed to hide their money at their Mount Meigs property before federal troops arrived on 14 April. Rush Jones buried a heavy wooden chest full of the family's silver deep in the ground, and Amelia hid $1,000 worth of gold (equivalent to nearly $20,000 today) beneath the brick pavements of her family's giant flower garden. Union soldiers then camped on the plantation and Bougier witnessed the destruction of her prison after nearly five years of incarceration. The troops set fire to 1,000 bales of cotton, demolished Jones's library, claimed his mules and horses and cut down his prized orchards of fruit trees and grape arbors. Without knowing their contents, Bougier saw the medical books and papers of J. Marion Sims's brother-in-law and former business partner burn.

But Bougier and her fellow captives' hope of meaningful liberation was cruelly undercut by the assassination of Abraham Lincoln in a Washington DC theatre later that night. The presidency fell to vice-president and Tennessee senator Andrew Johnson, an enslaver until August 1863 who favoured readmitting the former Confederate states to the Union with no demand that they guarantee African Americans' civil rights in their territories, and who tried to block key civil rights legislation. On 29 May, the new president issued an Amnesty Proclamation that offered a blanket pardon to all but

15,000 leading Confederates, and which allowed land confiscated in the South during the war to be returned to its former owners.[30] Ex-Confederates were returned to state legislatures and to US Congress later that year, and they quickly enforced a series of laws, known as 'black codes', that criminalized 'vagrancy' and entrapped freed people on their former prisons.

General Wilson's troops soon moved on from the Jones plantation and left its newly freed people behind. The soldiers never found the gold or silver. Once again, a *Clotilda* captor's treasure remained hidden. Like the tale of Washington Smith's Bank of Selma gold, the story of the Jones's buried treasure became an oft-repeated tale of Confederate victory amid defeat. The endurance of such narratives underscored their unspoken function: to celebrate the two families' equally successful concealment of their human 'treasures'. A woman who knew Bougier would later raise a toast from the silver goblets, and they went on display 65 years after their burial.[31]

When the fires on Rush Jones's property burned out and the smoke cleared from the mid-April air, Bougier and the other Africans imprisoned on his plantation found missing horses and livestock that no longer needed tending, and incinerated cotton and fruit that no longer needed harvesting. These things aside, their circumstances hardly changed. Alex Given and Rush Jones were among the small number of Confederates who did not benefit from the Amnesty Proclamation, wealth exceeding $20,000 ($375,000 today) being an exclusion from automatic pardon. But President Johnson personally authorized Given's pardon on 29 September and Jones's on 4 October 1865.[32] Liberation for the *Clotilda* survivors was bittersweet. With nowhere to go and no immediate help from the federal government, Bougier and her fellow shipmates were forced to remain on Jones's property.

Ella, the child *Clotilda* survivor sent to work as the Jones family's cook during slavery, and by now a 17-year-old mother, was also still trapped in their Montgomery property. Jones's daughter Susie claimed that Ella remained for years in the Jones household after the war ended and continued to serve her former captors as if freedom had never come. In fact, Ella probably did not stay long in the Jones's home. Against the odds, she managed to buy, before the decade was out, 35 acres of land, a mule and two cows in Elmore County, 7 miles northwest of the city, with her American-born husband Peter and their four small children.[33]

The end of the war brought with it a boom in railway construction, and Alex Given's former captive Reuben hired himself out as a labourer on the nation's rapidly expanding railway network, one of the few jobs available to freedmen in the South. Railroad labour was typically better paid than cotton picking, but the work was gruelling and dangerous, and the death rate was high. Reuben's work involved mining and blasting through rocks to carve out paths for the region's railway network. He then had to lift and align with precision countless heavy wooden ties before laying steel tracks on top. Reuben suffered physically more than most of his workmates. At just five feet tall, he was no John Henry, the legendary railroad worker who could hammer holes into rocks to build railroad tunnels faster than a steam-powered machine. When not laying tracks, Reuben was forced to return to his ex-enslaver's store on Commerce Street, a living space he now shared with another cotton merchant and former enslaver named John P. Dickinson, his wife Christianna and their four children.[34]

A teenage *Clotilda* shipmate named Komo, by now a 20-year-old man named Robert, was one of only two former Rush Jones captives to adopt 'Jones' as his surname. Komo hired himself out as a well-digger, digging deep holes in the searing heat to provide the people of Montgomery with fresh, clean water, work that was also arduous and dangerous. Another African-born well-digger, a man known to history only as 'Chinch', was killed when blasting rock for a well near the Alabama–Georgia border in 1895.[35] But newly liberated Komo refused to accept that his exile would be permanent. Nor did any of the other Montgomery Africans, including *Wanderer* survivor Jackson. Soon the young men and women would all be exploring the possibility of a way back home.

9

African Town

When the pregnant Kanko and the other Africans newly freed from Burns Meaher's plantation finally reached Mobile about a week after their liberation, their shipmates fashioned a new makeshift goatskin and wooden drum. The group had stopped using such an instrument during their enslavement for fear of attracting unwanted attention to themselves as foreigners, or worse, as 'heathens'. But on that cloudy mid-April day they did not mind how their pale-faced former captors, or even their African American neighbours, viewed them. After five years of terror, suffering and devastating losses, they were free, and they were determined to celebrate. As Kossula recalled, 'After dey free us . . . we so glad, we makee de drum and beat it lak in de Affica soil.'[1] One of the young men used the musical knowledge acquired during his military training to make the drum talk, and the others danced to its syncopated rhythms.

But the celebrations could not last. The approximately twenty-six Africans needed a plan, and the young men of the *Clotilda* quickly formed a meeting to work out what to do. They ached to go home, and they raged with the knowledge that passage back to Africa was the least their former captors owed them for their countless crimes against them. Yet sensing that Thomas Buford, William Foster, William Waldo Ingalls and the Meaher brothers would not help them, they resolved to save up their own money to leave. 'Now we want to go home and it takes a lot of money. You must help us save.

You see fine clothes – you must not crave them,' the men instructed their female shipmates after the meeting. '*You* see fine clothes and new hats – now don't you crave them either,' the young women indignantly replied. 'We will work together.'[2]

Eventually, Kossula became a shingle maker; the friend he called out to on the beach at Ouidah, Osia Keeby, hired himself out as a carpenter, and orisha initiate Polee became a lumber stacker at Blacksher Lumber Mill and later Magazine Hardwood Sawmill Company. They were initially forced to take on menial, arduous, dangerous and poorly paid labour on the land around them to earn money as freedmen. And they worked hard. Wiley G. Toomer, whose father William had alerted Timothy Meaher to the arrival of the *Clotilda* and its captives, employed some of the young men at his sawmill on Mobile's Commerce Street and remembered them as dedicated and reliable workers. Other shipmates laboured at the Meahers' sawmill, a local gunpowder mill, and on the railroad. Even in freedom, the Africans found they continued to be exploited and humiliated. They were forced to work eleven-hour days in the sawmills but were not paid for the final hour, and they were made to walk in the ditch rather than the road on their way to and from the Meahers' sawmill by former captors unwilling to respect their status as free men and citizens.[3]

The female shipmates got to work planting fruit trees and growing vegetables on the land around their cabins. They, too, found daily life a struggle. The Alabama earth was far less fertile than the soil of their homeland and raising crops much more difficult and laborious. But they succeeded in cultivating a wide range of foodstuffs, from peas, figs and potatoes, to corn, sugarcane and pumpkins. After harvesting their crops, they put their fresh produce in baskets, which they carried on their heads. They then walked the 3 miles south to town on Tuesdays, Thursdays and Saturdays, braving its strange and hostile white people, to sell their produce. They also sold baskets handwoven by their menfolk and for decades became a regular and visible presence in the centre of Mobile.[4]

Despite their strenuous labour, and the daily fears, indignities and sacrifices they endured, the shipmates found it impossible to save the hundreds of dollars they needed for a journey home. The men could each make up to $6 (equivalent to $110 dollars today) a week by working in the sawmills and selling their wares, but rental costs meant they could save no more than half that amount. 'We work hard and try save our money. But it too much money we need. So we think we stay here,' Kossula explained decades later. Forced to accept their fate, the Africans resolved to forge their own community on American soil. They felt strongly that their kidnapper and former enslaver should give them land after exploiting their labour for five years for free – and Timothy Meaher could well afford such compensation. Thanks to President Andrew Johnson's Amnesty Proclamation offering a blanket pardon to all but a small handful of the former Confederates and allowing them to keep all their non-human property, the Meahers still had all their wealth, including their steamboats and shipyard. It therefore fell to Kossula to confront his former captor – and current employer – with his community's demand. While the African man was still only 24 years old and looked younger, he was one of the most senior members of his community, and his years spent labouring alongside his captors on their steamboats made him the group's best male English speaker.[5]

One afternoon, Kossula found himself alone with Timothy Meaher. The African man was chopping wood for the Meahers' sawmill when the ageing white man sat down on the stump of a tree Kossula had just felled and began whittling a stick with his pocketknife. Kossula put down his axe and stared at his former enslaver. Aware of the sudden silence, Meaher looked up and saw the unhappy young man standing before him.

Timothy: Kossula, what makes you so sad?
Kossula: I grieve for my home.
Timothy: But you've got a good home.
Kossula: Captain Tim, how big is Mobile?
Timothy: I don't know, I've never been to the four corners.

> Kossula: If you give Kossula all Mobile, that railroad, and the
> banks of Mobile Kossula does not want them for this is not
> home. Captain Tim, you brought us from our country where
> we had land and home. You made us slaves. Now we are free,
> without country, land, or home. Why don't you give us a
> piece of this land and let us build for ourselves an African
> Town?

The human trafficker leapt up in indignation at the inference that he might owe his stolen workforce anything. 'Thou fool! Thinkest thou I will give you property upon property? You do not belong to me now!'[6]

Post-war Alabama was a dangerous place for the newly emancipated as resentful enslavers, including the *Clotilda* conspiracists, vented their anger at and sought to reassert their authority over their former captives. Furious at freed people's resistance to coercive labour contracts, they raged against the Freedmen's Bureau, an agency set up to aid freed people after the war, for materially empowering Black people by providing them with food and clothing. John Milton Dabney, who hid the *Clotilda* Africans on his Mount Vernon estate when they landed in Alabama, was brought before a grand jury in March 1870 charged with causing the deaths of two freedmen whose bodies were found in the Mobile River close to his property. One of the dead men had handcuffs around his wrists.[7]

Kossula's confrontation with his former enslaver was bold for another reason: Timothy Meaher's participation in the slave trade may not have ended with the close of the Civil War. When Tuskegee Institute secretary George Lake Imes interviewed the nine surviving Mobile shipmates in 1917, he learned that their fear of hiring themselves out to strange white men who might sell them back into slavery in Cuba or Puerto Rico was what incentivized them to invest in their own land. The shipmates' fear was substantiated by a Selma-based surgeon who reported a conversation he overheard among kidnappers in January 1866. Freed people were being hired as steamboat workers at landing points on the Alabama River that

Kossula knew only too well – Montgomery, Selma and Cahaba – and taken to Mobile, where they were rehired to go to Pensacola or New Orleans with the promise of increased wages. But to their horror, they found instead that they were being trafficked for up to $500 each in gold to Cuba, where slavery remained legal until 1886. According to the surgeon, the plotters were hoping to build a company and expand their Caribbean kidnapping 'enterprise'. There was no one better placed or with better form for committing such a crime than Timothy Meaher. During the war, the Meahers smuggled cotton to Havana and sold it to the British government, before returning to Mobile with sugar, tobacco, rum, coffee and tea that they could sell at inflated prices as they had become rare luxuries for Southerners due to trade embargoes.[8]

After Timothy Meaher's devastating refusal of their request for land, one of the Africans resolved to buy the territory from their former enslaver. The others followed their lead. 'If you are going to buy, we will too,' they said. They worked long hours and lived on a subsistence diet of molasses, cornbread and boiled cornmeal. They chopped down trees and carved out houses for themselves near the Meahers' sawmill between Chickasabogue Creek and Three Mile Creek, a bayou 3 miles north of Mobile. They built their first homes near the mouth of the Chickasabogue River, next to an overgrown prehistoric shell mound, in an area surrounded by ancient beech trees. Polee's granddaughter Ivory Hill explained how her grandfather carried on his back the wood for his property from the Meahers' mill to the site of his new home. The shipmates worked together to build houses for each other's families and chose a name for their community that reflected their determination to impress their stolen culture and heritage onto their foreign prison. As Kossula noted, 'We call our village Affican Town. We say dat 'cause we want to go back in de Affica soil and we see we cain go. Derefo' we makee de Affica where dey fetch us.' As newly freed people, they also adopted surnames. Osia Keeby managed to retain the second part of his name as his surname. Kossula tried to use his father Oluwale's name as his last name, but English speakers struggled to pronounce either of his names, and he became known as Cudjo Lewis. Charlie also adopted the surname Lewis, which was probably an anglicized corruption of Oluwale. Two other shipmates named Anthony and Archie both selected Thomas as their last names, orisha initiate Polee and his wife Rosallie chose Allen, and Gumpa, the Fon youth presented as a gift to William Foster, and his wife Josephine chose Lee. Abaché, the tall, round-faced woman with the centre parting, became Clara Aunspaugh.[9]

The mostly Yoruba-speaking community selected Gumpa as its leader. They created a system of law and order by appointing as their town's judges Charlie and a man with a nose ring named Jabez, the oldest Mobile-based male shipmates. Jabez also served as the community's onisegun, or doctor. As Yorubans, they believed that birth order dictated a person's social rank, and they transposed that worldview onto their community. Kossula explained the group's logic in selecting a Dahomeyan man as their leader to writer Zora Neale Hurston. 'We doan try get no king 'cause nobody among us ain' born no king. Dey tell us nobody doan have no king in 'Merica soil. Derefo' we make Gumpa de head. He a nobleman back in Dahomey. We ain' mad wid him 'cause de king of Dahomey 'stroy our king and sell us to de white man. He didn't do nothin' 'ginst us.'[10]

The Africans were mostly in their teens and early twenties when they forged the community they called African Town (later Africatown) out of the land that had held them prisoner. Yet they crafted a highly ordered society that drew on the social structures and teachings they learned as children in Yorubaland. They drew up their own laws to ensure there was no stealing, violence, or excessive drinking, which they disapproved of as a sign of ill-discipline, drunkenness having been forbidden back home. They held night-time hearings to arbitrate on misdemeanours and resolve disagreements, in which evidence was presented on both sides before being carefully weighed, and punishments for misdemeanours could be strict: a first offence prompted a formal warning and a second led to a whipping by Charlie, Gumpa or Jabez. The judges were not exempt from punishment, although as historian Emma Langdon

Roche found when she met the last surviving judge Charlie just before his death, the small, kind-faced man with high cheekbones and white goatee beard had a proud reputation for never having had a dispute with any of his shipmates.[11]

Not all the Mobile County Africans ended up in African Town. Little Kanko and her African American husband James Dennison saved up enough money to buy a homestead in the heart of downtown Mobile, at the corners of Delaware Street and Royal Street, whose northwest corner had once been the site of a slave market where captives were confined and displayed in a barred-windowed, three-storey brick building as they awaited their fates. The land lay between the courthouse and the constable's office. Kanko handled her finances so carefully that the couple managed to rent and eventually purchase more land around their property. They bought horses and mules to plough their garden so they could grow and sell vegetables. They raised cows, chickens and pigs so they could sell milk, eggs and bacon; they preserved the latter in their own smokehouse. Like her shipmates in African Town, Kanko took her wares to market, expertly balancing the goods she bought and sold on her head for long distances. Together with James, Kanko, probably drawing on her knowledge of the Yoruba saving systems ajo and esusu, invested money in the Freedman's Savings and Trust Company, or Freedman's Bank, a private savings institution designed to financially assist freed people. However, the bank failed in 1874 and depositors lost their savings. She also fought for, but never received, a pension for her husband's Civil War service.[12]

Yoruba culture remained central to Kanko's worldview and to the way she raised her children. She held onto her ancestral customs and dress habits and expected her descendants to follow them, too. She taught them Yoruba parables and made references to mermaids that were probably allusions to Yemoja, the water and mother spirit in Yoruba culture. Kanko and her family were model citizens, a fact in which she took great pride.[13]

A woman identified 67 years after her death as a *Clotilda* survivor became with her son Russell a major purchaser of land in Daphne,

Baldwin County, just across the bay from Mobile. At the time of her passing in April 1897, Lucy Dick owned just shy of 160 acres in that territory. Before her death, Lucy instructed her son to donate a section of the family's land to the Little Bethel Baptist Church in Daphne, where a new church building was erected in 1905. Historian Addie Pettaway would later identify the church, whose congregation included at least one other *Clotilda* survivor, Amey Greenwood/ Phillips, as part of the African Town community. A plaque placed outside the structure for the United States' 1976 Bicentennial commemorates Russell, who served as its deacon and sexton, and who was buried in its cemetery, as both the son of a *Clotilda* survivor and 'an outstanding and industrious citizen who acquired much land in the area. And once owned all the downtown of Daphne.'[14]

A few months after emancipation, Kossula proposed to Abile, the teenager who had so feared being eaten by her captors when she arrived in the United States. By that stage, the couple were among the few shipmates who had not yet married. Abile was now 20 years old, which meant she had reached marriageable age for a woman in Oyo, and she did not need much persuading. After a brief exchange in which Kossula promised to take care of her, she accepted his proposal. The pair had a traditional Yoruba marriage ceremony a month later, with drumming and feasting. 'Derefo', you know, we live together and we do all we kin to make happiness 'tween ourselves,' Kossula remembered.[15] Kossula built a four-room house for his new bride with the help of his shipmates. A hammer and saw were the Africans' only tools.

Kossula dug a well outside his house. He also erected eight gates around the property to recreate symbolically the protective gates that surrounded his town back home. Abile and Kossula had their first child two years after their emancipation. The baby was born on 4 July 1867: American Independence Day. The African Town shipmates gave most of their children both an African and an American name, and the new parents called their son Iyadjemi ('I suffered too much') to honour his Yoruban heritage, and Aleck to ensure he had a name comprehensible to English speakers.[16]

Abile would have a further four sons, including twins, and one daughter. She took great pride in their Yoruban ancestry, proclaiming, 'My childrens is all Africans.' Fon nobleman Gumpa and his wife Josephine also deeply valued their children's African heritages. Noah Hart, who had been enslaved as a house servant to Timothy Meaher, remembered their special treatment of one of their five daughters and three sons. 'Dey give it ebberything, and tote it ebberywhere, an' dey seem to make er kind er pres-dent outer it.' The child was born on the night of a new moon, which the elated Gumpa read as a powerful assertion of its Fon identity and a sign that his heritage had survived transatlantic erasure. Gumpa tattooed on the child's chest a crescent moon and an ouroboros, a circular symbol dating back to ancient Egypt of a snake eating its own tail, to symbolize its kinship to Mawu (the moon goddess) and Aido-Hwedo (the rainbow serpent).[17]

President Johnson's readiness to pardon the Confederates and readmit the seceding states into the Union without guaranteeing Black people's civil rights created a Republican backlash in US Congress, particularly among a faction of so-called 'Radicals' who supported immediate emancipation before the war and now wanted to secure equal rights for freed people. In early 1866, Congress overruled presidential vetoes to reauthorize and expand the Freedmen's Bureau and to pass the Civil Rights Act, which defined Black people as citizens with equal rights to public services. When the president questioned the constitutionality of the Civil Rights Act given that the US Supreme Court had ruled, in *Dred Scott v. Sandford* (1857), that Black people were not citizens, Congress drafted the Fourteenth Amendment to the US Constitution to reverse *Dred Scott* and secure equal citizenship rights for African Americans.

In March 1867, US Congress passed the first of four Reconstruction Acts that set out the terms of the South's readmission to the Union. The act dissolved state governments in the former

Confederacy, imposed federal control by dividing the region into five military districts and required states to draft new constitutions for approval by Congress, accord voting rights to all men and ratify the Fourteenth Amendment. The appointment of delegates to Alabama's constitutional convention, which was tasked with drafting the state's new constitution, gave Black men the right to vote locally and nationally for the first time while leading Confederates were disenfranchised for disloyalty. White Southern leaders responded by temporarily halting their campaign of terror and intimidation and adopting a new tactic: influencing Black men's votes. Timothy Meaher taught his former prisoners how to cast their ballots and explained why voting was important, but the shipmates and their African American neighbours weren't so easily manipulated. The Africans may even have been among the crowd of up to four thousand people that gathered to hear Pennsylvania congressman William Darrah Kelley, a 'Radical' Republican, speak at the corner of Royal and Government streets, about a dozen blocks directly south of Kanko's home, on the evening of 14 May that same year. The violent response that the majority Black political gathering provoked in the local white population became known as the 'Pig Iron' Kelley Riot. Shots were reportedly fired from the window of *Mobile Register* editor John Forsyth's office, and his son Charles was a suspect. One Black person and one white person were killed, and 20 others were injured.[18]

Such intimidation did not deter Anthony or Archie Thomas, or Charlie, Kossula, Osia Keeby or Polee from registering to vote in July 1867. Nor did it stop well-digger Komo, *Wanderer* survivor Jackson Smith and at least two other *Clotilda* survivors from registering as voters in Montgomery. Other *Clotilda* Africans were among the 3,712 Black Wilcox County residents, 4,210 Black Marengo County residents and 6,559 Black Dallas County residents who registered to vote that summer.[19]

Alabama's Black men voted for the first time in a statewide election that October and helped to appoint an overwhelmingly Republican set of delegates, including 19 Black men, to draft its new constitution. Komo and Jackson were almost certainly among those who cast their ballots, although their actions stirred up a newspaper backlash against 'unqualified' voters. The *Nashville Union and American* exaggerated the Africans' numbers to claim they were being used to manipulate the voting for the constitutional convention's delegates. 'Two hundred Africans in Montgomery and Autauga counties, who came over in the Wanderer [sic] and cannot speak English, were allowed to take an oath by touching a pen, for the purpose of voting for some registrar who would be a candidate for the convention.' A *Montgomery Mail* editorial suggested that, by striking off 'idiots, felons and native Africans who cannot speak', it could reduce the Black voting population.[20]

When another election to ratify the constitution was called for early the following February, the *Register* again attempted to terrify Black people away from the ballot box. 'Every colored man who votes in the election for the thing they call a constitution,' it warned, 'makes his record as an enemy of his white fellow citizens.' When the men of African Town went to cast their votes in favour of ratifying the constitution that winter, they were taking a huge risk. Those overseeing the count admitted that 'threats of discharge, invariably made, deterred negroes from voting.'[21]

The Mobile Africans were forced to contend with their former captor, too, when they went to vote for the first time that February. The young men set off early on election day to their nearest polling booth in Whistler, a neighbouring suburb north of Mobile. They walked in single file, a Yoruba custom that allowed them to navigate the narrow roads and forests back home more easily. But when they reached the polling station, they found Timothy Meaher waiting for them on horseback. 'See those Africans? Don't let them vote – they are not of this country,' he barked when he spotted them. They tried another polling booth manned by Judge John Maguire, a 33-year-old Irish-born cloth merchant, but Meaher predicted their movements and rode on ahead of them. The Africans were turned away again. When they discovered another voting booth on St. Stephen's Road, Meaher was there to meet them once more. 'Don't let those Africans vote – they have no right – they are not of this country.'[22]

Finally, the *Clotilda* shipmates found another voting booth on St. Francis Street and were able to cast their ballots after each handing over one dollar. One-third of Alabama's registered Black voters were turned away from the ballot box or terrorized into withholding their votes that winter, but the African men were among the 62,000 Black voters who made it to the polls. Each of them was so thrilled with their courageous act of civic engagement that they retained their voting papers for the rest of their lives. The *Register* discouraged white people from voting to ensure there were not enough votes to ratify the constitution, which needed to be approved by a majority of registered voters in the state, and the newspaper printed voters' names as it had threatened to do. Sadly, the Mobile Africans never again managed to vote, and they regretted that their single trip to the ballot box did not materially change their circumstances. Their votes were not completely wasted, however, as Congress passed a new Reconstruction Act a month after the election that allowed constitutions to be retrospectively ratified regardless of the overall voting tally. Six of the Mobile Africans also made sure they were beneficiaries of the Fourteenth Amendment, which was adopted on 9 July 1868. On 23 and 24 October that year, Polee, Osia Keeby, Kossula, Anthony and Archie Thomas and Charlie swore under oath to become United States citizens.[23]

Despite their newfound American status, the shipmates continued to keep their distance from the local African American community, which disparaged them as ignorant savages and even cannibals. But 'Free George', the emancipated man who warned them not to dance on Sundays during slavery, visited the group regularly to help them build their new community. Even at the end of their lives, the Mobile Africans still invoked and paid tribute to their ancestral orishas, and a West African philosophy of good and evil shaped their worldview. But 'Free George' wanted the group to convert to Christianity and brought them to the attention of Reverend Benjamin Franklin

Burke at Stone Street Baptist Church in Mobile. Kossula described on his deathbed his religious conversion, which he attributed to a conversation with Burke in 1869. When asked where he wanted to go when he died, Kossula pointed at the sky and replied, 'I want to go yonder.'[24] Burke then introduced him to God and the Bible.

Kossula and his shipmates' conversion to Christianity nine years after their displacement to Mobile was probably linked to an earth-shattering event that occurred at Stone Street Baptist Church in the spring of 1869. Abeokuta-based missionary Andrew Dickerson Phillips had returned to the United States after twelve unsuccessful years attempting to convert the city's residents to Christianity. War and persecution forced him to flee Abeokuta in 1867, and after a year-long respite in London, he landed in New York in January 1869. He made his way south, first to his relatives in Mississippi, and then on a lecture tour describing Yoruba culture to the region's Baptist churches to raise funds for a renewed missionary effort. His tour included African American churches because he believed that African Americans were particularly well placed to convert Africans to Christianity and because he wanted to teach Black Americans about what he considered to be 'the habits and condition of their own race in Africa'.[25] In April, Phillips arrived at Stone Street Baptist Church.

Dickerson Phillips was a large man in his early forties who liked to deliver his lectures with gusto.[26] But even without his trademark delivery, his approach was bound to touch the hearts and minds of 25 members of the congregation.

Baba wa ti mbẹ li ọrun
Ki a bọwọ fun orukọ rẹ.

Phillips's words were like magic to the *Clotilda* shipmates. Here was the Lord's Prayer in Yoruba. The Africans had slipped into the back of the church to avoid hostile attention from its African American worshippers, but in that moment they ceased to conceal themselves. They erupted in cries of delight. Here was a white man who knew their homeland and could speak their language. Perhaps he could take them home!

Despite their overwhelming excitement, the Africans quietened themselves and waited patiently for the missionary to finish his lecture. They then rushed up to him and introduced themselves as displaced Yoruba-speaking men and women. They begged the missionary to take them home and explained that they had been saving money for the trip. Please, they implored, could he help them? Phillips was unused to so much attention. He had spent a dozen years attempting to convert the residents of Abeokuta to Christianity but attracted just 30 followers in a city of 100,000 people. The group of young people now standing before him amounted to almost the same number. Believing them to be survivors of the slave ship *Wanderer*, he agreed to take up their cause. [27]

On 8 May at the Southern Baptist Convention in Macon, Georgia, Phillips raised the shipmates' situation publicly for the first time. He then gave a lecture in Raleigh, North Carolina, on 15 June that detailed life in Yoruba territory. He described enormous cities surrounded by farms that stretched for 30 miles and guessed the population of Yoruba speakers to be one million. He emphasized some supposedly exotic aspects of West African culture, including snakes worn around necks and worshipped, people wrapped in sections of cloth two feet wide and three feet long instead of dresses, shirts and trousers, and men with bare faces and shaven heads, except for 'fancy patches'. But he also described a society that fought 'fairly' in war, where people ate giant tubers much like Irish potatoes and raised cows, sheep, goats and turkeys, where the Quran was read in Arabic in northern territories, and where craftspeople smelted farming tools out of iron ore and butterflies out of gold. Phillips ended his speech by noting, 'In Mobile I saw 25 Yorubans, who came to this country in the "Wanderer" [sic]. They were delighted to see me speaking their tongue, and they desire to return with me. They are members of the Baptist Church in Mobile. Africans are firm in their convictions. I have seen them endure stripes and shed blood for their religion. We ought to help them.'[28]

Phillips's efforts to repatriate the Africans seemed to have some effect. After the Macon meeting, a religious newspaper suggested that 'measures are on foot to return them to the land of their fathers.' But his speeches came a few months too late. The American Colonization Society (ACS), which was established in 1816 by Presbyterian minister Robert Finlay with the purpose of relocating Black people in the United States to Africa, had spent five decades facilitating the migration of former bondspeople to Liberia but was running out of money and members. Between 1865 and 1869, the organization used up almost all its funds transporting to Liberia nearly two thousand four hundred emigrants, mostly from South Carolina and Georgia, and including at least one *Wanderer* survivor.[29] That meant it could no longer financially assist the *Clotilda* shipmates by the time Phillips highlighted their plight.

The ACS raised the Africans' situation with the United States government. But US Secretaries of the Interior Jacob Dolson Cox and Columbus Delano could find no legal precedent for repatriating displaced Africans, and an attempted appeal before Congress to change the law stalled.[30] The shipmates' case was probably hamstrung by the assumption they were *Wanderer* survivors. Their identification as victims of a later, unconfirmed and unprosecuted human trafficking voyage could have fostered greater interest in their plight, and even created an opportunity finally to prosecute their kidnappers.

The ACS continued to highlight the shipmates' story and its New York branch even drew on their predicament in late 1870 to raise funds for the colonization movement. While the branch agreed that repatriation to Liberia was theoretically possible, money was still an issue. In the 1870s, an adult emigrant's fare to Liberia cost $50 (around $1,400 in 2023), and the price for each of their children was $25 (around $700 today). By 1870, the 26 Mobile shipmates had at least 14 surviving children between them and although they had saved huge sums, the Africans could not fully fund their families' relocation. The New York branch ruled that a Liberian journey could only be undertaken 'if the necessary means are provided', and whether or not the *Clotilda* survivors could join it 'will depend very much upon the amount of means raised'. The Mobile Africans duly submitted applications for such a trip. But a 4 March letter from the ACS's corresponding secretary William Coppinger advised that 'no action be taken at present'. By then, the shipmates' advocate Dickerson Phillips was back in Africa on a new missionary expedition.[31]

After Phillips raised their hopes of repatriation, the Africans waited for a year before buying their first patch of land in Alabama. On 5 April 1870, African Town judges Charlie and Jabez and their wives Maggie and Polly co-purchased with African Americans Lucy Wilson and Horace and Matilda Ely 7 acres of the 82-acre property on which they had been enslaved. The Shades and Lewises shared their estate with their *Clotilda* shipmates Anthony and Uriba and their African American spouses. The woody territory, which cost the group $200 ($4,700 today) and became known as the Lewis Quarters, was located 2 miles west of the other Africans' property and bordered by railroad track and Three Mile Creek, the bayou 3 miles north of Mobile where the Africans first carved out homes for themselves. Their enslaver Thomas Buford died in 1866 at the age of 63; his body lay in a grave next to the land.[32]

As the Mobile Africans waited to hear from Phillips, Bougier and her surviving shipmates gathered in grim determination in Montgomery. Equally desperate to escape their circumstances and unwilling to give up on the possibility of going home, they agreed to meet annually in the city to strategize how to journey back across the Atlantic. Well-digger and registered voter Komo even taught himself to read and write in English, probably with the goal of advancing the group's objective.[33]

In the summer of 1872, Phillips sailed back to the United States. He returned to Mobile that autumn, where he learned of and reported on Bougier and her shipmates' annual Montgomery meetings, reigniting the Mobile Africans' hopes and the ACS's commitment to repatriating the shipmates. Although he still thought they were *Wanderer* survivors, Phillips now had a good sense of the number and locations of the *Clotilda* Africans, as he emphasized in a letter to Reverend John Orcutt, the travelling secretary of the ACS. 'It is reported that there are from fifty to one hundred of these people in the counties of Montgomery, Lo[w]nd[e]s, Dall[a]s, Wilcox, Conec[uh], and Mobile.' He explained that some of the shipmates were so desperate to go home that they had formed an organization, 'one provision of which was, that they should meet once a year in Montgomery, and do all in their power to return to their native land'. And he outlined his moving encounter with Fon nobleman Gumpa, 'an honest, faithful Christian man', and his oldest child Lucy, who was 'well educated, and very intelligent'. Poignantly, Phillips noted that Gumpa was 'almost wild with joy' when he suggested he might be able to return to Africa and promised to 'make me king!' if the missionary could facilitate his journey home.[34] Gumpa's emotive reaction to the possibility of repatriation underscored the hope Phillips instilled in the shipmates. Gumpa's claim that he could make the missionary his king was no idle promise; he was a Dahomeyan nobleman from the court of King Glele who was desperate to reclaim his rightful social status back home.

Phillips's letter brought the Africans' plight before the Pennsylvania branch of the ACS, which proposed to help them but initially took no action. Phillips visited the Africans again, and after a long conversation with them in Yoruba wrote once more to the ACS on 22 May 1873. 'They are very desirous to return to their own country,' he urged. The branch passed his message to ACS corresponding secretary William Coppinger, who asked the branch's president Eli Kirk Price to petition Congress again for a law facilitating their return home. New York reverend George Whitefield Samson took up the campaign. On 20 January 1874, he delivered an impassioned address at an event commemorating the fifty-seventh anniversary of the ACS in Washington DC, decrying that 'these captives, now asking return under American law, are yet unredeemed!' Tragically, however, Samson's words went nowhere, and Phillips, out of funds and unable to return to Abeokuta, gave up his missionary work and settled as a pastor in Tennessee.[35]

* * *

The *Clotilda* shipmates were not the only Africans in Alabama still battling to get home. *Wanderer* survivor Jackson Smith proved so skilled at his work in the *Montgomery Advertiser*'s pressroom that the secessionist newspaper made him a salaried employee when it was allowed to start printing again after the war. Desperate to return home, the young man saved his wages carefully as he continued for years to roll the latest editions off the newspaper's A. P. Taylor printing press. He even became an expert at fixing the machine when it jammed. An 1875 *Advertiser* article joked of its Congolese employee, by then in his late twenties, that 'our man, Jack, says that broiled monkey is the best meat he ever tasted – a point on which we make no issue.' South Carolina's *Columbus Enquirer* joined in, suggesting that Jackson's displacement and enslavement had 'reduced [him] to the low level' of Christian civilization while his countrymen endured as monkey-eating idol worshippers. 'The "barbarism of slavery" played the very mischief with his mental, moral and physical nature,' it sarcastically declared.[36]

Jackson was a Christian convert. Recognizing, like the *Clotilda* Africans, that support from religious leaders offered his best hope of returning home, and no doubt with encouragement from his American wife Amanda, who he married on 1 January 1867, Jackson joined the Old Ship African Methodist Episcopal Zion Church on Holcombe Street. Established in 1852, the white, two-storey church with a bell tower was the oldest African American place of worship in Montgomery. Formerly enslaved community leader Elijah Cook set up one of the city's first schools for African Americans at the Old Ship, and it was almost certainly there that Jackson learned covertly to read and write to boost his chances of returning home. Jackson knew and was probably taught by Reverend Solomon Derry, a freedman who was one of the first Black teachers in Montgomery, and whose work to establish a church in nearby Union Springs provoked a night-time visit from white supremacist group the Ku Klux Klan. Derry bravely stood his ground against the terrorists.[37]

As he continued to toil in the *Advertiser*'s pressroom, Jackson used language to navigate his circumstances and resist his employers' attempts to disparage his Congolese heritage. He openly challenged their racist assertions that Africans were barbarous cannibals. He even dared to curse in front of them, taking advantage of their incomprehension to express himself freely, and probably to debase them, in his mother language. As the newspaper admitted, 'He is tractable and good natured, but when thoroughly aroused never fails, as he says, to swear in his native tongue.' Even the *Advertiser* could not deny the African man's intellectual brilliance, noting that he learned to speak English within a few months of arriving in Alabama, and that 'his memory is remarkable, especially of dates and names, and [he] readily recalls the exact date of every change or extraordinary incident in his career since he landed in America.'[38]

The *Advertiser* also acknowledged that Jackson had a single-minded focus on returning home from the moment he arrived in Montgomery, and that he saved every spare dollar to pay for his journey. Jackson made it clear to his employers that he planned to live out his last days in his homeland. When in May 1880 the eldest of his five children, 12-year-old Jackson, Jr., suffered a fractured skull after being attacked from behind by another boy with that most American of objects, a baseball bat, the African man despaired.[39] The circumstances of the attack are not clear, but Jackson knew the child would not have experienced such violence back home. He determined more strongly than ever to keep saving.

In the summer of 1883, a quarter of a century after he was kidnapped, Jackson finally met his financial goal. He had put aside $150 (equivalent to $4,500 in 2023) from his modest *Advertiser* wages, which was enough to pay for his entire family's voyage to Africa, and he managed to secure passage on one of the ACS's final expeditions to Liberia. On 9 July, 23 years to the day after the *Clotilda* was scuttled and sunk in the Mobile River, the Smith family left their home at 131 Market Street for the last time and walked the half-mile to the city's Union Depot train shed. Jackson, Amanda, fourteen-year-old Jackson, Jr., ten-year-old Julia, six-year-old Magdelana, four-year-old Lucy and one-year-old George then boarded a train for New York City to begin their journey to Liberia.[40]

Before leaving Alabama, Jackson made it clear to the *Advertiser* office that he was not planning to return.

On 16 July, Jackson stood at New York Harbor, surrounded for the second time in his life by a vast expanse of ocean. He surely recoiled from the deceptively calm-looking water that had claimed the bodies of so many of his captive shipmates and nearly taken him, too. He knew the journey would be frightening, and it must have taken tremendous willpower to board the *Monrovia*, a New York-based, 543-ton steam/sail vessel that was on one of its 54 round trips to Liberia and Sierra Leone. The ship was horribly similar in appearance to the *Wanderer*, and the sight of the vessel bobbing on the water must have brought back a familiar terror. It would be a difficult journey. For the Smith family and most of the other travellers, their leisure and sleeping space was the ship's poop deck.[41] But the crowded open deck was still a world away from the *Wanderer*'s crammed, suffocating hold, and the fear and discomfort that Jackson felt was soon subsumed by elation. He was finally leaving the land that had robbed him of so much of his life and, if not able to return to the Congo of his childhood, then at least he was going back to the continent of his birth. For the first time in almost twenty-five years, he felt free.

The Smiths arrived at Monrovia, Liberia, on 21 August. The next day, they were taken by steamboat to Brewerville, their new home-town. Jackson and Amanda received the government's designated 25 acres of land for emigrants; their five children received 10 acres each. Jackson was so happy to be back in Africa that he sent an exuberant message to his fellow parishioners at Old Ship Church six months after he arrived at Brewerville, and the letter made its way to his former employers at the *Advertiser*. Jackson appealed to his African American friends to join him in his new life of freedom, and emphasized, 'You will please remember that we are not worrying over the thoughts of a civil rights bill, or any other bill. But we are in our own free country, where we have all the benefits of law and citizenship.' While admitting that he was not yet able to move into his new property or work due to an accident that had left him with a burned foot, Jackson stressed, 'I do not wish for you to ask for one nickle [sic] for me. I am in Africa.' He saved his strongest words for his old teacher Reverend Solomon Derry, who was suspicious of the ACS's agenda to remove Black people from the US and predicted the Smith family would die in Africa. 'The same God is here that you have there. So you all may stay and hug the rod that smites you and wear the yoke of oppression, but some will come.'[42]

The despairing *Clotilda* Africans began to resign themselves to permanent exile. On 30 September 1872, Kossula bought nearly two acres of land for $100 ($2,500 today) from Confederate veteran and railroad tycoon Colonel Lorenzo Madison Wilson and his wife Augusta Jane Evans Wilson. Colonel Wilson was the vice-president of the Mobile and Montgomery Railroad and one of Mobile's richest men. His wife Augusta, a Confederate nurse and propagandist who corresponded during the war with William Lowndes Yancey, was even wealthier. She was one of the most successful novelists of the nineteenth century, and the first female American author to earn $100,000 from her work. Her 1866 novel *St. Elmo* has been described as 'the *Gone with the Wind* of its day' and is thought to be the nineteenth-century US's third highest selling novel after *Uncle Tom's Cabin* (1852) and *Ben-Hur* (1880). On 21 October, Polee bought two acres of land for $200 ($5,000 today) from the Meahers. A week later, Osia Keeby bought two acres for $150 ($3,750 today) from the Meahers. All six acres were in territory north of Mobile that would later be named 'Plateau' by the Mobile & Birmingham Railroad. 'Dey doan take off one five cent from de price for us. But we pay it all and take de lan', Kossula remembered.[43]

The Africans had become practising Christians. But they so dreaded ridicule from the African American community for their West African accents and cultural behaviours that they built their own church. The modest two-storey white clapboard building, known as the African Church, and later as Old Landmark Baptist Church, was constructed on land next to Abile and Kossula's house.

The church faced east toward Africa, revealing the community's enduring desire to return home. It opened in February 1872 and Kossula recalled proudly that it was the first religious building in the area. To counteract accusations that they were savages, and to afford their children the best possible future, they even built a separate schoolhouse and asked the county to send them a teacher. Four years later, the Africans added a graveyard, which became known as Plateau Cemetery. Despite the presence of other Black churches in Mobile, the construction of a new church was still an incredibly brave thing to do. At least three African American churches in Mobile were set alight by white supremacists in the aftermath of the Civil War. Black worshippers were so fearful of an arson attack that the smell of sulphur, supposedly from a match being struck, caused a stampede at Stone Street Baptist Church in October 1867. Women and children were severely injured in the crush and three congregants suffered broken limbs when fleeing through the church's windows.[44]

The Africans were instructed by Reverend Burke to marry again when they converted to Christianity; they needed a licence for their living arrangements to be recognized in law. Reluctantly, they complied. On 8 March 1880, Reverend Burke married Abaché to her African American partner Samuel Turner at Stone Street Baptist Church. A week later, the reverend married shipmates Abile and Kossula, Polee and Rosallie, and Innie and Osia Keeby. Zuma, the young woman with the deep facial marks, finally followed her ship-mates and legally married her second husband, African American labourer John Livingston, in a Christian ceremony in June 1887. But Kossula made it clear after his wife's death that he considered the occasion only a formality; to him, the couple's Yoruba ceremony meant as much. 'I doan love my wife no mo' wid de license than I love her befo' de license. She a good woman and I love her all de time.'[45]

As the Africans began to acquire citizenship rights and buy land and build permanent homes, their former enslaver Timothy Meaher ended his steamboat journeys up and down the Alabama and Mobile rivers. 'I quit the river in 1870, when the colored citizens demanded cabin passage,' he explained to a journalist just before he died. His brothers left the business soon afterwards. Timothy Meaher spent the following years embroiled in legal disputes with tenants, railroad companies and oil tycoons over land he felt was his property. In December 1875, his legal fights exploded into violence, and he was brought before the Mayor's Court charged with assault with a deadly weapon at One Mile Creek, a small stream adjoining Three Mile Creek. Twenty-four-year-old William Thomas West had received permission from the Mobile and Ohio Railroad to build an oil warehouse on land he understood to be the railroad's property. Meaher and an unnamed relative camped on the land with guns. When West arrived to build the machine, Meaher shot him. His unnamed relative was probably his brother Burns, who had a reputation for dangerous behaviour with a gun. In the autumn of 1869, a newspaper reported that, while waiting in Mobile for his steamboat *Virginia* to be repaired, he 'amuses himself of nights by shooting at the river pirates who infest the wharves of that city'.[46] After retiring from the steamboat business, Burns Meaher operated a snag boat – a steamboat with a crane for removing obstacles – for the US government to clear trees and other debris from the Alabama River.

After years of displacement and frustrated hope, a sudden unexpected noise made the African Town residents feel less lonely, less lost. A group of shipmates were labouring outdoors one day when they heard the unmistakable sound of trumpeting elephants. A circus and its menagerie were passing by. The Africans wept and cried out in delight. 'Ile. Ile. Ajanaku. Ajanaku' (Home. Home. Mighty elephant. Mighty elephant). The sight of the animals gave the Africans hope that friendly villages were nearby. They fought to contain their desire to run after the giant creatures, and they spent the following days in excited anticipation. Perhaps they were not alone after all. Perhaps there was land nearby that was just like home. But the appearance of elephants in the United States was an unnatural sight. Like the shipmates, the animals had been dragged across the Atlantic for profit, held in captivity, and were doomed to live short, brutal lives in exile. As Kossula explained four years before his death, the elephants turned out to be the only friendly reminder of his childhood home for many years.[47]

By the early 1880s, the Africans' hopes of returning home were seemingly over. They had endured 20 years of displacement, and Archie, Polly, Zuma's first husband John Africa, and Uriba, the young girl who wept throughout the *Clotilda*'s voyage, had already passed on. Some of the shipmates had American partners; nearly all of them had American-born children. They had not heard from the Yoruba-speaking missionary Andrew Dickerson Phillips for a decade, and their secluded town three miles north of Mobile drew no attention from outsiders. Their lives and in some cases their labour were still overseen by their former enslaver and his family. The group's entrapment on the wrong side of the Atlantic seemed permanent. Yet two aspects of the group's predicament were soon to change. They were about to discover their community was not so hidden after all. They were also soon to discover how, amid tremendous despair, hardship and grief, there could be unimaginable joy.

10

Reunion

Matilda was seven years old when she first tasted the ecstasy of freedom. Except for a few terrifying hours in the swamps as a runaway from her enslaver Memorable Creagh on the eve of the Civil War, she had been imprisoned in Alabama for nearly all her life. Transatlantic slavery had radically reshaped her family. Her by now 15-year-old sister Sally, her protector throughout her captivity in the Black Belt, was still with her, but Matilda had no memory of her two eldest sisters, who were ripped away from her at John Dabney's plantation in Mount Vernon, nor of the two brothers left behind in the barracoon at Ouidah. Instead, she had a new half-brother named John, born to her mother Gracie and fathered by Guy, the shipmate Gracie was forced to marry when she arrived in the United States. A half-sister named Mary soon followed. Several other Black Belt *Clotilda* survivors, including fellow child captives Quilla and Redoshi, had become parents to US-born children too. Eighteen-year-old Dinah, however, was alone in Snow Hill. Not only had she lost her mother and brother at Mount Vernon, but the baby born of rape when she arrived in the Black Belt was gone, either dead or sold.

Matilda, Dinah and their shipmates' geographical isolation in the Black Belt meant they soon keenly felt the limits of their freedom. Vigilante patrols with bloodhounds conducted reigns of terror against the newly liberated people of Dallas, Wilcox and Marengo counties. Their victims were shot, drowned and hanged. By August

1865, 12 murders of freed people by white terrorists had been recorded near Selma. Major John P. Houston, who as provost marshal of federal forces administered the amnesty oath to ex-Confederates at Selma, documented the killings. He concluded that 'the cases of crime above enumerated, I am convinced, are but a small part of those that have actually been perpetrated.' He also noted, 'In a majority of cases the provocation consisted in the negroes' trying to come to town or to return to the plantation after having been sent away.' In the early twentieth century, a small, slight old woman who gave her name as 'Granny' to protect her anonymity admitted to living in a state of extreme terror in southern Alabama after the war: 'I was 'fraid all de time. An' when I was free'd I was 'fraid, too. Didn't do to say you was free. When de war was over if a n— say he was free, dey shot him down.'[1]

Bougier and her shipmates' entrapment further up the Alabama River in Montgomery County was also maintained by extreme violence. Future Republican governor of Alabama William Hugh Smith despaired at Montgomery's former Confederates. 'They show their contempt boldly and in every way for the federal government and its officers. This is manifest to every man there. They still persecute Union men and negroes. They whip the negroes, shoot them, hang them, kill them, now, for offences that under the old slave code they would not hang a white man for.' Surgeons J. M. Phipps and J. E. Harvey treated 14 freed people at Montgomery's Freedmen's Hospital who were shot, stabbed and beaten between April and August 1865 and lived long enough to seek medical aid. The patients included a man named James Taylor, who miraculously survived seven stab wounds, two bullet wounds and the severing of his lower arm, and a child known to history only as Ida, who was clubbed over the head by an overseer and died from her injury on 20 June.[2]

Bougier and her Alabama-born daughter Amanda were forced to stay on their former enslaver Rush Jones's Mount Meigs estate, confined to the tiny wooden cabin in which they had been enslaved, and which they shared with the now nine-year-old *Clotilda* survivor Nannie and Nannie's mother Sarah. Teenage shipmate Unsey and her Alabama-born daughter Hattie were trapped next door. If the group left the land that had held them prisoner, they would be homeless, landless and at potential risk of reprisals from their former enslaver. Ex-bondspeople who sought new lives of freedom in Montgomery were forced to build their own huts from any random bits of lumber they could find, or to seek shelter in abandoned houses and caves, or under sheds, gutters and bridges. The most unfortunate had to live outdoors. A law was passed at the Alabama State Capitol that autumn preventing freed people from squatting on land on which they did not work, with a member of the legislature admitting to a visiting reverend, 'We mean to keep them down; we do not mean to allow them to get up.' Ruthless employers doled out meagre salaries to those who remained or were forced back on the land, and deducted for food, lodging, dependants and any lost time or breakages. Tenants were forced to rely on credit and increasingly compelled to accept a share of the land instead of monetary payment, which bound them more closely to the land and made their chances of self-sufficiency even more unlikely. Conversely, some landowners drove their workers off the land instead of paying them when they finished harvesting their crops. Bougier, Sarah and Unsey all gave birth to babies with unknown fathers after the war; the circumstances of the children's conceptions are unclear, although neither Bougier nor Sarah remarried after they were violently separated from their husbands in West Africa and displaced to the United States.[3]

Following their emancipation, Matilda and her family left Prairie Bluff for Liberty Hill, a township in Dallas County known locally as Athens about ten miles northeast as the crow flies of the Creagh family cemetery. William and Siloma Hunt's former captives, teenage mothers Quilla and Lucy and their shipmate Ossa, remained for years on their enslavers' neighbouring Rehoboth estate, although Lucy eventually moved to Marengo County with her African American husband Jim and their eight children, presumably to be near shipmates living there.[4]

Matilda and her family's relocation brought them close to Bogue

Chitto and to Redoshi and her husband Yawith, and Cuffee and his wife Jinnie, the former captives of Confederate banker and legislator Washington Smith. Unlike Memorable Creagh's other former captives, who were still trapped in Marengo County and in Wilcox County, Matilda's family doubtless hoped they had left their Black Belt prison behind. But in Athens they were forced to work as propertyless farm labourers and found little improvement in their living and working conditions. Gracie and Guy were still expected to toil in the cotton fields from early in the morning until after nightfall, and the overseers who scrutinized their work were as sadistic as ever. Gracie and Guy worked as sharecroppers, which meant they laboured not for a salary but, rather, for a share of the cotton and corn they were required to plant and harvest, which was typically a third of the overall yield. By the age of 12, Matilda was made to join her mother, stepfather and sister in the fields.[5]

White landowners in the Black Belt controlled their Black workforces in the years after slavery was outlawed by controlling their sources of – and the amount they paid for – food, fertilizer, loans and other material necessities. Such items had to be bought from the plantation store or through a direct plea to the landowner. The strict division of land into tenant and sharecropper plots meant there was no free space to breed herds of roaming livestock that could have given the Africans and their African American neighbours an independent source of food and income. Instead, they were forced to intensively work small plots of land that required fertilizer bought on credit to remain productive, an expense that created a constant cycle of indebtedness in the 1880s, and which helped to fuel labour unrest in the 1890s.[6]

Just as they had endured during slavery, the Africans in the Black Belt were forced to inhabit crowded makeshift dwellings with inadequate clothing, bedding and furniture. When Tuskegee Institute graduate Dr. William James Edwards arrived in Snow Hill to build a school in 1893, he found a heavily mortgaged community that still lived in one- and two-room cabins. 'I remember that shortly after the founding of the school a Negro built a house and fitted it up with glass windows and people would go ten miles to see it,' he recalled.[7]

From the age of seven, Matilda took responsibility for her family's material needs to ensure their survival. Gracie and Guy's inability to communicate in English compelled the child to act as their interpreter when they bought items on credit at the local store owned by wealthy Irish-born merchant and farmer James McDonald, who was probably their landlord and employer. Whenever Gracie asked in Yoruba for two yards of coarse calico, a plug of tobacco, a box of snuff, meat and cornmeal, Matilda translated her request. Eventually, Gracie learned enough English phrases to shop independently of her daughter, but she always had to supplement her words with gestures to ensure she was understood.[8]

Freed people in Dallas County were so deeply bound to the land that a property's sale value was linked to the productivity of its labourers. Civil rights leader Amelia Boynton Robinson also identified a 'gentleman's agreement' between white men not to sell land to Black people in the Black Belt. On the rare occasions that African Americans had the opportunity to buy land, it would be priced at an extortionate rate. White landowners capitalized on Black people's lack of education and inability to scrutinize the agreements they made them sign, and fraudulent accounting ensured that Black farmers were never able to pay off the debts they owed their landlords. Their basic, monotonous diets of cornbread, condensed milk, strong coffee and salt pork contributed to their poor health and made them susceptible to catastrophic diseases such as tuberculosis.[9]

Redoshi, Yawith, Cuffee and Jinnie remained trapped on their former enslaver's plantation in Bogue Chitto, where they also raised vast quantities of cotton for little reward. Their limited English perhaps made them even more susceptible to exploitation than their African American neighbours. While Redoshi and Yawith's post-war farming output was not documented, Cuffee and Jinnie were forced to till 14 acres of land with just five dollars' worth of farming equipment. Yet they still raised 100 bushels of corn and eight bales of cotton in one year alone, a better return than all but one of their neighbours, who equalled their efforts. Despite this yield, the estimated value of their farm productions was just $100 (equivalent to $3,000 today) that year, a figure significantly lower than their neighbours' outputs.[10]

Yawith, who was probably in his late twenties at the time of his liberation, quickly deduced that his employer – and former enslaver – Washington Smith was not paying him and Redoshi properly for their labour. Entire bale-worths of cotton were being left off the accounting ledger. Yawith refused to tolerate such exploitation and worked out a way to fight back. He developed his own system for counting and checking his crop production that allowed him to circumvent his employer's undercount. Redoshi later explained his method to civil rights leader Amelia Boynton Robinson:

> He found that his cotton bales were not being counted correctly, but what the correct amount of counting was, he did not know. He began to keep up with the number of bales by putting a grain of corn in a jar each time he took a bale to the white man's gin. At the end of the gathering season, he would not ask the plantation owner how much cotton he had made; he would get someone else to count the grains of corn he had laid aside and tell the planter that he had so many bales ginned.[11]

Only former Snow Hill captive Dinah appears to have enjoyed a measure of autonomy from such abuses. After the war, she laboured for an African American couple on their $300, 30-acre farm in Bonham's Beat, a few miles away from present-day Vredenburgh and just east of Snow Hill. She continued to plant and pick cotton and corn, but she also grew sweet potatoes much like the yams that had been a speciality crop of her homeland.[12]

On 6 January 1872, the now 25-year-old Dinah secured her own small plot of land in Bonham's Beat when she married 22-year-old

Gasoway Miller. The couple managed 20 acres with a single mule, from which they succeeded in producing 150 bushels of corn and five bales of cotton per year. They also raised a handful of pigs and chickens; in 1880, their livestock was valued at $100 (equivalent to $3,000 today). By the end of the decade, Dinah and Gasoway had five children together.[13]

While the Africans battled to survive in the Black Belt, their former captors quickly regained their wealth and prestige, although they resented that they no longer had an abundance of fresh produce or a captive workforce to harvest it, collect it and deliver it to their door. Rush Jones had to walk the quarter-mile north from his home on Adams Avenue to the food stalls on Commerce Street. His middle daughter Jennie wailed decades later at the memory of his shopping trips. 'I felt we were forever disgraced and thought only the poorest people ever went to market, for the carts came from the plantations twice a week with meats, poultry, vegetables, fruits, melons, etc.' No longer able to make such lucrative income from his land without unpaid labourers, but still in possession of the large stash of gold and silver buried on his estate, Jones returned to medicine and reopened his Montgomery drug store. Jennie went to Augusta Female Seminary (now Mary Baldwin University), an elite private school in Staunton, Virginia, where she claimed to have befriended future US President Woodrow Wilson's sister Annie. The family's real upset came later: Jones's only son Rush, Jr., died before the decade was out, the trauma of a war-related chest injury having morphed into tuberculosis. Railway labourer Reuben's former enslaver Alex Given emerged from the conflict seemingly unscathed. He was still a cotton merchant with real estate valued at $10,000 and a personal estate valued at $25,000 in 1870 (a combined total equivalent to more than $800,000 today). He even took charge of the Exchange Hotel alongside Abram Phillips Watt, the brother-in-law of 'poet of the Confederacy' Sidney Lanier. Lanier worked briefly as a night clerk at the hotel under Given's management.[14]

Redoshi's former enslaver Washington Smith's Confederate banking operation folded when the war ended, but he soon formed a real estate agency with partners in New York, New Orleans and Alabama. In 1867, he established a New York banking business from his home in Selma. Matilda's former enslaver Memorable Creagh declared himself bankrupt to wipe off his debts in December 1867. But he was nowhere near as poor as he made out to his creditors. Seven months after the former enslaver's bankruptcy declaration, his mansion burned down, taking with it up to $15,000 worth of furniture (about $320,000 worth in today's money), several thousand dollars' worth of silver and the family's collection of fine clothing. Despite such a mishap, he still owned real estate valued at $2,800 and a personal estate valued at $30,000 in 1870 (a combined total equivalent to around $765,000 today).[15]

Washington Smith and Memorable Creagh navigated their business concerns alongside leading roles in post-war Alabama politics. Creagh became vice-president and temporary chairman of the Democratic and Conservative Club of Demopolis, a collective of former enslaver bankers, merchants and lawyers who sought to overthrow the Republicans at the 1870 mid-term elections. The group included former Alabama Confederate congressman Francis Strother Lyon, and future US congressmen James Taylor Jones and Richard Henry Clarke.[16]

Creagh also funded at least two anti-Northern newspapers. The *Star* operated out of Uniontown, a town 15 miles northwest of Bogue Chitto in Perry County, and *The Exponent / Southern Exponent* was based a further 20 miles west in Demopolis, Marengo County. Although the 'Salutatory' that Creagh wrote for the inaugural edition of the *Exponent* does not survive, a subsequent editorial, which promised to 'under all circumstances contend for the supremacy of the white race', and which 'appeal[ed] to the white men of this county to assist us', spelled out the newspaper's agenda.[17]

Washington Smith organized delegates to the National Union Convention in Philadelphia in August 1866, an event that sought to bolster support for President Andrew Johnson, who was seeking to readmit the former Confederate states to the Union without guaranteeing the rights of freed people in those territories. Smith also acted as an alternative to chairman of the state Democratic and Conservative Party James Holt Clanton at the 1868 National Democratic Convention, the pair having previously served together as electors for the Constitutional Union Party in the 1860 presidential election. Clanton was posthumously identified by his brother-in-law's daughter Susan Lawrence Davis as the first Alabamian grand dragon of the Ku Klux Klan, the white supremacist terrorist group that arose in response to the new Reconstruction Acts.[18]

The Ku Klux Klan emerged 20 miles north of the Alabama state line in Pulaski, Tennessee, in mid-1866, and its presence in Alabama was felt most strongly in the north of the state. The federal government's withholding of voting rights from former Confederate leaders as Black voters began to be registered for the first time to vote through a new progressive state constitution galvanized the Klan into an organized terrorist group. Wearing elaborate costumes designed to conceal its members' identities and terrify their victims, the Klan murdered, raped and mutilated both Black and white Republicans, set Black schools and churches alight, broke up political meetings and scared away political opponents. Newspapers, pamphlets, parades and songs celebrated the Klan before the Southern movement went underground in December 1868. In 1869 and 1870, Klan violence was worse in Alabama than in any other state except, perhaps, for North Carolina. Mass arrests and federal legal proceedings finally helped to suppress the terrorist organization in the early 1870s, although its disbandment also coincided with the Democrats' re-election to power in Alabama in November 1874; white elites in the state no longer needed to resort to violent vigilantism to assert their authority.[19]

Although it is not known if the *Clotilda* Africans were directly implicated in Klan violence, they were caught up in Klan-related propaganda. Former Confederate newspaper the *Memphis Daily Appeal*, which had been operating out of Montgomery at the end of the war, published a defence of the Klan in April 1868, and then reported in October – at the height of Klan violence and only two days after the Mobile Africans claimed their US citizenship – that Black people's freedom from slavery and perceived 'idleness' were fueling 'Vaudooism' or 'Hoodooism', to which it attributed the sickness of a white girl in New Orleans. One of two 'Congoes' from the *Clotilda*, it claimed, was responsible for the girl's ordeal. Albert Pike was the newspaper's editor between February 1867 and 30 August 1868; he was posthumously identified as one of the Klan's earliest leaders.[20]

In the early 1920s, Rush Jones's daughter Jennie described a tactic the Klan used to terrorize Montgomery's post-war Republican-led legislature. 'This mixed negro and carpetbagger [a disparaging term for Northerners in the post-war South] Legislature was about to pass a bill to wage war between whites and blacks. The Ku Klux heard of this and wrote a letter telling them if such a bill was passed that not one of this crowd would leave the Capitol alive.' Jennie added that a former captive of her uncle Constantine Jones was one of the letter's targets, and she claimed the man was so scared that he begged to go back to labouring for the Jones family.

> Dick (this plantation hand) who could neither read nor write, came to my father's office and said, 'Mas Rush want you vance me a plow and mule for a year?' Father said, 'Dick, I thought you were making so much money I felt I could call on you if I needed money.' 'Oh! Mas Rush legislature ain't no place for a n—and if I can git a mule and some land, town will never see Dick any more. I'se through with all the Yankees I know.'

Jennie's grotesquely racist story was a fabrication. There was no former Jones captive on the Alabama legislature, and the Republicans were not seeking to provoke a race war. But her knowledge of Klan activities underscored connections between the *Clotilda* captors and the terrorist group's leadership. When James Holt Clanton was killed in a duel with a former Union Army colonel in 1871, Reuben's former enslaver Alex Given was a member of a ten-man committee charged with leading the tributes to him and was one of his dozen pallbearers. Both Given and Jones made donations to Clanton's memorial fund.[21]

The Black Belt Africans worked to create a protective environment for each other amid such horrors and to counter such dangerous racist narratives. Despite never having seen a Christian place of worship before, they built a series of churches in Wilcox County either during or shortly after the end of slavery. Dinah's great-granddaughter Arlonzia understood that the shipmates worked single-handedly to build their churches, since all the people who worshipped there were 'just like [Dinah] was, all of them was slaves came from Africa'. She did not list the locations of the churches, but she noted that the first was near Gee's Bend, a community set in a loop of the Alabama River south of Bogue Chitto, east of Prairie Bluff. The Black Belt shipmates' efforts paralleled the work of the Mobile Africans, who built a space of worship separate from their African American peers, who they felt had internalized the anti-African prejudices of their former enslavers. Arlonzia described some of the pressures Dinah and her fellow Africans felt to convert to Christianity around the time of their emancipation. 'They wasn't Christians when they came here, but they had such a hard time they became Christians.'[22] Like Abile, her husband Kossula and their ship-mates in Mobile, the Black Belt Africans found their Yoruba customs and spiritual beliefs were viewed so negatively by their African American peers that conversion became a social necessity. Strikingly, Arlonzia claimed the structures were the first religious buildings in their community, just like Old Landmark Baptist Church in African Town.

The shipmates' first church was called Pleasant Hill Baptist Church and was made of brush arbour (a makeshift shelter forged from brushwood) with seating made from roughly hewn logs. The church was sited above a ditch, yet the Africans were so determined to worship their new Christian god that they gathered even when the seating flooded. They stood up to their knees in rainwater and continued to pray. When after a year the 'boss man', presumably the landowner, caught them worshipping, he burned down the church. Undeterred, they built another church in a different location. When that, too, was burned down, they moved to a different location and started again. The torching of the community's churches reflected a terrorist tactic employed frequently in post-Civil War-era Alabama by white supremacists, who recognized that the structures were sites of learning and spaces where calls for racial equality could be vocalized and shared. 'Didn't want them to serve God, 'cause they 'fraid they'd come free – and that's what they did,' Arlonzia explained.[23]

White elites, who had been actively hostile to the learning of enslaved peoples, continued to oppose the education of Black children in the Black Belt after the war. Attempts by the Freedmen's Bureau and missionaries to educate freed people were often met with violence, which meant children's learning in rural territories such as Wilcox County was neglected for decades. A Black student did not graduate from a Wilcox County public high school until 1955.[24]

Dinah raged against the violently enforced intellectual and spiritual poverty that limited the opportunities and dictated social attitudes to the Africans and their African American neighbours. '[T]hey catch you writing, they'll cut your fingers off,' Arlonzia explained. 'And they didn't learn them how to speak the language like they should. The boss man teach them to talk a bad way, then when the slavery was over with, they talked about how the black peoples didn't know how to talk. But they talked what they was taught ... They just had their African language when they got here.'[25]

On 22 February 1869, Washington Smith died suddenly at the age of 54 while on business in New York, although his death brought no change in the circumstances of Redoshi, Yawith, Cuffee and Jinnie, who continued to labour for their former enslaver's widow. His wife Susan managed her cotton crops closely, and her tenants had no control over how their debts were settled at the end of harvest season. Memorable Creagh died not long after, aged about sixty-five, in Demopolis on 21 May 1872.[26]

Matilda became a mother around the time of her former enslaver's death. Her teenage sister Sally left home to marry an African American man named John Walker shortly after emancipation, and Gracie and Guy's struggles to navigate the world around them meant they were no more able to protect Matilda from the sexual dangers of the post-war Black Belt than they could from long days in the cotton fields. Matilda was about thirteen years old when she fell pregnant in 1871 or 1872 with Eliza, the first of three daughters to a man whose name was documented as 'Bill Moze' and 'Willie Meyer' and who is likely to have been William R. Mayes. Mayes was a 20-year-old farmer living with his parents and siblings in Athens at the time Matilda fell pregnant. His father John was a wealthy Athens overseer-turned-landowner who established a system of abuse on his plantation early in his son William's childhood. He enriched his estate by buying an enslaved man and two teenage girls, seemingly with the intention of making the girls reproduce. The girls gave birth to nine children between them over an eleven-year period.[27]

Like their former enslavers, the Black Belt Africans began to die not long after achieving their freedom. Liza, the young woman who the Montgomery captives had sought to shield from arduous plantation labour when they arrived in Mount Meigs, and who Rush Jones's daughter Susie identified as an African queen, was still trapped on her former enslaver's estate after the war. Liza at first shared her property with an African American man named Joshua Ware. When Ware married in 1871, the African woman lived alone, except for the steer she needed to plough the heavy Black Belt soil, which in her accented English she pronounced ''teer'. Susie claimed her father gave Liza the steer and that it shared the cabin with her.[28] Her account of Liza's living arrangements was intended to frame the *Clotilda* survivor as an 'uncivilized' African, but unwittingly hinted at a Yoruba tradition of placing cattle in the inner courts of households to protect them from predators.

Slave cabins were usually made from wood and contained huge fireplaces, typically eight feet wide, that made them major fire hazards. As Northern journalist and architect Frederick Law Olmsted observed when he travelled through the South just before the war, 'The chimneys often catch fire, and the cabin is destroyed. Very little precaution can be taken against this danger.' In the mid-1930s, a woman who had been enslaved as a child in Virginia recalled, 'We didn't have houses like we do now. They were made out of trees cut down, and clay. Long chimneys, but not brick. We was afraid to make a big fire, for we was afraid the house would catch on fire.' But fires were vital. Food was cooked over the fireplaces, which were also the main source of light and warmth in cabins whose windows were often shuttered since there was no glass. Vinnie Busby, who grew up on a Mississippi plantation, remembered building 'big roarin' fires' that would 'light up de whole cabin bright as sunshine'.[29]

The Confederate cotton bale blaze that nearly burned down Rush Jones's house and the rest of Montgomery at the end of the war was a stark reminder to the Africans of the hazards of their Alabama prison. But there was little they could do to protect themselves from danger, and Liza's cabin caught fire one night while she was sleeping. The young African woman and her steer were killed in the blaze. Bougier and her fellow Africans woke one morning to the devastating sight of her destroyed cabin and the shock of the sudden, violent death of one of their beloved shipmates. Even Liza's former enslaver's daughter acknowledged that Liza's death was 'tragic': 'One night she went to sleep in front of the fire and a spark set her clothes on fire and she and the Teer were burned to ashes.' Liza's shipmates grieved that her sudden, violent death had denied her the funeral rites of a Yoruban woman. Susie recalled that Liza was one of the earliest of her father's captives to adopt Christianity. 'She was the first one of the Africans to accept the Christian religion and my mother said Liza had a wonderful conception of the power of Jesus Christ and the comfort it brought her in this strange land.'[30] But the shipmates never abandoned their West African worldviews even as they slowly began to embrace their enslavers' religion. To the

Africans' despair, there could be no proper burial for Liza and no means of putting her tormented spirit to rest.

Guy was probably in his forties when he died in Athens sometime in the 1870s. The cause of his death is unknown, but his wife Gracie succumbed to tuberculosis in December 1879. She was probably in her late forties or early fifties, too. Their US-born children John and Mary also disappear from the historical record in the 1870s; not only did Gracie lose two sons and two daughters to the transatlantic slave trade, but she was probably forced to bury her youngest children shortly before her own death. Gracie's oldest remaining child Sally became a mother at 17 to a child named William with her husband John, but the boy appears not to have survived childhood either. His father also soon died of an unknown cause. Matilda's sister and childhood protector Sally lost her family before she was 30; she never remarried.[31]

Matilda was only 19 or 20 when her mother Gracie died, but she had already given birth for the third time. Matilda named the little girl 'Winny' in a likely reference to her lost homeland of Owini Hill. Like Gumpa, who tattooed on his child's chest a crescent moon and an ouroboros to symbolize its kinship to moon goddess Mawu and rainbow serpent Aido-Hwedo, Matilda was probably seeking to memorialize her mother and affirm her family's African heritage in the United States.

Matilda played with language to assert power and autonomy as an African woman in the Black Belt in other ways, too. She posthumously nicknamed her former enslaver 'White Frost', which she assured a white journalist in the 1930s was his middle name and stemmed from his birth on the morning of a particularly heavy frost in Alabama. Matilda was teasing her interviewer and perhaps making fun of her former enslaver. Memorable Creagh's real middle name was Walker, and he was born in South Carolina on 4 July. Matilda and her parents inherited Creagh's surname after emancipation, but she eventually added a 'Mc' to the name to distance herself from her former captor, and to 'put the impress of her own personality upon it'.[32]

Redoshi also sought to retain control over language and, by extension, her identity. She taught her mother tongue to her daughter Lethe, who in turn passed the language onto her children. Like Matilda, Redoshi refused to forget where she was from, even as she adapted to her new, unchosen, life.[33]

At some stage after their emancipation, probably between 1880 and 1900 and likely without relocating from their Athens homes, Matilda and her sister Sally became tenants on the 1,700-acre estate of Atlas Jones Martin. Sally rented a cabin and Matilda rented land on the property. Martin's Station (also known as Martin Station) was a section of Athens that grew into an independent township by the early 1880s. Atlas Martin was one of the richest and most powerful men in Dallas County. He had been one of the region's biggest enslavers before the war, and his property was valued at $139,600 (equivalent to $5 million in 2023) around the time of the Africans' arrival in the United States. In 1868, he was appointed as County Commissioner, an elected official in charge of the county's governance.[34]

Despite Klan violence, Black men in the Black Belt continued to turn out in large numbers to vote in the years after emancipation. Three African American legislators, Benjamin Sterling Turner, James Thomas Rapier and Jeremiah Haralson, were elected to represent Alabama in US Congress in the early 1870s. The number of Black Alabamian state legislators fell from 31 in 1868 to 20 in 1870 as a result of Klan intimidation, but Black-majority counties played a decisive role in returning Republican candidates to every state office in 1872. The size of the Black voting bloc meant that the Republican Party, which had implemented legislation granting their freedom and voting rights, controlled the state's political apparatus until 1874, when Democratic elites, in many cases former enslavers, regained control of the state legislature amid charges of voter fraud.[35]

The voting system was now rigged against Black people in

Alabama. Quilla's shipmate and neighbour Ossa and other Black Belt Africans still sought to vote in the 1876 presidential election but were turned away from the ballot box. Their thwarted efforts led a US Congressional Senate Committee on voter suppression to query their presence in Marengo County. Attorney Henry Ashby Woolf, who lived close to two of the *Clotilda* Africans in the town of Linden in that county, denied before the committee there were any Africans in that area. 'I have lived there all my life . . . If there is a native African in Marengo County, I do not know it,' he declared. But Republican Marshall Greene Candee asserted there were 'quite a good many in Marengo County . . . who were brought there just before the close of the war', and who had been prevented from voting. Candee also stated that only 18 of the 138 Republican votes cast in that county were counted, while the number of Democratic votes had suspiciously risen sevenfold.[36]

Atlas Martin was the assistant registrar for Athens in the 1876 presidential election. African American US congressman Jeremiah Haralson recounted before a US Congressional investigating committee how Martin had suppressed the Black vote in that election. '[A]t that precinct one of the democratic inspectors, who keeps a store there, locked [the ballot boxes] up in his store . . . All the people were there, and they could not vote at all . . . I should say that we lost between *six and eight hundred* [votes] in one precinct – in the precinct of Liberty Hill [Athens].'[37]

Such voter suppression tactics ensured that Black legislators elected to power by newly enfranchised freed people after the war were not re-elected to represent Alabama in the 1876 election. The results of that contest were highly disputed. Republican Rutherford B. Hayes was eventually installed as US president over Democrat Samuel J. Tilden, but only following a deal with Southern Democrats that involved the removal of federal troops from the former Confederate states, an act that effectively ceded control in those states to the pre-war Southern political order. The Reconstruction era and the fight for Black people's civil rights in the South were over.[38]

Progress, it seemed, had come to a halt in the South. A gruesome public spectacle of white supremacy underpinned the Africans' loss of civil rights in the post-Reconstruction Black Belt. On 14 April 1882, the first documented lynchings occurred in Dallas County.[39] The killings took place in Bogue Chitto, and one of the two victims was Cuffee and Jinnie's 21-year-old neighbour Henry Ivy, who had grown up among the Africans.

In December 1881, a 75-year-old South Carolina-born former enslaver was fatally injured during a night-time robbery at his store at Brown's Station, a few miles north of Bogue Chitto. Jesse Benjamin Weisinger was a powerful figure in Dallas County. He was a Freemason, an election inspector and an election returning officer. Henry Ivy was a married farm labourer and son of a widowed mother.[40]

Ivy and a 35-year-old farmer named Sim Acoff were arrested after Weisinger's killing but quickly released for lack of evidence. Two other Black men were condemned to hang, and a teenager was imprisoned for Weisinger's death. But the accusation of killing a wealthy white man sealed Ivy and Acoff's fates, especially as the convicted teenager was Ivy's brother and his wife milked cows for Weisinger's son. As one newspaper admitted after the lynchings, 'Since their release they have been closely shadowed with a view to the conviction of all implicated.' Ivy made what was almost certainly a forced confession before seven white men a week after the convicted men's executions.[41]

Ivy and Acoff were held in a schoolhouse on 13 April by three of the seven men who extracted Ivy's confession. At two o'clock the following morning, a mob of 40 masked men rode up to the building on horseback, kidnapped the pair and hanged them from trees near Bell's Church in the west of Bogue Chitto, close to Redoshi, Yawith, Cuffee and Jinnie's cabins. Acoff's corpse could not be found in the hours after the murder, but Ivy's body was left in the woods until at least the next day to terrorize the Africans and their neighbours.[42]

Ivy and Acoff's deaths cruelly foreshadowed Cuffee and Jinnie's own bleak fates in Bogue Chitto. Before the end of the century, the couple were devastated to lose the homes and livelihoods they had forged in the hostile Black Belt landscape that had once held them prisoner. Their former enslaver's family had decided to drive them off their land, Washington Smith's descendants admitting years later that the Africans 'were not retained long on the plantation'. The landowners blamed the couple's expulsion on unspecified poor behaviour, which they linked to their African identities. They claimed they were members of a 'coast tribe' and 'entirely different in their characteristics' from Redoshi and Yawith, whose membership of an 'inland tribe' meant they were of a 'superior mentality and were trustworthy'.[43] Yet Gumpa was the only shipmate with links to the coast who was imprisoned on the *Clotilda*; Cuffee and Jinnie almost certainly were from the same Yoruba-speaking town as the rest of their shipmates.

A more probable reason for their expulsion was that, unlike Redoshi and Yawith, who in 1884 became grandparents to a boy named William after his African grandfather, they failed to produce children and were increasingly seen as a financial burden rather than an asset to their landlords as their strength began to fail and cotton prices plummeted in the mid-1890s. The couple's sudden homelessness recalled a practice during slavery of casting out captives when they grew old and their productivity declined. Abolitionist Frederick Douglass railed against the 'base ingratitude' shown to his grandmother, whose enslaver abandoned her to die in the woods when she became too frail to work.[44] With nowhere to go and no means of communicating with the world around them, Cuffee and Jinnie faced a dire future; they disappear from the historical record after the loss of their homes and livelihoods.

Exchange Hotel manager Alex Given's former captive also met a bleak end. By 1880, Reuben had escaped his former enslaver's grocery store and was boarding with an African American laundress named Hannah Taylor and her eight-year-old son, Henry. Soon though, the African man moved again, this time to 801 Adams Avenue, a property on the same street as the Jones's house. Reuben's new home, which was owned by another formerly enslaved woman, Lucy

Ann Lucas, lay one block south and east of the capitol building. Lucas was a brothel keeper, but Reuben had few choices about his domestic arrangements. He was now blind and could no longer work. The cause of Reuben's disability is unknown, but malnutrition, the hazards of railroad labour, and even years of excessive sunlight – a common cause of blindness among enslaved people – may have been factors in his loss of vision.

When Lucas died in 1895, she left behind a house, furniture, cow, calf and wagon, which together were valued at $3,000 (equivalent to nearly $110,000 in 2023). Lucas stipulated that half her property be left to her daughter Caroline ('Callie'), and the rest split equally between her servant Mollie Harmon and Reuben. Lucas's other daughter Missouri contested her mother's will, and the case was brought before a jury in December that year, which decided to award all the money to Callie and Missouri. The *Montgomery Advertiser* suggested that the Lucas sisters would take care of the blind, ageing and now impoverished man, but they soon disposed of the Pelham Street property, and may well have abandoned their financial rival, too. Reuben disappears from the historical record after the court case.[45]

Two *Clotilda* survivors managed to defy their shipmates' bleak fates and escape the post-war Black Belt on their own terms, however. William Hunt's widow Siloma held onto her dead husband's farm in Rehoboth until August 1881, when she relocated to Selma and set up a boarding house with her daughters on the corners of Selma and Green streets. She died three years later after a long illness at the age of 50. The sale of Siloma Hunt's farm and the loss of their land may have been the spark that set Ossa and Quilla, by then in their mid-thirties, on a daring 150-mile journey back down the Alabama and Mobile rivers. They had somehow heard that their fellow shipmates, including Ossa's sister Omolabi, were living in an 'African' township on the edge of Mobile. Ossa and Quilla scraped together the money for the journey south and set off to find them.[46] They brought with them their African American partners Clara and Ephraim and their eight young children.

There is no record of the Africans' meeting with their long-lost neighbours and relatives. But other accounts of such reunions, like that of anti-slavery activist Olaudah Equiano's brief reunion with his sister before his sale across the Atlantic, gives a sense of how Omolabi and Ossa must have felt. 'I had been travelling for a considerable time, when one evening, to my great surprise, whom should I see brought to the house where I was but my dear sister! As soon as she saw me she gave a loud shriek, and ran into my arms — I was quite overpowered: neither of us could speak; but, for a considerable time, clung to each other in mutual embraces, unable to do any thing but weep.'[47]

Ossa and Quilla's journey to Mobile was an emotional event for all the Africans, and Kanko named her new daughter Equilla in a likely tribute to her long-lost shipmate. The pair's return to the port city proved to the Mobile Africans that their separation and isolation was not necessarily permanent, and news of other shipmates still alive in the Black Belt served as evidence of the group's endurance. Suddenly, after more than twenty years of exile, the chance of other reunions seemed possible, the hope of finding their wider community less out of reach.

11

Burials

On 27 November 1886, a group of white Northerners landed in Mobile. Writers Charles Dudley Warner and Kirk Munroe, artists Charles Graham, John Durkin and Horace Bradley and publisher William Armitage Harper were halfway through a six-week tour of the educational establishments, mines, factories and cotton fields of the former Confederate states. The carefully choreographed propaganda project, whose participants were chaperoned in a private train, formed part of a wider effort by post-war Southern leaders to rehabilitate the region as a space for economic investment and a national centre of industry. As the trip's sponsor, New York magazine *Harper's Weekly*, which supported the Republican Party during and after the Civil War, acknowledged, 'The object of the visit was to see the "new south," to observe the social, industrial and educational changes of the last few years, in order that the actual condition of "the south" might be faithfully reported by pen and pencil.' The magazine reassured its Northern readers that 'political differences and the friction of races are yielding to the beneficent touch of healthy industrial enterprise and a fresh prosperity.'[1]

Kirk Munroe befriended banker and railroad tycoon George William Craik, an acquaintance of Rush Jones, on the tour. He visited Craik's home and wrote a story for *Harper's Young People* featuring the tycoon's nine-year-old daughter Julia and outlining the hospitality he enjoyed: 'we met with charming people, who were so kind to us, and who invited us to so many receptions, banquets, and other entertainments that they made the South appear a sort of fairy-land, where nobody has anything to do except have a good time'. Yet even Munroe was forced to admit that the South wasn't all leisure, banquets and fairy stories. When the 'New South' group arrived in Mobile, they were directed to African Town, very probably by Craik. Munroe became the first Northern visitor to interview the shipmates when he spoke to Abile and her husband Kossula. He suggested they would no longer recognize their homeland and were much better off in the United States. Abile quickly set him straight: 'Sun all de time; no cole. P'enty eat, p'enty drink, p'enty house, p'enty people; all brack, no white mans.' When he suggested her transatlantic displacement had at least gifted her with religious knowledge, the woman looked at him pityingly. 'White man, yo' no t'ink God in my country same like here?'[2]

The Africans' encounter with outsiders coincided with the deaths of their former captors. Kossula's enslaver James Meaher died on 8 February 1885. Kanko's enslaver Burns Meaher followed on 6 November 1889 and King Glele died in mysterious circumstances on 29 December that year, just as the French Empire sought to consolidate a territorial claim to the port city of Cotonou, 20 miles east of Ouidah.[3] His son Kondo, who took the name Béhanzin when he became king, fought the French army over Cotonou, which led to his capture and lifelong exile, first across the Atlantic to Martinique and finally to Algeria, and to the formal end of the Kingdom of Dahomey on 17 February 1900.

Timothy Meaher suffered a stroke near the end of his life and spent his final months partially paralyzed. Finally, on 3 March 1892, almost thirty-two years to the day after the *Clotilda* set sail across the Atlantic, the 79-year-old human trafficker died peacefully of old age at his home on Telegraph Road.[4]

Timothy Meaher's funeral two days later at St. Bridget Catholic Church in Whistler was well attended, and he was laid to rest in an expensive tomb in the 20-acre Stone Street Cemetery in Toulminville after the service officiated by Reverend Father John

F. Cassidy. The Mobile Africans were among the many witnesses to Meaher's funeral, and their presence at the burial ensured the former enslaver would not be laid to rest quietly. The shipmates did not hold back. The group's 'loud and weird lamentations' haunted proceedings and so unnerved their fellow mourners that it reached a local newspaper.[5] Their outburst was framed by an eyewitness as their way of paying tribute to a senior community figure. More likely, the death of the man who had stolen them from their homeland, forced them into servitude and had the wealth if not the inclination to take them home, resurfaced decades-long traumas and painfully underscored the permanence of their exile.

When Quilla reunited with her Mobile shipmates, she did not settle directly in African Town. Instead, she moved to nearby Toulminville on a street bordering Stone Street Cemetery and adjoining a road named after Confederate president Jefferson Davis.[6] Not only was she forced to bear witness to the opulent funeral of the man who had engineered her kidnap and enslavement, and who at his death was one of the richest and most powerful men in Mobile, but the presence of Timothy Meaher's grave must have served as a daily reminder of everything the former enslaver and human trafficker had taken from her.

African Town suffered its own devastating losses around the time of Meaher's death. Josephine was dead by the beginning of 1890, and none of her eight children with Gumpa lived long enough to see in the new century. Jabez followed his wife Polly to the grave before the new century began, and Maggie and Rosallie also died in the 1890s, leaving Charlie and Polee widowers. Two other shipmates, Adisa and Shamba, lost their American husbands around this time. Ossa, who changed his surname from Hunt to Allen in Mobile, perhaps because he was related to Polee and Rosallie, died a decade or so after his relocation to the city from Wilcox County. His sister Omolabi, who was forced to come to terms with the loss of her brother for a second time, adopted Ossa's orphaned son and namesake. Kanko's daughter Equilla Amy had only just turned 12 when an infected splinter in her foot caused the lockjaw that killed her in the autumn of 1891. Her distraught parents were forced to bury their youngest child and only daughter; they spent $8.35 (equivalent to nearly $300 today) on a fitting gravestone for their little girl. They kept the receipt for their terrible purchase for the rest of their lives.[7]

Abile and Kossula tragically lost their youngest child Celia/ Ebeossi to illness on 4 August 1893. Kossula recalled three and a half decades later the couple's desperate efforts to keep her alive and the shock of her death. 'My baby, Seely, de only girl I got, she tookee sick in de bed. Oh, Lor'! I do anything to save her. We gittee de doctor. We gittee all de medicine he tellee us tuh git. Oh, Lor'. I pray, I tell de Lor' I do anything to save my baby life. She ain' but fifteen year old. But she die . . . She doan have no time to live befo' she die. Her mama take it so hard. I try tellee her not to cry, but I cry too.'[8]

The grieving parents held a funeral for their daughter at Old Landmark Baptist Church. As the child lay in her open coffin, the congregation sang the hymn 'Shall We Meet Beyond The River'. Kossula had been a Christian for nearly twenty-five years, but the song felt like the wrong send-off for his daughter, and he could not join in. Instead, he recited in his head his grandfather's funeral song. Yoruba communities traditionally bury their dead deep underground on their homestead, but Celia was laid to rest in Plateau Cemetery. Kossula felt acutely his child's distance from home and built a protective fence around her grave. 'She lookee so lonesome out dere by herself — she such a li'l girl, you unnerstan' me, dat I hurry and build de fence 'round de grave so she have pertection.'[9]

In June 1893, two months before Celia's death, US Army captain Henry Romeyn became the second Northerner to visit African Town. Romeyn was in Alabama to oversee the confinement of religious and military leader Geronimo and about 400 other Chiricahua Apache prisoners of war, mostly women and children, following their surrender to the US Army in 1886 at the end of the Apache– US Wars, a series of military campaigns in which Apache groups fought to reclaim their ancestral homelands in the present-day southwest United States. The captives were being held at Mount

Vernon Barracks 30 miles north of Mobile, the same place the *Clotilda* shipmates were hidden when they first arrived in the United States. Tuberculosis and dysentery were so prevalent at the barracks that even Romeyn was forced to admit 'the death rate is enormous'. Just as the Africans experienced, Romeyn used the mission of 'civilization' to justify the Apache captives' suffering and the loss of their land, lives and heritages. He even compared the Africans' and Apaches' speech patterns.[10]

Leading *Clotilda* conspiracist Timothy Meaher's son Augustine led Henry Romeyn to African Town, safe in the knowledge that his recently deceased father and uncles could no longer be prosecuted for human trafficking. The army captain asked Gumpa which home he preferred. The nobleman instantly replied 'Dah-ho-mah', and repeated his answer three or four times for emphasis. Despite his sale into slavery by own kingdom, Gumpa was horrified when Romeyn told him that the French Empire was waging a successful war against Dahomey, and that 69 Dahomeyans, including 21 female warriors, were that summer on show for voyeuristic consumption at the World's Columbian Exposition in Chicago. The exposition, which was held to commemorate 400 years since the arrival of Christopher Columbus in the Americas and attracted 27 million visitors during its six-month opening, was the biggest national exhibition yet seen in the United States. 'Who catchee?' Gumpa cried. 'No! No! No man whip Dah-ho-mah. Got 'em too much men, got 'em too much fight-women. No man whip Dah-ho-mah.'[11]

An unidentified female shipmate echoed Gumpa's praise for Dahomey to underscore the deterioration of her living standards in the United States. 'In Dah-ho-mah, lan' all free, no buyee any, no paye any tax, go wok any lan' you want, nobody else work.' When Romeyn observed that Dahomey was an empire that launched slave raids against surrounding communities, she replied, 'Oh, no catchee all.' In her view, 'it was only my bad luck' to be caught; capture and enslavement were dangers but not inevitabilities. That fact alone did not make the United States a better place to live than Africa. Abile repeated the same position a few years later. Still desperate to return home almost forty years after her kidnap, she felt acutely the depreciation in her quality of life in the United States, reflecting that she would happily take her chances with the Dahomeyan army again as 'it is so much nicer there than it is here'.[12]

Despite their dire circumstances, the Africans worked to create the best possible environment for their families. African Town was a largely self-sufficient community. Strikingly tidy and brightly decorated cabins of up to five rooms in size were surrounded by picket fences and lovingly tended gardens and fields, which were chiefly cared for by the community's women. Abaché's plot included a rose garden. The homes' vibrant colour schemes – 'barbaric splendor' in the words of one outsider – testified to the endurance of the shipmates' Yoruba beliefs, as orishas are associated with specific colours.[13] While the men earned money at the nearby saw and shingle mills, the women maintained the crops and fed the chickens.

Polee's daughter Eva, who lived until 1992, recalled decades later a close-knit and industrious group that worked collectively to solve problems and helped each other in times of need. Eva, who was also Abaché's granddaughter, remembered an abundance of fruit and vegetables at her home. So skilled at gardening were the Africans that they grew their own greens, peas, potatoes, corn, peanuts, watermelon, cantaloupes and bananas. The community also had its own pear, plum, apple and fig trees and grape arbours. Once a week, they would gather around a dinner table in African Town to speak about Africa. Above all, the Mobile Africans' lives revolved around their two-storey wooden church, which they visited up to five times on Sundays, attired in their finest clothes. There, Kossula relived the horror of the attack on his town week after week and cried with Polee when talking of home.[14]

Innie, wife of Osia Keeby, was highly protective of her community and was mistaken by curious outsiders for its leader. A physically erect and highly dignified woman, so powerfully did she convey a sense of protective leadership that at least one intrusive stranger shrank from the sight of 'such overwhelming greatness'. Her husband learned to spell his own name and took pride in the literary abilities of the couple's nine children. Their eldest child Joiffu 'Joyful' eventually became the pastor of their church. Sad-eyed Osia Keeby, still with a fine head of hair but his carefully trimmed moustache now grey, was among several *Clotilda* survivors who sold their own crops. For more than a quarter of a century, he carefully cultivated a 2-acre garden outside his two-storey house, transforming the hard, lumpy soil into a rich, fertile patch of land that yielded fantastic produce. He worked from morning to night, precisely laying out each crop and clearing away the weeds before they threatened his plants and vegetables. He delivered his goods from door to door and developed his own written language for documenting his sales.[15]

Dark-haired Polee, the orisha initiate with the hoop earrings, also became a devoted gardener. Like Osia Keeby, he worked late into the night to tend his crops, which included herbs and medicinal plants. Polee was adept at identifying plants with medicinal properties and always kept leaves for a hot drink the community called 'life everlasting tea', which they drank with honey from his beehives. Like his male shipmates, he boosted his income by carving and selling wooden objects, including boats and furniture, a specialist skill perhaps learned back home, and was particularly well known for his walking sticks. Most of the Africans' handicrafts, including toys, baskets, storage chests and kitchen cabinets, were made from wood. Polee was also a minister at the Africans' church who always wore ties on Sundays and carried a Bible with him everywhere. His first wife and fellow *Clotilda* survivor Rosallie was the church's first Sunday School teacher. His daughter Eva grew up as one of ten children in her father's five-bedroom house, which he eventually owned outright, and never learned her father's language or used her Yoruba name, 'Jo-Ko', because her classmates laughed when she tried to speak it. But she appreciated how lucky she had been to grow up in such a talented and loving community, which she claimed lived 'like one family'. Reflecting on her experiences at the end of her life, she exclaimed, 'Lord, Jesus, that's the best life I ever lived. Jesus, I loved it.'[16]

African Town judge Charlie, a small, slender man with a kind face, high cheekbones, a goatee beard and a full head of silvery-white hair, also tended his garden from sunbreak till night at the end of his life. A deeply pious man known as 'Big Poppa' for his leadership role in the community, Charlie took time away from his garden every hour or two to pray. Charlie's English was limited to a few words, so he relied on his daughters Mary and Martha to sell his crops. The two women regularly walked the 3 miles to Mobile with their father's produce balanced on their heads. Charlie's green fingers and his daughters' labour meant he was by far the community's richest man, and he was always glad to help his neighbours when they needed financial aid.[17]

At least three women residents of African Town were smart businesswomen who earned decent incomes as travelling chefs. A woman named Alice Williams, who was probably the youngest of the Mobile Africans, a woman with high cheekbones named Shamba Wigfall, and Zuma, the woman with the deep facial marks, cooked rice and peas, stews, fish and chicken and carried the food in pots on their heads to sell to Black and white labourers at the local sawmills. In the mid-1890s, a journalist noted that 'Princesses Zuma and Camba make a regular business of supplying the mill hands with a freshly-cooked dinner, and have grown well-to-do on the proceeds.' 'The white folks would just love to eat her cooking,' Polee's granddaughter Viola Allen remembered of Zuma's efforts.[18]

In 1887, Abile and Kossula invested in an additional acre of land for $64.50 (equivalent to $2,000 in 2023) and their oldest sons Aleck and James opened a grocery store, which became the largest of six general stores in African Town. A 1900 newspaper report praised the Lewis Bros. Grocery Dealers, describing it as an exemplar of establishments in African Town 'owned and controlled by some able colored men', and where could be found 'a very fine stock and an exceedingly good trade'. When Aleck married a young woman named Mary Woods in October 1891, the family built a home for him on the family compound as was the Yoruba custom.[19]

By 1912, African Town's population grew to approximately two to three thousand. The residents' achievements were numerous.

There were at least a dozen stores, all owned by Black men, and nearly everyone owned their own homes. While most men worked at the Sheip Lumber Company, many also cultivated their own land, with plots of up to six acres. In 1910, with no state support, the residents singlehandedly raised $900 (equivalent to nearly $30,000 in 2023) for a new high school to accompany the schoolhouse the Africans built four decades earlier for their children. Mobile County Training School was presided over first by Tuskegee Institute founder Booker T. Washington disciple Professor Isaiah Josephus Whitley and then by Benjamin Baker, who expanded its focus from practical skills training to an emphasis on academic excellence.[20]

Despite such staggering progress, however, the *Clotilda* survivors never forgot the earth-shattering horrors of slavery and the ecstasy of freedom. Six months before he died, Gumpa raised his wrinkled hand to the sky and declared, 'I thank God I am free.' Zuma, hearing the small Fon nobleman's words, echoed her shipmate's sentiment. 'Oh, it is great to be free!' she declared. The *Clotilda*'s captain William Foster finally died on 11 February 1901, 20 days after his beloved Queen Victoria, news of whose passing caused him 'deep regret'. Foster's death closed the chapter on British involvement in the transatlantic slave trade, which began when privateer Sir John Hawkins, with the formal support of Queen Elizabeth I, captured 300 people from Sierra Leone and shipped them to Hispaniola (present-day Dominican Republic and Haiti) in 1562. But the African Town Africans were still trapped a stone's throw from the wreck of the *Clotilda* and the family of their former enslavers. Osia Keeby testified to the reality of his experience by pointing to a man in the road and stating, 'Thar goes the nephew of the man that brung us here.'[21]

As the Africans continued to celebrate their freedom through living relatively normal lives, new restrictions were being imposed on them. A nascent cross-racial populist movement fuelled by economic depression had posed a significant threat to the power of Alabamian elites in the 1890s. The populist platform promised to protect Black people's voting rights, implement labour reforms, end convict leasing, impose a graduated income tax, increase the supply of money and select political candidates via state-wide primaries rather than restricted party conventions. Democrat elites took extreme steps to cling onto power: voter suppression tactics included voter identification certificates, gerrymandering, gubernatorial appointments instead of elections, the elision of candidates' political affiliation from voting papers and the restriction of voting registration to the month of May. In September 1901, Alabama's political leaders met at the State Capitol in Montgomery to write white elite supremacy into law. They drew up the Constitution of the State of Alabama, which disenfranchised most of the state's Black men as well as many of its poor white men. Poll taxes, literacy tests, good character tests, property requirements and grandfather clauses (exemptions that applied only to men whose ancestors had voting rights before the Civil War and thus were not enslaved) were implemented to limit who could vote. The number of registered Black voters dropped from 181,000 in 1900 to less than 5,000 in 1903; nearly 40,000 poor white men were also cut from the voter rolls over the same period.[22]

The loss of political rights and legal protections amid rising racist violence, which created a culture of self-policing, and longstanding tensions between the African community and their African American neighbours combined to shape the sad fates of Abile and Kossula's children. On 9 August 1899, their youngest son Cudjo, Jr./ Feïchitan shot and killed an African American man named Gilbert Thomas at a party. The circumstances are unclear, but 27-year-old Cudjo and 26-year-old Gilbert grew up as neighbours, and Gilbert had a recent conviction for carrying concealed weapons. The killing may have stemmed from an attempted burglary on the brothers' grocery store, or from an enduring conflict. Kossula told Zora Neale Hurston that his sons were mocked as savages throughout their childhoods, which fuelled a reputation for fighting.[23]

Cudjo, Jr. was sentenced to five years in jail for manslaughter on

3 February 1900 and sent to Pratt Mines in Jefferson County, the largest coal mine in the South, to serve his sentence through Alabama's brutal convict leasing system, an exploitative system of labour akin to the plantation bondage his parents had endured. Convict leasing replaced slavery as a form of racialized social control in the post-war South and fuelled much of the region's industrial growth. The practice existed only in the South, and Alabama was the last state to abolish it, in 1928.[24] Many of its victims were Black people no longer bound to plantations who found themselves prosecuted for non-working-related 'crimes' such as vagrancy and loitering and then hired out for a profit. Pratt Mines, to which most of the convicts were leased, was owned by Tennessee Coal & Iron Railroad Company, of which Tennessee-born cotton industrialist John Hamilton Inman had been an investor and director until his death in 1896. Inman engineered the 'New South' tour that brought Kirk Munroe and his fellow Northerners to African Town to refashion the South's image as a leading industrial centre.

Cudjo, Jr. worked gruelling ten- to twelve-hour days underground dislodging, blasting, shovelling and transporting coal. African American prisoners, who made up most of the labourers, suffered brutal whippings at the hands of white guards and white prisoners, whose status as supervisors afforded them similar authority to plantation overseers. Explosions, falling rocks, runaway coal cars and diseases such as dysentery, pneumonia and syphilis combined to make death a constant threat.[25]

Cudjo, Jr.'s brother James made an appeal for his sibling's pardon, and on 25 July 1900 attorney Edward M. Robinson sent a petition for Cudjo's release to Alabama governor Joseph Forney Johnston. On 7 August, the pardon was approved.[26]

The petition dehumanized Gilbert as a social threat to and presented Cudjo, Jr. as an upholder of white supremacy. But other incidents revealed an unprotected Black community terrorized by apparent acts of racist violence and compelled to take the law into its own hands. Five months after Cudjo's release, his brother Aleck was one of three men and three women who were hit by a 'load of small shot' when a would-be assassin fired into a white man's grocery store, where a group of African Americans were congregating. The white law authorities quickly gave up trying to find the culprit. Six months later, an unknown assailant fired into Old Landmark Baptist Church during a service. A bullet ripped through Gumpa's thigh; another man and woman were also shot in the attack.[27]

Immediately after Gumpa's shooting, four of Kossula's five sons, Aleck, James, David and Cudjo, Jr., formed 'the Hickory Club', a vigilante group in African Town, to protect themselves from racist violence and to stop crime in the community. Members of the Hickory Club, which was based at the brothers' grocery store and whose members also included sawmill workers James Tunstall and Richard Winbush, patrolled the streets carrying revolvers and handcuffs and handed over troublemakers to the city's sheriff. At a time when Mobile's law enforcement was entirely white, the Hickory Club afforded its members a semblance of control and authority over their community. Even little Kanko fought to defend her town. As her granddaughter Mable explained, 'Someone believed to be the constable came by the house one day discussing some business property matters; my grandmother . . . physically picked up the constable and put the constable over the fence.'[28]

Gumpa's shooting presented him with huge economic challenges. He was doubly widowed at the time of the assault and was sole caregiver to his two surviving descendants, nine-year-old grandson Sidney and seven-year-old granddaughter Josephine, who he nicknamed Feeny. Yet he had barely recovered from his injury before his life came to a violent end.[29] On 11 September 1902, the small, slender man, who looked older than his 62 years, was hit by a train near his home and died either instantly or very shortly afterwards. The Fon nobleman's surviving shipmates were forced to come to terms with the sudden loss of a man deeply bonded to them despite his upbringing in the court of Dahomey, and who had been their town's leader and guiding authority for nearly forty years.

Gumpa's neighbour Nicholas Caffey took charge of Sidney and Josephine's welfare and went to Mobile County Probate Court seeking damages for the African man's death from the Mobile & Bay Shore Railroad Company. Gumpa left behind 2 acres of land, two cabins and other possessions valued at no more than $10 (equivalent to $350 in 2023). The location of his property was held by the court not to be desirable, and his estate was valued at a maximum of $40 (around $1,400 today). Judge Price Williams called Caffey's compensation claim 'doubtful, disputed and speculative', but he ultimately awarded him $500 (equivalent to $17,700 today), from which an allowance of $16 (worth around $570 today) was to be paid each month for the children's welfare.[30]

On 12 March 1902, Kossula was hit by a train, too. He rose early to plough a woman's garden for growing sweet potatoes, but was soon called home by Abile, who worried he was neglecting his breakfast and health. He then tricked Abile into helping him plant beans in his garden. 'You bringee me here for company,' she protested. 'Thass right,' he cheekily replied. After running out of beans and finding none at the local market, he travelled by wagon to Mobile to fetch more. Kossula bought the beans and set off for home. He was passing a slow rig on the railroad track at Government and Common streets when a switch engine, a small locomotive used for moving railroad cars, 'rushee down on me. Oh, Lor'! I holler to dem to stop 'cause I dere on de track, but dey doan stop . . . It rushee on and hittee de buggy an' knock me and hurtee my left side. Oh, Lor.'[31] Kossula's buggy was destroyed, and his terrified horse ran away; David, one of his twin sons, had to track it down the next day.

Kossula was carried to a doctor's office and given morphine. He spent the next 14 days in bed recovering from his injuries, which included three broken ribs. Kossula was left permanently disabled and could no longer work, so his shipmates made him sexton of their church, which they renamed Union Missionary Baptist Church a year after his appointment. Kossula felt lucky to be alive: 'It always a hidden mystery how come I not killed when de train it standing over me. I thank God I alive today,' he told Zora Neale Hurston. A white woman witness was so shaken by Kossula's near-death experience that she sent him a gift basket and checked in on him. She also visited the offices of the Louisville & Nashville Railroad Company to demand compensation on his behalf: the switch engine had travelled at speed through a busy street without using a whistle or bell and had seriously injured the ageing African man. When the company dismissed her campaign because the accident occurred in broad daylight, she advised Kossula to appoint a lawyer and sue the company.[32]

Kossula secured former Confederate lieutenant and US congressman Richard Henry Clarke as his attorney; he covered his legal fees by agreeing to share half the settlement. When the case went to court the following January, Kossula was stunned to find his lawyer had submitted a claim for $5,000 (equivalent to nearly $175,000 in 2023). The railroad company repeated its assertion that Kossula was at fault, but Clarke argued that the lack of warning on a busy street placed its citizens at grave risk and asked Kossula to show the injuries to his side that had left him unable to work for much of the past year. The judgment was so swift that Kossula was buying fish for Abile when he learned the jury had awarded him $650 (equivalent to $23,000 in 2023) that would be ready to collect the next day. But when David arrived at the lawyer's office, he found there was no money. 'De lawyer say dat too soon. Come back nexy week. Well, I send and I send, but Cudjo doan gittee no money.' No one explained to Kossula that there would be no money: Alabama's Supreme Court overturned the jury's ruling on appeal in October 1904.[33]

Sadly, there was to be little peace in the Lewis household over the next few years. Shortly after his father's train accident and about two years after his own pardoning, Cudjo, Jr. was shot by a 29-year-old African American man named Samuel Poe. Poe called himself a deputy sheriff, but there were no Black police officers in Mobile until the dawn of the civil rights movement. In fact, Poe was one of three members of the Blackthorn Club, which like the Hickory Club was a vigilante group set up 'for the preservation of peace and order at Plateau and vicinity'. Poe claimed that Cudjo, Jr. was wanted for a crime. But Kossula asserted that Poe made no attempt to arrest his son and instead hid in a butcher's wagon and shot him in cold blood when the wagon reached the family's grocery store. Cudjo was hit in the throat. His parents spent the next two days at his bedside praying and willing him to breathe. 'He try so hard to ketchee breath. Oh, Lor'! It hurtee me see my baby boy lak dat. It hurtee his mama so her breast swell up so. It make me cry 'cause it hurt Seely so much.' Kossula wished he 'could die in place of my Cudjo'.[34] Samuel Poe was never prosecuted for the killing and a few years later became the pastor of Hay Chapel (now First Baptist Church) in Prichard. Kossula tried to forgive him but felt that, as a man of God, Poe had a moral duty to apologize for the murder. Kossula was still waiting for an apology at the end of his life.

Sometime after this, Kossula's son David met a violent and sinister death over the Easter weekend. David came home from work hungry that late April day. Abile refused to serve her son's baked fish dinner until Kossula was ready to eat, so David took over his father's woodchopping. He then had a bath and told his parents he was going to Mobile to collect laundry. He promised to be back quickly. But David never made it to the city. He was decapitated by a train at Plateau Station. Kossula refused to believe that the headless body belonged to David until he saw his dead son's face. But Abile recognized her son's body straightaway and cried out in agony. 'My wife lookee at my face and she scream and scream and fell on de floor and cain raise herself up. I runnee out de place and fell on my face in de pine grove. Oh, Lor'! I stay dere. I hurtee so. It hurtee me so to hear Seely cry.' Abile's trauma was so upsetting to Kossula that he returned home only when his shipmates could promise she had stopped screaming.[35]

David's brother Polee Dahoo was overcome. His twin – and according to Yoruba belief half his soul – was dead. He demanded his father sue the railroad company, but Kossula was still chasing compensation for his own accident. Polee was furious, bereft, and fantasized about his parents' lost homeland. 'He say when he a boy, dey (the American Negro children) fight him and say he a savage. When he gittee a man dey cheat him. De train hurtee his papa and doan pay him. His brothers gittee kill. He doan laugh no mo'. Shortly after David's death, Polee left home saying he was going on a fishing trip. He was spotted heading towards Twelve Mile Creek, close to where the wreck of the *Clotilda* lay buried, and then disappeared. 'My boy gone,' Kossula told Zora Neale Hurston.'He ain' in de house and he ain' on de hill wid his mama. We both missee him. I doan know. Maybe dey kill my boy. It a hidden mystery. So many de folks dey hate my boy 'cause he lak his brothers. Dey doan let nobody 'buse dem lak dey dogs. Maybe he in de Afficky soil lak somebody say. Po Cudjo lonesome for him, but Cudjo doan know.'[36]

Kossula's second-oldest son James had just completed a 20-month jail sentence, almost certainly at Pratt Mines, for a charge of assault with intent to murder at the time of David's death and Polee's disappearance. (The victim and circumstances of the incident are not clear.) The experience – combined with the loss of his brothers – devastated James's health. He fell ill and died on 17 November 1905 aged just 35, leaving behind his wife Ella and two small daughters. Kossula recalled the death of his second son: 'we putee him in de bed. I do all I kin and his mama stay up wid him all night long. We gittee de doctor and do whut he say, but our boy die . . . He die holdin' my hand.' Abile and Kossula buried James near his siblings in Plateau Cemetery and inscribed his headstone with the message 'Sleep On And Take Thy Rest. God Called Thee Home. He Knoweth Best. Glory Be to God.'[37] They then returned to an empty house.

In late September 1906, a devastating hurricane swept through Mobile County, killing scores of people and causing millions of dollars-worth of damage. Communication to and from Mobile was cut off for five days and the city was plunged into darkness. Ships were wrecked and flood waters rose to seven feet in parts of the city's business district. The surrounding communities of Coden, Port and Bayou La Batz were almost destroyed. African Town emerged largely unscathed, with most of the devastation confined to Mobile's southwest coast. But the community would not be allowed to forget the white supremacist whirlwind that followed.

Although African Americans comprised most of the storm's dead, they were made its scapegoats by a fractious white community whipped up by racist fears and emboldened by a massacre in Atlanta two weeks earlier, in which white mobs attacked the city's African American community and killed at least 25 people. Black Mobilians were blamed for pillaging damaged property and armed militias patrolled the city with instructions to kill on sight. At least one African American man was beaten almost to death in the street. But the most brutal act of racist violence occurred on 6 October, when 17-year-old Cornelius 'Dick' Robinson and 20-year-old Will Thompson were snatched from a train by 200 men wearing white masks and armed with shotguns, revolvers and rifles. Robinson and Thompson were accused of assaulting white girls, but both died protesting their innocence. The youths were hanged just after noon from two live oak trees near Prichard Station, halfway between Quilla's home and African Town, and close to the site of David's death.[38]

Hundreds of white people gathered at the murder scene. One newspaper described the roads leading to the site as a 'mass of people' and estimated that the crowd numbered at least 2,000 by late afternoon. People cut off pieces of bark from the trees and clothing from the bodies. Some shot bullets at the dead youths; others shot photographs. At least one postcard featuring a dozen white men in suits and bowties posing around the bodies was widely circulated. The public spectacle of Black death fuelled a rumour that African Town was rising in revenge. In fact, the mob killings so traumatized the local Black community that the residents of Toulminville would continue to recall its horror 30 years later.[39]

At two o'clock one Sunday morning in late September 1907, almost a year to the day after Robinson and Thompson's deaths, a group of masked men bearing shotguns and pistols dragged an African American man accused of burglary through a rainstorm to the same cluster of oak trees from which the youths had been hanged. The mob wrapped a clothesline around the neck of Moses

Dossett and left his body to hang in the darkness for several hours. Dossett was not from African Town; his killing near there was intended to instil further terror in the all-Black community.[40]

Dossett's lynching placed African Town in significant danger. A rumour that its residents were holding secret uprisings to avenge his death was spread by white workers at a nearby factory, prompting a company of 25 militiamen to march on African Town at 4.45 a.m. the morning after Dossett's death. They encountered several community members with rifles and arrested them, but they released the men when they explained the weapons were for defence only. White men had been travelling to African Town to frighten the residents and they were worried they would be run out of town. Newspapers quickly dispelled rumours of a Black uprising. The *Birmingham News*'s summary was typical: 'The reports were started by persons of no authority and there was not the slightest occasion for sending for troops.' But Louisiana newspaper the *Daily Signal* made clear the violence that awaited the town's citizens: 'If armed negroes, who are in force near Whistler, Ala., prepaatory [sic] to attacking the whites of that town, in reprisal for the lynching of a negro last Saturday, move on Whistler, they will be given a warm reception. Four hundred farmers, armed with Winchesters, are awaiting the attack, and among them are some of the best shots in the South.'[41]

Amid such terrors, the Africans were forced to bury more of their shipmates. Innie passed away on 25 July 1906. She was probably about fifty-six years old. Her husband Osia Keeby bought her a gravestone whose message still clearly reads, 'A precious one from us has gone. A voice we loved is stilled. A place is vacant in our home which never can be filled.' Two other African Town shipmates, a woman named Adisa Wiggfore/Bruntson, who relocated to the community in the 1880s or 1890s from the village of Mauvilla about twelve miles away, and a man named Samuel Johnson died around that time, and Abaché buried Samuel, her American husband of four decades. Another African Town African, Anthony Thomas, died on 13 January 1910, leaving behind a sizeable estate for his second wife Susan and five adult children. Around the same time, Zuma was forced to bury her shipmate and son-in-law Sampson Martin, who was living in her household. Sampson, who also appears to have been a late migrant to African Town, was about sixty at the time of his death and left behind three young children, Jim, Zema (or Zuma) and Abraham, who are probably the three children who appear alongside their African grandmother in a photograph taken by Emma Langdon Roche.[42]

Grief for her lost children compounded Abile's physical deterioration, and she began to have dreams in which she found they were cold. Like Kossula, Abile felt acutely her children's isolation in the church graveyard. She took care of her sons and daughter when they were young by pulling up the quilts that she lovingly made for them to cover their chins as they lay in bed. In the final week of her life, she returned to the graveyard where four of her children were buried. Kossula found her walking up to each grave and re-enacting her bedtime gesture. Abile explained through tears that she did not want to leave him behind, but she was about to die as she needed to be with her children. 'She cry 'cause she doan want me be lonesome,' Kossula recalled. 'But she leave me and go where her chillun. Oh Lor'! Lor'! De wife she de eyes to de man's soul. How kin I see now, when I ain' gottee de eyes no mo'?' Abile died from chronic interstitial nephritis in the early hours of on 14 November 1908 at the age of 63.[43]

The devastated Kossula devised Yoruba-style parables to process his wife's death. He shared his first composition with his shipmates eight days after she died, thoughtfully bowing and then raising his balding head as he launched into his story:

Kossula: Suppose Charlee comes to my house and wants to go on to Pole[e]'s. He has an umbrella which he leaves in my care. When he comes back he asks for his umbrella – must I give it to him or must I keep it?
His shipmates: No, Kazoola! You cannot keep it – it is not yours!
Kossula: Neither could I keep Albine; she was just left in my care.

But everything about the couple's home reminded him of her. When he found two corn stalks knotted together in his garden, he could not bear to pluck them as he felt they symbolized the couple's relationship.[44]

Kossula's suffering was compounded by yet more sorrow. His oldest and last remaining child Aleck died of a short illness at the age of 41 on 9 December 1908, only a few weeks after his mother's death. Kossula was left alone with Aleck's widow Mary and her three children, who he persuaded to stay on the family compound, telling her that the land would be hers when he died.[45]

The *Clotilda* survivors who had endured such devastating hardships throughout their lives were dying, and those who remained now recognized that Africa was out of reach. They were torn between their lost homelands and loved ones who lay buried in Plateau Cemetery. As Emma Langdon Roche observed, 'Kazoola says he often thinks that if he had wings he would fly back; then he remembers that all he has lies in American soil – the wife who came from his native land, who was his helpmate and companion through the many years, and all his children.'[46]

Early in the twentieth century, Tuskegee Institute founder Booker T. Washington and his white assistant, pioneering sociologist Robert E. Park, visited African Town and interviewed Osia Keeby. Park was concerned about the rise of international Black social movements when he finally wrote about the encounter in 1919. He was so unwilling to acknowledge Africanist influences on US culture or that Black people might be forging identities beyond the nation that he dismissed the community's African language and cultural retentions. He also claimed Osia Keeby rejected Yoruba-speaking missionary Andrew Dickerson Phillips's repatriation efforts 50 years earlier because 'I crossed the ocean once, but I made up my mind then never to trust myself in a boat with a white man again.' Park used his meeting with Osia Keeby to argue that 'the slave had in fact very little desire to return to his native land'. Yet Park's story contrasted profoundly with the homesickness Osia Keeby described to Washington when he asked the ageing African man if he ever contemplated returning home. 'I goes back to Africa every night, in my dreams.' Unlike Park, the clearly moved Washington felt that 'I had discovered the link by which the old life in Africa was connected with the new life in America.'[47]

The *Clotilda* captives were not the only Middle Passage survivors who continued to dream of home well into the twentieth century. In 1904, a man named Cilucangy, who was one of the *Wanderer*'s many child captives and was known in the United States as Ward Lee, distributed a written plea to the public to help him reach Africa. Claiming to have received a vision from God a year earlier instructing him to go home, Cilucangy appealed to his readers' Christian charity. The agony of Cilucangy's exile was evident in his letter, in which he stated that he hoped 'to go back to Africa soon as I can get off to go' and 'beg[ged] every one who will please help me'. Cilucangy's repatriation campaign was unsuccessful, and he died 10 years later.[48]

In the final years of her life in the early twentieth century, Kanko's two-storey, three-bedroom house in the heart of Mobile was well furnished with a sofa, wardrobe, dressers and hat rack. A large cabinet safe held her crockery and cutlery; another safe held decorative dishes, including her china jug and silverware. The living room had two fireplaces, and framed photographs hung on the walls. Kanko also had a phonograph, and she so adored ragtime music, whose syncopated rhythms owed much to West African music, that she bought instruments for her son Napoleon's five oldest children. The Dennison band featured a cornet, trumpet, flugelhorn, trombone and euphonium; all the children could play instruments. Alongside her kitchen cookstove, Kanko also operated a large outdoor fireplace, which she used to boil clothes, cook and preserve meats and roast nuts and potatoes. As she cooked outdoors at night, Kanko often told her family Yoruba stories. She was a skilled craftswoman who carried on her person homemade black and white chequered handkerchiefs. Her aprons were made from coarse crocus sack, but she trimmed them with braid. In the cold months, she wore a velvet, beaded, dark brown overcoat.[49]

Even in old age, Kanko usually walked the four miles from her home in the centre of Mobile to Union Missionary Baptist Church, although in bad weather she caught the streetcar or horse and wagon. Every first and third Sunday of the month after his wife's death, Kossula travelled into Mobile by streetcar after church to have dinner and long conversations with Kanko and her family. The Africans spoke about their childhoods and explained their Yoruban customs to their families. The pair liked to walk the streetcar tracks together to explore their surroundings and catch up with other shipmates and were said to walk so briskly they exhausted their children and grandchildren. Afterwards, Kossula would return to clean the church and ring the evening bell.[50]

Kanko led an incredibly busy life. Emma Langdon Roche noted in 1912 that she 'works as a man' and continued to rear a fine breed of pigs for bacon. However, arthritis meant that Kanko now walked with a little metal cane, and wore glasses. Her mobility issues made it increasingly hard for her to walk the city with Kossula. Kanko was about seventy years old when she died on 16 April 1917, 18 months after her American husband James. She was buried alongside her husband and their daughter Equilla Amy in Plateau Cemetery.[51]

Like Kanko, Zuma walked with a cane by early 1917, although Christian Frederick Klebsattel, the German-born principal of the Emerson Institute, Mobile's oldest school for African Americans, judged her to be 'still quite active' when he counted her among the 'members of this original cargo, nine in number', who 'still survive and live in and near Plateau'. Yet when Tuskegee Institute secretary George Lake Imes met Zuma later that year, he remarked on her 'kindly, beaming face', but also on how her physical infirmities had rendered her immobile. Her useless body was a cruel reminder of her stasis. There was now no hope she would return home. Zuma died shortly after that encounter, with her US-born second husband John by her side. Two other shipmates died around the same time. Ossa's sister Omolabi died on 10 October 1919, and Abaché, the woman with the centre parting, followed her to the grave 13 days later.[52]

On 11 June 1922, the body of an elderly African woman was borne three miles from her home on St. Charles Avenue in Toulminville. Members of local Black masonic lodge St. Paul No 5 turned out in full to pay their respects to Quilla on that stifling yet cloudy summer day. The impressive turnout was a testament to the deep impression the elderly woman and her children had made on her community in the forty years since her return to Mobile County. Her son Albert became an engineer's assistant, and her carpenter son William was described as a 'well known' and 'respected citizen' of Toulminville when he died eight years after his mother. Chief among Quilla's mourners was Ephraim, who had been her husband for nearly fifty years, and who would follow his wife to the grave a mere seven months later, much as he had followed her to Mobile decades before.[53]

Like Zuma, who never forgot her mother's lullaby, Baldwin-based *Clotilda* survivor Amey Greenwood/Phillips shared a song from her homeland for her descendants right up until her death on 2 May 1923. The song left such an impression on Amey's great-granddaughter Eulean Marino Knight that she repeated the West African melody and words to a Mobile journalist just before her own death at the turn of the twenty-first century. 'My father Bailey Marino's grandmother, Amy [sic], would sing a song from Africa for the children. I was 8 years old, and I can remember it,' she explained as she launched into the tune. Kossula, Polee and Charlie also adapted a spiritual song from their homeland into a Christian prayer. They kept the original melody, but they turned the words into a plea for salvation.[54]

In the early 1920s, the Mobile Africans' church had a congregation of about two hundred. Osia Keeby was the pastor, and Kossula continued to serve as sexton, always ringing the bell to summon its worshippers. Polee's daughter Eva remembered the careful attention Kossula paid to his role: 'Every week Uncle Cudjo had a bench out there at the church. He would take all the lamps out there and set them on that bench. He'd wash the globes and fill the lamps and take them back in the church. Those lamps would be sparkling clean.'[55]

Dark-haired orisha initiate Polee died of pneumonia on 19 August 1922. 'Even to the day he died, he talked about going back to his home over there in Africa,' Eva recalled. According to Eva, the last words of all the survivors she spoke to were that they wanted to go home. Travelling chef Alice Williams passed away on 19 November 1922. Sad-eyed Osia Keeby, who was doubly widowed after marrying again in August 1913, died of influenza on 22 February 1923. Kossula was alone, and his daughter-in-law Mary worried that he might not recover from the loss of his last companion. The grieving African man, still bright-eyed but now slightly stooping, pointed to Plateau Cemetery a week after Osia Keeby's death and stated simply, 'All buried there.'[56]

12

Gee's Bend

In the summer of 1893, for the first time since her arrival in the United States 33 years earlier, Dinah stepped boldly back onto the Alabama River. Now aged 46, she had decided to relocate to the cotton fields of Gee's Bend, a community just across the water from her home in Bonham's Beat. Accompanying her on the water-borne journey were her three sons, nineteen-year-old Shad, nine-year-old John Henry and seven-year-old Jimmie. Her seventeen-year-old daughter Sally had gone to the town of Camden to find work but eventually joined her mother after starting a family; her adult daughter Minerva remained behind in Bonham's Beat. Gee's Bend was an 11,000-acre section of Wilcox County just east of Prairie Bluff and just south of Rehoboth that was framed by a loop in the Alabama River. The lower 7,500-acre section of the bend known as Primrose consisted of Black tenant farmers and a single white family of landowners. Gee's Bend was only three and a half miles north of Camden on the other side of the river, but there was no bridge to get there. Instead, travellers relied on a raft made from hollow logs whose front and back sections had no railings, which could only be used at low tide, and which was only access-ible via a narrow and winding dirt road that descended precipi-tously to the water. 'The steep descents to the ferry are actually terrifying,' wrote one 1930s visitor, who observed that 'no one ever uses it unless it is almost a necessity'.[1]

Dinah clung tightly to her little boys as they were borne across the water. She had paid a dime for the journey, the same amount she claimed was paid for her when she arrived in the United States. Despite the traumatic memories the trip might have evoked, Dinah bore the journey stoically so as not to frighten her children. Dinah had been without her US-born husband Gasoway for nearly five years following the couple's divorce in November 1888. Their 16-year marriage had been unhappy. Gasoway fathered a daughter out of wedlock and he married an African American woman named Mary Washington a month after his divorce.[2]

The remote, Black-majority neighbourhood of Gee's Bend, a community of around twelve hundred people at the turn of the twentieth century, afforded Dinah with a sanctuary from such misery. Poor transport links forced Gee's Bend to be a largely self-sufficient and highly skilled community. Like the African Town Africans, the residents built their own wooden houses from the local environment, covering the roofs with hand-cut pine shingles, and filling the cracks in the walls with clay to keep out the cold. Presbyterian minister Renwick Carlisle Kennedy remarked in wonder when he visited the community a few years after Dinah's death that 'in some of their houses the only purchased material used is a sack of nails.' Flair with handicrafts was a central feature of the community: the men and women made their own bedding and clothes and built their own furniture. Kennedy was deeply impressed by the people of Gee's Bend. 'Certainly they are underprivileged. But they are excellent people who have done remarkably well for the chance they have had.' Kennedy also found that residents were passionate about their nearly all-Black community despite its isolation. Dinah and her children were typical of its settlers, who unlike in other sections of the Black Belt where tenants moved frequently, opted to stay in Gee's Bend with their families for years and who 'love[d] their homes'.[3]

In the early twentieth century, Dinah established herself as one of the leading artists of Gee's Bend, a collective of Black Southern women whose visionary approach to quilt-making is now recognized as an important part of the United States' artistic heritage.

Historians have suggested that African American patchwork quilts generally, and Gee's Bend quilts specifically, may have been influenced by strip weaving, a traditional method of cloth production throughout West Africa in which strips of cloth are sewn together into a single fabric. Yoruba men and women both traditionally engaged in strip weaving. While men used large horizontal looms that produced narrow strips, women used a smaller vertical loom that produced broad pieces of cloth known in Oyo as kijipa.[4]

Although governmental aid workers visiting the community at the height of the Great Depression overstated Gee's Bend's geographical isolation and by extension its cultural exceptionalism, the many close connections between the Black Belt *Clotilda* survivors and the Gee's Bend quilters highlight the shipmates' enduring presence and influence in the region. Substantial African linguistic patterns were identified in Gee's Bend well beyond the end of the Civil War and even into the middle of the twentieth century. As late as 1939 a federal government pamphlet recorded, 'Even today some of the older people can speak a language that outsiders cannot understand – probably an African dialect.' The minister Renwick Carlisle Kennedy described Primrose, the 7,500-acre lower portion of Gee's Bend where Dinah settled with her children, as an 'Alabama Africa' when he visited the community in 1937, and he noted that other African Americans labelled members of the community 'Africans'. Kennedy noted only 'slight differences of speech' and a practice of burying a dead person before holding their funeral, but he remarked on 'pronounced variations' in the community's customs.[5]

In Gee's Bend, quilts were intrinsic to forging a sense of individual and communal identity in the wake of the traumas of the Middle Passage and slavery. For the community of Gee's Benders as well as other women in the African American South, these textiles were multi-generational documents of struggle and endurance. Across Dinah's lifetime in Alabama, most Gee's Bend quilts were made from work clothes. Much like the quilts that Abile imagined pulling over her children's gravestones, quilts formed from the clothes of lost loved ones served as acts of memorialization. 'I can point to my dead brother's pants or my father's shirt. Or I can point to my grandmother's dress and tell my kids what she did in that dress. We didn't have cameras growing up. We had quilts,' explained Lucinda Pettway Franklin. 'When we had babies to die, you'd see this little piece of baby clothes in the quilt. It was a meeting place for us.' Poignantly, Kossula kept boxes filled with 'ragged quilts' in his home at the end of his life; although they no longer had use value after his wife and children's deaths, he could not bear to part with them.[6]

Quilting was an essential artform for Black women in the South in the nineteenth and early twentieth centuries that was passed on from mothers to daughters. Gee's Bend quilts stand out for their improvisational blend of bright colours, abstract shapes and mixed materials, and have been likened by art historians to Abstract Expressionism, a mid-twentieth-century New York-based art movement broadly characterized by abstract representation, painterly spontaneity and emotional expressivity, a comparison that highlights the quilts' artistry even as it risks obscuring their deeper significances. The quilts were crafted in a community that lived in such poverty that its members were forced to repurpose worn-out cloths to stay warm. Yet the creativity of their patterns expresses something of the beauty in their lives that the red cloth flown on the *Clotilda* had promised to its captives, but which they were denied in the United States. Cloth was a highly prized commodity in West Africa.[7] If the racialized social structure of the Black Belt would not allow its Black residents to share in the wealth their enforced labour created, then the Gee's Bend community nevertheless forged its own forms of visual beauty.

Dinah's family had an extensive influence on the Gee's Bend community. Although her oldest son Shad soon relocated to nearby Canton Bend, her middle son John Henry eventually became the manager of the Gee's Bend estate, and her daughter Sally served as the community's midwife. Sally had 12 children of her own, who in turn had many children, including celebrated quiltmakers Loretta Pettway and Qunnie Pettway, who was the mother of another lauded quiltmaker, Loretta P. Bennett. Sally's granddaughter Arlonzia, who was also an important quiltmaker, estimated late in her life that she had thirty-two grandchildren and about thirteen or fourteen great-grandchildren.[8]

Dinah was not the only *Clotilda* survivor with close connections to Gee's Bend. Quilla, Ossa and their shipmate Lucy Hunt were enslaved to William H. Hunt in Rehoboth (now Route 1, Alberta), the 'land bridge' to Gee's Bend, and which art critics identified as part of its quilting community. Quilla's daughter Sudie married into what would later become Gee's Bend's largest quilting family. Quilla's son-in-law Richmond Anthony was the cousin of one Emma Coleman *née* Greer and shared a household with her when they were children. Emma in turn was the great-grandmother and guardian of Agatha Bennett, one of Gee's Bend's most celebrated quilters. Matilda lived less than ten miles away from Rehoboth. Redoshi lived 2 miles further north in Bogue Chitto, where she was enslaved alongside Alfred Moseley, who was the father, grandfather and great-grandfather of many of Gee's Bend's leading quilters. Another *Clotilda* survivor, Cresia Dansby, lived in Rehoboth with her African American husband Ned; her shipmate Peggy Crear lived 3 miles south of Gee's Bend in Camden after the war. Although their residences were officially Prairie Bluff and Boiling Springs, census data also show two other *Clotilda* captives, Rachel Taylor and Caroline Winters/Perkins, living and renting land next door to Quilla and Cresia with their African American husbands in 1880. Caroline died there sometime in the 1910s.[9]

Rehoboth's significance as a quilting centre in fact rivalled that of Gee's Bend in the mid-twentieth century. It was the official base of the Freedom Quilting Bee, an important – and overlapping – quilting cooperative that emerged among voting campaigners during the civil rights movement, and which drew national attention to the region's quilts for the first time. In December 1965, Episcopal priest Francis X. Walter of the Selma Inter-religious Project visited Possum Bend, 2 miles west of Camden, to document acts of Black voter intimidation, and was so struck by the artistry and originality of quilts hanging from a clothesline that he secured a $700 grant from the

Episcopal Society of Cultural and Racial Unity to buy 70 of them. 'From Highway 5 in Alberta down to Gee's Bend, there really were quilts piled up on the side of the road and people standing there waiting and I handed out ten dollar bills,' he recalled. Those quilts were sold at auction in New York and exhibited at the Smithsonian. Walter brought the money from their sales back to the region's quilters, who used it to establish the Freedom Quilting Bee to financially empower themselves and their families. The cooperative endured until 2012.[10]

The Mobile Africans also had reputations for artistry. According to Polee and Rosallie's great-granddaughter Beatrice Ellis, who was herself an artist and quiltmaker, 'They were very crafty people.' Polee's daughter Eva learned how to sew and crochet from her mother Lucy, who was Polee's second wife and Abaché's daughter. Eva earned money from her work from the age of 11 and made all her community's wedding dresses. As Addie Pettaway noted of the African Town community, 'Quilting was a favorite pastime for the women . . . Brilliantly colored pieces of cloth were hand-stitched into a variety of patterns.' Their descendants formed the Silver Leaf Sewing Circle to develop their skills and display their art.[11]

None of Dinah's quilts are thought to have survived, but a quilt created in the 1940s by her daughter-in-law Gertrude Miller was, for Arlonzia, reminiscent of her great-grandmother's treasured African cloth. Squares of fabric are laid together in long lines across the quilt. Laid diagonally on top of these squares are strips of bright-coloured string, creating an intricate pattern that appears visually to move back and forth across the quilt. Strikingly, the quilt's diagonal design echoes the intricate woven patterns of raffia material, a palm fibre used by Yoruba women and their ancestors to make cloth, ropes, baskets, hats and possibly shoes for thousands of years.[12]

Shortly before Dinah's relocation to Gee's Bend, the Black Belt Africans attracted the attention of outsiders for the first time. Knoxville College, a leading Black college in Tennessee established by the Presbyterian Church at the end of the war, set up a series of mission schools in Wilcox County in the 1880s and 1890s. The first school, initially named Prairie Bluff Mission and then Miller's Ferry Mission, was located halfway between Prairie Bluff and Gee's Bend and framed in both directions by the Alabama River. Much like the worship under the arbours that Dinah described to her great-granddaughter Arlonzia, the Miller's Ferry Mission began in the open air. Community members congregated on long benches under a giant live oak tree for four years before the school finally secured a permanent building in 1888. Such was the hunger for learning among Black people in the Black Belt that the school attracted students from Alabama and beyond. Prairie Mission, just across the river from the Miller's Ferry station and a mile north of Prairie Bluff, by then a ghost town, was chosen as the site of a second school and 600-acre farm in 1894. A church was added there four years later.[13] The Prairie Mission building still stands and was added to the National Register of Historic Places in 2001.

Knoxville College's work drew the support of the Black Belt *Clotilda* Africans, who recognized the schools as a belated chance to improve the lives of their children and grandchildren. The shipmates shared their stories of transatlantic kidnap, separation and enslavement with the missionaries, who were horrified to find they had landed in the heart of a recent transatlantic human trafficking operation. They were equally appalled to learn of the abuses the community still endured. 'In some sections of the surrounding country,' despaired Knoxville College president Ralph Wilson McGranahan, 'there is almost as great cruelty practiced by the plantation owners as when their tenants were their own property and liberty is a misnomer for the kind of life they live.'[14]

In the 1890s, the Africans' suffering was particularly acute. Cotton prices were already at extremely low levels when the United States entered a four-year recession in what became known as the Panic of 1893, the worst economic crisis in the nation's history until the Great Depression. What compounded the Africans' desperate situation was voter fraud, voter restriction legislation and outbreaks of racist terrorism as attempts to counter a nascent cross-racial populist movement. Black people had continued to vote in large numbers in the Deep South in the 1880s, and class-based party alliances of Black and poor white voters secured as much as 32 to 49 per cent of the vote in 10 Southern states that decade, posing a real threat to the business and landowning elites who controlled the Democratic Party in the South. When a third-party agricultural movement emerged in 1892 to contest the Democrats' hold on power in Alabama, the party machine responded with voting legislation, ballot stuffing and violence.[15]

In the 1930s, civil rights leader Amelia Boynton Robinson watched the cotton statistician for Dallas County gloat and laugh as he recounted how ballots were stuffed and swapped to invalidate Black people's votes at the turn of the twentieth century. Future Speaker of the US House of Representatives William Brockman Bankhead recorded in his diary a method of voter fraud as practised in the 1894 election by a law student in nearby Conecuh County, who was rewarded with a government job for his work: 'one of his methods was to place the Democratic tickets in the bottom of the ballot box, and cover them over so as to give it the appearance of being the bottom of the box. When the votes were to be counted, he would take up the paper cover off the tickets and count them as if voted, in the meantime having pocketed as many Republican votes as he had placed Democratic in the box.' Political alliances among Alabama's Black and poor white voters would have defeated the Democrat elites and elected populist leader Reuben Kolb as the state's governor in 1892 and 1894 if not for such voter fraud and voting restriction legislation. Kolb sought to overturn landowners and industrialists' stranglehold on the state's wealth and power by implementing fairer taxation and industrial worker rights; he also initially promised to protect Black people's voting rights, although he reneged on such a promise in 1894. Nearly fifty thousand fewer votes were cast in 1894 than in 1892 due to an 1893 law introduced by Montgomery legislator and future Alabama Supreme Court Justice Anthony Dickinson Sayre that handed the power to appoint election officials to the state governor, implemented highly restrictive voter registration, mandated that election officials rather than trusted friends assist blind and illiterate voters and removed references to party affiliation from the ballot.[16]

At 10.00 p.m. on 4 May 1895, the first of two acts of racist violence struck at the heart of the Africans' community when the Miller's Ferry mission was deliberately set alight. Pine kindling and oil were used to turn the pine structure into what one witness described as a 'mass of flames'. Everything was destroyed, and the Africans and their neighbours were left in terror and despair. 'We never felt safe at home nor was it prudent to leave home,' one missionary recalled. William Henderson, a red-haired, Scottish-born, Reconstruction-era probate judge who owned the land on which the school was built and aided the mission's work, tried to prosecute the crime before a grand jury. But the jurors dismissed the case despite compelling evidence the culprit was 43-year-old Prairie Bluff overseer-turned-Possum Bend farmer Clark Lyles. When Henderson publicly named Lyles as the arsonist, the farmer went armed to the Scotsman's store with his brother John and fired three shots at him from close range. Two of the bullets somehow missed their target; the third tore through Henderson's undershirt but missed his flesh. The school's principal, Peter Cooper Cloud, who gathered much of the evidence confirming Lyles's guilt, fled to a new mission school in Summerfield, Dallas County, to escape a similar attack.[17]

The surrounding community of mostly cashless sharecroppers resolved to build a new school despite the dangers and spent a painful year at the height of a depression scraping together $84 (equivalent to $3,000 in 2023) and then reconstructing the property. Community members hauled lumber through the winter rain on roads and footpaths that had turned to heavy mud. At least one man laboured through the cold without rest in just a worn coat and thin shirt, such was his determination to provide an education for his children. 'I can't learn 'em myself, so I must help fix a place for them what can,' he declared.[18]

The second act of racist violence that terrorized the Africans occurred around the time of the reconstructed school's completion. In July 1896, Matilda's neighbours Israel Mobley and William 'Little Billy' Hunter were lynched in Bogue Chitto. Thirty-nine-year-old farm labourer Mobley and 29-year-old servant Hunter were accused of attempting to kill Colonel Charles Davis Hunter, one of the region's largest landowners. Their public executions served to warn followers of Reuben Kolb's populist movement, which sought to break wealthy white landowners' and businessmen's political stranglehold on Alabama, that resistance to the political status quo would not be tolerated.[19]

Charles Hunter was an outspoken racist who described white supremacy as the reason to vote for Democratic banker and industrialist Joseph Forney Johnston in his 1896 campaign to defeat the populists and become Governor of Alabama. Hunter had recently advertised for 50 German farmer families to settle on his property. Blaming Black labourers for the dramatic fall in cotton prices precipitated by the Panic of 1893, he sought to restaff his black prairie soil with white people. The grapes, pears and apples in his 20-acre fruit orchard and the Jersey cows that grazed on his Bermuda grass and clover also signalled his shift away from a cotton economy built on African American labour. Hunter hoped that Black workers would be forced to the bottomlands of Mississippi and eventually 'crowded to the wall'.[20]

The Black Belt Africans entered a new century marked by fear and despair, which was compounded by the deaths of several of their shipmates and relatives. Many of the Africans and their descendants died in poverty and isolated misery. At the turn of the twentieth century, the Black Belt economy was framed even more strongly than it had been during slavery around a single crop: cotton. In 1900, only 390 Black families in Dallas County owned their properties. Matilda and Redoshi were rarely able to venture beyond the two stores in the tiny township of Rehoboth, ten miles southeast of Bogue Chitto, eight miles southeast of Martin's Station and three miles above the loop in the river leading down to Gee's Bend. The streets in the Black section of Selma remained unpaved well into the twentieth century, and the only roads in the surrounding countryside led to the white landowners' gates.[21]

Matilda was one of about seven hundred tenants living and working on Atlas Martin's land in Athens at the turn of the twentieth century, an estate so vast that a newspaper report likened it to a 'small city'. Matilda continued to labour at Martin's Station when Atlas Martin died in May 1908 and the land passed to his son-in-law, Victor Boardman Atkins. Atkins was one of the most powerful men in Selma and was mayor of the city at the time of his father-in-law's death. His store, V. B. Atkins Grocery & Commission Company, was located directly opposite the Alabama River and was one of nine major wholesale grocery businesses in the Black Belt. Businessmen such as Atkins served as commission merchants and cotton buyers, buying – and setting the price of – cotton while they sold groceries.[22]

Redoshi and her husband Yawith were still trapped on their former enslavers' land in Bogue Chitto at the turn of the twentieth century, too, and their captors' youngest daughter Ida still lived in the Lapsley Street mansion where the Africans had been forced to labour during slavery. In June 1908, Ida's husband, Colonel William Washington Quarles, gave a lecture on tuberculosis at a school in Selma, mobilizing the language of science to justify the South's slavery-based past. Desperate living conditions and a lack of access to medical care meant the Africans and their neighbours were particularly susceptible to infectious diseases such as tuberculosis, which killed Matilda's mother Gracie and quite possibly her shipmate and husband Guy and their children John and Mary. Quarles's talk formed part of a special exhibition on the disease, chaired by Matilda's landlord and employer Victor Boardman Atkins, in response to growing concerns about its prevalence.[23]

Noting that tuberculosis rates between 1901 and 1905 were twice as high among Alabama's Black population as among its white population, Quarles asserted how much better off Black people were during slavery, when enslavers intervened in their labourers' health to maximize their productivity. 'Then, they were well-housed, amply clothed, sufficiently fed, forced to abstain from excesses of habit and living, in every way well-cared for by a master who valued each as a precious nugget of gold.' Remarking with no intended irony that Black people did 'ninety-nine per cent' of the labour to keep households such as his Lapsley Street mansion clean, Quarles accused the state's Black population of slovenly behaviour and of spreading germs everywhere. His talk was judged to be 'scholarly in its grasp of the vital subject'.[24]

Three months after his speech, Quarles was struck on the knee by a large rock as he walked down Broad Street in Selma. It was thrown by a 12-year-old Black child and future First World War soldier named Leon Lindsey, who was arrested and fined $15 (equivalent to $500 in 2023) plus court costs for his act. Lindsey mimicked Quarles's pained reaction to the blow when he appeared before the court.[25]

While the son-in-law of Redoshi and Yawith's enslavers used the language of pseudo-science to blame Black tenant farmers for their poverty and poor health, the daughter of Quilla's enslavers also drew on her lived experiences to promote a narrative that Black people were better off during slavery. William and Siloma Hunt's youngest daughter Mamie Hunt Sims relocated from Selma to Chicago in the early twentieth century. Her move coincided with the racist massacre in Atlanta in September 1906 that killed at least 25 African Americans. The massacre drew the North's attention to the South's culture of racist violence, which stirred Hunt Sims to write a book that sought to downplay the mass killings by romanticizing the social order that had held the Africans in bondage. *Negro Mystic Lore* (1907) was a collection of 17 short stories written in imitation Black Southern dialect that purported to document Hunt Sims's memories of life on her mother's plantation immediately after the war. Hunt Sims emphasized in the book's foreword that her purpose was 'to show the real kindly feeling existing between the people of the South and the *better class* of the negroes'. She read her stories and other tales written in imitation Black Southern dialect throughout Illinois, Indiana and Michigan, and her book received sufficient notoriety for anthropologist Arthur Huff Fauset to list it in the seminal Harlem Renaissance text *The New Negro* (1925) as an example of 'Negro Folk Lore'.[26]

In April 1917, the United States entered the First World War after the German government tried to forge an alliance with Mexico and German submarines began sinking US-flagged merchant ships to counter British trade embargoes. Matilda could only look on as all five of her sons were called before the draft board on different dates over the next 18 months, including her 'baby boy', 20-year-old Thomas, who was conscripted into the US Army. Many of the men of Gee's Bend, Dinah's son John Henry among them, were also called before the board.[27]

As Matilda anxiously awaited her youngest child's wartime fate, Redoshi suffered her own loss. Yawith died in the cabin in which he had been enslaved on 12 October 1918, nearly sixty years after his kidnap and transplantation to Alabama.[28] His death record listed his age as 100, but he was probably in his early eighties at the time of his passing. Redoshi was left to come to terms with the loss of her lifelong protector and beloved husband, who laboured alongside her throughout her years of exile in the United States, and who she guided around their property with the aid of a wooden cane as he became increasingly frail. Yawith had never been able to escape his enslavers' family and remained in debt bondage to them throughout his life.

With the help of her widowed daughter Lethe and her grandchildren William and Josie, Redoshi buried Yawith's body deep underground on her property according to Yoruba custom, to ensure his spirit stayed close to her. She then planted bottles face-down around his grave. She arranged the half-buried objects in geometrical formation to mirror the circular layout of her hometown's houses before surrounding them with flowers. Redoshi selected each bottle for its ability to catch the sun and they stood in sight of the worn but still enduring picket fence that Yawith had built years before. Much like the gate that Kossula constructed for his teenage daughter Celia/Ebeossi, Redoshi laboured to create a protective outline for her lost husband's grave.[29] She then prepared to face the future alone.

13

Cocolocco

On a cool, damp morning in late October 1895, Bougier decided to go to town. She put on a warm cap, placed a chequered apron over her thick jumper and filled a hand-woven basket with long twisted sticks of sassafras root. She took in the plant's sweet, cinnamon-like aroma as she draped the basket on her arm. She then walked briskly to the brand-new Prattville Junction railway stop next to her home to catch a train six and a half miles south to Montgomery.[1] Bougier was now nearly sixty years old. Her homeland was as far out of reach as ever, and more than three and a half decades had passed since she had last held her three lost children. But she was still determined to re-enact as closely as possible the regular trading trips to Ogbomosho that she undertook in her youth. She wanted to inhabit once again the life of a mid-nineteenth century Yoruban woman. She prepared to take her wares to market.

Bougier had been perfecting her trips to town since following her shipmate, former child cook Ella, to Elmore County along with her young daughters Amanda and Mary roughly two decades earlier.[2] Unlike the more isolated Mount Meigs, Elmore County had long been linked to Montgomery via rail and was a popular destination for affluent white tourists, who came to hunt, barbecue and swim in the nearby Jackson Lake. But the new station, which had been built to replace the little railway stop 2 miles north at Coosada, presented novel challenges to the small, dark-skinned woman.

Buying a ticket meant testing out on an unfamiliar and potentially hostile white ticket inspector her English language skills, which remained a struggle throughout her life. Trains arrived not just from Nashville in the north and Louisville in the south, but also now from Prattville in the west, and Bougier had not only to locate the right train, but also work out where to stand on the platform to ensure she was in the right place to board the separate 'Coloreds' carriage.

The dangers and humiliations endured by Black travellers in the South were increasing rapidly in the 1890s as the region's white elite adopted a policy of *de jure* segregation to cement its grip on political power. Local laws segregating railway cars first began appearing in the South in the late 1870s and 1880s and gained federal approval six months after Bougier's first trip to Prattville Junction's new station, when the United States' Supreme Court shut down a challenge to Louisiana's 1890 Separate Car Act by a light-skinned Louisiana Creole man named Homer Plessy. The Supreme Court's *Plessy v. Ferguson* (1896) ruling held that segregated state facilities were acceptable, provided such facilities were equal.

But the reality of public travel for African Americans in the South was profoundly unequal. As a Black woman, Bougier was consigned to her trains' front carriages. Front coaches were the most danger-ous sections of trains as they were the most exposed in the event of a crash. They were also the most crowded, worn out and dirty. The front carriage was typically where luggage was stored, and most railroads simply recycled their old and discarded coaches to avoid having to purchase separate carriages for Black passengers. Soot and smoke from the trains' coal- and wood-fired engines poured into the front compartments, blasting noxious fumes into Bougier and her fellow passengers' lungs and staining their clothing. In his 1920 book *Darkwater*, celebrated scholar and activist W. E. B. Du Bois raged against the indignities he was forced to endure when travel-ling south. 'The "Jim-Crow" car is up next the baggage car and engine. It stops out beyond the covering in the rain or sun or dust. Usually there is no step to help you climb on and often the car is a smoker [smoking carriage] cut in two and you must pass through the white smokers or else they pass through your part, with swagger and noise and stares. Your compartment is a half or a quarter or an eighth of the oldest car in service on the road. Unless it happens to be a through express, the plush is caked with dirt, the floor is grimy, and the windows dirty.'[3]

At Prattville Junction, Bougier found her way onto the Montgomery train and disembarked onto the open platform when it pulled into the city's Union Depot less than an hour later. When Bougier first began travelling to the Union Depot, there was, according to the *Montgomery Advertiser*, 'a ladies' waiting room, [and a] gents' waiting room', spaces she knew that, as a Black woman, she could not use. But for the past 10 years, there had been three waiting rooms, 'one for the ladies, one for gentlemen and one for colored people'.[4] Bougier now had access to a washroom, but she had to share it with men.

The trip back to Prattville Junction was extremely hazardous for the ageing African woman. The Union Depot tracks were narrow and crowded, and trains arrived haphazardly at the platforms, making it hard to know which one to catch. Though Union Depot was finally replaced by a new, improved Union Station building in 1898, the segregated women's toilet facilities were rarely cleaned and frequently blocked. Even worse, as station employee and future civil rights leader Edgar Daniel ('E. D.') Nixon despaired, the segregated drinking water was 'carried in one of the buckets used for mopping the men's rest room'. The penalty for a Black person 'trespassing' or 'loitering' in the wrong section of the segregated station was a day in court and a dollar fine. Remarkably, Bougier learned not only to navigate the station's strictures and humiliations, but by persuading its white staff to give her nickels when she fell short of the 15-cent train fare home, she even found a way to make it compensate her.[5]

Bougier exited the Union Depot and stepped onto Commerce Street, the area's main throughfare since its founding as 'East Alabama Town' in 1818, catching sight of the riverfront and the site of her smuggled landing from one of the Meahers' steamboats 35 years earlier. The city's financial district had changed drastically in the years since her arrival. The once dusty walkway was now paved with cobblestones. Solitary yellow carriages shot about as if by magic in directions prescribed by the long black strings that stretched above them, the mules that were initially needed to pull them having long since been retired. The First National Bank founded 40 years earlier by *Wanderer* survivor Jackson Smith's enslaver Josiah Morris had become a six-storey 'skyscraper', the first high-rise building in the city. Montgomery's population had more than tripled in size since the *Clotilda* voyage, and Bougier had to plot a course through the unforgiving crowds of people, streetcars and wagons also seeking to traverse the city's busiest street. For an ageing Black woman, walking these streets was a particular challenge: whenever she encountered a white pedestrian heading in the opposite direction, she had to step out of their way.[6] Bougier walked purposefully past Montgomery's banks, barbers, jewellery shops and newsagents, and found her regular trading spot amid the busy market stalls selling fruit and vegetables.

During the 50 years she spent traversing Commerce Street, Bougier became an avid consumer as well as a trader. She bought tins of loose tobacco, which she smoked through a wooden pipe, as well as snuff and chewing tobacco. Bougier learned to smoke a pipe and chew tobacco in the United States, but the taking of snuff was a habit she brought with her from home. Her lunch was often a grocery store-bought cheese sandwich and a Coca-Cola. This was her favourite drink, although she could never pronounce its strange American name. 'Cocolocco,' she ventured when asked. Bougier never knew that part of its name derived from the West African kola nut, an important trading crop, flavouring ingredient and spiritual object for the Yoruba that was frequently used in sacred offerings to the orishas. Nor did she ever know how closely the drink's history was linked to her own. On 16 April 1865, two days after General James Harrison Wilson's troops ransacked Rush Jones's plantation and liberated Bougier and her fellow *Clotilda* captives, the same soldiers fought pharmacist and Confederate home guard John Stith Pemberton at the Battle of Columbus, inflicting a gunshot wound and a saber wound across his chest and abdomen that were said to have caused his lifelong morphine dependence, although his addiction may also have been linked to earlier chronic health issues. After the war, Pemberton became fixated on the kola nut, whose active ingredient is caffeine, as a potential morphine-free painkiller. He first included kola nut extract in his French Wine of Cola tonic. When his adopted home city of Atlanta passed an 1885 law severely restricting alcohol sales, Pemberton moved into the soft drinks industry and used the nut to create Coca-Cola.[7]

Bougier did not find many buyers on Commerce Street that late October day. In warmer months, she gathered bunches of home-grown mint to sell. At the height of summer, her split-wood basket held river-fed berries, plums and other wild fruit that she foraged from around the oak trees and lakes below Prattville Junction. Bougier's handpicked berries were fat and succulent and always sold well in Montgomery. She was especially proud of their quality. But the sassafras roots, which she used for medicinal purposes, held less obvious appeal to the city's white consumers, and she typically sold them to stables, which turned her produce into horse fodder.[8]

After a short while, Bougier moved on to her other regular trading spot on what had once been known as Market Street and was now called Dexter Avenue. She walked past Commerce Street's intersection with Bibb Street, where Alex Given's grocery store and John Miles Smith's furniture shop once stood, and where Reuben and Jackson had been forced to live and labour. Sixty years in the future, 15-year-old Claudette Colvin would be roughly arrested and handcuffed at that exact spot for refusing to move to the back of the bus because a 40-year-old white woman did not want to sit along-side a Black child. Bougier walked on and reached Court Square, where the Exchange Hotel still stood.[9] It was at Court Square that Rosa Parks, following Colvin's example, refused to give up her seat to a white man and was arrested, igniting the 1955−6 Montgomery

Bus Boycott that reversed *Plessy v. Ferguson* and rendered travel segregation unconstitutional. Bougier walked past the square's artesian well where enslaved families had once been sold and separated. The watering space had recently been beautified with a cast-iron fountain adorned with birds and Narcissus-like figures and topped with a statue of Hebe, the Greek goddess of youth.

Bougier turned left onto Dexter Avenue to continue selling her wares. Stretching in front of her at the end of the vast walkway was the giant white Greek Revival Alabama State Capitol, the first home of the Confederacy and, 60 years in the future, the end point of the Selma to Montgomery marches, the campaign that stirred US President Lyndon B. Johnson to pass the 1965 Voting Rights Act and outlaw the discriminatory practices that had for so long denied the vote to Black people throughout the South. Just in front of the capitol was the Second Colored Baptist Church. The red-brick building, which would later be renamed the Dexter Avenue Baptist Church, was completed in 1889 and became the site of Dr. Martin Luther King, Jr's first pastoral appointment in 1954. It was from that building's basement that Dr. King led the Montgomery Bus Boycott.[10]

Although Bougier did not live to see the end of segregation, she witnessed the determined resistance to its birth. A two-year boycott of Montgomery's streetcars arose in response to an ordinance, championed by the *Montgomery Advertiser* and effective from 10 August 1900, that segregated the vehicles' passengers. Bougier watched as the autonomous yellow carriages fell empty for months. Black people walked long distances and waited for mule-driven wagons in the blazing sun rather than board streetcars. African American hackmen lowered their prices to provide affordable travel to their protesting passengers. People picketed streetcars, handed out flyers and badges, and placed signs around the city to promote their campaign. African American newspapers galvanized protesters to continue their efforts. The boycott, which was one of many such protests in every ex-Confederate state, was remarkably tenacious and successful. Over the first 21 days of the campaign, the Montgomery Street Railway Company lost more than $1,400 (equivalent to more than $50,000 today) in fares, and even had to close one of its lines. One visitor to the city was impressed that what they termed a 'universal boycott' was still in place after nine months, and the city's streetcar company was so hard hit financially that it temporally suspended its segregation policy. African American newspaper *Southwestern Christian Advocate* rejoiced. 'We are gratified to know that our people united at something long enough to win a victory for the race.'[11]

But in 1903, city authorities introduced a repressive law that criminalized the campaigners' activities, forcing its leaders to risk heavy fines or months of hard labour. Protesters waiting to board wagons instead of streetcars could be charged with vagrancy, and it became illegal even to mention that a boycott was underway or planned. Suddenly, boycotting became too challenging and danger-ous to undertake. The law would bring anti-segregation crusades to a thudding halt for more than fifty years.

Bougier was not the only *Clotilda* shipmate to witness – and perhaps even participate in – Montgomery's streetcar boycott. One of the trolley lines went past 350 South Jackson Street, a house two blocks east and one and a half blocks south of the capitol that had, for at least 20 years, been the home of Komo, the 15-year-old boy renamed Robert by his kidnapper Rush Jones who became a well-digger and taught himself to read after his liberation. Komo was a widower living alone at the time of the boycott, but by 1904 he was sharing the property with his new bride Clara. By the end of the decade, after saving up his wages as a well-digger, gardener and labourer, he finally managed to buy the home outright after renting it for years.[12]

Komo's South Jackson Street house placed him at the heart of Montgomery's prosperous Black middle class. At the bottom of the street was the State Normal School for Colored Students, later Alabama State College and now Alabama State University, whose faculty members Professor Jo Ann Robinson and Mary Fair Burks were the first people to call for a bus boycott after Rosa Parks's arrest. In 1920, the house immediately opposite Komo's property,

309 South Jackson Street, became the Dexter Parsonage, the home of 12 Dexter Avenue Baptist Church pastors, including civil rights leader Vernon Johns and, later, Dr. King. The Kings rose early to watch the first empty bus pass their home at the start of the 1955–6 bus boycott, and Dr. King's wife Coretta Scott King and her ten-week-old daughter Yolanda narrowly escaped harm when white supremacist terrorists bombed the building during the campaign. As Coretta recalled, 'I thanked God that we were yet alive . . . A few feet had spared our lives.'[13]

Bougier continued to travel to Montgomery throughout the new century, where her daily labours also brought her close to the court-house and her captors' old home. Rush Jones died in 1887, but in March 1893 a memorial window dedicated to the enslaver and bearing the inscription 'B. Rush Jones, M. D.' was placed at the First Presbyterian Church just across from his property. The tribute, which was visible on entry to the building, coincided with a grow-ing practice of venerating the Confederacy which, sometime later, Bougier would find herself caught up in. Confederate memorializa-tion began immediately after the war and was led by elite Southern women, including Jones's widow Frances Amelia Taliaferro Jones. Its roots lay in Civil War nursing, which brought upper-class women into the public sphere for the first time. Montgomery's central loca-tion in Alabama made it an important medical centre during the Civil War. Jones worked as a surgeon in the city's Confederate hospi-tals, and Amelia was drawn to caring for wounded Confederate soldiers by her husband's occupation. Labour shortages meant the couple's captives were compelled to work in the hospitals, too. Their African child cook Ella was probably one of the enslaved women and girls who were made to clean, cook and tend to patients in the three-storey, 265-bed Ladies' Hospital on Commerce Street.[14] After the war, elite women mobilized this newfound experience as public organizers and political actors by spearheading a cultural narrative that deflected attention from Southern leaders' abandonment of the

Union and obscured the horrors of slavery by valorizing the Confederacy.

Sophie Bibb, who worked alongside Amelia Jones and her captives at the Ladies' Hospital, led the Montgomery campaign to venerate the Confederacy. Bibb was president of the Woman's Hospital Association during the war. After the conflict, she organized the Society for the Burial of the Dead, serving as president of the Montgomery branch of what became known as the Ladies Memorial Association (LMA). Amelia and Alex Given's younger daughter Sarah Whiting were both early members of the Sophie Bibb Chapter of the LMA.[15]

The LMA devoted itself to memorializing the Confederate dead, and the elaborate tombstones and annual ceremonies in Montgomery's Oakwood Cemetery, as well as the statue to honour Montgomery's Confederate dead that was unveiled on the grounds of the capitol on 7 December 1898, and which confronted Bougier every time she walked down Dexter Avenue, were the results of its efforts. The centrepiece of the monument, a 70-foot shaft topped with a woman bearing a sword and flag, was made in its members' image. The female figure, who stood above four pedestals bearing an infantryman, cavalryman, artilleryman and sailor, was intended to signify 'Patriotism'. As the LMA acknowledged, 'In one hand is held a flag, the other a sword, as if a mother tendered the blade to her sons for her defense.'[16]

The LMA branches morphed into the United Daughters of the Confederacy (UDC) in the mid-1890s. A Sophie Bibb chapter of the UDC was established in 1896. The goal of the new organiza-tion, in the wake of the failed populist movement of the 1890s and in parallel with the implementation of *de jure* segregation and African American and poor white disenfranchisement, was to cement the Southern elite's power by defending its history. Monuments to Confederate leaders in carefully selected public places including town squares, parks and courthouses sought to dictate the historical narrative, and the UDC played a central role in raising funds for them. The UDC worked to ensure its members' husbands, fathers and grandfathers were memorialized not as human traffickers and abusers who committed treason by seceding from the Union to prolong human bondage, but, rather, as brave men who fought vainly to defend a noble heritage, or 'Lost Cause'. As the organization grew, so did the number of Confederate statues, approximately half of which were placed between 1903 and 1912 alone. Would-be UDC members were also expected to study history, and history discussions and programmes were key components of group meetings.[17] State and local chapters set up history committees and appointed historians with specific responsibilities for documenting the past.

Bougier became ensnared in the UDC's Lost Cause propaganda when she appeared in a 1907 *Selma Times* newspaper supplement dedicated to elite Confederate women. The call for submissions to the supplement was led by Thomas McAdory Owen, founder of the new Alabama Department of Archives and History, the first US state archive, which was housed in the state capitol. The project formed part of a campaign by the Confederate Veterans, Sons of Veterans, Memorial Associations and the UDC to narrate upper-class Southern women's actions during the war, and an edition was planned for every major Southern city newspaper. Revenue from the supplements' sales was intended to help fund a Confederate women's monument, but they were also intended as stand-alone histories. As Owen explained, 'It will be the special design of the editor to collect the scattered historical fragments and materials pertaining to them for *permanent preservation* in the Alabama supplements.'[18]

UDC Sophie Bibb Chapter historian Toccoa Page Cozart rewrote Bougier's history for the supplement. Drawing on Bougier's status as a local celebrity and her own friendship with the Jones's daughters – she boasted in her narrative about drinking from one of the family's buried silver goblets – Cozart reimagined the Yoruban woman's liberation from the Jones plantation to falsely position her as a devoted servant who resisted her freedom.

Cozart's story served as a public, if coded, admission that Rush

Jones imprisoned Africans. But her narrative implicated Bougier in Lost Cause mythologizing in ways that wilfully obscured both her origins – she was simply an 'old "pure African"', seemingly transplanted to Alabama decades before the war – and the horrors of her enslavement. In Cozart's fantasy narrative, Bougier, who was still in her twenties and the mother of a small daughter at the time of her liberation, was reconceived as an elderly woman who defended her captors and who spoke in a crude Southern dialect instead of her monosyllabic, heavily accented English. According to Cozart, the small woman boldly confronted the Union Army and threatened, in barely comprehensible language, to 'sen' town, ha' yo' Yank' rasc'l rest' ('send to town and have you Yankee rascal arrested'), which provoked the soldiers' laughter. When the soldiers' plundered goods were engulfed by flames, Cozart claimed the Yoruban woman thanked a Christian God that the property of 'Old Mare', the man she called 'Lushey' in real life because she never mastered English well enough to pronounce the 'r' in 'Rush', would not fall into their hands. Cozart insisted that Bougier continued to take satisfaction from her action even after being ordered by the soldiers to her cabin. 'But aw had de las' wud, I did!' she still claims.[19]

As Cozart rewrote Bougier's past, one of the historian's elite male counterparts acted to control the African woman's public image on the streets of Montgomery. In early February 1907, a month before the *Selma Times* supplement went to press, Bougier was accosted on the street by George William Craik, the railroad tycoon and banker who had played host to the 'New South' artists and writers 20 years earlier and who very likely led the group to African Town. Craik's father-in-law William Owen Baldwin was Rush Jones's fellow surgeon and business partner. Craik brought with him an unfamiliar white man in his mid-thirties with sideswept brown hair, round glasses and a moustache almost as thick as his own. Ray Stannard Baker, founder of the new periodical *American Magazine*, was one of the early twentieth-century US's most highly regarded journalists, a social reformer, or 'muckraker', whose views on public policy earned him visits to Theodore Roosevelt's White House.[20]

Baker was travelling through the South in the winter of 1906–7 to conduct the first major investigation by a mainstream journalist into America's racial divide, the Atlanta race massacre that incited the lynchings of Dick Robinson and Will Thompson near African Town having drawn national attention to the South's racist violence and sparked fears of a race war. The threat of a major journalistic investigation into Southern racist violence worried the region's white elites, who followed Baker's work closely. They had little cause for concern. Despite his progressive reputation, Baker wrote with the dominant race and class prejudices of his age. He sought to placate Southern elites, relied heavily on them for his sources and failed to grasp the ways in which the terror of lynching was deployed as a form of social control. He even stayed at the Exchange Hotel, where he wrote to W. E. B. Du Bois asking for biographical information to substantiate his views on the limits of African American social mobility.[21] That made it easy for Craik to steer Baker's thinking when he introduced him to Bougier.

Despite explaining that she was 'secretly landed at Mobile', Craik told Baker that Bougier was a *Wanderer* survivor and framed her in a way that led the journalist to believe Southern slavery was ultimately beneficial to 'ignorant' Africans. Baker failed to meaningfully interview Bougier, concluding that 'she speaks very little English, and I could not understand even that little.' Instead, Craik forced the 70-year-old African woman, despite her passionate resistance, which Baker read as 'superstitious terrors', to have her photograph taken, and made her daughter Amanda pose for the camera, too. Bougier held herself proudly in the white headscarf and loose-fitting robe she wore over her shirt and jumper. As the camera's shutter clicked, she turned her head away from the lens in a defensive gesture, revealing on her cheek the facial mark she acquired as a child.

Baker used the photographs as Craik intended: to create a pseudo-ethnographic visual narrative of American assimilation and 'progress' in an article that mused on whether 'a mere century or two in America has really operated to whiten the blackness of thousands of years of jungle life', but which concluded: 'It is certain that the darkest American Negro is far superior to the native African Negro.' The picture caption did not name Bougier but referred to her simply as a '*typical* African Negro woman and her daughter'. Ray pointedly noted that Amanda was married to a 'respectable-looking' farmer; over the course of a generation, the family had 'progressed' from 'jungle life' to 'civilized' Americans.[22]

Over the next few years, Bougier's former shipmates – and Rush Jones's former captives – would die, Komo while labouring on the Autauga plantation of William 'Will' Adams Gunter, Jr., one of the most powerful men in Montgomery. Gunter served as Montgomery's mayor from 1910 to 1915, around the time of Komo's death, and again from 1919 until his own death in 1940. The pro-secessionist Gunter family were among the region's most powerful enslavers before the Civil War. Will Gunter's grandfather Charles Grandison Gunter was so deeply invested in slavery that he moved to Brazil after the war because it was still legal there. Komo's death on Gunter's plantation underscores the striking proximity between the slave trade and the development of car and air travel in Alabama. Gunter's family purchased the city's first automobile in 1908, and he was such a keen promoter of air travel that he was named 'the father of commercial aviation in Montgomery'. Gunter Air Force Station was named after him.[23]

Unsey, the teenage shipmate who like Bougier fell pregnant to an unknown man shortly after her arrival in Montgomery, passed away 60 miles southeast of Mount Meigs in Spring Hill, Barbour, on an unknown date early in the new century. Nannie, the four-year-old girl who survived the Middle Passage with her mother Sarah, was sharing a home on Pike Road in Mount Meigs with her mother when she died on 22 April 1910, surrounded by her Alabama-born brothers Ben Smith and Sam Pettiway and their large families.[24]

Ella, the child forced to labour as a cook in the Jones household during slavery, was a widow who lived alone after her daughter

Victoria moved out to marry in December 1900. But at least four of the African woman's five surviving children lived near her home on Reese Ferry Road in Autauga County. Her oldest and youngest sons were her immediate neighbours. Peter and George were successful farmers who managed an estate on Reese Ferry Road on land probably inherited from their father. The brothers' business was so prosperous that when the Gillespie Auto Company organized a tractor demonstration and barbecue to encourage African American farmers to invest in the new machinery, their property was chosen as the venue.[25]

Ella died at her Reese Ferry Road home on 6 November 1918, five days before armistice brought an end to the First World War. She was surrounded on her deathbed by a vast extended family, including her children Victoria, Peter, George and Joseph, and at least 20 grandchildren. Peter and George purchased a sturdy headstone to commemorate their mother, which still stands at her resting place in McQueen Place Cemetery (also known as Whiting Cemetery) in Prattville. The thick stone slab records that she was 70 years old when she died. Carved at the top of the headstone were the simple words 'Mother of Peter and George', which expressed succinctly both the brothers' love for their mother.

The passing of Bougier's shipmates meant that the African woman was alone. At the close of each long day in the city, Bougier travelled back to the Prattville Junction home she shared with Amanda. But still she set out determinedly each week to sell her wares in the city. As late as 1925, a newspaper article acknowledged that Bougier was 'known to practically every man, woman and child in the city . . . and her customers were numerous'. Walking for Bougier had become a physical challenge, but she still travelled to the capital every Thursday and Saturday morning from Prattville Junction. Even her fear of the speedy automobiles first introduced to Montgomery by the city's mayor – and Komo's employer – Will Gunter's family in 1908 and now a regular sight on Commerce Street and Dexter Avenue did not stop her visits to the city. At least Bougier knew that if she had a bad day and failed to sell enough produce to pay for her train fare home, after 40 years she could still claim a nickel from Union Station's long-serving ticket agent Samuel Tate Suratt, who she called the depot man. Before Suratt's retirement in the mid-1920s, Bougier presented him with a large basket of sassafras roots as thanks for his kindness.

In the summer of 1923, a young journalist named Clare Hagedorn, aware that 'everybody, almost, knows Ole Bulja', figured that the African woman would be a fitting subject for a *Montgomery Advertiser* profile. Hagedorn tried in her article to mould Bougier into an early twentieth-century white Southern fantasy of Black womanhood. But the woman that the journalist encountered could not have been more different from Cozart's racist fantasy, and Hagedorn was confounded by her refusal to play into stereotypes. Bougier was neither 'placid' nor 'gentl[e]', but instead met her enquiries with 'shrewdness' and suspicion. Nor was Hagedorn, who lived until 1996, especially interested in the horrors that had brought the elderly African woman to Alabama. Instead, she gleaned most of the *Clotilda* survivor's story from Susie Jones Waller, daughter of Bougier's former enslaver, who repeated the lie that Bougier was a *Wanderer* survivor to conceal her father Rush's crime. Hagedorn was, however, forced to acknowledge that Bougier's distrust was 'aroused perhaps by her early experiences' and that she still met her US prison with firm resistance. As the journalist noted, 'the years have not thoroughly succeeded in taming her spirit, despite her industrious habits'.[26]

Hagedorn's failure to conduct a meaningful interview with Bougier was partly the result of communication issues. English was still a challenge to Bougier. Those ignorant of her language battles perceived her as taciturn. As the *Montgomery Advertiser* later noted, 'She is an odd old soul given more to silence than speech.' But Bougier toyed with the young journalist, too. As a member of a society conditioned to value its Black residents only in terms of their labour, Hagedorn noted that the nearly ninety-year-old woman had a reputation for being industrious. Bougier denied that was true. 'I know nothin' 'bout work. When I tired, I quit,' she replied. When Hagedorn, who sought to frame Bougier as an historical anachronism, asked her if she was 100 years old, the African woman laughed. 'I dunno. Two hunderd, mebbe,' she suggested.[27]

In the spring of 1925, two years after Hagedorn's interview and a full 65 years after the *Clotilda*'s voyage, Bougier became seriously ill. Her family rushed her to Hale Infirmary, the only hospital for Black patients in the city. Surgeons at the two-storey building on Lake Street, seven blocks east and one block south of Komo's former home, were forced to amputate her leg following an infection of that limb, and she spent several weeks recuperating at the infirmary from the trauma of her operation. Bougier's absence from Montgomery's streets was soon noted, and the *Montgomery Times* ran an update on the state of her health three days after she returned to her Prattville Junction home.[28]

For the first time since her kidnap, Bougier had once again to confront physical confinement in a small space. Her small, frail body was too weak for crutches, and she could no longer leave her cabin, let alone venture into the city to sell her wares. Hearing of Bougier's plight, an African American maid at Union Station resolved to help the woman she had watched come and go from the station for years. Eugenia Streety launched a fundraising campaign at the station to pay for a wheelchair. She managed to secure contributions from both Black and white employees, and quickly raised $22.50, equivalent to $400 today.[29] Streety had never received a formal education, and like Bougier endured a daily battle against humiliation and social marginalization; yet her campaign to make the segregated station provide for a formerly enslaved African woman meant she was one of the few people who achieved any kind of meaningful redress for a *Clotilda* survivor.

Just under two months after Bougier left hospital, an African American porter at Union Station delivered the wheelchair to the elderly African woman. The man may well have been future civil rights leader E. D. Nixon, whose willingness to mount a court challenge to bus segregation using Rosa Parks as a test case led to the Montgomery Bus Boycott, and who almost led the anti-segregation movement before the 26-year-old Dr. King took over. Nixon was at the time a former baggage handler-turned-Pullman car porter at the station, and he probably knew Bougier and her shipmate Ella from childhood.[30]

The porter lifted Bougier up gently, laid her in the chair and pushed her into her yard. The elderly woman was deeply grateful to be freed from her cabin and whispered her thanks to the young man. 'First time I been in the sun since I been home. Thank you all, very much.' The *Montgomery Advertiser* celebrated the achievement as a joyful end to Bougier's story. The newspaper even looked ahead to her death and imagined the chair being passed to another 'charity case'. 'The wheel chair is to be hers as long as she needs it – and when "Ole Bulja" shall have gone "beyond the sun" the chair will be bestowed upon some other worthy unfortunate.'[31] But in reality the gift was a small mercy that underscored the lifelong injustice she endured and the finality of her separation from her homeland. Bougier could get about now, but her world had shrunk immeasurably. She would never again be able to travel even the short distance to town.

For the next five years, Bougier wheeled herself as best she could around Prattville Junction. Finally, on 27 June 1930, she died in the shade of her cabin, surrounded by her two American daughters and her many grandchildren and great-grandchildren. The mercury hit the ceiling on the day of Bougier's death, just as it had 70 years earlier when she was first displaced to Alabama.[32]

14

The Courthouse

The dredger *Alabama* arrived in Mobile on 25 May 1925. Kossula watched as the machine spent months sucking up sand from the riverbed to transform the low-lying land and waterways around African Town. The State of Alabama had decided to turn 550 acres of what one journalist described as 'useless swamp' north of the city into a factory site and rail and ocean terminal system, and the dredger soon began churning up parts of the elderly Yoruban man's former home. Kossula started selling sections of his estate after family members' deaths. He sold a plot one week after Abile's passing to the physician who reported her death, probably to pay for her medical and funeral bills. His sales in 1920 and 1922 of three other plots coincided with the death from tuberculosis of his 23-year-old grandson Emmit Lewis, and the death of Emmit's daughter Bertha May Lewis at just 25 days old. But government pressure rather than immediate need drove Kossula's surrender of land to Mobile County in November 1926 to make way for what became the Alabama State Docks and the Cochrane Bridge and Causeway, a continuous paved highway running ten and and a half miles in length from Magazine Point to Baldwin County.[1]

Having witnessed the destruction of his hometown in his youth, Kossula watched the community he forged become commercialized by a state that continued to disregard him. The Meaher family still owned much of the land in the area and all the mill sites. They leased about a hundred acres next door to African Town to the International Paper Company to build what would become one of the largest – and most polluting – papermill sites in the world. Other highly polluting industries sprang up around the waterfront. The developments brought jobs but few other benefits; the community had to wait until 1960 for indoor plumbing, running water and paved and lit streets.[2] Yet the highway that now cut through his home brought Kossula unprecedented visibility in the last decade of his life, which he used to assert his community's history and cultural beliefs and even to forge unexpected connections with his remaining shipmates and homeland.

One of the first professionally trained anthropologists of African descent arrived in African Town three months after the *Alabama*. Twenty-six-year-old Arthur Huff Fauset was collecting Black Southern folktales for the American Folklore Society and wanted to speak with the last known African-born slavery survivor. Kossula demonstrated the endurance of his Yoruba heritage by sharing with Fauset one of his parables, 'T'appin' (Terrapin). The tortoise is the most popular animal in Yoruba folklore, a substitute for humankind whose misbehaviours warn against moral failings. In Kossula's story, the tortoise tricks his fellow animals into sharing their food during a famine but runs out of food for his family when he then tries to feed his whole village. Kossula's parable appeared between poems by Langston Hughes and Countee Cullen and artwork by Aaron Douglas in Alain Locke's edited collection *The New Negro* (1925).[3] *The New Negro* was the key text of the Harlem Renaissance, an interwar explosion of Black art, literature, music and dance.

Fauset was only interested in documenting folklore, however. It fell to fellow anthropologist and *The New Negro* contributor Zora Neale Hurston to record Kossula's story. Hurston was one of the first people to cross the Cochrane Bridge and Causeway when, on the instructions of her tutor, the pioneering anthropologist Franz Boas, she followed Fauset to African Town in a two-seater Nash coupé she nicknamed 'Sassy Susie' in late July 1927. Although Hurston was the first trained scholar to document the *Clotilda* conspiracy, she was also an inexperienced researcher whose essay on Kossula consisted mainly of unattributed text from Emma Langdon Roche's 1914 book on the slave ship.[4] The *Journal of Negro History*, unaware of the plagiarism, published Hurston's essay that October, where it caught the attention of an elderly white patron of Black artists named Charlotte Osgood Mason.

Mason sent Hurston back to interview Kossula as part of what would become a 27-month collecting trip through the African American South. On 14 December 1927, the writer boarded a train at New York Penn Station bound for Mobile, and she began interviewing the elderly man two days later. Over several visits, Hurston documented Kossula's life story and collected a series of his parables. She received a 16mm camera as part of her work contract, which she used to shoot a three-minute film of the African man – possibly the first professional recording by an African American woman filmmaker. The partially overexposed silent footage shows the 86-year-old, in patched trousers, a dark jacket and with a wide-brimmed hat covering his by now nearly bald head, stepping onto, and speaking on, his porch before wielding an axe at a woodpile to demonstrate his enduring strength. He bows his head to tell a parable, gesturing expressively and smiling at Hurston as he speaks. Kossula also agreed to be photographed and asked that the graves of his beloved wife Abile, and their children Aleck, Celia, Cudjo, Jr., David, and James be included in the frame. He prepared for the photo shoot by dressing in his best suit but also by removing his shoes, as he wanted to look like he was in Africa, 'where I want to be'.[5]

Mason ultimately expected Hurston to write a book on Kossula that adhered to her own fantasies of a static African past, which she saw as an escape from 'weakening white civilization . . . whose spiritual life is choked by the love of material possessions and material power' and a 'flaming pathway' back to the 'Truth'. Hurston chafed against her patron's expectations, against a work contract that demanded she collect but not creatively interpret folkloric material, and against the limits of historical enquiry to capture the beauty and artistry of Black folk cultures. The writer went so far as to distance herself from her work with Kossula in a May 1928 magazine article. 'Slavery is sixty years in the past. The operation was successful and the patient is doing well, thank you . . . Slavery is the price I paid for civilization.' But slavery wasn't sixty years in the past for Kossula, who forever ever mourned his homeland. He begged Hurston to reach out to his lost family, who he wanted to believe were still alive. His voice broke as he explained, 'I lonely for my folks . . . I know they hunt for me.'[6]

As Hurston interviewed Kossula, the *Alabama* dredged up objects that were identified as parts of the *Clotilda*, and visitors to Mobile Bay claimed bits of wood which were supposedly from the slave ship. In an 8 March 1928 letter to her friend Langston Hughes, Hurston wrote that she had sent wood from the schooner to Mason, who was also Hughes's patron, and joked about sending four to six more boards of wood from the vessel to the elderly woman so a frieze outlining the history of slavery, starting with 'capture in battle in Africa' and ending with Hughes's celebrated poem 'The Weary Blues', could be carved on it. On 10 May, Hurston also sent a piece of wood to Alain Locke that she claimed was from the *Clotilda*.[7]

The Alabama State Docks were formally opened on 25 June 1928. A *Birmingham News* reporter identified the docks as the largest pier in the nation and called their opening 'one of the greatest steps taken by the state in many years'. Three months later, another *Birmingham News* reporter effused that, since the project's completion, 'the former swamp and jungle north of Mobile, where released savages from the last of the slave ships found a congenial home, has become one of the busiest spots in Alabama'. An anchor supposedly belonging to the schooner was displayed at the docks and photographed for a local newspaper in 1933.[8]

A week after the docks opened, Hurston drove in a Chevrolet coupé paid for by Mason from Mobile to Bogue Chitto, where she found 80-year-old Redoshi and her 66-year-old daughter Lethe. Bougier, Dinah, Matilda, Redoshi and possibly also a man named Nathanael Brown over in Snow Hill at that stage were probably the last living *Clotilda* survivors outside Mobile.[9] The docks' opening drew crowds from across the state and beyond, and Hurston may have learned of Redoshi's existence and location from a visitor there.

Redoshi readily shared her life story with the anthropologist. But Hurston told only Langston Hughes of her visit to the African woman. At the end of a 10 July 1928 letter to her fellow writer, Hurston reported that she had met one of the 'original Africans', claiming – inaccurately – to have encountered her on the Tombigbee River. Describing Redoshi as 'most delightful' and a 'better talker' than Kossula, Hurston nevertheless asserted to Hughes that 'no one will ever know about her but us'. Hurston's secrecy probably represented an attempt to wrest some of her collecting material from her patron, and she may have planned to insert Redoshi's memories and stories into *Mule Bone*, a play she and Hughes were working on together against Mason's wishes.[10]

Hurston's belief that Redoshi would remain hidden was mistaken, however, for less than a year later the Yoruban woman befriended a 23-year-old African American woman named Amelia Isadora Platts (later Boynton Robinson). Boynton Robinson, who died in August 2015 a week after her 110th birthday, was a Georgia-born Tuskegee Institute graduate who relocated to Dallas County in April 1929. Boynton Robinson and her future husband Samuel William Boynton arrived in Bogue Chitto as US Department of Agriculture county extension and home demonstration agents charged with teaching Black Southern farmers how to improve the health of their crops and homes. Frustrated by the futility of such work, they soon sought to effect more meaningful social change. Together with her husband and six others, Boynton Robinson founded the Dallas County Voters League and spent 30 years spearheading a Black voter recruitment drive from her home on Selma's Lapsley Street, the same street where Redoshi's former enslaver Washington Smith had his mansion and where the African woman had laboured during slavery. In fact, Boynton Robinson's invitation to Dr. Martin Luther King, Jr. to visit Selma after her husband Samuel's death in 1963 culminated in the Selma to Montgomery marches, which in turn precipitated the 1965

Voting Rights Act. Dr. King and his fellow activists used Boynton Robinson's Lapsley Street property as their campaign headquarters. Boynton Robinson was one of the marchers beaten by state police for attempting to cross the Edmund Pettus Bridge during the first Selma to Montgomery march on 7 March 1965, which became known as 'Bloody Sunday'. A photograph of the 59-year-old woman's unconscious body was published around the world, which fuelled international outrage and support for the marchers' campaign.[11]

Bogue Chitto left a deep impression on the burgeoning civil rights activist. Boynton Robinson later described the township as a 'fearless community' where people taught themselves to read and where ministers instilled in their congregations the importance of registering to vote. Shortly after Boynton Robinson arrived, the Ku Klux Klan marched to a man's house with the intention of lynching him for failing to doff his hat to a white man. But they were met by a hail of bullets and fled in terror. The Klan never dared return to Bogue Chitto.[12]

Boynton Robinson's account of the radicalism of Redoshi's community at once underscored the injustices the African woman endured throughout her life, but it also highlighted her remarkably close association as a Middle Passage survivor with the US Civil Rights Movement. Selma Voting Rights leader Bernard LaFayette, Jr. emphasized Bogue Chitto's significance to his campaign's success in the mid-1960s. He recalled that the area was nicknamed 'Freetown' and was so renowned for its pride and independence that it was selected as the location of a voting registration drive when application numbers in Selma began to drop. The residents of Bogue Chitto responded so enthusiastically to the campaign that more Selma residents were inspired to register.[13]

The young Boynton Robinson was particularly inspired by Redoshi, and she described her visits with the African woman as 'among my richest experiences in the early 1930s'.[14] Redoshi asked the young woman for her company one summer afternoon during those years before the home demonstration agent's monthly education meetings. As Boynton Robinson stepped onto Redoshi's property, she marvelled at the elderly woman's immaculate yard and the half-buried objects arranged in geometrical formation and surrounded by flowers to mark Yawith's grave, and the still-enduring picket fence built by Yawith years earlier.

Boynton Robinson sat near Redoshi on a bench held up by two ageing trees, and noticed the newspaper that covered the dark boards of her two-room cabin. The elderly woman used the makeshift wallpaper for insulation and probably for aesthetic reasons, too. Photographs show that Kossula and the Gee's Benders used newspaper for the same purposes in the 1920s and 1930s. Struck by the neatness of the wallpaper, Boynton Robinson learned that Redoshi used flour and water combined with copper sulphate to deter cockroaches and mice. Boynton Robinson recognized such ingenuity as evidence of how much she could learn from Bogue Chitto. 'I remembered that the county agent had told me I could learn a lot from these people.'[15]

Redoshi smiled as she rocked in her rocking chair and began a conversation with the young woman:

Redoshi: We are going to have much rain real soon.
Boynton Robinson: How do you know?
Redoshi: Yesterday's sunset, last night's moon, and the clouds
    always tell me what we're going to have. You know what the
    moon bring us? Not what you call a lady all the time. She do
    lot controlling. Moon come up, big and full, then she get
    fuller, then she get down. She take all she can from earth's
    surface and us. Then she turns this way and that way. When
    you see her ends up, she's full of water and on her back. Soon
    much rain come, she let it out and keep on 'til she point to
    the earth. Then her cup is empty and upside down and start
    picking up more water. The sun help too, picking up much
    water the moon drop.[16]

In March 1930, Hurston returned to New York to draft her book on Kossula. But she chose not to complete revisions to *Barracoon* that might have led to its publication in her lifetime, despite a determined effort from Charlotte Osgood Mason, with the aid of Alain Locke, to find a publisher for the project. Unlike Mason, who demanded that she document what she saw as a disappearing African past, the anthropologist wanted to show that Black Southern cultures were dynamic, not static. Hurston was also unaware of the extent to which Europeans' guns and hunger for African labour precipitated the demographic breakdown and turn to militarism that drove the transatlantic slave trade. Nor did she recognize that slave traders on the African continent would not have understood their victims as 'Africans' but, rather, as members of alien societies with whom they were at war. Thus, she reacted badly to learning from Kossula and Redoshi that they had been kidnapped and sold by their fellow Africans. As she admitted in her 1942 memoir, 'the inescapable fact that stuck in my craw, was: my people had *sold* me and the white people had bought me. . . . my own people had butchered and killed, exterminated whole nations and torn families apart, for a profit before the strangers got their chance at a cut.'[17]

Like many of her Harlem Renaissance contemporaries, Hurston ultimately found the subject of slavery too difficult to confront. Aside from 'T'appin's' insertion in *The New Negro* and Alain Locke's allusions to slavery-era stereotypes and demand in that text that African Americans not be viewed through the 'dusty spectacles of past controversy', African American writers rarely engaged directly with slavery in the 1920s. Authors concerned with proving their right to citizenship were keen to distance themselves from a past marked by oppression and perceived social stigma. Equally, Hurston's writings sought to avoid expressions of Black bitterness against white racism, which she felt disempowered Black people by reinforcing their status as victims.[18] *Barracoon*'s publication also risked spotlighting Emma Langdon Roche's *Clotilda* book and exposing Hurston's plagiarism of that text. Yet Hurston's abandonment of *Barracoon* meant that Kossula's voice and the crime of the *Clotilda* would continue to be obscured for decades. *Barracoon* would not be published until 2018.

Kossula continued to draw interest from elsewhere, though. In mid-May 1930, white South Carolina writer Julia Peterkin interviewed the African man. Peterkin had just won the Pulitzer Prize for *Scarlet Sister Mary* (1929), a novel about the Gullah people, a South Carolina community with strong African cultural and language retentions. Accompanying her was Doris Ulmann, a New York-based photographer who had immortalized in sepia some of the most famous writers, artists and intellectuals of the age, including poets Robert Frost, William Butler Yeats and the Meaher brothers' cousin Edna St. Vincent Millay, Alabamian disability rights advocate Helen Keller, singer-activist Paul Robeson, sociologist Max Weber and Albert Einstein.[19]

Kossula agreed to be photographed by Ulmann, who sought to capture the psychology of a formerly enslaved subject in the manner with which she depicted New York's leading artists and thinkers. Her picture shows a sitting man with visible marks on his cheeks and above the bridge of his nose gazing away from the lens in contemplation. He wears a clean white shirt with buttons and a pocket and patched trousers. He holds a cane in his right hand and rests a pile of patchwork in his lap as if he has just been interrupted by the photographer's presence. Sewing was a male Yoruba tradition that Kossula carried with him to the United States. During their 43-year marriage, Abile would wash his clothes and Kossula spent his evenings patching them.[20]

News of Kossula's meeting with Ulmann and Peterkin caught the attention and concern of Charlotte Mason, who had been conspiring to conceal the elderly man from other researchers. In early September 1930, Kossula dictated an apologetic letter to Mason to thank her for her generosity – she had been providing him with a monthly allowance – and to assure her that he had resisted sharing his history for three years on Hurston's instructions until Ulmann and Peterkin's visit: 'the young Lady told me you said not to there fore I dont let any one see it any more . . . I only Did that so they Would Help me But there is no one Did for me as you.'[21]

As Mason schemed to conceal Kossula, Boynton Robinson

arranged a meeting for Redoshi's benefit. In January 1931, the young woman brought an African student and anticolonial activist to Dallas County to observe her educational work and to visit the elderly woman. Thirty-year-old Danieri (Daniel) Kato was the first Ugandan to enroll at Tuskegee Institute, where he was completing a degree in agriculture. Kato's overseas education formed part of a wider African interest in Black US learning institutions as models for achieving independence from European rule. He brought information about the National Association for the Advanced of Colored People (NAACP) back to his home country, which led to correspondence between his older brother Joseph R. Kamulegeya, secretary of the Young Baganda Association, and the NAACP's research director, W. E. B. Du Bois. The Young Baganda Association was an anticolonial protest movement that inspired sister associations in neighbouring Kenya.[22]

Redoshi was overcome with joy at meeting a fellow African and shared stories and memories of her lost homeland. Boynton Robinson was so moved by Redoshi's happiness that she could still recall the encounter nearly four decades later, although she misremembered the East and West Africans as members of the same ethnic group.

> We took [Kato] to meet Aunt Sally, and they began to talk about Africa in general. Suddenly she screamed with delight, the two of them were from the same tribe! This was the first time she had met anyone from Africa who could speak and understand her language since she had left her home more than 80 years before. She was filled with joy. As they talked about their country, the village, the nearby rivers, speaking many times in their own language, I sobbed aloud with happiness for her.[23]

Redoshi was a Yoruba-speaking woman from present-day southwest Nigeria; Kato was a Bantu-speaking member of the Ganda people from Uganda's capital Kampala. But Redoshi's pleasure at meeting a fellow African after seven decades in exile was still immeasurable. Kato provided her with a vital psychological connection to her lost homeland and showed it was possible to travel back and forth between continents. Even her former enslavers' family was forced to admit that Redoshi 'was always homesick for her old home. She always said that she would like to go back home'.[24]

Meanwhile, Kossula's old cabin was falling into disrepair, his clothes were worn and the front sections of his shoes flapped when he walked. He could no longer refuse attention from visitors other than Hurston. The *National Geographic*'s assistant editor Frederick Simpich arrived in Alabama in February 1931 on a six-week visit to research a major feature on the state. Simpich's trip overlapped with the arrest, near-lynching and first trial of the Scottsboro Boys, nine Black youths who were falsely accused of raping two white women on a freight train. The sentencing of eight of the youths to death by an all-white jury in early April of that year caused national outrage. Yet Simpich's article paid no attention to the case. Unlike Ray Stannard Baker 24 years previously, the Northern journalist had not come to investigate Alabama's race relations; his goal was to promote its tourism and industry, just as the 'New South' group had sought to do 45 years earlier. The president of the Chamber of Commerce at Bayou La Batre, a city just east of the Point aux Pins peninsula where the *Clotilda* first anchored with its kidnap victims, welcomed the *National Geographic*'s 'additional publicity', which he predicted would help to 'bring in hundreds of visitors, new capital and permanent residents'.[25]

Simpich treated Kossula as a historical 'curiosity' and his article barely mentioned slavery. But in meeting him, he caught something of the tragedy of the African man's plight. Simpich found Kossula had never stopped speaking and thinking in Yoruba over the many months and years since the deaths of his shipmates. He counted to 10 and named the objects in his home for the journalist. The pain of no longer being able to share his language was acute and mixed with existential fear. 'I got nobody talk with. I forget Dahomey talk,' he declared.[26] For Kossula and the other displaced Africans, his language was his identity. If he lost his language, it would sever his last connection with his homeland.

On the evening of 21 October 1931, the Big Zion AME Zion Church in Mobile held a fundraiser and ninetieth birthday celebration for the man widely thought to be the last living African-born slavery survivor. Large numbers of Black and white Mobilians gathered to hear speeches by the city's former mayor and other leading dignitaries, spirituals by Franklin Street Baptist Church choir, and an account of Kossula's story as well as a Yoruba song delivered by the man himself. Local bakeries donated cakes for the occasion, which raised $65.72 (equivalent to $1,300 in 2023) to provide Kossula with a weekly allowance and to cover his medical costs.[27]

Kossula's benefit drew the attention of Walter Hart Blumenthal, a self-proclaimed authority on 'American Aboriginal life' whose wife Claudine hailed from Mobile. Blumenthal interviewed Kossula for the New York *Evening Post* in November 1931, and the article was quickly reprinted in the *Literary Digest*, a magazine with a readership of 1.4 million in 1930. Simpich's article appeared concurrently in the December issue of the *National Geographic*, whose circulation in 1930 was 1.3 million. Seventy-one years after his trafficking, Kossula was suddenly famous across the United States. Opportunists sought to turn his story into a New York vaudeville attraction, but he turned down their offer to appear on stage.[28]

News of Kossula's press and public attention somehow reached Matilda and Redoshi. Perhaps a sympathetic reader with knowledge of both Kossula and Redoshi put the pair in touch with each other to remedy the isolation that Kossula described to Simpich. Regardless of how the news reached them, that December, Matilda and Redoshi traveled 150 miles south for a reunion with their shipmate.[29]

When Redoshi had last seen Mobile Bay as a young girl 71 years earlier, she was disoriented, emaciated and sick with dehydration. Now, it looked very different. The river's banks had been relocated since its dredging, and the once lonely, tree-strewn waterway around Twelve Mile Island had been transformed into a major industrial development. But the Mobile River and the terror it represented were still horribly familiar to the elderly African woman.

For Matilda, the visit was different but no less difficult. She had no memory of her transatlantic kidnapping as a 2-year-old and encountered the site of her trafficking to the United States as if for the first time. Matilda's visit to Mobile represented what one journalist termed 'one of the great events in Tildy's life, for [it] represents to her a link with her childhood', and she used the trip to explore the brutal circumstances of her arrival in the United States with Kossula, who described his own remembrances of their transatlantic incarceration.[30]

Matilda still lived and worked on the Atkins estate at Martin's Station, the land having passed from Victor Boardman Atkins to his son Victor Bethune Atkins upon the former's death in 1915. By now in her seventies, she would stoop to clear away the weeds from the cotton plants with her long, slim fingers for her son Thomas, who ploughed the fields. But Matilda's posture and energy even in old age were striking. She stood tall, walked with a 'vigorous stride' and spoke in a voice that was deep and husky but still clear. Her eyes bore signs of cataracts, but her skin was smooth, and she wore her grey-white hair in short braids decorated with brightly coloured ribbons, perhaps in a Yoruba style learned from her mother Gracie.[31]

Twelve Mile Island proved such a cruel reminder of the crime that wrecked the lives of Matilda and her family, and for which they had received no justice or even public acknowledgement as victims, that it galvanized the African woman to act. A week before Christmas 1931, Matilda set off along 15 miles of dirt roads from her home in Martin's Station with her sons Joe and Thomas to reach Dallas County Courthouse in Selma. She had decided to request an appointment with probate judge Watkins Mabry Vaughan.[32] She wanted to inform one of the state's chief lawmakers that she was a survivor of the last US slave ship and deserved compensation.

Matilda entered the courthouse, an imposing two-storey Gothic-style structure with a 40-foot wooden clocktower, and waited patiently in its corridor to see the judge. As a trafficking and slavery victim who had endured decades of hardship and poverty in the United States and witnessed the premature deaths of her mother, stepfather and most of her children, she felt sure she deserved financial support like the crowd-funded aid Kossula had just received. Matilda was one of the last survivors of the Middle Passage, as confirmed by her crow-foot facial mark, and she arrived at the court-house at the height of the Great Depression. As a Black tenant farmer from the Black Belt, her financial circumstances are likely to have been desperate. Joe and Thomas also raised with the judge the First World War veterans' bonus, a military service payment that one US congressman was seeking to unlock 13 years early in the face of a mounting economic crisis.[33]

Matilda and her sons' financial demands were quickly dismissed. According to local journalist Octavia Wynn, who witnessed her appeal, Matilda struggled to forcefully articulate her case to the intimidating white judge. 'Tildy believed that being snatched from her home in Africa, while yet an infant, called for a little reimburse-ment, but she could not, or would not, make this ancient claim vocal to the Judge,' the journalist reported.[34]

Wynn was a wealthy white woman and a member of the United Daughters of the Confederacy (UDC). She downplayed the radic-alism of Matilda's act and emphasized her deference, noting her defeated reply of 'I don't spec I needs anything more'n I got' when Vaughan dismissed her reparations claim.[35]

Matilda was forced to leave the courthouse empty-handed. Yet her claim for compensation foreshadowed key activities in the civil rights movement. As the probate judge for Dallas County, Watkins Vaughan was responsible for overseeing who could vote. He was also a veteran of Alabama's constitutional convention of 1901, which withdrew the vote from most Black men and many poor white men in the state. Whether or not Matilda understood the full range of Vaughan's powers, her call for redress before a leading participant in Black voter suppression preceded by 33 years the demands of the Selma Voting Rights campaigners. Even more remarkably, the encounter took place in the same building at which those same campaigners later queued for the right to vote. Matilda's act anticipated the daring efforts of activists such as Amelia Boynton Robinson and Annie Lee Cooper, who were violently arrested outside the courthouse for demanding their civil rights.[36]

What made Matilda's march to the courthouse even more extraordinary was that her landlord/employer Victor Bethune Atkins oversaw Black disenfranchisement in the pre-Civil Rights-era South and proudly acknowledged her home's status as one of the least democratic places in the country. Martin's Station was the first Alabamian electoral precinct to declare results in the 1932 US presidential election, in which Democrat Franklin Delano Roosevelt defeated Republican incumbent Herbert Hoover, because only seven white people in a Black-majority district of more than 1,200 persons could vote. When Octavia Wynn asked Victor Atkins in a tongue-in-cheek article what made his precinct so special that it could return its results so quickly, the Selma First Ward councilman emphasized the place's ordinariness and made a telling joke: its only exceptional feature was that the Black labourers who worked his land had just won prizes at an annual poultry show. Atkins was chairman of the Board of Registrars at Dallas County Courthouse during the Selma Voting Rights campaign. When forced by federal law to register Black voters in the summer of 1965, he declared ominously, 'We're going to obey the law. And then we'll see what comes later.'[37]

Matilda and Redoshi's journey to Mobile and Matilda's subsequent courthouse visit caught the attention of another Selma-based journalist. *Montgomery Advertiser* reporter Sidney Flock set out to correct the *Literary Digest*'s assertion that Kossula was the *Clotilda*'s only living survivor by documenting Redoshi's memories. The African woman was only too glad to share her history with the baby-faced, grey-eyed 20-year-old. But key aspects of the white journalist's account of her life were unreliable and at times demonstrably false. Redoshi spoke in stilted English, and her recollection of her traumatic past proved exhausting. Eventually she put out her hands in a plea for the young man to leave. 'Me tired. Go now,' she declared. Just as Clare Hagedorn had done when documenting Bougier's life, Flock leaned heavily on Redoshi's enslaver's daughter Ida Smith Quarles and other prominent Selma citizens to fill in the gaps in the African woman's story. He emphasized her apparent gratitude to her former enslaver, claimed she lived in a 'jungle' on the Congo River basin and asserted that she was not a child trafficking victim, but, rather, a 25-year-old married woman who dreamed of her dislocation in a 'huge canoe of gigantic flapping wings' seconds before her kidnap.[38]

Redoshi still managed to express her trauma clearly and forcefully to the young reporter, who noted that 'advanced age has not dulled the keen intelligence of her mind and she graphically relates the incidents concerning her capture in Africa and journey to America.' She described her kidnap by Dahomey warriors, the journey to the coast, her transportation to the *Clotilda* by canoe, the darkness of the slave ship's hold, the death of a man and child at sea and the captives' concealment upriver amid the woods and swamps when they arrived in Alabama. Redoshi also conveyed her anger and indignation at being reduced to a chattel. 'Me no trash. My father, he to Tarkar what you call lawyer here.'[39]

The money held in trust for Kossula lasted less than six months, and Black Mobile newspaper the *Press-Forum Weekly* sponsored a second benefit for the elderly man at Franklin Street Baptist Church on the evening of 11 May 1932. Five choirs performed spirituals at the event, and Kossula shared his life story once again with the crowd. The audience was smaller, but the attention Kossula enjoyed reminded him of Charlotte Mason's instruction not to talk to outsiders.[40]

The publicity Kossula received from the *Literary Digest* and *National Geographic* nevertheless drew another significant visitor to African Town in March 1933. Mary Ellen Caver was a 36-year-old white woman from Birmingham who had spent two years between

1925 and 1927 as a Baptist missionary in Ogbomosho, a city Kossula visited regularly as a child. When Caver asked him if he had heard of Nigeria or its then capital city Lagos, he replied that he had not. She then asked Kossula if he knew the Yoruba people. Instantly, his posture changed, and he broke into a smile. 'You been to Yoruba land? You know Yoruba language?' he asked breathlessly. 'Alafia [peace]', she replied, before describing other Yoruba phrases and names. Seventy-three years into his exile, Kossula had become visibly frail. But he came to life with Caver's words. Here, at last, was a sign from home. Sobbing with joy, the 92-year-old raised himself from the ground and began to pray. 'Dear Jesus I thank you that I have at last heard from home.'[41]

Then it was Kossula's to turn to act as interviewer. Caver answered his many questions about the people and culture she had come to know. Kossula listened through his tears, at times too overcome to speak when he heard fresh descriptions of the homeland that had existed only in his mind for the past seven decades. Caver was an imperfect witness. Her understanding of Africa was framed through a missionary's ethnocentric biases. But Kossula still recognized the land she was describing, which proved to him that his countryfolk had endured. Caver was so moved by their conversation that she described the day as one of the happiest of her life. 'They were bright memories for Uncle Cujo, loaded with bright memories of home, mother and freedom. His prayers had at last been answered,' she recalled. Kossula begged Caver to return to Nigeria one day to share his story with his people.[42]

Kossula and Matilda were not the only surviving shipmates who sought to counter their historical erasure in their final years. In the early 1930s, Dinah forced her great-grandchildren to endure a daily dinner-time ritual in which she recited the horrors of her kidnap and enslavement as they bowed before her. So profound was Dinah's rage at the abuses she endured that her descendants would not be allowed to forget them either. Her great-granddaughter Arlonzia recalled that her ancestor would 'take a switch' to the children 'if we didn't listen' to her memories of enslavement. Dinah literally beat her life story into her offspring. Violent memories were re-enacted and passed on through violence. For Dinah, the visceral horrors of her past needed to be viscerally impressed upon her descendants to be meaningfully comprehended. Arlonzia was particularly haunted by her great-grandmother's story of her journey from Africa. 'I was real small when she told me the story, but it startled me so I kept it,' she explained seven decades later.[43]

On 31 July 1933, seventy-three years, three weeks and three days after the *Clotilda* docked on the edge of Mobile Bay, Dinah died in her two-bedroom log cabin in Gee's Bend. The 86-year-old had spent the final months of her life on the brink of starvation. In 1931, creditors took away everything Gee's Bend's all-Black community of tenant farmers owned because they could not meet their rent payments. Plummeting cotton prices after the First World War coincided with a boll weevil infestation that destroyed crops throughout the South. When the stock market crashed in October 1929, prices reaching an all-time low. Residents were still recovering from major flooding seven months before the crash, which caused the Alabama River at Primrose, the lower section of Gee's Bend where Dinah lived, to swell from approximately 100 yards to 10 miles in diameter.[44] Bereft of the tools and livestock they needed to live off their land, Gee's Benders were forced to forage and hunt to survive. Although it is not clear to what extent malnutrition hastened Dinah's death, the enforced suffering she experienced at the end of her life served as a tragic bookend to the enforced suffering she was made to endure at its start.

At the time of Dinah's death, quilting in Gee's Bend was more important than ever. Gee's Benders were only saved from starvation in the winter of 1932–3 by the Red Cross, which provided them with flour, meat and cornmeal. In those dire circumstances, quilting became even more central to the Gee's Benders' lives as women travelled between houses to quilt with one another. It was a practice that became the community's central social activity and its chief means of social and spiritual survival. Resident Georgiana Bennett Pettway described a scene of extreme poverty and grim collective determination. 'Those old folks would quilt the quilt, they sung the song, they prayed the prayer, they ate what they could eat around the quilt. That was really their daily occupation.'[45]

In the final months of his life, Kossula continued to make money from his gardening and grew sugarcane as a treat for his twin great-granddaughters Martha and Mary. The African man was a very popular member of his community. Neighbour John C. Randolph remembered that he always had time for the local children, who enjoyed spending time with him. 'He was a very generous person,' he said. 'If you would ask for something from his garden, he would give it to you.' Kossula continued to earn an income by sharing his life story with local audiences and was by now so famous that he received random visitors from out of state. 'He was confined to bed and was being taken care of by relatives, but his mind was active,' Dorcas Ransom of Stillwater, Oklahoma, remembered of her encounter with Kossula. Even in his final months, he continued to express his desire to go home but, as a newspaper acknowledged, 'the money for the trip was never available'. He still travelled into Mobile to visit Kanko's family, and he always sat in the same spot on the faded blue bench on her porch. 'We were always happy to hear or see Cudjo come to our home,' recalled Kanko's granddaughter Mable Dennison. 'Cudjo continued to visit until he became too ill to do so.'[46]

Until the end of 1934, Kossula still rang the church bell of Union Missionary Baptist Church twice on Sundays. But as he approached death, he finally gave up hope of going home, as he explained in his last interview. When asked if he wanted to return to Africa, he sat for a long time in silence, slowly rubbing his swollen, arthritic hands along the patches of his ragged trousers. Eventually, he spoke. 'No fadder, no mudder, no sister, no brudder, no child there to meet Cudjo. Cudjo not even know where his home was. It was a home many days from de coast, but Cudjo not know where. It had corn and beans and beeg yams, but Cudjo not know where. And now Cudjo stay here. Cudjo's wife she buried here. Cudjo's sons buried

here. Cudjo he be buried here. No more he go back to Africa.'
Kossula turned away from the journalist. 'No more he see the beeg,
beeg yam. No more he eat the beeg melon. No more he see his
people. No more he see his people.'[47]

In January 1935, Kossula's health began to fail, although he still
received visits from curious outsiders. Emma Langdon Roche
returned to see him and brought with her a white New Orleans-
based writer, Roark Bradford. The writer's condescending fantasy
of Black Southern life, *Ol' Man Adam an' His Chillun* (1928), had
become a Pulitzer Prize-winning play titled *Green Pastures* (1930)
that was on tour in Mobile that month. The play was about to be
made into a Hollywood film. At the time of his encounter with
Kossula, Bradford was working to adapt the story of African
American folk hero John Henry into a Broadway musical.[48]

As Kossula's strength declined and his breathing became increasingly laboured, he sat up in his rocking chair to mark the sunset, just
as the sick were raised up to watch the sunset during his childhood
in West Africa. Roche came to visit him again in his final days, and
he sang for her the spiritual song from his homeland that he, Polee
and Charlie had adapted into a Christian prayer:

> Jesus Christ, Son of God,
> Please, Jesus, save my soul.
> I want to go to heaven
> When I die,
> Jesus Christ, Son of God.

After a week of deteriorating health, Kossula's heart finally gave out and
he died in his four-room house at 5.00 p.m. on Friday 26 July 1935. He
was 94 years old. Kossula's funeral was held three days later before a
packed congregation of his townsfolk at Union Missionary Baptist
Church. His 32-year-old granddaughter Angeline Lewis tolled the bell,
just as the African man had done for so many of his shipmates.[49]

* * *

The Courthouse

On 24 September 1936, two filmmakers from the United States Department of Agriculture arrived at Redoshi's log cabin in Bogue Chitto to document her on celluloid. Raymond Evans and Eugene Tucker were making a 23-minute instructional film called *The Negro Farmer: Extension Work for Better Farming and Better Living* (1938) in collaboration with the Tuskegee Institute. Just like the government-funded work of Amelia Boynton Robinson and her husband Samuel Boynton, the production was designed to teach Black Southern farmers who were struggling to survive during the Great Depression how to improve the health of their crops and homes. Believing Redoshi to be the oldest person in Dallas County and keen to document a 'historical curiosity' of the antebellum era, the two men sought to include the Middle Passage survivor in their film.

Redoshi permitted Evans and Tucker to record her. In the film, she sits, draped in a patchwork quilt, in her rocking chair on the porch of her cabin. Aside from Hurston's footage of Kossula, the 18-second recording is the only known cinematic document of a Middle Passage survivor. Redoshi spoke and sang for the camera in her mother tongue, although of course her voice cannot be heard in the silent film.[50]

Roughly ten weeks later, on Sunday 13 December, Redoshi died in her cabin surrounded by her daughter, grandchildren, great-grandchildren and great-great-grandchildren. The African woman's death in the same place she had been held in bondage was a particularly cruel ending for a woman whose life had been defined by injustice and loss. Redoshi was never able to escape her poverty and only nominally did she escape slavery. Her home throughout her life was a dark one-room and kitchen hut with two small windows and front and back doors that were just big enough for a grown man to fit through, and which she decorated with newspaper to hide the dark wooden boards and shut out the cold. The elderly woman never came to terms with her displacement on a Black Belt plantation and tears streamed down her face when she was asked to recall the home that had been so brutally snatched away from her as a child. She never gave up hope of returning to her peaceful existence in West Africa, where her community had lived 'together like one family'.[51]

Funeral services took place the day after Redoshi died, and she was buried on her former enslaver's estate, which was still owned by his daughter Ida. The 1,800-acre plantation was eventually sold in 1955 to Miller and Company, Inc for $90,000 (equivalent to $1 million today) in what the *Selma Times-Journal* described as 'one of the country's largest cash transactions involving farm property'.[52]

Around the time of Redoshi's death, a three-and-a-half-page summary of her life appeared in *Our Home Land*, a school textbook intended to provide eight-year-old Alabamians with an introduction to the history of their state. The presence of a survivor of the hidden crime of the *Clotilda* in a segregation-era school textbook was remarkable. Yet like Toccoa Cozart's account of Bougier, *Our Home Land*'s portrait of Redoshi was part of a wider propaganda mission to aggrandize Alabama's enslaver elite and frame its Black population as unworthy of citizenship. Even the book's layout mimicked the segregated structure of mid-century Alabamian society: Redoshi appeared in a separate 'Negroes' section that was disconnected from the rest of the state's history.

Our Home Land's co-author Marie Bankhead Owen was one of the most powerful people in Alabama in the first half of the twentieth century. Her Klansman father John Hollis Bankhead, Sr. served for 33 years as a Democratic US congressman and then a senator. He also strengthened Alabama's convict leasing system during his four years as warden of the state penitentiary, turning the unpaid, dangerous labour of mostly Black prisoners like Cudjo Lewis, Jr. into a major source of state revenue. Her middle brother William Brockman Bankhead was Speaker of the US House of Representatives – and thus third in line to the US presidency – at the time of Redoshi's death; her oldest brother John Hollis Bankhead, Jr. was the author of the Alabama Election Law of 1902, which disenfranchised most of the state's Black voters for most of the twentieth century. He was also a US senator responsible for the structure and funding of the New Deal, an enormously consequential federal relief programme introduced by President Roosevelt during the Great Depression. Bankhead ensured most aid went to white recipients.[53]

Marie Bankhead Owen's own political authority stemmed from her marriage to Thomas McAdory Owen, founder of the Alabama Department of Archives and History (ADAH). She became head of the ADAH for 35 years following her husband's death in 1920 and completed his four-volume *History of Alabama and Dictionary of Alabama Biography* (1921), the first comprehensive history of the state. She worked to shape understandings of Alabama's past. Such was her influence that she even selected the state's motto with the words – 'We Dare Defend Our Rights' – encapsulating her pro-Confederate views. She also helped organize and lead the Southern Anti-Suffrage Association, so fearful was she that granting women the franchise would reopen the debate around Black people's voting rights.

Marie Owen's work on *Our Home Land* built on Lost Cause mythologizing promoted by the UDC and ADAH since the 1890s, which sought to indoctrinate the region's children into accepting as normal the region's race-based class inequalities. The reform of public-school education in the South in the early twentieth century led to the emergence of local school boards and administrators and to the standardization of textbooks according to an upper-class white Southern worldview. The UDC took charge of monitoring textbook content and some UDC chapters formed their own text-book committees. Rush Jones's youngest daughter Susie set up the Sophie Bibb UDC Chapter's first Children's Chapter for such a purpose on 8 June 1897. In 1939, an NAACP survey highlighted in vain the negative power of such texts and how their 'miseducation' would lead children to grow up 'with the fixed notion that Negro citizens are inferior to white citizens'.[54]

It is true that aspects of *Our Home Land*'s story matched claims Redoshi and her shipmates made elsewhere. Redoshi apparently 'lived in the hills of Africa'. Dahomey warriors killed her townsfolk in a night-time attack after a previous visit claiming friendship. Her journey to the coast took two weeks, which fitted with Kossula's claim that the distressing march to Ouidah took 16 days in total. The textbook also noted that Redoshi's kidnappers 'hid the slaves in the swamps' when they arrived in Mobile Bay and sold them quickly to avoid being caught.[55]

Such details suggest Owen at least consulted Redoshi before writing her biography. But the textbook provided no sense of the terrors of the Middle Passage even though it acknowledged that Redoshi 'remembered everything that happened'. Horror was reframed as sorrow to play down the injustices she endured. The name of the *Clotilda* and the date of its arrival were not mentioned. The text acknowledged that it was 'against the law to bring *any more* slaves, but some bad men brought them anyway', an admission of criminality that nevertheless located the wrongdoing not in the act of human theft but, rather, in Redoshi's kidnappers' participation in trafficking after the legal trade ended, and which protected their anonymity by failing to name those 'bad men'.[56]

Owen's narrative infantilized Redoshi, intimated that her kidnapping 'saved' her by giving her religious knowledge and displaced her sense of injustice onto two fictional Dahomey men supposedly kidnapped alongside her and sent to work in the fields with her. Redoshi was homesick, but she had a 'good home' and a 'kind master' who seemingly played no part in her trafficking, and whose daughter 'took care of her faithful old servant until the end'. The text acknowledged that Redoshi married one of her shipmates but did not admit to her outraged claim that her traffickers sold her as a child bride; instead, she was a 'grown woman' when she was kidnapped and 'over a hundred years old when she died'. *Our Home Land* reassured its young readers that 'everyone loved Aunt Sally because she was so good.' The text was still being taught in Alabama's schools into the 1950s.[57]

As part of the New Deal, cotton fields such as those belonging to Victor Atkins were transformed to pastureland. The crop's dominance in the Black Belt came to an end, and African American sharecroppers and tenant farmers were driven off the land by a lack of work and into cities such as Selma. That probably explains why Matilda, a woman who spent her life working in the cotton fields of Wilcox and Dallas counties, ended up relocating to her youngest daughter Emma Hollins's house in the centre of the city in 1936. Matilda was living in the Green Street property when she suffered a stroke in September 1939. The African woman lived on for another four months before her death on Saturday 13 January 1940 at the age of 81 or 82.[58] One mile away, the building that for years housed her former employers and landlords the Atkins' grocery store still stood at 1100 Water Avenue. A few feet south of the store, a new Alabama River crossing was nearing completion. The Edmund Pettus Bridge, which was named after a famous Confederate and Klan leader and later became one of the most iconic sites of the civil rights movement, was formally opened on 25 May.

Matilda never achieved formal recognition as a Middle Passage survivor in her lifetime, and she never received compensation for the many crimes she and her family endured. The last *Clotilda* survivor and last known Middle Passage survivor was buried without public fanfare on 16 January surrounded by her remaining children and grandchildren amid the trees in Martin's Station Cemetery.[59]

Epilogue

On 12 January 2023, almost eighty-three years to the day after Matilda's death, a tornado passed through Martin's Station and then struck Selma. Winds of up to 130 miles per hour injured 25 people and damaged hundreds of properties and businesses, including the home of Matilda's 86-year-old grandson Johnny Crear. The devastation, which led authorities to declare Selma a major disaster area, rubbed salt in the wounds of a city already suffering from decades of decline. Today, around 30 per cent of Selma's population of 17,000 people, 84.2 per cent of whom are African American, live in poverty. The city's median household income in 2021 was just under $30,000, a figure more than $40,000 below the median national household income for that year. The struggle to rebuild the city – residents were still waiting for help to clear their streets of debris a month after the disaster – underscored struggles that the *Clotilda* survivors' families and their wider communities continue to endure, as well as their resistance in the face of adversity. When confronted with the damage to his roof and windows, Johnny stoically insisted that 'all [is] repairable'.[1]

Johnny has lived in Selma for nearly his whole life. At one time, he lived in a house on Lapsley Street, the same street where Washington Smith had his mansion and where Redoshi laboured during slavery, but also one minute's walk from the home of Amelia Boynton Robinson, which Dr. Martin Luther King, Jr. and his fellow activists used as their campaign headquarters during the Selma to Montgomery marches. When Johnny returned to Selma from university in the early 1960s, he travelled, like his grandmother before him, to Dallas County Courthouse. He wanted to join the tiny number of African Americans in the state with the right to vote. As he was leaving the courthouse that day, a member of the three-person registration board approached him and asked if he was Joe Crear's son. When Johnny said he was, Victor Bethune Atkins mentioned that he had grown up alongside Joe at Martin's Station and they had played together as boys – Atkins later inherited the estate on which Matilda and her son laboured. Johnny still believes that personal connection is why the registration board afforded him the right to vote.[2]

The residents of Selma played a critical role in the civil rights movement, and Johnny was an active participant in that fight. On 18 September 1963, he was arrested by sheriff of Dallas County Jim Clark at an anti-segregation rally because he refused to allow a white man who was trying to incite a riot to push a garter snake in his face. As an administrator at Selma's Good Samaritan Hospital, Johnny also witnessed injured people, among them Amelia Boynton Robinson, being brought in to be treated at the hospital in the aftermath of Bloody Sunday, 7 March 1965. That day, Alabama state troopers and state police led by Sheriff Clark assaulted 600 peaceful marchers with batons and teargas as they attempted to cross the Edmund Pettus Bridge during the first Selma to Montgomery march.[3]

At least three of Matilda's great-grandchildren also played key roles in the civil rights movement. Sisters Dot Slones, Gwen Gamble and Deborah Smith were among the more than five thousand children who were arrested and beaten in Birmingham, Alabama, for participating in what became known as the Children's Crusade, or Children's March. The industrial centre that child *Wanderer* survivor Jackson Smith's enslaver Josiah Morris bankrolled and allegedly named was in 1963 the key battlefield in the civil rights movement. On the morning of Thursday 2 May that year, more than 1,000 children walked out of school and gathered at 16th Street Baptist Church to demand an end to segregation in the city. Just after noon, the children left the church carrying placards, locking arms and singing freedom hymns, and marched eight blocks towards the city's business district. State police arrested 959 child marchers. When more children joined the campaign over the following days, officers set fire hoses, police dogs and batons on marchers as young as six years old. Images of children being assaulted so shocked the world that on 10 May, city officials reached an agreement with Dr. King's Southern Christian Leadership Conference to desegregate schools, lunch counters, restrooms and drinking fountains.[4] Members of a local Ku Klux Klan chapter responded with murderous fury on 15 September, a week after the first school was integrated, placing a timed bomb at 16th Street Baptist Church that ignited just before a Sunday school class. The explosion killed 11-year-old Carol Denise McNair and 14-year-olds Addie Mae Collins, Carole Rosamond Robertson and Cynthia Dionne Wesley. Addie Mae's 12-year-old sister Sarah Collins was also badly injured and partially blinded by the explosion. The bombing sparked the anti-segregation march that led to Johnny's arrest.

Redoshi and Dinah's old homes were also important sites in the civil rights campaign. Not only was Bogue Chitto the enthusiastic centre of a major voter registration drive in the mid-1960s, but by the early 1940s members of that community were already holding political gatherings and meetings at schools and churches to show people how to fill out voter applications. As Amelia Boynton Robinson, who spent 30 years helping people in the region to vote, recalled, 'They were often the first in line to register, even after driving 20 miles to get there. They were among the first groups to march for freedom and the first to go to jail.'[5]

Wilcox County's population was 75 per cent Black in the early 1960s, yet it had no Black voters. In 1963 and after a year of planning, a group of men from Gee's Bend marched to Dallas County Courthouse determined to change that. Ten men were ultimately allowed to fill out registration forms, although the documents were immediately rejected by Matilda's former landlord Victor Bethune Atkins's registration board. The community continued its fight through legal filings until it finally was successful in 1966. As a punishment for their voting rights fight, the makeshift ferry between Gee's Bend and Camden, which Dinah used to relocate to the community with her sons nearly seventy years earlier, was shut down in 1962. That made it very difficult for Gee's Benders to exercise their right to vote, and to access other vital services, including schools and medical care. The service was not restored until 2006. According to Wilcox County sheriff Lummie Jenkins, 'We didn't close the ferry because they were black; we closed it because they *forgot* they were black.'[6]

To counter the racism the community endured, and to encourage their fight for their voting rights, Dr. King preached to Gee's Benders at Pleasant Grove Baptist Church in February 1965, telling them, 'I come over here to Gee's Bend to tell you you are somebody . . . You are as good as any white person in Wilcox County.' 'It's true, it's true,' his applauding congregation of 300 replied. Almost exactly a year later, more than sixty local quilters and voting rights campaigners, including Estelle Witherspoon and Nettie Young, who were both jailed for marching alongside Dr. King, established the Freedom Quilting Bee to financially empower themselves and their commu-nity. Such were the feelings of affinity between the Gee's Benders and Dr. King that the mule-drawn wagon that transported the civil rights leader to his funeral was made in Gee's Bend.[7]

Descendants of the Mobile *Clotilda* survivors laboured to preserve and celebrate their West African heritages, even while those herit-ages were being erased. Since the publication of *Barracoon* in 2018 and the identification of the wreck of the *Clotilda* next to Twelve Mile Island in 2019, there have been documentaries, books, news reports and a play about African Town (now Africatown). Descendants' group the Clotilda Descendants Association (CDA) has held a 'Spirit of Our Ancestors Festival' every February since 2019 to celebrate its members' family history. After decades of silence, two descendants of Timothy Meaher even agreed to meet with members of the CDA at the end of 2022, and while Hurricane Katrina damaged and shut down the community's original Welcome Center in 2005, a new multi-million-dollar Welcome Center and Heritage House was opened in Africatown in July 2023.[8]

Epilogue

Efforts to preserve the legacy of Africatown go back much further, however. In July 1959, the Progressive League of Plateau, led by local historian Henry C. Williams, who knew Kossula, and which included several of the *Clotilda* survivors' descendants, held a celebration to mark what they believed to be the centenary of the Africans' arrival in Mobile. The group raised $5,000 (equivalent to more than $50,000 today) for a bronze bust of Kossula for that anniversary, which was placed outside Union Missionary Baptist Church. In 1961, acting under the false belief that they had an ancestral link to Ghana, the Africatown community invited the Ghanaian ambassador for a visit. In February 1982, the first Africatown Folk Festival was held. That same year, Prichard's mayor John H. Smith arranged a twin-city agreement with Ouidah, and Beninese diplomats and artists became regular visitors. The community even received formal apologies for their ancestors' enslavement from the Catholic Archbishop of Cotonou, Isidore de Souza, descendant of the notorious Brazilian slave trader Francisco Félix de Souza, and from Simon Pierre Adovelande, director of Benin's Agency for Reconciliation and Development. The Africatown Direct Descendants, Inc. (a forerunner of the CDA) was established in 1984, and in 1997 the Africatown Community Mobilization Project, Inc. was created to help preserve and promote Africatown. Many descendants also laboured for years to conserve their ancestors' individual stories. Kanko and James's granddaughter Mable Dennison documented her ancestors' histories across two 80-page booklets, Polee's daughter and Abaché's granddaughter Eva spoke of her memories and gave a taped interview, and Charlie and Maggie's great-great-granddaughter Lorna G. Woods has provided guided tours of Africatown and toured schools to promote her family's history.[9]

Following a campaign begun by Henry C. Williams in the late 1970s, sections of Africatown were finally added to the National Register of Historic Places in 2012, although the officially recognized sites still do not include Lewis Quarters, the first permanent home established by the Mobile *Clotilda* survivors. The recognition also came far too late to save most of the original community from destruction. Perhaps around fifteen or sixteen properties built by the Africans, including most of Gumpa's home, were demolished in the late 1980s to make way for the Cochrane Bridge's replacement, the Cochrane-Africatown USA Bridge. Gumpa's chimney is the only structure built by Africatown's founders that still survives. A five-lane highway was added to the Cochrane Bridge redevelopment in the early 1990s, which paved over part of the Old Plateau Cemetery that the shipmates established in 1876. Residents believe some of the Africans' graves were dug up as part of that development.[10]

The Mobile Africans were not the only shipmates whose graves were destroyed in the decades after their death. On 3 May 1923, one day after she died, 81-year-old Amey Greenwood/Phillips was buried in the Yancey Crane Cemetery in Daphne, Baldwin County, a region close to Mobile County where the Meaher family also have extensive land holdings. Twelve Mile Island, where the *Clotilda* also lies buried, is in Baldwin County. The Black section of that cemetery was destroyed in or around 1970, and buildings were placed on top of the *Clotilda* survivor and her children's graves. The white section of the cemetery was left untouched. As of 2023, Amey's great-great-great-great-grandson Marquis Watkins is working with the City of Daphne to add a historical marker to the site to serve as a permanent memorial to his ancestor.[11]

The legacies of the *Clotilda* survivors and their descendants is being undermined in other ways, too. In 2013, the US Supreme Court ruled in the case of *Shelby County, Alabama v. Holder* that states and localities with a history of voter discrimination were no longer required – as had been dictated by Section 5 of the Voting Rights Act – to gain clearance from the federal government before making changes to their voting systems. Since then, the Alabama legislature has purged hundreds of thousands of people from voting rolls, shut down polling sites in majority-Black counties and failed to publicize a change in the state's felony disenfranchisement law that clarified thousands of people's right to vote. The legislature implemented a voter ID law in 2014 and then shut down dozens of motor vehicle licence offices in predominantly Black counties, making such documentation difficult to obtain. Alabama Republicans were also ruled to have illegally discriminated against Black voters when they drew the state's seven new congressional districts in 2021 and packed a third of such voters into a single district. That district incorporated but also extended beyond all the rural Black Belt counties and included Birmingham, Montgomery and Tuscaloosa, three of the state's five largest cities. Unlike in other states, absentee voting in Alabama is only permitted for a limited number of reasons, and the deadline for submitting ballots by mail was reduced in 2021 from five to seven days before election day. As US President Joe Biden acknowledged when he visited tornado-damaged Selma on 5 March 2023 to mark the fifty-eighth anniversary of Bloody Sunday, 'This fundamental right [to vote] remains under assault.'[12]

A 2021 study found schools in the Black Belt to be slightly more segregated than they were in 1990. After desegregation, white elites in the Black Belt and throughout the South created racially exclusive private schools that became known as 'segregation academies'. The state subsidization of private schools was ruled unconstitutional in 1967, and the slight rise in segregation in recent years can be attributed to demographic changes: there has been a much larger drop in the number of white children relative to the number of Black children in the region. Yet as the authors of that study also note, 'the academies themselves can still be found across the South and they still maintain overwhelmingly majority-white enrollments'. While rich families, mostly white, can afford to send their children to private schools, poor children, mostly Black, must make do with underfunded public schools that are judged to be 'failing'. As of November 2022, 40.5 per cent of the state's 'failing' schools are in the Black Belt.[13]

The train that Bougier caught twice weekly from Prattville Junction no longer runs. The last train stopped at Union Station in 1979, just over two decades after the Montgomery Bus Boycott reversed *Plessy v. Ferguson* and rendered travel segregation unconstitutional, integration having coincided with falling demand for rail travel. The red-brick and limestone building still stands – it was declared a National Historic Landmark three years before its closure – but there has been no passenger rail service in Alabama's capital since 1995. There is still a limited bus service in the city, but buses run on their routes only every 60 to 90 minutes on weekdays, even less frequently on Saturdays, and not at all on Sundays. Alabama is one of five states in the country that sets aside no money for public transportation; the service is funded entirely at the local and federal level. Like Komo's employer Mayor Will Gunter and his family, who introduced automobiles to the city in 1908, those who can afford to do so own cars. Alabama is the most car-dependent state in the country. But higher rates of poverty among Black households limit their access to such vehicles and thus their mobility. A 2020 study found that 12 per cent of Black households in the state have no access to a car, compared with only 4 per cent of white households.[14]

Governmental investment is even more markedly absent in other sections of the Black Belt. In 2017, a United Nations official visiting Lowndes County, a region just east of Selma and Snow Hill and just west of Montgomery where Rush Jones's mother owned land, found communities functioning without reliable electricity access or public sewage or water supply services. Instead, they were forced to make do with homemade sewage systems that were releasing raw sewage back into waterways, backyards and children's playing areas and fuelling high rates of diseases such as E. coli and hookworm. Philip Alston, who was then the UN's Special Rapporteur on extreme poverty and human rights, was so shocked by the deprivation he encountered in that county that he judged it among the worst he had ever witnessed. 'I think it's very uncommon in the first world. This is not a sight that one normally sees,' he declared. In his subsequent report, Alston also noted how strikingly different were the average poverty, earnings, infant mortality, unemployment and incarceration rates of African Americans compared with white Americans and concluded, 'These shameful statistics can only be explained by long-standing structural discrimination on the basis of race, reflecting the enduring legacy of slavery.'[15]

A view up Market Street (later Dexter Avenue), Montgomery in 1867. The artesian well where slave auctions were held is in the foreground. The Capitol Building is in the background.

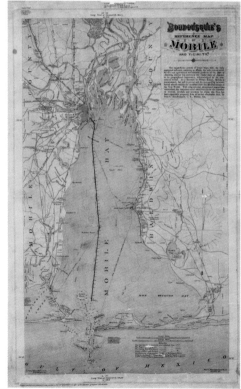

Boudousquie's 1889 reference map of Mobile and Vicinity, which shows an 'African Colony' at Magazine Point.

Group sketch of African Town residents on their way home from church, *c*.1893.

Sketch of Shamba, *c*.1893.

Sketch of Zuma, *c*.1893.

Sketch of Osia and Innie Keeby's home, 1897.

Zuma on her porch, *c*.1916.

The cable ferry between Camden and Gee's Bend in 1939.

Gee's Bend quilters Jennie Pettway and another girl with the quilter
Jorena Pettway, April 1937. Newsprint wallpaper is visible on the walls.

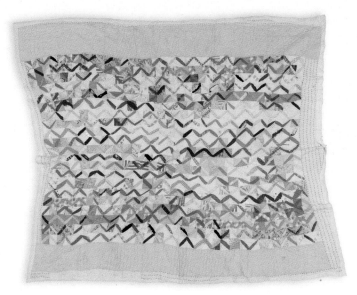

'Zigzags': a *c.*1940 quilt by Gertrude Miller that was likened
to her mother-in-law Dinah's treasured African cloth.

Dinah's daughter Sally, the midwife of Gee's Bend, in 1939.

Ray Stannard Baker's 1907 photographs of Bougier and her daughter Amanda.

An anchor falsely named as the *Clotilda*'s on display
at Alabama State Docks in August 1933.

Kossula in his cabin in
the late 1920s.

Doris Ulmann's 1930
photograph of Kossula.

The old Gothic-style Dallas County Courthouse, where Matilda
went to demand reparations in December 1931.

Redoshi being interviewed 80 days before her
death for the film *The Negro Farmer* (1938).

The residents of Africatown have been plagued by their toxic environment for decades. After renting 100 acres of land bordering Africatown to the International Paper Company in 1928, the Meaher family leased another 134 acres to the Scott Paper Company to build a second papermill in 1940. Until their closure in 2000, Africatown's two papermills were among the world's most productive – and polluting. The plants' sulphurous odour was some-times so strong that it was difficult for residents to breathe. Ash – or salt cake – from the plants, which was corrosive enough to rust cars, rained down on vegetable gardens and the very food they were eating. Water used in paper production was dumped back in Africatown's waterways, polluting the water with dioxin which, as investigative journalist Nick Tabor notes, is 'one of the most toxic compounds ever tested'. In 1978, the addition of three oil-tank farms, a chemical manufacturer and a cement company brought new toxic substances and new forms of pollution to the area. From 1988 onwards, the US Environmental Protection Agency began compiling a Toxic Release Inventory report (TRI) of emissions, which showed that International Paper and Scott Paper were among the nation's top 200 air polluters. In 1988 alone, they released 964,000 pounds of chloroform and 1.8 million pounds of hydrochloric acid, both of which are known carcinogens, into the air around Africatown. TRI data from 1992 showed that the discharge of chemicals associated with birth defects was far higher in Mobile County than anywhere else in the nation, and that, chiefly thanks to Scott Paper, Mobile County had the highest rates of cancer-causing chemicals in the state. Residents, including direct descendants of the *Clotilda* survivors, report extremely high rates of cancer and premature death.[16]

Since the publication of *Barracoon* and identification of the *Clotilda* in the Mobile River, Africatown and the health issues its residents face have belatedly achieved national and international recognition. But such attention has also coincided with a growing attempt by state legislators, mostly in the US South, to police the teaching of slavery and its legacies, an act that risks resuppressing histories such as those of the *Clotilda* survivors. In January 2023, Alabama Republican legislator Ed Oliver sponsored House Bill 7, which seeks to ban 'divisive concepts', including those 'relating to race', from school and university classrooms. Such legislation, which free speech advocacy group PEN America has described as an attempt to 'make patriotism – or more specifically, a knee jerk and uncritical form of patriotism – compulsory', echoes the 'Lost Cause' propaganda of the pre-Civil Rights era, which shaped US Southern history according to an elite white worldview to indoctrinate the region's children into accepting as normal its race-based class inequalities. That effort to police the past was so successful that the *Clotilda* was still being dismissed as a hoax or ignored by historians until well into the twenty-first century. Kanko's granddaughter Mable Dennison, who laboured for years to recover her ancestor's story, articulated the devastating personal effect of such erasure. 'For an individual to know nothing about his or her heritage can help reduce, crush or even eliminate the basic desirable qualities of one's identity.'[17]

To deny the story of the *Clotilda* is also to deny a history that extends far beyond Alabama, and even the United States. The voyage of the *Clotilda* and its aftermath provide a mere snapshot of African-born slavery survivors' experiences. The ship's journey was just one of around thirty-six thousand documented slave ship voyages that were made across the Atlantic from the start of the sixteenth century until perhaps well into the 1870s. Its captives numbered merely 110 of the more than 12.5 million people who were forced onto slave ships during that period. Compared to the vast majority of those who endured the transatlantic slave trade, the shipmates' experience of bondage was brief. The fact that they landed in the United States was atypical too: more than 96 per cent of all Middle Passage survivors were sent to other regions in the Americas.

Yet archival material relating to the *Clotilda* and its survivors collectively represents by far the most detailed record of a single slave ship voyage and its legacies. Moreover, it is the *only* Middle Passage story that can be told comprehensively from the perspective of those enslaved. The *Clotilda* shipmates' individual voices and stories therefore serve as a necessary corrective to dominant histories of transatlantic slavery that have framed personal horrors, traumas, griefs and the battle to adapt and survive in terms of numbers and statistics.

And the stories that the *Clotilda* survivors tell are remarkable. Their lives document the manifold ways, big and small, that a group of enslaved children and young adults resisted their imprisonment, impoverishment and geographical isolation and asserted their West African identities in the United States both during and after slavery. Most of the survivors lived long enough to witness not just freedom, but also *de jure* segregation. The last of them contributed to the Harlem Renaissance and even the activist beginnings of the civil rights movement.

The *Clotilda*'s voyage stemmed from a long-rumoured bet after all. But the slave ship's origins went much deeper. When questions over the morality of slavery were rising to the fore in the mid-nineteenth-century United States, some of Alabama's richest and most powerful men decided to charter a slave ship and sail it across the Atlantic and then back to Alabama. The schooner's journey highlights the endurance of an illegal slave trade to Brazil and Cuba for decades after the trade's ban, a sordid history of human trafficking in which US ships and citizens played key roles. Equally significantly, the *Clotilda*'s voyage was a major event in the lead-up to secession, a crime of which future Confederate leaders had knowledge and even personal interests. The story of the *Clotilda* and its survivors also shows that leading promoters of the Lost Cause narrative in late nineteenth- and early twentieth-century Alabama knew that their parents and their friends' parents enslaved African young people, including children as young as 2 years old. When they defended the Confederacy's legacy, they did so in the knowledge that transatlantic child trafficking was a still-visible component of that legacy to the extent that they were prepared to rewrite its victims' experiences in a newspaper supplement and school textbook.

The stories of the *Clotilda* survivors nevertheless show that their lives were so much richer than the countless crimes committed against them. They were loving parents and partners and community-minded men and women who gave generously and fought for their rights and the rights of those around them. Even as they embraced Christianity, their Fon and Yoruba belief systems remained central to how they lived and interpreted the world and shaped how they raised their children. They survived in their alien and hostile environment by mobilizing agricultural and herbal knowledge, craftsmanship and trade and hunting skills from back home. As Polee's daughter Eva recalled, 'They worked hard and made the most of what they had.'[18] While Burns Meaher was killing time shooting at 'river pirates' – perhaps displaced freed people – in the autumn of 1869, *Clotilda* shipmates were carving out homes for themselves amid the woods and swamps to the north of Mobile, all the while diligently saving up money in an ultimately frustrated effort to return home. While future chairman of Alabama's Board of Registrars Victor Bethune Atkins was gloating that only seven people from his electoral precinct voted in the 1932 US presidential election, Matilda McCrear, by then in her mid-seventies, was still labouring on his land, stooping to clear away weeds from his cotton plants to aid her youngest son.

Ultimately, the story of the *Clotilda*'s survivors is a tale of enduring tragedy and loss. The shipmates forgot neither the shock of their displacement nor the traumas of their lives in bondage. Their misery was plainly visible on their faces even decades after their kidnap. But the story of the *Clotilda* shipmates is also an extraordinary account of survival and endurance. They resisted their experiences of enslavement and transatlantic dislocation and sought to hold onto their West African identities. They left important creative and spiritual legacies in Alabama, and their stories and actions foreshadowed the Montgomery Bus Boycott, a crucial early event in the civil rights movement, and the Selma Voting Rights campaign, which led directly to the 1965 Voting Rights Act. Many traces of their presence can still be found throughout Alabama, and their legacy, and their descendants, remain across the United States.

Acknowledgements

This book owes an immeasurable debt of gratitude to many, many people, but I'd like to start by thanking my late mother, Elizabeth, who, more than anyone else, set me on the path to undertake this work. And it certainly would not exist without the incredible time, support, and information shared by countless *Clotilda* survivor descendants and their families, including but by no means limited to Chanelle Blackwell, Johnny Crear, Joycelyn Davis, Bobby Dennison, Jeremy Ellis, Elizabeth Fay, Patricia Frazier, Gwen Gamble, Devin Kennedy, Thelma Kennedy-Malveaux, Delisha Marshall, Nikki Short, Dot Slones, Blanche Smith, Deborah Smith, Gail Stallworth, Charmaine Anderson Taylor, Clarence Wall, Jr. and Marquis Watkins.

The research contained in this book builds on ground-breaking archaeological, historical, and genealogical work relating to the *Clotilda*, its survivors, and the community of Africatown by James P. Delgado, Mable Dennison, Sylviane A. Diouf, Zora Neale Hurston, Addie Pettaway, Ben Raines, Natalie S. Robertson, Emma Langdon Roche, John H. Smith, Nick Tabor, Llewellyn (Lew) Toulmin and Henry C. Williams. I'm especially grateful to James Delgado and Nick Tabor, who readily shared their *Clotilda* research materials without me ever having to ask. Baldwin-based historian Arnetta Sims, whose ancestor Wallie Valrie, Sr. was enslaved alongside *Clotilda* survivor Amey Greenwood/Phillips, was also a fantastic source of knowledge and support.

Many other people and organizations have helped to promote and support the research contained in this book. I was the lucky recipient of a British Library Eccles Centre Visiting Fellowship that I sadly did not have time to use during the pandemic. Sean Coughlan at the BBC not only reported on the research from which this book stemmed three times but also took unpaid time away from his day job to join me in a virtual Africatown event. Mike Foster, one of Africatown's biggest supporters since learning he's related to the *Clotilda*'s captain William Foster, has for three years kept me abreast of his and the community's work to promote its history. Barton Bernstein, Keith Cartwright, Kelechi Dibie, Alston Fitts, Joey Jenkins and Vanessa Mongey all aided my previous work on Redoshi and Matilda McCrear. Tommy Boyd shared his own knowledge of and enthusiasm for Redoshi's story, and Ty Wright called my attention to Redoshi's appearance in the schoolbook *Our Home Land*. I am forever grateful to Amelia Boynton Robinson's granddaughter Carver Boynton and great-grandson Professor Kimeu Boynton for allowing me to reproduce material from *Bridge Across Jordan* and to Loretta Pettway Bennett for granting permission to reproduce Gertrude Miller's quilt.

This book drew on vital archival material held at the following locations: Alabama Department of Archives and History; Amistad Research Center, Tulane University; Doy Leale McCall Rare Book and Manuscript Library, Mobile, Alabama; Library of Congress; Mobile Public Library; Moorland-Spingarn Research Center, Howard University; National Archives and Records Administration, Atlanta, Georgia; and the Souls Grown Deep Foundation. I am especially grateful to Elizabeth Theris-Boone at Mobile Public Library and Scott Browning at the Souls Grown Deep Foundation for help with my repeated queries. Some of the material in this book was compiled while I was a Guest Researcher at Linnaeus University in Sweden. I began identifying *Clotilda* survivors while I was a Leverhulme Early Career Research Fellow at the University of Nottingham and most of the book's research was undertaken while I was employed by Newcastle University.

I was the lucky beneficiary of the most wonderful editors imagin-

Acknowledgements

able. At Amistad: Tracy Sherrod, Jennifer Baker and Rakesh Satyal and Assistant Editor Ryan Amato. At William Collins: Shoaib Rokadiya and Arabella Pike, and Editorial and Publisher's Assistants Sadé Omeje and Sam Harding. Katy Archer was the book's UK project editor, Richard Collins was the copyeditor, Julian Humphries designed the book's UK jacket, and the book's UK publicist is Lizzie Rowles. Stephen Brayda and Mike McQuade created the book's US jacket, and the book's US publicity and marketing team are Sarah Schoof and Lucile Culver. The maps are the great work of John Plumer.

My incredible literary agent Max Edwards inspired me to turn my academic research into something a wider audience might want to read and provided boundless enthusiasm and support for the project from start to finish. I am also deeply indebted to Gus Brown, Vanessa Kerr and Tom Lloyd-Williams at ACM UK, and Mark Kessler at Susanna Lea Associates.

Many wonderful friends and colleagues have championed this book along its journey, especially Celeste-Marie Bernier, Catherine Hackett, Jade Montserrat, Jennifer Orr, Alan Rice, Fionnghuala Sweeney and Helen Taylor. The final word of thanks belongs to my fantastic family: my father Gerard, my siblings Frances, Joseph and Samuel, their partners Rob, Jenny and Gonia, and my nieces Elizabeth ('Lily'), Emily and Hazel. Not only have they enthusiastically helped and supported the book in countless visible and invisible ways, but they make everything worthwhile.

Notes

The *Clotilda* Africans

1. Historian Addie Pettaway recorded in the early 1980s that this man was also known as 'Uncle Dear Sir'. The surname 'Africa' – and probably also Maggie's alternative forename 'America' – were most likely invented by census-takers who felt unable to comprehend and transcribe the *Clotilda* survivors' actual names. Pettaway, 'The Folklife', 26.

2. A visitor to Mobile wrote down the shipmates' birth and initiation names as they heard them in an undated manuscript. The anonymous author did not pair the group's African names with their US names, so it is unclear who among them was Anthony Thomas, for example. However, 'Absha' is identifiable as Abaché, 'Bossah' as Bose, 'Cozaloo' as Kossula, 'Deza' as Adisa, 'Foloroah' as Parloro, 'Koloco' as Kanko and 'Goobee' as (Osia) 'Keeby'. 'Lahla' was probably Abila, 'Somee' likely Zuma, 'Esso' may have been a variant of Ossa/Osia (and therefore either Charlie or Ossa Allen) and 'Gocby' (Gohoby means 'interim chief' in Yoruba) perhaps African Town's leader Peter Lee, whose Fon name was recorded posthumously as Gumpa. Historian Sylviane A. Diouf has found Yoruba translations for six of the other names recorded in that document: 'Ahdabee' (Ahdabi: 'we have arrived here'); 'Alloko' (a name given to a child whose mother has lost several children); 'Fahboom' (Fabumi: 'given by the *fa* or oracle'); 'Ockballa' (Okégbalê: 'top of the shrine'); 'Ojo Facha' ('born during a rainfall'); and 'Sacahrahgo' (Sakaru). The other names were transcribed as Ajemo, Cooyaka, Gockilago, Iyouha, Messa and Sanalowa. 'Religion of the Dahomans', n.d. The Museum of Mobile, cited in Diouf, *Dreams*, 261, n. 72.

3. Two African-born men named Peter Johnson with different approximate ages — 32 and 50 — and differently named wives were documented living close to *Clotilda* enslaver Memorable Walker Creagh's McKinley estate on the 1880 census. Peter Johnson, 1880 Census, Shiloh, Marengo, Alabama; Peter Johnson, 1880 Census, Jefferson, Marengo, Alabama.

4. Jones, *Love and Loyalty*, 346; Fitts, *Selma: Queen City*, 10; Clara Hagedorn, 'Ole Bulja Is Interesting Character Well Known on Streets of Montgomery', *Montgomery Advertiser*, 3 June 1923, 26.

Chapter 1: Kidnap

1. Roche, *Historic Sketches*, 81.

2. The Agojie/Ahosi ('King's Wives'), or Mino ('Our Mothers'), were an important feature of nineteenth-century Dahomey that may have emerged because its population was much smaller than its greatest regional enemy, the Oyo Empire, and because of transatlantic slave traders' general preference for young male captives. Many, or if not most, women warriors were not Dahomeyan by birth, but rather foreign captives who were recruited into the army's ranks. Dahomey also struggled to compete militarily with the Oyo Empire's commanding cavalry as the tsetse fly meant horses could not survive on the coast. James Saxon Childers, 'From Jungle to Slavery – and Freedom', *Birmingham News*, 2 December 1934, 44; Hurston, *Barracoon*, 45; Alpern, *Amazons*, 37, 52–61, 65 and 67–8; Hurston, *Dust Tracks*, 166; Bay, *Wives of the Leopard*, 205.

3. Byers, 'The Last Slave-Ship', 743; S. L. Flock, 'Survivor Of Last Slave Cargo Lives On Plantation Near Selma', *Montgomery Advertiser*, 31 January 1932, 13; Boynton Robinson, *Bridge Across Jordan*, 32.

4. Klebsattel, 'Slaves Captured', 517-18; Hurston, *Dust Tracks*, 166.

5. Hurston, *Barracoon*, 45–6.

6. 'Osie' is the name listed on Matilda's death certificate. Sylviane A. Diouf identifies the name Zora Neale Hurston recorded as 'O-lo-loo-ay' as Oluwale, a name also shared by the man known in Mobile as Osia Keeby. Conversely, Natalie S. Robertson suggests it may have been a corruption of Obalolu/Obaloluwa, meaning 'where there is a king, the king is as God.' However, Kossula denied that he and his fellow *Clotilda* Africans were of royal lineage. 'Nobody among us ain' born no king', he reported. Diouf identifies the name Hurston recorded as 'Ny-fond-lo-loo' as Fondlolu, although her translation is based on a mistaken interpretation that Kossula and his family were members of the Isha

sub-group of Yoruba of western-central Benin; conversely, Robertson identifies it as Ninfoluwa, which translates broadly as 'have something for God; give something to God; make gifts to God' in Yoruba. Owen and Mitchell, *Our Home Land*, 76; Matilda Crear Death Certificate, Selma, Dallas, Alabama, 13 January 1940; Hurston, *Barracoon*, 38 and 46−7; Diouf, *Dreams*, 43; Robertson, *The Slave Ship Clotilda*, 95−6 and 148; Alpern, *Amazons*, 66.

7. The captives' hometown was spelled variously by historians and journalists as A'tarco, Ataka, Attako, Taccou, Taccow, Takko, Takkoi, Tekke, Tekki, Tika and Tiko, but most commonly as Tarkar. Kossula's two-year-old shipmate Matilda named her third daughter 'Winny' in a likely tribute to her lost homeland. Both previous studies on the *Clotilda* mistakenly place Tarkar far from 'Whinney', but for different reasons. As Kossula once referred to his homeland as 'Whinney', Robertson does not include him among the residents of Tarkar, even though he stated that he was from Tarkar in his other interviews. Robertson instead connects Tarkar to the Takad chiefdom in southern Kaduna, central Nigeria. Conversely, Diouf recognizes that Kossula was from Tarkar, but does not recognize *Harper*'s 'Gossolaw' as Kossula. Diouf posits instead that 'Whinney' might be Ouémé/ Weme or Ouinhi in present-day south Benin and that Tarkar might be near Banté, a region in the west of present-day Benin, given the similarity between the name Kossula and the Banté town Kossola. Diouf also interprets 'A'tarco' as Atakora in the far north of Benin to suggest some of the *Clotilda* Africans came from there, but it is most likely a variant spelling of Tarkar. Caver, 'A Lone Survivor', 6; Byers, 'The Last Slave-Ship', 743; Henry Romeyn, 'The Last Slaver', *Times-Democrat*, 1 April 1894, 25; Hurston, *Barracoon*, 3; 'Last Slave Ship Sunk Here Raised', *Mobile Register*, 25 February 1917, 12A. MPL. http://digital.mobilepubliclibrary.org/items/show/1792; Hurston, 'The Last Slave Ship', 355; Henry Romeyn, 'Last of the Slavers', *Altoona Tribune*, 19 February 1903, 2; 'Lonesome, But With Confidence, Last of Africans Awaits Call', *Andalusia Star*, 9 March 1923, 8; Imes, 'The Last Recruits', 355; Roche, *Historic Sketches*, Ch. 5; Winny Creagh, 1880 U.S. Census, Liberty Hill, Dallas, Alabama; Robertson, *The Slave Ship Clotilda*, 79−80 and 115−18; Diouf, *Dreams*, 32 and 36.

8. Childers, 'From Jungle'; Roche, *Historic Sketches*, 75−6; Hurston, *Barracoon*, 38; Christopher Pala, 'Town says Last Slaves Brought There', *Atlanta Constitution*, 15 May 1983, 2; Cammie East,

'Africatown Works Toward its Future, Honors its Past', *Mobile Press-Register*, 5 July 1981, 4-B. MPL. https://digital. mobilepubliclibrary.org/items/show/1846.

9. Missionary Richard Henry Stone noted such buildings' imperviousness to fire, observing that 'after a big fire the people go out to the farms, get a supply of poles, grass, reeds and vines, and in a few days everything is as before.' Roche, *Historic Sketches*, 75–6; Berger, 'Cugo Lewis'; Hurston, 'Cudjo's Own Story', 650–1; Stone, *In Afric's Forest*, 26; Delany, *Official Report*, 32; Hurston, 'The Last Slave Ship', 351; Johnson, *The History of the Yorubas*, 98–9.

10. Byers, 'The Last Slave-Ship', 743.

11. Boynton Robinson, *Bridge Across Jordan*, 32; Dennison, *A Memoir*, 71.

12. Robertson points out that the word is likely a reference to the abobaku ('one who is expected to die with the king'), an officer of the king who was expected to die with him to serve as his attendant in the afterlife. Dennison, *A Memoir*, 71; Hurston, 'Cudjo's Own Story', 654; Flock, 'Survivor'; Robertson, *The Slave Ship Clotilda*, 95; Johnson, *The History of the Yorubas*, 57; Owen and Mitchell, *Our Home Land*, 76.

13. Usman and Falola, *The Yoruba*, 243–4.

14. Ibid., 243; Reverend A. D. Phillips, 'Lecture on Africa', *Biblical Recorder*, 30 June 1869, 1; Childers, 'From Jungle'; Hurston, 'Cudjo's Own Story', 649.

15. Phillips, 'Lecture'; Childers, 'From Jungle'; Usman and Falola, *The Yoruba*, 248–9; Stone, *In Afric's Forest*, 21 and 23; Pettaway, 'The Folklife', 68.

16. Burton, *Abeokuta*, 131; Roche, *Historic Sketches*, 75.

17. 'The Trade of Yoruba'.

18. Cowries were used in protection and health rituals and added to each household's altar to Ori, the Yoruba orisha (spirit) of fate and destiny. When Europeans keen to profit from the transatlantic slave trade realized cowrie shells' value to Africans, they transported them in vast quantities to the continent to trade for enslaved people. Dennison, *A Memoir*, 29; Roche, *Historic Sketches*, 76–8; Akinwumi Ogundiran, 'Cowries and Rituals of Self-Realization', in *Materialities of Ritual in the Black Atlantic*, 74–5; Green, *A Fistful of Shells*, 19 and 314–15.

19. Law, *The Oyo Empire*, 206; Hurston, *Barracoon*, 20–3.

20. Kossula was the second child born to Oluwale and his second wife. Kossula had five full siblings and twelve half-siblings. Hurston, *Barracoon*, 38–40; Usman and Falola, *The Yoruba*, 247–8.

21. Kanko's mother's name was given as Conco on Kanko's death certificate. Lottie Dennison Death Certificate, Mobile, Alabama, 16 April 1917; Usman and Falola, *The Yoruba*, 291; Dennison, *A Memoir*, 38.

22. Ibid., 19.

23. There was some misunderstanding in Mable's account: the name Lagos was given, although Yoruba-speaking Kanko would have known the city as Eko, and her home was supposedly separated from Congo by the East African River Nile. Diouf concludes that 'Kanko' was a misspelling of the female Yoruba name Kêhounco. Conversely, Robertson suggests 'Kanko' was a corruption of 'Kaninkon', a community in the northern Nigerian state of Kaduna, indicating she came from that place. But that is unlikely given the strong evidence of Kanko's Yoruba origins. Ibid., 19 and 35−6; Diouf, *Dreams*, 35; Robertson, *The Slave Ship Clotilda*, 108.

24. Ninety-six per cent of all surviving captives landed in the Caribbean and South America. By far the largest share – just under five million people – disembarked in Brazil. The next highest share of Middle Passage survivors – more than a million people – landed on the British island of Jamaica. About three-quarters of a million people were displaced to the French colony of Saint-Domingue (present-day Haiti). An additional three-quarters of a million people were sent to the Spanish island of Cuba. Only about 389,000 Africans – less than 4 per cent of all Middle Passage survivors – disembarked in the present-day United States. 'Trans-Atlantic Slave Trade – Estimates'. Trans-Atlantic Slave Trade Database.

25. Ibid.; French, *Born in Blackness*, 8.

26. The reasons for Britain's shift from dependency on, to prevention of, the slave trade were complex and evolved over time, although economic self-interest and imperialism are considered to have played important roles alongside genuine humanitarianism. Slavery was not abolished in the British Empire until after the passage of the 1832 Reform Act, which expanded the franchise, limiting pro-slavers' power in parliament and creating new constituencies in the industrial North of England, where abolitionist feeling was strong. The British government spent £20 million – 40 per cent of its annual expenditure – compensating former enslavers for the loss of their human 'property', and King William IV was so opposed to emancipation that he had to be assured of its certain failure before he would sign the 1833 Abolition Act into law. When the act came into force on 1 August 1834, only enslaved people below the age of six were

immediately freed; full emancipation was not granted until 1 August 1838. Wills, *Envoys of Abolition*, 5–10; Taylor, *The Interest*, 271–2, 275 and 310.

27. 'Trans-Atlantic Slave Trade – Estimates'.

28. Kpengla is named Adahoonzou by the source of this quotation. Dalzel, *The History*, 217; French, *Born in Blackness*, 267–8.

29. Oyo was one of the largest slave trading entities in the Bight of Benin until its collapse in the 1830s. Lovejoy, 'Mapping Uncertainty', 131.

30. Hurston also later reported that 'Kossula and his fellow Takkoi tribesmen were placed in one barracoun [sic] by themselves'. The number of captives on board the *Clotilda* varied considerably across different primary sources, although 110 is likely to be accurate as that was the figure their kidnapper William Foster admitted to trafficking. That was also the number recorded by George Lake Imes when he interviewed nine of the shipmates in 1917. Conversely, Richard Hines, Jr. learned from head of the conspiracy Timothy Meaher that 160 Africans were forced onto the *Clotilda*, a figure Henry Romeyn repeated a few years later when he visited the Mobile Africans in the company of Augustine Meaher, Timothy's son. Emma Langdon Roche, who knew some of the *Clotilda* survivors and interviewed William Foster's widow, understood that he bought 130 Africans and boarded 116, which was the same number S. H. M. Byers reported when he interviewed Abaché, Abile and Kossula. Wiley G. Toomer, whose father William Henry Toomer helped to hide the captives, recalled that 93 people were trafficked to Alabama, although he also claimed that 'nearly all' of them were 'young males'. Film director George Frederic Wheeler reported after interviewing Polee and Zuma that 92 Africans were landed in Mobile, but he also asserted that Zuma was a 125-year-old Zulu woman. Hurston, *Barracoon*, 53, 65, 71 and 92; Hurston, *Dust Tracks*, 167; Hurston, 'The Last Slave Ship', 355; Foster, 'Last Slaver', 9; Imes, 'The Last Recruits', 355; Hines, 'Last Slave Cargo', *Pittsburgh Dispatch*, 30 November 1890, 15; Romeyn, 'The Last Slaver'; Roche, *Historic Sketches*, 87–8; Byers, 'The Last Slave-Ship', 743; 'Last of Slave Business', *Buffalo Commercial*, 7 Feburary 1901, 4; 'Booker T. Washington Book the Background', *Birmingham Reporter*, 15 September 1917, 2.

31. The historical capital of the Ijesha is Ilesa, a town in present-day Osun State, 60 miles east of Owini Hill and 55 miles southeast of Ogbomosho. The Nupe's historical territory lies just northeast of Ogbomosho. One of the *Clotilda*'s oldest male survivors, whose name

was recorded as Jerry on the 1870 census, J. B. on the 1880 census and his son's death record, Jabez by the son of his kidnapper, and posthumously by his shipmates as Jaybee, had a nose ring that indicates he was probably a Fulani or Nupe tradesman. Jaybee has previously been identified as a member of the so-called 'Jaba' or Ham people of Kaduna State in northwest Nigeria. But 'Jaba' is an ethnic slur for the Ham people and translates roughly as 'stinking house rat'. Most likely, he took the biblical name Jabez in the US, which his shipmates knew as 'Jay-bee', just as they knew Alice as 'Allie', Charles as 'Charlie', Inez as 'Innie' and Josephine as 'Josephin-ah', because Yoruba words do not end with consonant sounds or contain the letter 'z'. Pettaway, 'The Folklife', 95; Diouf, *Dreams*, 38; Robertson, *The Slave Ship Clotilda*, 111–15; Roche, *Historic Sketches*, 82; Jerry Sha, 1870 US Census, Beat 3, Mobile, Alabama; J. B. Shaid, 1880 US Census, Kosters, Mobile, Alabama; Frank Shade, Deaths and Burials Index, Prichard, Mobile, Alabama, 5 June 1958; Meaher to Donaldson; John, 'Narratives of Identity', 20–2.

32. Law, *Ouidah*, 222.

33. As Robertson notes, a journey following the path of the Ogun River, which flows just west of Oyo down to Lagos, would have been the most logical route for Africans kidnapped in Oyo. When implored by a British naval officer in 1863 to halt the transatlantic slave trade, King Glele explained why he had no intention of doing so. He emphasized that selling people was a generations-old practice that he had inherited and was dependent on to feed his people and hold his kingdom together, the palm oil trade being an inadequate financial substitute. 'I cannot stop it all at once: what will my people do? And besides this, I should be in danger of losing my life.'

Jamaican traveller Robert Campbell was in Abeokuta in March 1860 to witness the aftermath of an earlier attempted assault on the city: 'We found Abbeokuta in considerable commotion. Only a few days before, the Dahomians were known to be advancing against the city, but informed doubtless by their spies of the reception that was prepared for them, they suddenly wheeled about and retraced their steps, not without committing much depredation among the people through whose territory they passed.' Ibid., 233; Alpern, *Amazons*, 181; 'Summary of News – Foreign', *Guardian*, 17 April 1860, 2; Robertson, *The Slave Ship Clotilda*, 99; 'Despatches from Commodore Wilmot', 835; Campbell, *A Pilgrimage*, 124.

34. Richard Henry Stone spent two years in Abeokuta in the late 1850s and early 1860s, where Oro ceremonies were occasions to administer

legal punishments and resolve political matters. Nineteenth-century historian Reverend Samuel Johnson, whose father Henry Erugunjinmi Johnson was an omoba (prince) of the Oyo Empire, recorded that the principal Oro worshippers among the Oyo Yoruba lived in Jabata, a province in New Oyo, and in Iseyin, a neighbouring town. Simpich, 'Smoke', 740; Stone, *In Afric's Forest*, 88; Johnson, *The History of the Yorubas*, 32; Hurston, *Barracoon*, 41–3.

35. The use of agbajigbeto ('hunters in the reception area'), spies who may have originated in their place of espionage, and who could describe the organization of its army and the location of its gates and major households, was an important Dahomey military tactic. Flock, 'Survivor'; Klebsattel, 'Slaves Captured', 516; Hurston, *Barracoon*, 43–5; Bay, *Wives of the Leopard*, 131–2; Imes, 'The Last Recruits', 355.

36. Byers, 'The Last Slave-Ship', 743; Boynton Robinson, *Bridge Across Jordan*, 32; Campbell, *A Pilgrimage*, 115.

37. Alpern, *Amazons*, 181.

38. Hurston, *Barracoon*, 47–8; Baquaqua and Moore, *Biography*, 38.

39. Hurston, *Barracoon*, 48.

40. As the captives drew closer to Ouidah, they passed a Dahomeyan village, where they were disturbed to see the heads of other recent victims of its army mounted on poles, and skulls devoid of their flesh. The display of skulls was a key expression of Dahomeyan military power. Ibid., 48–9. Emphasis in original; Roche, *Historic Sketches*, 82; Bay, *Wives of the Leopard*, 134.

41. Diouf questions the veracity of Kossula's map because Dahomey had not conquered Lagos or Badagry and it was taboo for its king to travel by sea. But all three cities are set back from the sea by a long lagoon system and Kossula's map shows the Africans passed north of the waterways that separated the ports from the coast. Moreover, Lagos, Badagry and Porto-Novo's nominal independence and Dahomey's coastal influence meant its army was unlikely to encounter obstructions to those territories. British missionary Frederick Forbes visited the West African coast in 1849 and 1850 and reported that, although Ouidah was the only slave port belonging to Dahomey, 'the king claims the beach and the right of embarkation, and enforces tribute from the European traders at the ports of Porto Novo [sic] and Badagry on the east'.

Hurston, who believed when she drafted her posthumously published manuscript *Barracoon* that 'Tarkar' was Takon (formerly Itakon), a region 40 miles north of Porto-Novo in present-day Benin, recorded in that document that the captives also spent a few days at Abomey (identified as 'Lomey' in *Barracoon* but unequivocally as 'Abomey' in her memoir *Dust Tracks on a Road*), where their captors had a feast and where Kossula supposedly caught sight of the king's house, which he noticed was made from skull bones. But that claim was almost certainly false; Abomey was 150 miles west of Oyo, was not on Kossula's map, and Redoshi also reported that the captives were marched directly to the sea. Crucially, Hurston appears to have corrected that assertion in a 1943 *American Mercury* article, noting instead that '*Travelers* reported that the palace at Abomey was made of bleached skulls', and recording only that the captives passed through Lagos, Badagry and Porto-Novo before arriving at Ouidah. Most likely, Hurston sought to add historical detail to *Barracoon* by embedding into her narrative Roche's more general observation that the 'King of Dahomey's house was built of skulls'. A letter Hurston sent to her benefactor Charlotte Osgood Mason shows she thought Glele's skulls were an important detail, and Kossula's fleeting references to Abomey in *Barracoon* appear to paraphrase other sources. His allusion to 'fresh head high on de stick' echoes Roche's report that, 'As they passed near one of Dahomey's villages . . . they caught sight of fresh heads raised on poles', and his strikingly vague description of the annual festival the captives supposedly witnessed there – 'Everybody sing and dance and beatee de drum' – sounds like the historical source Hurston cited, which called it an event 'with music, dancing, and singing'. The captives could not have been in Abomey during the May to June festival as they reached Ouidah by early May. Diouf suggests the Dahomey army 'always went back to Abomey or Cana to dispose of its prisoners'. But Italian missionary Francesco Borghero understood that survivors of a March 1862 assault on a town near Abeokuta who were not sold into slavery at Ouidah would *then* be taken to Abomey for sacrifice. Borghero bought and liberated several children and 10 adult men to save them from such a death march. Robertson, *The Slave Ship Clotilda*, 99 and 104; Diouf, *Dreams*, 48; Forbes, *Dahomey and the Dahomans*, 11 and 18; Roche, *Historic Sketches*, 74–5 and 82; Mann, *Slavery*, 42; Hurston, *Barracoon*, 52; Hurston, *Dust Tracks*, 164–5; Owen and Mitchell, *Our Home Land*, 76; Hurston, 'Last Slave Ship', 353–4. Emphasis added; Hurston to Mason, 25 March 1931, in *Zora Neale Hurston*, ed. Kaplan, 214; Alpern, *Amazons*, 181; Marc Shiltz, 'Cosmopolitanism in the Nineteenth-century Missionary Encounter', in *We the Cosmopolitans*, 122.

42. Kossula told a journalist that he had never seen the sea before he was forced across it. Simpich, 'Smoke', 740.

Chapter 2: The Conspiracy

1. The steamboat *Roger B. Taney*, which was built and launched in 1857, and the year 1858 were later named as the site and date of the *Clotilda* bet, probably to create the false impression the *Clotilda* conspiracists were acting on impulse rather than out of pro-slavery zealotry. That the conspiracy was long in the planning was underscored by the fact that the schooner's owners insured the vessel four years in a row, signalling they intended it for international trade. As archaeologist James P. Delgado has noted, such a practice was incredibly rare at the time as it was costly and meant the vessel had to adhere to rigid standards. 'It is No Slight Evidence . . .', *Daily Delta*, 29 October 1852, 2; Ayer, *The Reminiscences*, 38; 'The Roger B. Taney', *Clarke County Democrat*, 14 May 1857, 2; Hines, 'Last Slave Cargo'; Archaeological Investigations, 18–19; Delgado, 'Diving for the Clotilda'; Delgado, *Clotilda*, 104–5.

2. 'The Weather'. *Cahaba Gazette*, 11 January 1856, 2; 'The Weather', *Sumter County Whig*, 9 January 1856, 2; 'We Expected to . . .' and 'Weather', *Clarke County Democrat*, 31 January 1856, 2; 'For Several Days . . .', *Daily State Sentinel*, 9 February 1860, 3.

3. Walter Johnson has pointed out that slavery was a 'stock topic of conversation' on steamboats, making them important platforms for disseminating and ultimately reinforcing attitudes to race and slavery in the US South. Ayer, *The Reminiscences*, 38–9; Romeyn, 'The Last Slaver'; Johnson, *River of Dark Dreams*, 135.

4. Gosse, *Letters*, 26; English, *Civil Wars*, 8; Johnson, *River of Dark Dreams*, 5 and 10; Beckert, *Empire of Cotton*, xix, 109 and 205.

5. Anon., 'Origin of Slaving'; Russell, *My Diary*, 185.

6. Malcolm Lee Johnson suggests that Chubb 'may have still actually been transporting slaves when the *Royal Yacht* was captured on the night of November 7–8, 1861, during the Civil War, since he was imprisoned at Fort Lafayette in the north and condemned to death for engaging in the slave trade'. Chubb's sentence was eventually commuted.
'St. Charles . . .', *New Orleans Crescent*, 8 January 1856, 1; Fremantle, *The Fremantle Diary*, 54; Johnson, *Texas Tales*, 53; 'Arrival of the Connecticut', *New York Times*, 18 December 1861, 5.

7. Ferrer, *Cuba*, 110; Johnson, *River of Dark Dreams*, 397.

8. Harris, *The Last Slave Ships*, 3–6 and 24; Ferrer, *Cuba*, 110; Thomas, *The Slave Trade*, 762.

9. Harris, *The Last Slave Ships*, 221 and 240–1.

10. See, for example, 'New York', *Times-Picayune*, 29 June 1872, 1; 'Another International Complication', *Charleston Daily News*, 29 June 1872, 1;

'Slaves Landed', *Daily Commonwealth*, 29 June 1872, 1; House of Commons, 19 April 1872, in *Hansard's Parliamentary Debates*, 1563; Sir Henry Morton Stanley, 'Whydah', *New York Daily Herald*, 23 April 1874, 13; de la Riva, *El monto de la immigración forzada*, 16; Franco, *Comercio clandestino de esclavos*, 178; Thomas, *The Slave Trade*, 771 and 784.

11. William Foster was very likely the 25-year-old Pictou-born ship's carpenter who arrived in Rhode Island on 3 June 1844, and almost certainly the same carpenter who arrived in Rhode Island from Pictou on 2 July 1845, one day before his mother and seven of his siblings. His father and oldest brother, both named George, arrived in Rhode Island together on 20 July 1844; his oldest sister Ann arrived seven weeks later. Foster probably named the schooner after St. Clotilde (*c.*474–545), who helped to establish Christianity in Western Europe by converting her husband, King of the Franks Clovis I (*c.*466–511), from paganism to Roman Catholicism. Clovis is widely regarded as the founder of the French monarchy. Taylor, *Rhode Island Passenger Lists*, 75–6; 'Capt. Wm. Foster, Commander of Last American Slave Vessel Buried Yesterday', *Prichard Herald*, February 1901. MPL. https://digital. mobilepubliclibrary.org/items/show/1789; William Foster, 1900 US Census, Whistler, Mobile, Alabama; *Clotilda's* Original Certificate of Registry; Delgado, *Clotilda*, 96 and 102.

12. Emma Langdon Roche, basing her knowledge on local rumours, felt 'certain' that other trafficking voyages were undertaken by the Meaher brothers and William Foster. Roche, *Historic Sketches*, 71–2; Delgado, *Clotilda*, 125 and 134–5; Tabor, *Africatown*, 31.

13. Sledge, *The Mobile River*, 262.

14. Hines, 'Last Slave Cargo'; Russell, *My Diary*, 187.

15. Roger Eastman was Timothy's four-times-great-grandfather and Max Eastman's five-times-great-grandfather. Millay's great-grandfather John Millay and Timothy's mother Susannah Millay Meaher were siblings. O'Meagher, *Some Historical Notices*, 175–6.

16. A newspaper report lamented that clerk Thomas C. Daniel was a popular man who had been forced to retaliate against his physically intimidating boss; the steamboat captain 'was to blame'. Ibid., 176–8; 'The Funeral of Captain Timothy Meaher', *Mobile Daily Register*, 5 March 1892. MPL. http://digital.mobilepubliclibrary.org/items/ show/1834; Olmsted, *A Journey*, 567; 'Unfortunate Difficulty', *Cahaba Gazette*, 7 July 1854, 2.

17. Ayer, *The Reminiscences*, 38; *Ayer's American Almanac*, n. p.

18. Judge Walter B. Jones, 'Off The Bench', *Montgomery Advertiser*, 15 February 1954, 4; *History and Directory*, 23; 'Church History of Montgomery', *Montgomery Advertiser*, 22 August 1921, 3; 'Democratic and Anti-Know-Nothing Meeting', *Weekly Advertiser*, 2 January 1856, 3.

19. Halstead, *Caucuses of 1860*, 5; Brown, 'The Orator of Secession', 613 and 616; 'Death of William L. Yancey', *Montgomery Weekly Mail*, 12 August 1863, 1.

20. Spratt's grandmother Margaret Taylor Polk was the sister of the president's grandfather Ezekiel Franklin Polk. 'The Southern Convention', 317; Sinha, *The Counterrevolution*, 127−8, 137 and 140−1; Wells, *The Slave Ship Wanderer*, 50−1.

21. For example, cotton and woollen textile production was 17 times greater in the North, bar, sheet and railroad iron production was 13 times greater, pig iron production was 20 times greater, firearms production was 32 times greater, and unlike the North, the South had no factories for making munitions, steel, car wheels or sewing machines. Southern political economists also bemoaned that the South produced two-thirds of the nation's exports but only one-tenth of its imports. Ignoring the comparative underinvestment in Southern manufacturing and the extremely low subsistence levels of enslaved people, who made up nearly half the populations of Alabama, Louisiana and Mississippi yet had no wages to help grow the economy, Southern elites railed against what they saw as Southern wealth being diverted North. For discussions of the links between land exhaustion and the Civil War, see Mauldin, *Unredeemed Land* and Silkenat, *Scars*. Roland, *An American Iliad*, 44; Beckert, *Empire of Cotton*, 103; Johnson, *River of Dark Dreams*, 8, 11 and 282−5.

22. James De Bow to Edmund Ruffin, 29 June 1859, cited in Mitchell, *Edmund Ruffin*, 124. Emphasis in original.

23. Slave trade advocates had been attempting to bring a slave trade debate to the floor of a Southern Convention every year since 1855; 1858 was the year they finally succeeded. Johnson, *River of Dark Dreams*, 396; 'Southern Commercial Convention', *Independent American*, 7 April 1858, 2; Walther, *William Lowndes Yancey*, 219; Sinha, *The Counterrevolution*, 148−9.

24. The Upper South was a net exporter of enslaved people, and the Deep South was a net importer of enslaved people. For that reason, most of the slave trade reopening advocates resided in the Deep South. Keri Leigh Merritt has identified as one of the causes of the Civil War the growing militancy of a poor white underclass in the Deep South,

which, finding itself shut out of an economy centred on slavery, began to form labour organizations in the 1850s. She observes that, 'the master class was already strenuously defending the peculiar institution from attacks by northern abolitionists and by slaves themselves. When poor whites created a three-front battleground, slaveholders had few viable alternatives other than secession to protect their main source of wealth and revenue'. In 1860, Alabama had 33,730 slaveholding families, a sizeable proportion of its total white population of 565,000. Nevertheless, much of the region's wealth and most of its enslaved population were concentrated in the hands of a tiny elite. Eighty-five per cent of all cotton picked in the South that year was harvested on estates of more than 100 acres, and 91.2 per cent of all people enslaved in the region were imprisoned on those estates. Walther, *William Lowndes Yancey*, 216–18; Wells, *The Slave Ship Wanderer*, 12–13; Johnson, *River of Dark Dreams*, 404; Merritt, *Masterless Men*, 4–6; Colcord, *The History of Pig Iron Manufacture in Alabama*, 2; *Alabama: A Guide to the Deep South*, 77; Beckert, *Empire of Cotton*, 110.

25. Scroggs, *Filibusters*, 212; Walker, 'General Walker's Policy',166; Johnson, *River of Dark Dreams*, 417.

26. Du Bois, *The Suppression*, 176; Johnson, *River of Dark Dreams*, 396; Walther, *William Lowndes Yancey*, 231.

27. *Agricultural Experiment Station*, 35; Roche, *Historic Sketches*, 84; Foster, 'Last Slaver', 1; Final Outbound Manifest for the *Clotilda*; Hines, 'Last Slave Cargo'.

28. Crews recruited after the 1808 slave trade ban typically were not told the purpose of their voyage because their work was nasty and brutal, sickness and death rates were high and they risked incarceration or abandonment in Africa or prosecution back home. A handwritten note held by the History Museum of Mobile records the first and second mates as George Duncan and J. B. Northrup. However, as Nick Tabor has suggested, those names were probably intended to provide cover for the voyage's actual participants. 'Capt. Wm. Foster'; Crew List for the *Clotilda*'s Final Voyage; Hines, 'Last Slave Cargo'; Tabor, *Africatown*, 303.

29. Walter Smith, 1860 US Census, Mobile Ward 1, Mobile, Alabama; B. R. Jones and Elizabeth V. Smith Marriage Certificate, Montgomery, Alabama, 16 December 1863; 'Long Grabs', 'Montgomery, Ala. Feb. 26, 1860', *Lancaster News*, 7 March 1860, 2.

30. Roche, *Historic Sketches*, 84; Foster, 'Last Slaver', 1–2.

31. Portugal made little effort to enforce anti-slave trade laws. Diouf thus speculates that Foster may have embellished his accounts of near

capture by two Portuguese anti-slavery vessels. Robertson notes that Praia's US Consul only ever reported the capture of one slave ship, the brig *Falmouth* in June 1860. Ibid., 3; Roche, *Historic Sketches*, 85; Diouf, *Dreams*, 29; Robertson, *The Slave Ship Clotilda*, 35.

Chapter 3: The Coast

1. Foster counted 4,000 prisoners in Ouidah's barracoons and suggested there were 1,000 people in Redoshi's enclosure. A British Commissioner estimated that the barracoons at Ouidah could hold 3,000 captives. Flock, 'Survivor'; Foster, 'Last Slaver', 7; 'Sailed 4 Mar . . .', 2; 'Slave Trade', in *Annals of British Legislation*, 107.

2. Stanley, 'Whydah'.

3. W. M. Hutton, 27 July 1843, cited in Law, *Ouidah*, 140; Horton, *Physical and Medical Climate*, 34–5.

4. Skertchly, *Dahomey*, 56–7.

5. 'Trans-Atlantic Slave Trade – Estimates'; Law, *Ouidah*, 2.

6. Baquaqua and Moore, *Biography*, 39.

7. Hurston, *Barracoon*, 53.

8. Montejo, *The Autobiography*, 37 and 41–2.

9. Ibid., 42.

10. Hurston, *Barracoon*, 53.

11. The *Clotilda* Africans gave away little about the site of their prison. Emma Langdon Roche gathered only that it was behind a 'white house on the river-bank'. The precise location of Ouidah's barracoons remains unknown, although contemporary chroniclers placed them near the residence of notorious Brazilian slave trader Francisco Félix de Souza. According to a Wesleyan missionary, 'Mr. De Souza's premises occupy at least three acres of ground, surrounded by a substantial swish wall, two feet thick and twelve feet high. Inside this wall are his slave-barracoons. His house stands in front of his premises; and, being coloured white, is visible from the sea.' The white-painted Fort of São João Baptista de Ajudá (Fort St. John the Baptist of Ouidah) was built by the Portuguese Empire as a base for its slave-trading activities before being taken over by de Souza when the trade was criminalized. Visitors to Ouidah today will find the sites of the barracoons 'officially' located at the western Zomaï quarter of Ouidah and another place called Zomaï in the village of Zoungbodji south of Ouidah and 1 mile north of the sea, because the name 'Zomaï', which translates as 'Fire (or Light) prohibited', has been taken to mean that captives were held there in darkness as a means of controlling them. However, nineteenth-

century travellers learned that the name 'Zomaï' referred in Ouidah not to barracoons but, rather, to where de Souza's gunpowder stores were held. Nor are there records of a barracoon at Zoungbodji, and Henry Romeyn understood they had to be further north, 'to be safe from [anti-slavery] cruisers' fire or any casual observation'. Huntley, *Seven Years' Service*, 116; Fox, *A Brief History*, 114; Law, *Ouidah*, 137–8; Law, 'Commémoration de la Traite Atlantique à Ouidah', 21; Roche, *Historic Sketches*, 82–3; Romeyn, 'The Last Slaver'.

12. Stanley, 'Whydah'; Campbell, *A Pilgrimage*, 137.

13. Lloyd, *The Navy*, 30; Rediker, *The Amistad Rebellion*, 49.

14. Bay, *Wives of the Leopard*, 47.

15. Foster, 'Last Slaver', 6.

16. Ibid., 6; Diouf, *Dreams*, 55–6.

17. In Vodun, Dangbe is the physical manifestation of the rainbow serpent Aido-Hwedo, guardian of life, movement, stability and childbirth, who served as agent to the goddess Mawu when she created the earth. Law, *Ouidah*, 123 and 249; Foster, 'Last Slaver', 7.

18. Foster gave no details of his momentous encounter with King Glele or its purpose. The kings of Dahomey normally remained at their palace at Abomey while their administrators sold captives on their behalf at Ouidah. As Robin Law has observed, 'European ships' captains did sometimes travel to Abomey to see the king, but only when they had some specific problem or dispute to resolve with him.' Hurston firmly asserted that Foster 'did not meet the king', but only because Roche never mentioned such a meeting in her brief account of the slave ship captain's stay in Ouidah. Ibid., 7; Skertchly, *Dahomey*, 141–2; Stanley, 'Whydah'; Burton, *A Mission*, 407; Law, *Ouidah*, 127; Hurston, *Barracoon*, 8; Roche, *Historic Sketches*, 85–6.

19. Childers, 'From Jungle'.

20. 'Sailed 4 Mar . . .', 2.

21. Foster, 'Last Slaver', 7.

22. Hurston, *Barracoon*, 53.

23. Hagedorn, 'Ole Bulja'.

24. S. H. M. Byers, who interviewed Kossula, his wife Abile and Abaché, noted that 'Few of the captured ones had been more than twenty at the time of their enslavement.' Such a high number of child sales was not unusual; 46.1 per cent of Africans sold across the Atlantic after 1810 were under the age of 15. In other words, around half the victims of the illegal slave trade were children. The *Clotilda* was reported in federal documents to be carrying around fifty adults and fifty children

when it arrived in the United States, but as David Eltis has noted, the criterion for distinguishing enslaved adults from children in nineteenth-century courts was 'sexual maturity as assessed by physical appearance, which for most Africans at this time would probably occur in the mid-teens'. According to such a measurement, a typical 15- or 16-year-old might be classified as an adult. The definition of 'child' used by the British Royal African Company in the late seventeenth- and early eighteenth century was even stricter: a 'child' was a person aged 10 or younger. Byers, 'The Last Slave-Ship', 742; Fett, *Recaptured Africans*, 8; David Eltis, 'Trans-Atlantic Slave Trade — Understanding the Database: Methodology', Trans-Atlantic Slave Trade Database.

25. Robertson has identified the patterns as Abaja marks. 'Clotilda — Sailed from Mobile . . .', 2; Foster, 'Last Slaver', 7–8; Roche, *Historic Sketches*, 124; Robertson, *The Slave Ship Clotilda*, 97; Oyeniyi, *Dress*, 76.

26. Stanley, 'Whydah'; Hurston, *Barracoon*, 53–4.

27. The Middle Passage was so named because it historically represented the middle leg of the triangular slave trade between Europe, Africa and the Americas in which African people were forcibly displaced to the Americas.

28. Ibid., 54.

29. 'Kru', or 'Kroo' (perhaps originating from the British word 'crew'), was an umbrella term for autonomous groups of expert swimmers, canoe-makers and canoeists originating from present-day Liberia and southwest Côte d'Ivoire whose seafaring skills proved vital to European traders during the transatlantic slave trade era. Their tattoos, which ran from the hairline to the bridge of the nose, were intended to mark them out from captive Africans. Ibid., 54, and 165, n. 5; Frost, *Work and Community*, 7–10; Gunn, *Outsourcing African Labor*, 15–16, 20–1 and 55–6.

30. Gronniosaw, *A Narrative*, 5; Simpich, 'Smoke', 737 and 740.

31. Hagedorn, 'Ole Bulja'; Equiano, *The Interesting Narrative*, 70; Baquaqua and Moore, *Biography*, 42.

32. For example, a British slave ship sailor in the 1760s recalled how Africans on his voyages repeatedly told him they were 'all stolen'. Cited in Rediker, *The Slave Ship*, 106; Boynton Robinson, *Bridge Across Jordan*, 31–2.

33. Hurston, *Barracoon*, 54.

34. 'Take us in little boats to big boat', Redoshi recalled plainly. Flock, 'Survivor'; Skertchly, *Dahomey*, 41; Baquaqua and Moore, *Biography*, 42.

Notes

35. Captives were shaved to prevent lice infestations at sea. Roche, *Historic Sketches*, 87; Diouf, *Dreams*, 57; Hurston, *Barracoon*, 54–5; Hurston, 'The Last Slave Ship', 358.

36. Judith Byfield, 'Dress and Politics in Post-World War II Abeokuta (Western Nigeria)', in *Fashioning Africa*, 32; Roche, *Historic Sketches*, 126; Babasehinde A. Ademuleya, 'Body Adornments and Cosmetics', in *Encyclopedia of the Yoruba*, 48.

37. Flock, 'Survivor'.

38. Roche, *Historic Sketches*, 86.

39. William Arnett, 'Dinah the Slave and Her Descendants: Missouri and Arlonzia Pettway', in *The Quilts of Gee's Bend*, 92; Mary M. Friend, 'Sawnee', *Times-Democrat*, 19 November 1893, 16; 'Last of Slave Business'; Hagedorn, 'Ole Bulja'.

40. Reminding her readers that cotton was 'once a rare and costly textile fiber in Europe and elsewhere', Colleen E. Kriger points out that 'modern industrial manufacture has not only transformed the way human labor is thought of and remunerated, but it has also changed our sense of the value of manufactured goods, especially the cloth we wear.' Dinah was not the only Middle Passage survivor who recalled the colour red as a traumatic symbol of their kidnapping well into the twentieth century. Pucka Geata was a survivor of the *Wanderer*, the penultimate slave ship to land in the United States, which docked at Jekyll Island, Georgia, on 28 November 1858. Shortly before his death in Augusta, Georgia in 1915, Pucka frightened a little girl by waving a red pocket handkerchief at her and exclaiming, 'I liked to had ya, I liked to had ya.' When asked shortly before her death in 1990 why she had been so scared, she explained that the four *Wanderer* survivors that she knew told her 'that's the way they brought 'em over here from Africa'. Floyd White, a longshoreman from St. Simon's Island, Georgia, also recalled *Wanderer* Africans telling him that 'Dey trap em on a boat wid a red flag'. Kriger, *Cloth*, 2 and 36; Baldwin, *Great & Noble Jar*, 82–3; *Drums and Shadows*, 184; Beckert, *Empire of Cotton*, 36 and 51.

41. Foster, 'Last Slaver', 8.

42. Kossula told a different version of the story to Emma Langdon Roche: a Dahomey warrior stole him after his sale to Foster and hid him under the whitewashed house that stood next to the barracoons. But Kossula was intrigued by the sound of the choppy seawater. He ran away from the house and climbed up the outside of one of the barracoon's walls to see what was happening. 'I hear the noise of the sea on shore, an' I wanta see what maka dat noise, an' how dat water worka – how it fell

on shore an' went back again.' When he saw his townsfolk in a canoe, he called out to them, drawing the attention of Foster, who pulled him from the wall and out to sea, making him the last captive to leave. That story is unlikely to be true in a literal sense. The barracoon was several miles and a neck-high lagoon away from the ocean. Foster was already on board the *Clotilda* when his captives were forced into the canoes. But for Kossula, who had come to rely on parables to make sense of the many losses in his life, the meaning of the story was the same as the remembrance he shared with Zora Neale Hurston: he would still be in Africa if not for a cruel twist of fate. Hurston, *Barracoon*, 54; Roche, *Historic Sketches*, 113.

43. Foster, 'Last Slaver', 9.

Chapter 4: The Sea

1. 'Booker T. Washington Book'; 'Eva Jones Remembers Father Who Helped Found Africa Town', *Montgomery Advertiser*, 3 December 1985, 21; Roche, *Historic Sketches*, 125.

2. John Beardsley, 'Pettway', in *Gee's Bend: The Women*, 218.

3. Henry Romeyn also noted that 'all [were] ironed at the ankles.' Typically, only men were shackled, although women and children's comparative mobility below deck brought with it vulnerability to sexual abuse at the hands of their captors. Klebsattel, 'Slaves Captured', 517; Byers, 'The Last Slave-Ship', 743; Flock, 'Survivor'; Romeyn, 'The Last Slaver'; Diouf, *Dreams*, 65.

4. Kossula recalled that the Africans were not certain they would see land again. Klebsattel, 'Slaves Captured', 517.

5. Hurston, *Barracoon*, 55.

6. There were a few exceptions, such as the mothers Bougier and Gracie. William Foster falsely claimed the youngest on board was 12 years old, presumably to obscure the extent to which the *Clotilda* voyage was a child trafficking enterprise. Riggins, *Riggins Family Ancestry Book*, 8; Byers, 'The Last Slave-Ship', 743; O. S. Wynn, 'Woman Survivor of Last Slave Ship, Erect and Vigorous at Advanced Age, Walks Fifteen Miles for Gov'T Help', *Selma Times-Journal*, 20 December 1931, 11; 'Clotilda – Sailed from Mobile . . .', 2.

7. Archaeologist James Delgado estimates that the tiny space allotted to each captive adhered closely to slave ship regulations introduced in the late eighteenth century by the British government: six feet by one foot six inches for men; five feet by one foot four inches for women; and five feet by one foot for children. Archaeological Investigations, 16; Roche,

Historic Sketches, 88; Delgado, 'Diving for the Clotilda'; Delgado, *Clotilda*, 169; Klebsattel, 'Slaves Captured', 517.

8. Clementine was sent to Brunswick, Georgia, where she lived until 1923. Lifelong Brunswick resident Maria Campbell Blain (1845−1936) reported the circumstances of Clementine's birth to local historian Margaret Davis Cate a few years after the African woman's death. Yet Cate insists that Clementine and her brother Tom Floyd were 'about grown' when they arrived in the United States in her published account of Blain's remembrances. Calonius, *The Wanderer*, 104; Wells, *The Slave Ship Wanderer*, 27 and 31; McCash, *Jekyll Island's Early Years*, 153 and 243, n. 6; Cate, *Our Todays and Yesterdays*, 154.

9. One slave trader estimated the temperature in his ship's hold reached between 120 and 130 degrees Fahrenheit (49 to 50 degrees Celsius). Childers, 'From Jungle'; Imes, 'The Last Recruits', 355; Kenneth F. Kiple and Brian T. Higgins, 'Mortality during the Middle Passage', in *The Atlantic Slave Trade*, 324; Hurston, *Barracoon*, 55.

10. Boynton Robinson, *Bridge Across Jordan*, 32; Wynn, 'Woman Survivor'; Thomas, *The Slave Trade*, 415; Foster, 'Last Slaver', 9−10.

11. Boynton Robinson, *Bridge Across Jordan*, 32.

12. Dennison, *A Memoir*, 25 and 38−40; Hurston, *Barracoon*, 38.

13. Beardsley, 'Pettway', 218; Romeyn, 'The Last Slaver'; Campbell, *A Pilgrimage*, 58; Stone, *In Afric's Forest and Jungle*, 125; Diouf, *Dreams*, 44−5.

14. Zora Neale Hurston recorded their god's name, which she transcribed as 'Alahua'. The Yoruba creator-God is also known as Olorun or Olodumare. Diouf traces 'Polee' to the ritual name 'Kupollee'. Conversely, Robertson suggests that Polee's name derived from Kupolu, Kupolusi, or Kupolokun, which were not initiation names, but, rather, birth names meaning 'one born after the death of the Olu (chief) of the house'. Hurston, *Barracoon*, 19; Usman and Falola, *The Yoruba*, 271−4; Diouf, *Dreams*, 44−5; Robertson, *The Slave Ship Clotilda*, 161.

15. Roche surmised that Zuma was 'possibly the last 'Tarkbar' and thus Nupe, a Muslim ethnic group her Yoruba shipmates knew as 'Takpa'. Diouf supports such an origin by identifying her name (which was also transcribed as Juma, Juna, Kazooma, Saner, Zinnia, Zimmer, Zooma and Zunia) as Arzuma/Juma'a, which means 'born on a Friday' in Arabic. But Roche's account is unreliable. She failed to communicate with the usually friendly African woman and turned instead to William

Foster's widow Adelaide, whose racist framing of Zuma as a socially isolated 'unregenerate' encouraged Roche to play up the large, dark-skinned woman's physical differences from her shipmates. Roche noted that while the other Africans had 'three [marks] on the cheek' and two lines above the nose, Zuma had 'three deep gashes' that accentuated 'all her fat, brutal old ugliness.' Yet the style of her markings, which met 'at the bridge of the nose', before 'running diagonally across each cheek', echoed her shipmates' Abaja patterns. Henry Romeyn reported that Zuma was captured by 'L'Ascatha' (Tarkar) before being sold to William Foster, but also impossibly claimed she was from 'Loandi' (Luanda/Loanda), a major slave port more than two thousand miles south of Oyo. Zuma's later devotion to Christianity – a neighbour described her as 'pow'f'u'l in pra'er' – also raises questions about her origins; as Diouf has also noted, it would have been extremely unusual for a Muslim to convert. Jones, *Love and Loyalty*, 347; Imes, 'The Last Recruits of Slavery', 358; 'Booker T. Washington Book'; Chris McFadyen, 'Legacy of a "Peculiar Institution"', *Azalea City News & Review*, 15 September 1983, 4. MPL. https://digital.mobilepubliclibrary.org/items/show/1813; Saner Africa, 1870 US Census, Beat 3, Mobile, Alabama; James Weir, Jr., 'The Last Slaver and Its Queer Cargo of Devil Worshipers', *Courier Journal*, 18 April 1897, 19; Zimmer Leveston, 1900 US Census, Precinct 9, Whistler, Mobile, Alabama; Roche, *Historic Sketches of the South*, 114 and 126; '115-Year Old Negro Dies at Mobile', *Clarke County Democrat*, 22 November 1923, 1; Diouf, *Dreams*, 34 and 169; Romeyn, 'The Last Slaver'; Jones, 'Editorial Correspondence', 53–5.

16. Childers, 'From Jungle'; Hurston, *Barracoon*, 55; Foster, 'Last Slaver', 10; Klebsattel, 'Slaves Captured', 517.
17. Hurston, *Barracoon*, 55; Hagedorn, 'Ole Bulja'.
18. Boynton Robinson, *Bridge Across Jordan*, 33.
19. Roche, *Historic Sketches*, 123.
20. Equiano, *The Interesting Narrative*, 72, 85 and 97; Cugoano, *Thoughts*, 8–9; Piersen, *Black Legacy*, 11–12.
21. Abile and Kossula's fears may have been deliberately stoked by Foster. Slave ship captains used sharks to terrorize and thus control both their captives and their crews. Rediker, *The Slave Ship*, 37 and 39; Roche, *Historic Sketches*, 114.
22. Hurston, *Barracoon*, 56; Klebsattel, 'Slaves Captured', 517; Romeyn, 'The Last Slaver'; Roche, *Historic Sketches*, 90.
23. Flock, 'Survivor'; Harris, *The Last Slave Ships*, 221; Roche, *Historic Sketches*, 89–90.

24. Klebsattel, 'Slaves Captured', 517; 'Last Slave Ship Sunk'; Imes, 'The Last Recruits', 356; Berger, 'Cugo Lewis'; 'Lonesome, But With Confidence'; Hurston, *Barracoon*, 55–6; Boynton Robinson, *Bridge Across Jordan*, 32.

25. Flock, 'Survivor'; Wynn, 'Woman Survivor'.

26. Another note, written from Foster's perspective but not in his hand, stated simply, 'lost a girl of 14'. It's not clear if the 'girl of 14' and 'girl of 16' were the same person. *Mobile Daily Register* journalist Richard Hines, Jr.'s handwritten interview notes with Foster and Timothy Meaher record that '1 Negro died on passage', but he omitted that information from his published article. Conversely, Henry Romeyn reported in 1894 that two captives died at sea, which was the same number recorded by Emma Berger and James Saxon Childers when they interviewed Kossula in the 1920s and 1930s. Emma Landon Roche omitted any reference to deaths at sea from her 1914 book on the *Clotilda*, which gave few other specific details about the horrors of the transatlantic voyage, prompting Zora Neale Hurston to include in *Barracoon* an erroneous and likely fallacious claim by Kossula that nobody died, or was even sick, on the slave ship. 'Clotilda – Sailed from Mobile . . .', 2; 'Lonesome, But With Confidence'; 'Africans Around', *Montgomery Mail*, 16 July 1860; 'Sailed 4 Mar . . .', 1; Hines, 'Last Slave Cargo'; Hines, 'Annotated as Told . . .', 1; Romeyn, 'The Last Slaver'; Berger, 'Cugo Lewis'; Childers, 'From Jungle'; Roche, *Historic Sketches*, 89–91; Hurston, *Barracoon*, 56.

27. Campbell, *A Pilgrimage*, 71; Hurston, *Barracoon*, 33.

28. 'The Last Slave', *The Dothan Eagle*, 4 December 1935, 4.

29. Roche, *Historic Sketches*, 90.

30. Foster, 'Last Slaver', 10.

31. *United States v. Burns Meaher*, Writ of Seizure and Summons; Roche, *Historic Sketches*, 90–1; Hurston, *Barracoon*, 55–6.

Chapter 5: Arrival

1. James Delgado cites Foster's knowledge of Tampico as a port where he could overhaul a slave ship as potential evidence the *Clotilda* was involved in human trafficking before its final voyage. Delgado, *Clotilda*, 136.

2. Roche, *Historic Sketches*, 91; Delgado, *Clotilda*, 158; William Foster, 'Last Slaver', 10–11; 'Clotilda – Sailed from Mobile . . .', 3.

3. 'Last of Slave Business'; Hines, 'Last Slave Cargo'; Scott, 'Affika Town', 60.

4. Timothy Meaher named the *Taney* after US Chief Justice Roger Brooke Taney, who ruled in the notorious Supreme Court case *Dred Scott v.*

Sandford (1857) that Black people were not citizens, and thus not entitled to the rights of citizens, and that slavery therefore could not be prohibited in the nation's territories.

5. Emma Langdon Roche recorded a different story: Hollingsworth was meant to be waiting for the *Clotilda*'s arrival at Point aux Pins with his steamboat. Regardless of whether Hollingsworth was ignorant of the plot when he was summoned, he was surely aware from the *Clotilda*'s overpowering smell of urine, vomit and excrement that locked in its hold were scores of transatlantic trafficking victims. Hines, 'Last Slave Cargo'; Roche, *Historic Sketches*, 94; Dennison, *Biographical Memoirs*, n.p., 23 and 56.

6. 'The Weather and Crops', *Cahaba Gazette*, 13 July 1860, 3; 'Correspondence of the Advertiser', *Weekly Advertiser*, 25 July 1860, 1.

7. Hurston, *Barracoon*, 56.

8. Roche, *Historic Sketches*, 96.

9. Flock, 'Survivor'.

10. Roche, *Historic Sketches*, 96.

11. Roche probably gained this information from Adelaide Foster, Foster's widow. On 16 July 1860, the *Montgomery Mail* claimed the 103 captives it reported were collectively worth '$103,000'. William Toomer's son Wiley G. Toomer suggested that $1,000 was a conservative estimate for the captives; Foster himself intimated their individual value was $1,400. Ibid., 92; Russell, 'My Diary', 187; 'Africans Around', *Montgomery Mail*, 16 July 1860; 'Last of Slave Business'; 'Sailed 4 Mar 1859 . . .', 2.

12. Ben Raines notes that the use of fatwood, or 'lighter wood', the dead central trunk of a tree containing highly combustible sap, would have ensured the blaze was visible as far south as Mobile. Roche photographed for her 1914 book a wreck she identified as the *Clotilda*, which archaeologists believe matches the size and shape of the slave ship. Hurston, *Barracoon*, 56; Hamilton, *Mobile of the Five Flags*, 285; Roche, *Historic Sketches*, 97 and 103; Raines, *The Last Slave Ship*, 80; Byers, 'The Last Slave-Ship', 745; 'Answers to Inquiries', *Evening Sun*, 29 March 1911, 5; Imes, 'The Last Recruits', 356; Klebsattel, 'Slaves Captured', 517; Berger, 'Cugo Lewis'; Delgado, *Clotilda*, 11.

13. Elizabeth Taylor Moore Dabney's maternal grandmother Elizabeth Aylett, *née* Henry, was Patrick Henry's daughter.

14. Imes, 'The Last Recruits', 356; Hurston, *Barracoon*, 56.

15. Roche, *Historic Sketches*, 97.

Notes

16. *Harper's Weekly*, *Diario de la Marina* and the *Anti-Slavery Bugle* all repeated a hoax claim, first reported by the New Orleans *Daily Delta*, that the Africans were the 11 adults and 11 children auctioned by slave trader Julian Neville outside the St. Charles Hotel in New Orleans at noon on 13 July. In fact, at least seven members of that group, which included skilled blacksmiths Henry and Ned, a woman named Maria and her small children Green and Charity, and two unaccompanied 12-year-olds named Charlotte and Maria, had European ancestry. Neville forced the *Daily Delta* to print a correction on the day of the group's sale. *Harper's Weekly* claimed in October 1859 that its weekly circulation of up to 93,000 copies per week was more than double that of other illustrated newspapers. The *Clotilda's* trafficking voyage was also reported in British newspapers the *Leeds Mercury*, the *Kirkcudbrightshire Advertiser and Galloway News* and the *Huddersfield Chronicle*. 'Clotilda – Sailed from Mobile . . .', 4; Romeyn, 'Last of the Slavers'; Byers, 'The Last Slave-Ship', 745; 'Arrival of a Slaver at Mobile', *Times-Picayune*, 10 July 1860, 2; 'Arrival of a Slaver at Mobile', *New Orleans Crescent*, 10 July 1860, 1; 'Arrival of a Slaver at Mobile', *Daily Delta*, 10 July 1860, 2; 'Safe Arrival of a Slaver', *Wisconsin State Journal*, 10 July 1860, 1; 'New Orleans, July 9 . . .', *Janesville Daily Gazette*, 10 July 1860, 2; 'New Orleans, July 10 . . .', *Vicksburg Daily Whig*, 10 July 1860, 3; 'New Orleans, July 9 . . .', *Buffalo Daily Republic*, 10 July 1860, 3; 'From New Orleans', *Buffalo Commercial*, 10 July 1860, 3; 'Arrival of a Slaver at Mobile', *Brooklyn Evening Star*, 10 July 1860, 3; 'New Orlans [sic], July 10 . . .', *Daily Empire*, 10 July 1860, 3; 'New Orleans, July 9 . . .', *Republican Banner*, 10 July 1860, 3; 'New Orleans, July 9 . . .', *The Tennessean*, 10 July 1860, 3; 'Arrival of Africans', *Memphis Daily Appeal*, 10 July 1860, 3; 'New Orleans, July 9 . . .', *Louisville Daily Journal*, 10 July 1860, 3; 'Cargo of Africans Landed', *Alexandria Gazette*, 11 July 1860, 3; 'The Schooner Clotilde . . .', *Hartford Courant*, 11 July 1860, 2; 'Arrival of Africans', *Oxford Intelligencer*, 11 July 1860, 3; 'African Slaves Landed in Mobile Bay', *Evening Star*, 11 July 1860, 3; 'Arrival of a Slaver', *Lynchburg Daily Virginian*, 11 July 1860, 3; 'Afrikanische Sklaven Gelandet', *Baltimore Wecker*, 11 July 1860, 2; 'A Cargo of Africans Landed in Alabama', *Chicago Tribune*, 11 July 1860, 4; 'Arrival of Negroes', *Rock Island Argus*, 11 July 1860, 2; 'Arrival of Africans', *Quad-City Times*, 11 July 1860, 1; 'Arrival of a Cargo of Negroes', *Morning Democrat*, 11 July 1860, 1; 'The Slave Trade Reviving', *Muscatine Evening Journal*, 11 July 1860, 2; 'Arrival of a Slaver at Mobile', *Daily Constitutionalist*, 11 July 1860, 3; 'Africans Arrived',

Macon Daily Telegraph, 11 July 1860, 2; 'Successful Landing of a Slave Cargo', *Richmond Dispatch*, 11 July 1860, 3; 'New Orleans, July 9 . . .', *Wheeling Daily Intelligencer*, 11 July 1860, 3; 'New Orleans, 9th', *Bangor Daily Whig and Courier*, 11 July 1860, 3; 'African Slaves Landed in Mobile Bay', *Daily Exchange*, 11 July 1860, 1; 'Cargo of Negroes Landed', *Boston Evening Transcript*, 11 July 1860, 1; 'Sch. Clotilde . . .', *Fall River Daily News*, 11 July 1860, 2; 'Arrival of Africans', *Detroit Free Press*, 11 July 1860, 1; 'African Slave Trade', *Burlington Times*, 11 July 1860, 2; 'African Slaves Landed in Mobile Bay', *Baltimore Sun*, 11 July 1860, 2; 'The African Slave Trade', *Syracuse Daily Courier and Union*, 11 July 1860, 3; 'New Orleans, July 9', *Buffalo Morning Express*, 11 July 1860, 2; 'From New Orleans', *Cleveland Daily Leader*, 11 July 1860, 4; 'Arrival of Africans', *Richmond Daily Whig*, 11 July 1860, 3; 'Cargo of Slaves', *Daily Milwaukee News*, 11 July 1860, 4; 'More Africans Landed', *Harper's Weekly*, 4.186, 21 July 1860, 455; 'More Africans at New Orleans', *Harper's Weekly*, 4.187, 28 July 1860, 473; 'Una Buena parte de los negros . . .', *Diario de la Marina*, 18 July 1860, 2; 'Items of Mention', *Daily Delta*, 12 July 1860; 'Julian Neville's Sales', *Daily Delta*, 12 July 1860, 3; 'We Would Call Particular Attention . . .', *Daily Delta*, 13 July 1860, 2; 'The Key West Negroes', *Anti-Slavery Bugle*, 28 July 1860, 3; 'Our Serials and our Circulation'; 'America', *Liverpool Mercury*, 23 July 1860, 2; 'America', *The Standard* (London, UK), 23 July 1860, 5; 'America', *Leeds Mercury*, 24 July 1860, 1; 'America', *Kirkcudbrightshire Advertiser and Galloway News*, 27 July 1860, 2; 'Miscellaneous News and Home Gossip', *Huddersfield Chronicle*, 28 July 1860, 2.

17. *Mobile Register*, 12 July 1860, cited in *The Anti-Slavery History*, 16–17, emphasis in original; 'African Negroes Openly Imported into Mobile', *Mobile Register*, 14 July 1860, emphasis in original; 'More Full-Blooded Africans', *Mobile Mercury*, 23 July 1860, emphasis added.

18. Thaddeus Sanford to Howell Cobb, 13 July 1860, NARA, cited in Tabor, *Africatown*, 65.

19. Owen, 'Missionary Successes', 237.

20. Boynton Robinson, *Bridge Across Jordan*, 32; Montgomery, 'Survivors', 620.

21. Flock, 'Survivor'.

22. Meaher and his former captive Noah Hart both reported that Meaher was arrested, although there is no contemporaneous evidence that he was ever charged with a crime. Sanford to Cobb, 18 July 1860, NARA, cited in Tabor, *Africatown*, 67; Hines, 'Last Slave Cargo'; Scott, 'Affika Town', 61; Romeyn, 'The Last Slaver'.

Notes

23. Nick Tabor speculates that future Confederates Godbold and Sandford may have been genuinely concerned to uphold the law, or that they may have been keen to be seen to be doing so by Washington DC. As Tabor also notes, Sandford edited the *Mobile Register* immediately before John Forsyth. Sanford to Cobb, 18 July 1860; Tabor, *Africatown*, 65 and 67−8.

24. Southern unity probably prevented the seizure of the shipmates. Henry Romeyn reported three decades after the *Clotilda*'s landing that 'While many of the more conservative class of citizens did not favor the importation none would furnish any information which would tend to imperil the neck of a neighbor.' As Tom Henderson Wells observed of the *Wanderer*, which landed in Georgia 19 months before the *Clotilda*'s arrival, 'The only signs of Southern disapproval were silence and the worried letters from [chief conspirator Charles Augustus Lafayette] Lamar's father.' About one hundred and seventy survivors of that ship – more than 40 per cent of the group – were taken to Aiken County, South Carolina, where they were 'conspicuous and should have been easily seized'. 'Clotilda – Sailed from Mobile . . .', 4; Hines, 'Last Slave Cargo'; 'Collission [sic]', *Cahaba Gazette*, 17 July 1857, 2; Romeyn, 'The Last Slaver'; Wells, *The Slave Ship Wanderer*, 44−5.

25. 'The Mobile Importation of Africans', *Times-Picayune*, 29 July 1860, 3.

26. Roche, *Historic Sketches*, 99−100; Owen and Mitchell, *Our Home Land*, 77.

27. The *Mobile Mercury* reported on the sales as they were taking place, noting on 23 July that 25 people of 'pure, unadulterated African stock' had been sent north 'the other day'. The *New Orleans Crescent*, *Cincinnati Enquirer* and *New York Times* reprinted the story a few days later. 'More Full-Blooded Africans'; 'More About the Wild Africans', *New Orleans Crescent*, 25 July 1860, 4; 'More Full-Blooded Africans', *Cincinnati Enquirer*, 28 July 1860, 1; 'More Full-Blooded Africans in Alabama', *New York Times*, 31 July 1860, 8.

28. Memorable Creagh was also the likely enslaver of other *Clotilda* Africans with strikingly alliterative bondage names: couple Alex and Alice, Angus, Caroline, Cransy, Cresia, Mahala, Mary, May, Pat, Peggy, Penelope, Peter, Pinkney, Rachel and York. Although most of the shipmates were from the same Yoruba-speaking town, the *Clotilda* Africans identified some of their shipmates as Fulani, Hausa, Ijesha and Nupe. The Ijesha speak a Central Yoruban dialect, but the Fulani, Hausa and Nupe languages are distinct from Yoruba. Yoruba itself was not standardized until the Bible's translation into Yoruba in 1884. As Toby Green notes, 'in regions such as Ekiti in southern Nigeria, to this

day, neighboring villages speak mutually incomprehensible forms of the "Yorùbá" language'. Boynton Robinson, *Bridge Across Jordan*, 33; Green, *A Fistful of Shells*, 388 and 391.

29. The Africans quickly learned that polygamy was widely viewed in the United States as a sign of cultural backwardness. Kossula and Osia Keeby defended the practice by citing the biblical examples of Solomon and David and explaining that loyalty to one's wives was paramount; to look upon another woman was met with severe punishment. Kossula also explained that wives selected subsequent wives so they could take over their labours in the home: 'I am growing old – I am tired – I will bring you another wife.' Johnson, *The History of the Yorubas*, 103 and 113–16; Roche, *Historic Sketches*, 78–9; Boserup, 'The Economics of Polygamy', in *Perspectives on Africa*, 384 and 391.

30. Creagh may also have been the original purchaser of Lucy, Ossa and Quilla, a trio of captives who soon became the property of his neighbour William H. Hunt. Ossa's sister Omolabi was left in the hands of the Meahers. Gracie's agonies at losing two more of her children were not recorded, and Matilda was too young to remember her sale or her two oldest sisters, who she never saw again. However, the experience of a Kentuckian mother named Lucy, as remembered in the narrative of formerly enslaved abolitionist Lewis Clarke, gives a clue to how Gracie must have felt. Lucy lost seven of her eight children to slave traders. Clarke watched the separations in horror: 'the mother and infant were first sold, then child after child – the mother looking on in perfect agony; and as one child after another came down from the auction block, they would run and cling, weeping, to her clothes. The poor mother stood, till nature gave way; she fainted and fell, with her child in her arms . . . When she came to, she moaned wofully [sic], and prayed that she might die, to be relieved from her sufferings.' Clarke and Clarke, *Narratives*, 106–7.

31. Arnett, 'Dinah', 92.

32. Hurston, *Barracoon*, 56–7; translation by Elisée Soumonni, in Diouf, *Dreams*, 82 and 266, n. 33.

33. Judy and Mary's status as *Clotilda* Africans is not certain but is likely given their proximity to the other Baldwin County Africans and given that Mary's daughter married Judy's son. Census information for Judy and Mary is unreliable. Mary was identified only as the daughter of Africans on the 1880 census. Conversely, Judy was identified as African-born on that document but was reported to be 72 years old despite having a 9-year-old child. Both women were listed as Alabama-born on

the 1870 census. The Mobile shipmates told George Lake Imes that
Foster received eight captives, Emma Langdon Roche recorded that he
received 10, an anonymous 1890 note suggested he received 14, and
Zora Neale Hurston reported that the figure was 16. Imes learned that
the Meaher brothers claimed more than 50 of the other captives, while
Hurston noted that Burns took 20 and Timothy took 32 of them.
Conversely, Erwin Craighead learned from Timothy Meaher that the
captives claimed by Timothy, Burns and Foster comprised 30 people in
total, a figure that tallies closely with the number of *Clotilda* Africans
living in Mobile after the war. Mary Langman, Holland Lott (Lott Holland)
and Lida Lott, 1880 US Census, Court House, Baldwin, Alabama; Judy
Holland, 1880 US Census, Court House, Baldwin, Alabama; Judy Hollan
[sic], 1870 US Census, Township 5, Baldwin, Alabama; Mary Langman,
1870 US Census, Township 4, Baldwin, Alabama; 'Jefferson Buford', in
Owen and Owen, *History of Alabama*, 3 and 251–2; Imes, 'The Last
Recruits', 356; Roche, *Historic Sketches*, 97; 'Captain Foster Sold the
Clotilda . . .'; Hurston, *Barracoon*, 56; Craighead, *Mobile*, 358.

34. Scott, 'Affika Town', 61.
35. Ibid., 61.
36. Ibid., 61.
37. Roche, *Historic Sketches*, 123.
38. *United States v. Jno. M. Dabney*, Writ of Seizure and Summons; *United States v. Burns Meaher*, Writ of Seizure and Summons; *United States v. William Foster*, Summons; *United States v. William Foster and Richard Sheridan*, Summons and Complaint.
39. Judge Jones ruled that because Horatio N. Gould had not actually trafficked the African woman he enslaved, he was not liable for prosecution under federal law. Ben Raines notes that Foster's case was mentioned twice in 1866 federal court documents, but that there is no record of him ever paying a fine for customs law violations. 'The United States vs. Horatio N. Gould', 531 and 536–7; *United States v. Jno. M. Dabney*, Writ of Seizure; Romeyn, 'The Last Slaver', 25; Raines, *The Last Slave Ship*, 93.

Chapter 6: The River

1. Hurston, *Barracoon*, 59–60; James M. Meaher, 1860 Non-population Schedule, Northern Division, Mobile, Alabama.
2. Byrne [sic] Meaher, 1860 Agricultural Census, Grove Hill, Clarke, Alabama; Imes, 'The Last Recruits', 356–7; Roche, *Historic Sketches*, 102.

3. Scott, 'Affika Town', 61.

4. Ibid., 61; Byfield, 'Dress and Politics', 32; Riggins, *Riggins Family Ancestry Book*, 9—10.

5. Hurston, *Barracoon*, 59. Emphasis in original.

6. Scott, 'Affika Town', 62—3; Riggins, *Riggins Family Ancestry Book*, 9.

7. Two years earlier, Fernando Mareno had turned away from that port another seized slave ship, the brig *Echo*. Anon., Interview with Percy Phillip Mareno; 'Amy', 'Robert' and 'Caroline', 1866 Alabama State Census, Baldwin County; Caroline Grigsby Deaths and Burials Index, Daphne, Baldwin, Alabama, 13 November 1930; Benito Julian Moreno, Wills and Probate Records, Escambia, Florida, 9 February 1866; Coker, 'The Mareno Family', 103; Fett, *Recaptured Africans*, 70, 81 and 85; *Forty-Fourth Annual Report*, 16; 'Stirring Up the Barracoons', *Montgomery Mail*, 7 July 1860.

8. Ingalls falsely claimed the Africans were freed on arrival in the United States to create the impression that the young woman worked willingly in his household and was not enslaved. Burns Meaher's other *Clotilda* captives very likely included a 10-year-old girl named Appy or Abbie, whose name appears twice across genealogical data. The 1870 census shows Appy living in St. Stephens, Washington County, a county bordering Clarke County and just 10 miles away from the community of Bigbee, where Kanko was forced to marry James Dennison during her enslavement to Burns Meaher. Appy's home was the plantation of Tennessee-born Edward P. Royle, from whom she took her surname and who may have purchased her from the youngest Meaher brother. The 1900 census shows Appy living in the region of Selma's Mulberry Road and Division Street; like her housemate and possible daughter Ida, Appy probably relocated with Edward when he moved to that city in 1873 to open the Royle House hotel, on the corner of Broad Street and Alabama Avenue. Dennison, *A Memoir*, 30–1; Atticus Mullin, 'The Passing Throng', *Montgomery Advertiser*, 1 July 1948, 14; Appy and Ida Royle and Edward P. Royal, 1870 US Census, St. Stephens, Washington, Alabama; E. P. Royle and Ida Royle, 1870 US Census, Bellevue, Dallas, Alabama; Abbie Royal, 1900 US Census, Selma Ward 5, Dallas, Alabama; 'Royle House (advert)', *Times-Argus*, 26 September 1873, 2.

9. Kennedy, 'Life at Gee's Bend', 1072.

10. Hurston, *Barracoon*, 61; Buchanan, *Black Life on the Mississippi*, 71; J. R. McDaniel, 'Congo Slaves', *Nashville Banner*, 7 May 1913, 8; DeLeon, *Four Years*, 49.

11. Hurston, *Barracoon*, 60—1.

Notes

12. Jackson, *Rivers of History*, 81; DeLeon, *Four Years*, 50; 'Capt. Tim Meaher's Sketch of His River History', *Clarke County Democrat,* 12 June 1890, 1.

13. *Scientific American* counted 474 deaths on US steamboats in 1860, two-thirds of which were collision-related. The worst steamboat disaster occurred on 27 April 1865, when the *Sultana* exploded and sank in the Mississippi River, killing approximately 1,169 people, mostly Union Army soldiers recently released from Confederate prisons. Hurston, *Barracoon*, 60; 'Loss of Life by Steamboats', 371; 'Accident to the Taney', *Watchman*, 3 August 1860, 2; 'Accident to the Steamer Taney', *Weekly Advertiser*, 8 August 1860, 1.

14. Hurston, *Barracoon*, 60.

15. Ibid., 62.

16. Ibid., 62.

17. London *Times* reporter Sir William Howard Russell noted the appalling conditions of the women and children who labored at the landing sites. Russell, *My Diary*, 187.

18. 'The Alabama River', *Alabama State Sentinel*, 5 December 1860, 2; McDaniel, 'Congo Slaves'.

19. 'Which Way the Wind Blows', *Weekly Advertiser*, 19 December 1860, 2.

20. The cost of the *Southern Republic* is not known, but early steamboats typically cost between $20,000 and $40,000 to build (equivalent to $750,000 to $1,500,000 today). William Russell understood that the *Southern Republic's* financing came from the *Clotilda* voyage. 'Editorial Correspondence', *Alabama State Sentinel*, 19 December 1860, 2; William H. Russell, 'The Civil War in America', *The Times* (London, UK), 7 June 1861, 5; Kotar and Gessler, *The Steamboat Era*, 104; Jackson, *Rivers of History*, 110—11.

21. 'The Southern Republic', *Southern Champion*, 4 January 1861, 3; DeLeon, *Four Years*, 42; 'The "Southern Republic"', *Weekly Advertiser*, 30 January 1861, 3; 'Marine List', *Mobile Daily News*, 18 February 1861, 3.

22. Russell, 'The Civil War in America'; DeLeon, *Four Years*, 42.

23. Johnson, *River of Dark Dreams*, 103; DeLeon, *Four Years*, 48.

24. 'We Return Our Thanks . . .', *Southern Champion*, 15 February 1861, 3; 'Food for the Rifles', *Cahaba Gazette*, 31 May 1861, 3; Hurston, *Barracoon*, 61; Cox, 'Mobile in the War', 209.

25. US Army captain Henry Romeyn and US Army major S. H. M. Byers both reported that some of the Africans were commandeered into working for the Confederacy, although Romeyn also believed that the rest of the group were freed and 'left to shift for themselves' by the

time the war started. The Africans themselves made no mention of any fortification work. Hogs roaming wild in the US South adapted to the dangerous conditions by becoming very aggressive. They were incredibly dangerous prey for hunters. Hog Bayou, which is located at the northern part of Africatown, acquired its name from the hogs that were hunted there. Berger, 'Cugo Lewis'; Byers, 'The Last Slave-Ship', 742; Romeyn, 'Little Africa'; Silkenat, *Scars*, 35–6; Raines, *The Last Slave Ship*, 168; Roche, *Historic Sketches*, 101; Hurston, *Barracoon*, 61–2.

26. William Lowndes Yancey's friend and biographer Joel Witherspoon DuBose reinforced that lie in the early twentieth century when he identified the Africans he had seen on the Meahers' steamboats and who later settled in Mobile as *Wanderer* survivors. The influential Alabamian historian likely knew the truth, however: in 1860, he was living alongside 129 enslaved people on his father Kimbrough's vast estate in Marengo County, close to where several of the *Clotilda* Africans were imprisoned. McDaniel, 'Congo Slaves'; J. W. Du Bose, 'Letter to the Editor', *Birmingham News*, 20 October 1909, 4; K. C. and John DuBose, 1860 US Census, Township 17 Range 4 East, Marengo, Alabama; Kim C. Dubose, 1860 Slave Schedule, Township 17 Range 4 East, Marengo, Alabama.

27. The identity of 'Bully' is unclear. He was too young to be any of the known shipmates who gathered north of Mobile after freedom was declared, which raises the possibility that, like 'Ecotah', he drowned while labouring on one of the Meahers' steamboats during slavery. Russell sought to distance himself from his fellow diasporic Irishman by racializing his appearance. He noted that the enslaver had 'a very Celtic mouth of the Kerry type'. Russell was insinuating that, unlike the Dubliner, who was descended on his father's side from Ireland's Anglo-Protestant elite, Meaher's forebears came from the west of Ireland, a space Othered in the nineteenth-century British imagination for being predominantly Catholic, Celtic, Irish-speaking and poor. Meaher's father was from Rathcash/Ráth Chaise, a townland in southeast Ireland. Russell, *My Diary*, 185 and 188–9.

28. Canada became the only certain site of safety for people fleeing slavery after the passage of the 1850 Fugitive Slave Act, which ruled that former captives in the North must be sent back to their enslavers. Ibid., 189.

29. Ibid., 189.

30. 'Accident to the Southern Republic', *Montgomery Weekly Post*, 5 June 1861, 3; Hurston, *Barracoon*, 60.

31. The oldest, and perhaps most accurate, census on which Kanko's name appears lists her birth year as 1848. Dennison, *A Memoir*, 29; Dennison, *Biographical Memoirs*, 28; Lottie Jordan, 1870 US Census, Mobile Ward 5, Mobile, Alabama.
32. Dennison, *Biographical Memoirs*, 28; Dennison, *A Memoir*, 31.
33. Dennison, *Biographical Memoirs*, 37–42; Roche, *Historic Sketches*, 102.
34. Hurston, *Barracoon*, 62.

Chapter 7: The Black Belt

1. 'Rambles in Old Wilcox', *Wilcox Progressive Era*, 11 November 1896, 2; Zo. S. Cook, 'In the Past', *Clarke County Democrat*, 29 November 1888, 1; 'Thomas Bivin Creagh', in Owen and Owen, *History of Alabama*, 3, 422; W. M. Creagh, 1860 Agricultural Schedule, Western Division, Wilcox, Alabama.
2. McGranahan, *Historical Sketch*, 51.
3. The captives transplanted to Prairie Bluff included Caroline, Cransy, Cresia, Martha, May and Rachel. Peggy Crear, another shipmate who ended up 15 miles south in Camden after the war, was probably sent there, too.
4. The captives sent to McKinley were Alex, Alice, Angus, Mahala, Pat, Penelope, two men both named Peter, Pinkney and York. Early twentieth-century author Katharine Hopkins Chapman rewrote the horror of the Marengo Africans' arrival to depict them as a subhuman threat to white Southern racial 'purity'. Chapman's husband John was born in McKinley three years after the *Clotilda*'s landing, and the couple were neighbours of the widow and daughter of Redoshi's enslaver. In her callous reimagining, Chapman suggested that the traumatized youngsters 'sulked' when they arrived in McKinley, and her account shows how, much like their forced transatlantic nakedness, the shipmates' desperate hunger was used as 'evidence' of their savagery. Chapman claimed that the captives were so primitive that not only were they 'utterly unused' to cooked food, but they were also 'semi-amphibious' and that, when sent to work in a field, they abandoned their labours and dived for hours in a nearby swamp: 'they rushed into the water waist deep, began feasting on frogs, worms and small fish, and there they remained until sundown'. Katharine Hopkins Chapman, 'Some Spicey Sundays: Contrasting Congregations', *Birmingham News,* 30 June 1906, 5.
5. 'A Friend', 'Obituary', *Daily Selma Reporter*, 13 July 1864, 1; William Hunt, 1860 US Census, Western Division, Wilcox, Alabama; William H. Hunt, 1860 Slave Schedule, Western Division, Wilcox, Alabama.

6. English, *Civil Wars*, 7–8; McCarty, *The Reins of Power*, 25.

7. Pargas, *Slavery and Forced Migration*, 139–40.

8. 'Effects of the Drouth', *Montgomery Advertiser*, 8 August 1860, 2; 'The Weather', *Cahaba Gazette*, 27 July 1860, 3.

9. Fitts, *Selma*, 26; Forner, *Why the Vote*, 6.

10. In 1860, Smith's real and personal estates were collectively valued at $125,000, a figure equivalent to $4,500,000 in 2023. Wash M. Smith, 1860 US Census, Selma, Dallas, Alabama; 'Quarles Rites Wednesday at Three O'Clock', *Selma Times-Journal*, 11 January 1949, 1 and 3; Brewer, *Alabama*, 226 and 384; Allen Furniss, 'History Filled Home Recalls War Stories', *Selma Times-Journal*, 5 July 1964, 9C; 'Plantation Sold For Large Figure', *Selma Times-Journal*, 14 December 1955, 1; 'Turpentine Distillation', *Tuskegee Republican*, 25 January 1855, 2; 'Historical Group Starts Sessions In City Today', *Selma Times-Journal*, 22 April 1960, 10; Elizabeth Via Brown, 'Plantation Home Attracting Tourists', *Montgomery Advertiser*, 25 March 1979, 2C.

11. While many slave trade reopening advocates supported human trafficking as part of a wider commitment to pro-slavery disunionism, others claimed the trade's reopening would help equalize the North and South's economies and keep the Union together. The pro-secession *Montgomery Advertiser* lampooned Smith for his efforts to position the CUP as a pro-slavery party. 'He utterly failed to sustain his sinking cause, and when called upon . . . he stood up and confessed that [CUP presidential candidate John] Bell had uttered abolition sentiments in Congress on the question of slavery in the District of Columbia. But still he said that the party to which he belonged had for its chief object the extension of slavery. O, consistency!' Neither Jefferson Davis, the president of the Confederacy, nor Robert E. Lee, its most celebrated military general, was a secessionist, but both chose allegiance to their state over loyalty to their country. Johnson, *River of Dark Dreams*, 396–7; 'H.', 'Messrs. Editors . . .', *Weekly Advertiser*, 29 August 1860, 1; Patricia A. Hoskins, '"The Best Southern Patriots": Jews in Alabama during the Civil War', in *The Yellowhammer War*, 157.

12. Brewer, *Alabama,* 233; Washington M. Smith Clemency Plea, Alabama, 12 September 1865; 'Quarles Rites Wednesday', 1 and 3; W. M. Smith, 'Letter to W. A. Dunklin, Wm. Shearer and R. S. Smith, Selma, Alabama', *Selma Daily Reporter*, 19 June 1862, 3; Fitts, *Selma*, 55 and 65.

13. Smith enslaved one man, four women and four children in Dallas County before he bought the four *Clotilda* captives. W. M. Smith, 1860 Slave Schedule, Selma, Dallas, Alabama.

14. Boynton Robinson, *Bridge Across Jordan*, 31; Banks and Pennington, *A Narrative*, 50–1.

15. Flock, 'Survivor'.

16. 'Washington Smith-Quarles House', *Selma Times-Journal*, 24 March 1983, 21; Furniss, 'History Filled Home', 9.

17. Flock, 'Survivor'.

18. 'And when that molasses was made, they had poplar trough to pour that molasses in. No barrels at all. I never seed a barrel 'long then, nothing but troughs', Moseley recalled. Sonkin, Audio Interview with Isom Moseley; Covey and Eisnach, *What the Slaves Ate*, 69–71; William Campbell, 1870 US Census, Rehobeth [sic], Wilcox, Alabama; William Arnett, 'Interview with Lizzie Major', in *Gee's Bend: The Women*, 299.

19. Boynton Robinson, *Bridge Across Jordan*, 33.

20. The 1870 and 1880 censuses suggest that Alice, who lived until 1925, was as young as seven in 1860. Aleck and Alice Burns, 1870 US Census, Linden, Marengo, Alabama; Alec and Allice Burnes, 1880 US Census, Jefferson, Marengo, Alabama.

21. Dinah may have been one of the captives claimed by Timothy Meaher when the shipmates arrived in Alabama. She probably wasn't the only Snow Hill *Clotilda* survivor. In 1920, 55-year-old African-born Nathanael Brown was living with his wife Caroline and adopted 9-year-old son Howard in Furman, a former section of Snow Hill. Nathanael died in Selma in July 1930. Arnett, 'Dinah', 92; 'Trips in the County', *Wilcox Progressive Era*, 19 February 1914, 1; Nathanael Brown, 1920 US Census, Furman, Wilcox, Alabama; Nathanial Brown Death Record, Selma, Dallas, Alabama, 29 July 1930.

22. Wes Smith, 'Resilient Alabama Town Weaves Its Own Artistic Magic', *Orlando Sentinel*, 25 December 2002, A1 and A16.

23. David Holt, 'New Town Born in Monroe', *Birmingham News*, 14 September 1911, 2.

24. Charles Tait was a second cousin of US Secretary of State Henry Clay. Sellers, *Slavery in Alabama*, 32; Jackson, *Rivers of History*, 46; Charles Tait to James A. Tait, 27 January 1827, cited in Moffat, 'Charles Tait', 229–30.

25. Gosse, *Letters*, 251; Arnett, 'Dinah', 93; Edwards, *Twenty-Five Years*, 27.

26. The whip was not the only form of violent terror that Dinah witnessed in Snow Hill. Enslaved men were subjected to sadistic games that led to violence if they were not fast enough on their feet. Arlonzia understood that 'the mens had to take this kind of a training program to see how fast they could run. They put this dog in the pen with a

man, and the man had to run fast enough to jump the fence and get out before the dog gets him. Dog bite him bad if he didn't get out – tear him up.' Arnett, 'Dinah', 93.

27. *Mobile Daily Register*, 10 May 1859, cited in Sellers, *Slavery in Alabama*, 248–9; McGranahan, *Historical Sketch*, 58; 'We Learn From the Camden . . .', *Weekly Advertiser*, 28 April 1858, 2; Williamson, *March On!*, 66–7.

28. The smartly dressed white men arrived at Memorable Creagh's plantation on large chestnut horses on 28 January 1861, six months after the shipmates' arrival and one week before delegates from Alabama and six other Southern states gathered in Montgomery to form a slaveholding confederate republic. Matilda and Sally's escape attempt counters the pro-slavery *Advertiser*'s claim that none of Creagh's captives wanted to flee and that they reported the Underground Railroad's activities. 'Negro Theives [sic] and Incendiaries About', *Weekly Advertiser*, 13 February 1861, 2.

29. 'Weather, River, Boats', *Daily Confederation*, 7 February 1861, 3; Gosse, *Letters*, 252; Drew, *The Refugee*, 248; 'A Runaway in Jail', *Clarke County Democrat*, 29 October 1863, 1.

30. Gosse, *Letters*, 252; Ovington, 'Slaves' Reminiscences', 1134.

31. Bordewich, *Bound for Canaan*, 111; Drew, *The Refugee*, 249.

32. The father of Lucy's son was nominally a young man called Jim who laboured in the fields with her. But the baby was named Sandy, hinting that his real father was a white man and possibly even Hunt. Sandy was two months old when Hunt died, as was the enslaver and his wife Siloma's only son, William, Jr. 'Obituary', 1; W. H. Hunt, Civil Appointments, Wilcox, Alabama, 16 June 1864; William H. Hunt, Alabama Wills and Probate Records, 1 November 1864.

33. Quilla's oldest child Albert was born in September 1865. Price, *The Life*, 38; 'Administratrix's Sale', *Daily Selma Reporter*, 18 November 1864, 1; Albert Holman, 1900 US Census, Kosters, Mobile, Alabama.

34. Friend spent much of the war on the plantation where Sawnee and Miller were enslaved, and her article is the only known document of their existence. Friend, 'Sawnee'; La Fayett [sic] Minor, 1860 Agricultural Schedule, Southern Division, Pickens, Alabama.

35. *Cotton Sold*, 46; Scott, *The War*, 417–18.

36. McIlwain, *Civil War Alabama*, 254 and 383, n. 19.

37. *Wanderer* shipmates August and Wembo Congo rushed to take up arms against slavery as soon as the federal government began recruiting Black soldiers. The pair enlisted as privates in the 2nd Louisiana Native

Guard Infantry Regiment when it was organized in New Orleans in October 1862. They could hardly speak English, but they quickly established their bravery. Their African American Lieutenant Robert Hamlin Isabelle affirmed that they 'have proved as good soldiers as we can find in the whole three colored regiments'. Another *Wanderer* shipmate, Charles Carr, who was kidnapped from Congo with his brother and sister and enslaved near Savannah, Georgia, signed up for a three-year term with the 34th US Colored Infantry in January 1865, days after his emancipation. But his military career ended abruptly when white Southerners, resentful of African American troops' social status, spread fearful rumours about the dangers of Black men with guns. Carr was honourably discharged in February 1866. Rex Miller identifies the Battle of Munford as the site of the war's last casualties. August Congo in the Civil War Soldier Records and Profiles, 1861–1865; Wembo Congo, Civil War Soldier Records and Profiles, 1861–1865; 'Native Africans Enlisting', 829; Charles Carr, Colored Troops Military Service Records, 1863–1865; Charles Carr, Freedman's Bank Records, 1865–1874; Keenan, *Wilson's Cavalry Corps*, 203–10; Miller, *Croxton's Raid*, 80–1.

38. When the *Wanderer* arrived in Georgia in December 1858, the Forrest brothers were the biggest slave traders in and around Memphis and Nathan was one of the region's richest men. Nathan Forrest later admitted to a journalist his participation in the *Wanderer* children's trafficking. 'I had an interest in the *Wanderer*, and we brought over 400; only six per cent died [the real death toll was closer to 20 per cent]. They were very fond of grasshoppers and bugs, but I taught them to eat cooked meat, and they were as good n——s as any I ever had.' Two of the Africans enslaved by the Minter family were named Conner and Fongo. The third person's identity is unknown. Anthony Minter, who died in July 1859, supposedly bought the Africans, which suggests they were not *Clotilda* survivors. 'Forrest', *Republican Banner*, 11 March 1869, 1; Wall, 'Direct from Congo', 74–8; Eiland, 'The Unspoken Demands', 58–9; 'Minter Homestead, Near Burnsville, Dates Back to Period Before War', *Selma Times-Journal*, 20 October 1929, 5; Mrs. J. W. Dennard, 'Memories of Dallas County', *Selma Times-Journal*, 16 March 1941, 11; Mrs J. W. Dennard, 'Memories of Dallas County', *Selma Times-Journal*, 23 March 1941, 5; Mrs J. W. Dennard, 'Memories of Dallas County', *Selma Times-Journal*, 25 May 1941, 5.

39. Brown, 'Plantation Home'.

40. Andrews, *History*, 258; F. Salter, 'History of the Campaign of the Cavalry Corps, M. D. M., in Alabama and Georgia, from the Twenty-second of

March to April Twentieth', in *The Rebellion Record*, 706; English, *Civil Wars*, 27.

41. Memorable Creagh resisted paying at least 50 of his former captives for the first 11 months of their freedom. The men and women lodged a complaint with the Freedmen's Bureau, an agency set up to aid newly freed people, which ordered Creagh to pay them $1,625, a figure equivalent to about $600 per person in 2023. Sonkin, Interview with Isom Moseley; 'Creagh', United States, Freedmen's Bureau, Records of Freedmen's Complaints, 12 March 1866; Smith Clemency Plea.

Chapter 8: The Capital

1. Although it misidentified the *Clotilda* as the *Wanderer*, an 1895 *Montgomery Advertiser* article recorded Bougier's journey from Mobile to Montgomery: 'the parties interested in the cargo of negroes . . . met the "Wanderer" with a small boat out in the gulf and brought the human property to a point below Mobile, where they were brought ashore, then carried through the country to some secluded landing on the Alabama River and brought to Montgomery by one of the river steamers.' 'Lucas Will Contest Now On', *Montgomery Advertiser*, 18 December 1895, 7; 'Weather, River, &c', *Weekly Advertiser*, 25 July 1860, 3.

2. The two largest slave markets nationally were New Orleans in Louisiana and Natchez in Mississippi. The South's other major slave trading cities included: Baltimore, Maryland; Charleston, South Carolina; Lexington, Kentucky; Savannah, Georgia; and St. Louis, Missouri. Rogers, *Confederate Home Front*, 5 and 50; Sellers, *Slavery in Alabama*, 154–6.

3. Russell, *Pictures*, 15. Emphasis added; 'A Rare Importation', *Memphis Daily Appeal*, 27 April 1859, 3.

4. Russell, *Pictures,* 16–17 and 19.

5. Montgomery had already witnessed three major fires during its 40-year existence. An 1838 blaze destroyed much of Court Square and Court and Montgomery streets; an 1846 fire destroyed half of Market Street; and an 1849 fire destroyed the first Capitol Building. Punishments meted out to enslaved people were severe. A blacksmith named Jade was whipped for nearly 15 minutes on the eve of the Civil War for stealing money to fund his flight north. His cries of agony echoed up to his enslaver Will Wright's mansion. Jade died of his injuries three days later. 'Montgomery', in Owen and Owen, *History of*

Alabama, 2, 1037; Blue, *A Brief History*, 24 and 27–8; Russell, *Pictures,* 27–8; Farrior, 'Interview with Caroline Holland'.

6. The group of mostly little boys and a few girls, women and men reached the city via train from Macon, Georgia, on Christmas Eve 1858. After four days in the city, 34 of them were carried, again via wagon, to the steamboat *St. Nicholas*. They stopped at Benton, an Alabama River landing point between Montgomery and Selma. From there, they were transplanted 11 miles south to the village of Collerine, where they were sold to local enslavers. Two members of the group were dead within hours of their arrival at Collerine. Others were 'reduced to the grave's brink' according to one Montgomery newspaper. 'Gone West', *Independent American*, 5 January 1859, 2; 'The Wanderer's Africans Going West', *Baltimore Sun*, 13 January 1859, 1; 'The Wanderer and Her Cargo of Africans', *National Era*, 6 January 1859, 3; 'Editor Remembers Shipment of Slaves', *Luverne Democrat*, 27 October 1932, 2; 'The Montgomery Confederation . . .', *Alexandria Gazette*, 5 January 1859, 2; 'Dissolution of Partnership', *Weekly Advertiser*, 19 January 1859, 3; B. R. Jones, 1860 Slave Schedule, District 1, Montgomery, Alabama.

7. du Mont, *du Mont de Soumagne*, 82; 'Long Grabs', 'Montgomery, Ala.'; B. C. Jones, 1860 Agricultural Schedule, District 1, Montgomery, Alabama; B. C. Jones, 1860 Slave Schedule, District 1, Montgomery, Alabama.

8. Victoria/Ella appears inadvertently to have passed on her racist name to her daughter, who was registered on her death certificate as Victoria Queen Avery. Victoria Queen Avery Death Record, Montgomery, Alabama, 24 April 1949; Hagedorn, 'Ole Bulja', 26.

9. Reuben's enslaver was identified as 'the late John Givens [sic]' in an 1895 newspaper article. But Reuben's home after the Civil War was Alex Given's grocery store and there were no other families named Given or Givens living in Montgomery County in 1860. A. F. Gieven [sic], 1860 Slave Schedule, District 1, Montgomery, Alabama; Mears & Turnbull, *City Directory*, 41; A. F. Givon [sic], 1860 US Census, Division 1, Montgomery, Alabama; 'Lucas Will Contest Now On', *Montgomery Advertiser*, 18 December 1895, 7.

10. William Foster and Adelaide Vanderslice Marriage Record, Montgomery, Alabama, 6 September 1860; 'Capt. Wm. Foster'; Blue, *A Brief History*, 26; 'Talladega Springs Has Changed Owners', *Montgomery Times*, 7 September 1911, 3; Sulzby, *Historic Alabama Hotels*, 125–6; Rogers, *Confederate Home Front*, 8; 'Montgomery', in Owen and Owen, *History of Alabama*, 2, 1039.

11. Jennie Jones Vass, 'Montgomery Girl's Recollections Of the War and General Lee', *Montgomery Advertiser*, 30 April 1922, 4.

12. The Republican Party's stance was so strongly opposed by Southern elites that Lincoln was absent from the ballot in 10 slave states; his victory was facilitated solely by Northern and Western voters. 'Mass Meeting of the Citizens of Montgomery', *Weekly Advertiser*, 14 November 1860, 2; Du Bose, *The Life*, 540. Emphasis added; 'Great Secession Meeting at the Capitol!', *Weekly Advertiser*, 21 November 1860, 2.

13. Jackson mastered English so quickly that the *Montgomery Advertiser* remarked on his achievement years later. Nichols, *Forty Years*, 236; 'A Montgomery Negro Off for Africa', *Montgomery Advertiser*, 23 June 1883, 5.

14. John M. Smith, 1860 US Census, District 2, Montgomery, Alabama; 'A Montgomery Negro'; 'The Wealthiest Man in Alabama . . .', *Knoxville Daily Tribune*, 21 June 1890, 2.

15. The *Advertiser* later recorded the start date of Jackson's employment as 10 May 1868, presumably because the newspaper did not want to admit it had enslaved a trafficked African child. 'The Gentlemen from Africa', *Cahaba Gazette*, 28 January 1859, 2; 'A Montgomery Negro'.

16. The selection of a permanent president of the convention on 7 January was also a close contest. William M. Brooks of Perry County, who called for immediate secession, won the vote 53−45 against Robert Jemison, Jr. of Tuscaloosa, who wanted to consult with other states before any decision was made. Walther, *William Lowndes Yancey*, 276−7; 'The Rubicon is Crossed', *Weekly Advertiser*, 16 January 1861, 3; Blue, *A Brief History*, 30; Rogers, *Confederate Home Front*, 20.

17. Vass, 'Montgomery Girl's Recollections'; 'Luncheon Will Be Feature of Inaugural Celebration', *Troy Messenger*, 17 February 1936, 3; Rogers, *Confederate Home Front*, 27−8; Kenneth W. Noe, 'Introduction', in *The Yellowhammer War*, 3.

18. As W. E. B. Du Bois observed, 'when it came to actual hostilities, the South sorely needed the aid of Europe; and this a nation fighting for slavery and the slave-trade stood poor chance of getting'. Before negotiations with the UK even began, British consul in Charleston Robert Bunch warned British Foreign Secretary John Russell that William Lowndes Yancey wanted to reopen the slave trade. Historian Hugh Thomas emphasizes that the South was so reliant on enslaved labour that 'had the South won the Civil War, the African [slave] trade would indeed have been reopened.' Johnson, *River of Dark*

Dreams, 419−20; Du Bois, *The Suppression*, 187−8; Robert Bunch to Lord John Russell, 21 March 1861, Russell Papers, FO5/750, Public Record Office, The National Archives, UK; Thomas, *The Slave Trade*, 766.

19. Toccoa Cozart, 'What the Women of Montgomery Did', *Selma Morning Times*, 13 March 1907, 11; 'Fruit Exhibitions', *Weekly Advertiser*, 11 July 1860, 3.

20. Nichols, *Forty Years*, 237; Farrior, 'Interview with Martha Bradley'.

21. Ibid.

22. Hagedorn, 'Ole Bulja'.

23. DuBose, *Notable Men*, 30; 'Murder and Its Punishment', *Tuskegee Republican*, 31 August 1854, 2; 'Murder − Burning of the Murderer!', *Weekly Advertiser*, 30 August 1854, 2. Emphasis in original; 'Public Meeting at Tallahassee', *Weekly Advertiser*, 6 September 1854, 1; 'Public Meeting', *Tuskegee Republican*, 12 October 1854, 2.

24. After witnessing failed surgeries on the same group of women and girls for three years, Rush Jones joined other members of Montgomery's medical community, including Sims's apprentices, in distancing himself from the surgeon's work. Jones's concern was not for the captives but, rather, for his brother-in-law's reputation. 'I must tell you frankly that with your young and growing family it is unjust to them to continue in this way, and carry on this series of experiments. You have no idea what it costs you to support a half-dozen n——s, now more than three years, and my advice to you is to resign the whole subject and give it up. It is better for you, and better for your family', Jones warned. The gynaecologist ignored his brother-in-law and continued the surgeries for another year. Sims, *The Story*, 242; Sims, 'The Treatment of Syphilis', 448−9; Hagedorn, 'Ole Bulja'.

25. As historian William Garrott Brown acknowledged in the 1890s, 'his passing was little marked'. 'Death of Hon. Wm. L. Yancey', *Weekly Advertiser*, 5 August 1863, 1; Brown, 'The Orator of Secession', 615; Jones, ed., 'The Journal', 241.

26. Jones, *Yankee Blitzkrieg*, 108−10.

27. Jones, ed., 'The Journal', 230; Jones, *Yankee Blitzkrieg*, 111; Vass, 'Montgomery Girl's Recollections', 4.

28. Jones, *Yankee Blitzkrieg*, 111, 112 and 114−15; Fleming, *Civil War*, 220.

29. Rogers, *Confederate Home Front*, 149; Jones, ed., 'The Journal', 234; Jones, *Yankee Blitzkrieg*, 114 and 116−17.

30. Only an oath of allegiance was needed for most Confederates to secure a pardon and the restoration of their property.

31. It is unclear whether General Wilson encountered the Africans on Rush Jones's estate, but he is understood to have met child *Wanderer* survivor Frank Bambush (*c*.1847−74) when Union forces reached Columbus two days after departing Mount Meigs. Frank's captor, a pro-Union enslaver named Randolph L. Mott, allegedly tried to hand over the youth to the general, who refused to take him. The Jones's daughter Lucy Ellen Jackson donated the goblets and pitcher to the Montgomery Museum of Fine Arts. The objects were among the first items placed on display when the museum opened in 1930. 'Jackson to Relate War Recollections', *Montgomery Advertiser*, 4 April 1934, 3; Cozart, 'What the Women', 3; Vass, 'Montgomery Girl's Recollections'; Causey, 'Sleuthing through Columbus History', 30; Bellware, 'Africans in Columbus', 18; Swift, *The Last Battle*, 28; 'Fine Arts Museum Announces New Treasures', *Montgomery Advertiser*, 7 December 1930, 19.

32. A. F. Given, Pardons Under Amnesty Proclamations, 1865−1869; B. R. Jones, Pardons Under Amnesty Proclamations, 1865−1869.

33. Ella and Peter's estate yielded 200 bushels of corn and six bales of cotton in the autumn of 1869. Ella Duncan, 1870 US Census, Township 17, Elmore, Alabama; Peter Duncan, 1870 Agricultural Schedule, Township 17, Elmore, Alabama.

34. Like *Wanderer* survivor Jacob Sango, who was kidnapped aged 11 and who grew to only four feet seven inches in height, Reuben's short stature indicates he was one of the *Clotilda*'s many child captives. It also suggests that diet-related malnutrition was one of the many cruelties he endured during his enslavement. Dickinson was a brick mason and contractor who, before the war, had been an architect. Arnesen, *Brotherhoods of Color*, 6 and 10; Brannon, 'A Study in Folk Lore'; Jacob Sango, 1870 US Census, Hogg Island, Russell, Alabama; Jake Vangue Death Record, Seale, Russell, Alabama, 12 August 1920; 'Business Cards', *Daily State Sentinel*, 28 December 1867, 1; Reuben Govan [sic], 1870 US Census, Montgomery Ward 5, Montgomery, Alabama.

35. Chinch's Georgia family connections suggest he was a *Wanderer* survivor. Jim Taylor, an elderly African American well-digger living in early twentieth-century Montgomery, miraculously survived a three-hour burial beneath 2,500 pounds of brick, mortar and earth, but drowned eight years later when water burst through another well and the rope that he hooked to his body to pull him out ripped through his ragged clothes. 'Opelika', *Montgomery Advertiser*, 13 September 1895, 3; 'Buried Alive', *Montgomery Times*, 31 August 1904, 1; 'Old

Negro Well Digger Drowned While At Work', *Montgomery Times*, 25 January 1913, 7.

Chapter 9: African Town

1. 'The River News', *Times-Picayune*, 15 April 1865, 8; Hurston, *Barracoon*, 65.
2. Roche, *Historic Sketches*, 114–15. Emphasis in original.
3. Cudjo Lewis, 1880 US Census, Whistler, Mobile, Alabama; Orsa Keebie, 1880 US Census, Whistler, Mobile, Alabama; Anon., Audio Interview with Clara Eva Bell Allen Jones; 'Last of Slave Business'; Hurston, *Barracoon*, 66; Robertson, *The Slave Ship Clotilda*, 139–40.
4. Roche, *Historic Sketches*, 101; Pettaway, 'The Folklife', 57; Hurston, *Barracoon*, 66–7; Scott, 'Affika Town', 59.
5. Roche, *Historic Sketches*, 114–15; Hurston, *Barracoon*, 66; Mullin, 'The Passing Throng'.
6. The Africans also reported in 1917 that they offered William Foster $1,000 (equivalent to $20,000 today) to take them home, but he refused their money, telling them that he would expect to profit from such a journey and that $1,000 was nowhere near enough to cover his expenses. Roche, *Historic Sketches*, 115–16; Imes, 'The Last Recruits', 357.
7. Assistant superintendent of the Freedmen's Bureau Lieutenant Colonel George E. Yarrington counted 38 murders of Black men in Alabama's six southern counties over three months in 1865. He also described the shocking fate of a woman and her three small children who were among a party of freed people who journeyed to the Tombigbee River – a route just taken by a pregnant Kanko and her son Willie – in search of federal forces. A white man named Bill Odam confronted the unlucky woman. 'Where are you going? Down the river, ain't you?' When she replied 'Yes, sir', he exclaimed, 'I will show you the way through hell.' He cut the throats of the woman, her 9-year-old son and her 7-year-old daughter and threw their bodies and the woman's helpless baby in the water. Another woman and her children were nailed into a hencoop before being thrown alive in the Tombigbee River. Feldman, *The Irony*, 7; *Report of the Joint Committee*, 4, 65; 'Mr. John M. Dabney . . .', *Selma Morning Times*, 22 March 1870, 3; 'Alabama News', *Times-Argus*, 31 March 1870, 3; *Mobile Daily Register*, 19 March 1870 and 23 April 1870, cited in Tabor, *Africatown*, 63.
8. Imes, 'The Last Recruits', 357; General A. L. Chetlain, Washington DC, 14 March 1866, in *Report of the Joint Committee*, 3, 150; B. B. Cox,

'Mobilian Tells of This City in Civil War Days', *Mobile Register*, 1 November 1914, 5A. MPL. https://digital.mobilepubliclibrary.org/items/show/1804.

9. Polee's daughter Eva asserted that her father took his surname from a man who enslaved him during the war, but she could not recall the enslaver's first name. Diouf draws this conclusion about Charlie's surname origins, although her study confuses Charlie with Osia Keeby, who also bore the name Oluwale. Antoinette Wakeman and George Lake Imes both recorded that the name Cudjo Lewis was a corruption of the name Kossula, which Wakeman transcribed as 'Consouloa' and Imes spelled 'Cusolu'. Abaché acquired her unusual surname from, and was likely enslaved to, Captain Peter Francisco Aunspaugh, who served alongside Timothy Meaher and the kidnapped Africans on the *Southern Republic* and worked as Burns Meaher's steamboat clerk after the war. Roche, *Historic Sketches*, 104 and 116–17; Anon., Audio Interview with Clara Eva Bell Allen Jones; Robertson, *The Slave Ship Clotilda*, 143; Hurston, *Barracoon*, 68 and 72; Diouf, *Dreams*, 134; Antoinette V. H. Wakeman, 'Simon-Pure Africans', *Paxton Record*, 18 June 1896, 6; 'Imes, 'The Last Recruits', 359; 'The "Southern Republic"', *Weekly Advertiser*, 30 January 1861, 3; 'River Intelligence', *Mobile Daily Times*, 30 May 1867, 5.

10. Hurston lampooned royal lineage claims, which she saw as a Eurocentric obsession rooted in snobbery and lies. Meaher to Donaldson; Usman and Falola, *The Yoruba*, 20; Hurston, *Barracoon*, 66; Hurston, *Dust Tracks*, 167.

11. Roche, *Historic Sketches*, 117–18; Hurston, *Barracoon*, 68; Campbell, *A Pilgrimage*, 55.

12. Aso was a form of savings bank where money could be deposited with and withdrawn from a creditor at any time, and esusu was like a credit union whose members pooled their savings. Dennison, *A Memoir*, 34–5, 45, 57, 63–6 and 71; Sellers, *Slavery in Alabama*, 154; Green, *A Fistful of Shells*, 434.

13. Another African man living in downtown Mobile after the war was also very likely a *Clotilda* survivor. Peter Johnson worked like so many of his shipmates as a wood sawyer and lived with his American wife Julie, daughter Mary and baby son, also named Peter, in the Old Dauphin Way Historic District of the city, a popular living quarter for steamboat captains, merchants and maritime pilots. Julia soon died, however, and in spring 1876 the African man broke his ankle, probably in a work-related accident. The injury was so bad that Peter lost his ability to walk and therefore to work and ended up with his 6-year-old

son at the Mobile County Asylum for the Poor. Four years later, both father and son, who was registered as 'mute' on the 1880 census, were still trapped in the asylum, where conditions were atrocious. An early twentieth-century inspector of the asylum likened its cooking and drinking water to sewage. The outraged inspector suggested it was 'nothing short of criminal to compel the inmates of that institution to drink this water'. Peter disappears from the historical record after 1880; he probably died in the asylum before the end of the century. The fate of his son is unknown. Dennison, *A Memoir*, 38, 41−2 and 72; Dennison, *Biographical Memoirs*, 19; Jean Martin, 'Vacation in Alabama the Beautiful', *Selma Times-Journal*, 1 May 1983, 21; Peter, Julia, Mary and Peter Johnson, 1870 US Census, Mobile Ward 8, Mobile, Alabama; Peter and Peter Johnson, 1880 US Census Schedules of Defective, Dependent, and Delinquent Classes, Mobile, Alabama; Peter and Peter Johnson, 1880 US Census, Kosters, Mobile, Alabama; 'Oates Goes After Commissioners', *Progressive Age*, 2 January 1913, 2.

14. As Polee's daughter Eva also noted, not all the Africans belonged to the same church in the early twentieth century. 'No, not all of them was members of [Old Landmark Baptist Church in African Town] − it was different churches then.' Scott, *Daphne*, 209; Lucy Dick, General Land Office Records, Baldwin, Alabama, 23 June 1898; Russell Dick, General Land Office Records, Baldwin, Alabama, 23 June 1898; Russell Dick, Sworn Affidavit, Baldwin County Deeds and Records, December 1911; 'Dots from Daphne', *Baldwin Times*, 19 January 1905, 2; Pettaway, 'The Folklife', 51; Anon., Audio Interview with Clara Eva Bell Allen Jones.

15. Johnson, *A History of the Yorubas*, 103; Hurston, *Barracoon*, 72.

16. Kossula's effort to reconstruct a feeling of home echoed the craftsmanship of another of the United States' last Middle Passage survivors. Tahro, who was known in the United States as Romeo Thomas, was one of more than a hundred *Wanderer* captives who were sent to Edgefield, South Carolina. Using construction techniques he learned as a child in Congo, the Kikongo speaker recreated in Edgefield the house from which he had been so cruelly wrenched as a youth. If Tahro could never again see his lost homeland, then he was determined to recreate the physical sense of living there. The single-room, windowless dwelling was woven together from lath held in place by twine netting and supported by a timber frame. The roof was made from straw thatch. The house was completely waterproof and was so robust that it stood until at least 1907. Tahro's neighbour Lucinda Thurmond, who died in 1990, remembered playing in it as a child. Tahro's skills extended to

broom-making, and he also designed a carved walking stick that recorded the year of his capture and whose many notches probably recorded the number of years he spent in exile. At the end of Tahro's life, he gave up hope of returning home, believing it was no longer possible to reunite with his kinsfolk, but he never stopped speaking of his beloved homeland. Tahro died in Edgefield on 20 February 1923. Hurston, 'The Last Slave Ship', 351; Cudgenle, Pheny and Alice Adams, 1870 U.S. Census, Beat 3, Mobile, Alabama; Eleck V. Lewis, Findagrave. com. https://www.findagrave.com/memorial/116892993/aleck-lyadjemi-lewis; Owen Alderman Duncan, 'The Last Survivor of Slave Cargo of the Last Slave Ship', *Aiken Standard*, 18 November 1927, 5; Baldwin, *Great & Noble Jar*, 83; Romeo Thomas Death Record, Edgefield, South Carolina, 20 February 1923; Hurston, *Barracoon*, 72–3.

17. After the birth of their second child, James/Ahnonotoe, Abile and Kossula had twin boys, David/Adeniah ('prince') and Polee Dahoo ('Polee the elder'). Polee's name probably indicates that he was the older twin. Around the same time, Abaché gave birth to twins Ed and Susie to her African American husband Samuel Turner. Twins (ibeji) are considered a blessing in Yoruba culture; they are sacred to the thunder orisha Shango and are believed to share a soul. If Ed and Susie received African names, they were not documented, but if they had been born in their mother's homeland, they would have been called Taiwo (first-born) and Kehinde (second-born). Yoruba people have among the highest rates of twin births in the world, and the shipmates' ethnicity likely explains the frequency of twins in African Town. The Nigerian town of Igbo-Ora, less than 70 miles southwest of Owini Hill, describes itself as the 'twins capital of the world.' Zuma gave birth to John and Mary in December 1879. Polee's 11 children with Abaché's daughter Lucy included twin girls Alma and Elma. Dinah Miller and Redoshi were both grandmothers to twin girls and Abile and Kossula had twin great-granddaughters; strikingly, all three sets of twins were named Martha and Mary. Dinah's great-grandchildren Pimy and Mack Pettway were also probably twins.

According to the Fon, the moon (Mawu) is the creator goddess. Mawu is said to have created the world on the back of or in the mouth of the rainbow serpent Aido-Hwedo. She then assigned Aido-Hwedo to hold up the heavens by coiling herself around the earth. Noah also claimed the *Clotilda* Africans threw their newborn babies in the creek and only retrieved them if they struggled for life. Noah had little respect for the Africans' cultural traditions, and his amanuensis, wealthy white writer Mary McNeill Scott, had even less. Nevertheless, he may have been recalling a belief that developed in the Dahomey royal household, and perhaps was expressed by Gumpa, that babies with physical deformities were tohosu ('king of the water'), powerful, dangerous deities who needed to be returned to the water from which they were believed to have come. The Fon nobility's belief in such deities is thought to have arisen in response to extreme drought and famine in the mid-eighteenth century. Only rarely were such babies allowed to live.

Noah also suggested the Africans' burial traditions were strikingly different from the funerals Kossula knew in Tarkar, although his account is unreliable given that, except for 'Ecotah', who was lost in the Alabama River, few of the Africans, and perhaps only Archie Thomas, died before the group established a church cemetery. Noah claimed that, instead of burying their loved one at home, the Africans dug graves 15 feet deep on the tops of hills, which they filled with tree bark. They wrapped the corpse with strips of sapling bark, carried the body above their heads, laid it in the grave and then added more tree bark and earth on top to create a 'roun' flat moun''. They then folded their arms, caught each other's hands and danced, sang and wept in a ring. Noah also asserted that the group had an annual tradition back home that involved swimming out to an island and allowing each other to drown as a way of weeding out their community's oldest, weakest members. Such a practice would have been at odds with the Yoruba tradition of burying a loved one at home to ensure their continual spiritual attachment, as an ancestor, to their family. Clara, Ed and Susie Turner, 1870 US Census, Beat 3, Mobile, Alabama; Alexis Akwagyiram, 'Nigeria's Twin Town Ponders Cause of Multiple Births', *Reuters*, 9 April 2019. https://www.reuters.com/article/us-nigeria-twins-idUSKCN1RL1A9; Diouf, *Dreams*, 136–7; Zuma, John and Mary Livingstone, 1880 US Census, Whistler, Mobile, Alabama; Alma and Elma Allen, 1910 US Census, Precinct 9, Mobile, Alabama; Mary and Martha Petway, 1920 US Census, Gees Bend, Wilcox, Alabama; Mary and Martha Moore, 1910 US Census, Mitchell, Dallas, Alabama; Pimy and Mack Peteway, 1940 US Census, Gees Bend, Wilcox, Alabama; Wakeman, 'Simon-Pure Africans'; Scott, 'Affika Town', 63–4; Herskovits and Herskovits, *Dahomean Narrative*, 30–1; Bay, *Wives of the Leopard*, 93.

18. Tennessee, which was the last state to secede from the Union, was the only exception to this rule. That state's legislature ratified the

Fourteenth Amendment on 18 July 1866 and was readmitted to the Union the following week. Roche, *Historic Sketches*, 119; Burnett, *The Pen*, 157–8; Severance, *Portraits*, 311.

19. Bogue Chitto's male citizens cherished their new voting rights and turned out in huge numbers to cast their ballots. Yawith was likely among them. He may well be the 'William Smith' who registered to vote in Marion Junction in 1867. Three other *Clotilda* Africans, Alex Burns, Angus Cheney and Pinkney Claiborne, registered to vote in Marengo County in June 1867. 'Beast' Porter and William Seay were the other Montgomery Africans who registered to vote. Archie and Tony Thomas 1867 Voter Registration, Election District 1, Precinct 1, Mobile, Alabama; Charles and Cudjo Lewis, 1867 Voter Registration, Election District 2, Precinct 3, Mobile, Alabama; Arthur Kebee, 1867 Voter Registration, Election District 2, Precinct 3, Mobile, Alabama; Pauli Allen, 1867 Voter Registration, Election District 2, Precinct 3, Mobile, Alabama; Boynton Robinson, *Bridge Across Jordan*, 29; William Smith, 1867 Voter Registration, Marion Junction, Dallas, Alabama; Alick Burns, 1867 Voter Registration, Marengo, Alabama; Angus Cheeney, 1867 Voter Registration, Marengo, Alabama; Pinkney Claiborne, 1867 Voter Registration, Marengo, Alabama; Bease [sic] Porter, 1867 Voter Registration, Elmore, Alabama; Jno Smith, 1867 U.S. Voter Registration, Montgomery, Alabama; Robt. Jones, 1867 Voter Registration, Montgomery, Alabama; Willis Sea, 1867 Voter Registration, Montgomery, Alabama.

20. Specifically, the *Mail* suggested it could reduce the number of Black voters from 62,160 to 60,000. Well into the twentieth century, the *Clotilda* survivors' presence in post-war Montgomery was still being used as a reason to deny Black people the franchise. Future Alabama senator Albert Gallatin Taylor Goodwyn repeated the story of benighted Africans at the ballot box ahead of Alabama's 1930 gubernatorial election in his role as commander-in-chief of Confederate Army veterans' group the United Confederate Veterans. He recalled in a letter to the *Montgomery Advertiser* that, 'In socalled [sic] Reconstruction I saw hundreds of negroes brought to the polls in my native voting precinct under the leadership of a carpet bagger [sic] from Maine and voted as he directed. Several of these negroes were native Africans, brought over here unlawfully by a New England ship called "The Wanderer" [sic]. These innocent and pitiful Negroes were numerously armed with shotguns and pistols. The great mass of the representative Whites was disenfranchised.' Goodwyn lived near six of

the *Clotilda* survivors in 1867, although the shipmate derogatorily named 'Beast' by his enslaver was the only African-born registered voter in his precinct. 'The Registration Swindle in Alabama', *Nashville Union and American*, 2 October 1867, 4; 'How the Constitution Can be Defeated', *Greenville Advocate*, 19 December 1867, 1; 'Letters To The Editor', *Montgomery Advertiser*, 19 October 1930, 4.

21. Burnett, *The Pen*, 160–1; 'Mobile County', in Election in Alabama, 25.
22. Maguire likely would have turned the Africans away even without Meaher's instructions; he was part of a Constitutional Executive Committee whose members were charged with 'defeating the so-called Constitution'. Emma Langdon Roche recorded that only Kossula, Osia Keeby and Polee went to vote, but those were the only Mobile-based male shipmates still alive to speak to when she wrote about the incident. It is likely that all or most of the men of African Town voted, and certainly all of those whose names are identifiable on 1867 voter registration documents. Roche, *Historic Sketches*, 119–20; John McGuire [sic], Affidavit, 25 March 1868, in Election in Alabama, 64–5; 'The Constitutional Executive Committee', *Mobile Daily Times*, 15 January 1868, 3.
23. Although court data does not confirm that their applications were granted, Osia Keeby was a naturalized US citizen according to both the 1900 and 1910 censuses and Kossula was naturalized according to the 1920 census. Charlie was recorded as an 'alien' on the 1900 census, but the census-taker was unable to confirm information directly with him as the African man could not speak much English. Anthony Thomas was wealthy enough to pay poll tax prior to his death in 1910, which should theoretically have afforded him voting rights, at least until 1901, when specific restrictions such as literacy tests debarred most Black men and many poor white men from voting. Burnett, *The Pen*, 161; Roche, *Historic Sketches*, 120; Mobile City Court Records, 23 and 24 October 1868; Tony Thomas, Wills and Probate Records, Mobile, Alabama, 9 January 1911; Osie Keeby, 1900 US Census, Precinct 9, Whistler, Mobile, Alabama; Osia Kerby, 1910 US Census, Precinct 9, Mobile, Alabama; Cugo Lewis, 1920 US Census, Whistler, Mobile, Alabama; Charles Lewis, 1900 US Census, Precinct 10, Kosters, Mobile, Alabama.
24. Emma Langdon Roche recorded that the Africans continued to believe in a benevolent spirit named 'Ahla-ahra' ('ala' means 'dream' and 'dara' means 'good' in Yoruba) and a malevolent spirit named 'Ahla-bady-oleelay'. Diouf notes that 'n'bady' ('bad') is a word specific to the Isha

Yoruba of Banté to support her contention that the shipmates came from western Benin. However, Robertson offers an alternative and fuller translation of 'Ahla-bady-oleelay': that it was an allusion to the trinity of Fon spirits Alasa, Gbade and Akele, who were assistants to Fon deity of thunder Xevioso. Two years before his death, Kossula gave a slightly earlier conversion date of 1868. Hurston, *Barracoon*, 68—9; Roche, *Historic Sketches*, 79—80; Diouf, *Dreams*, 41; Robertson, *The Slave Ship Clotilda*, 166—7; Emma Roche, 'Last Survivor of Slave Ship Deeply Grateful to God, Man', *Mobile Press*, 18 August 1935. MPL. http://digital.mobilepubliclibrary.org/items/show/2195; Caver, 'A Lone Survivor', 6.

25. Tupper, *A Decade*, 23; 'Rev. A. D. Phillips', *Baptist and Reflector*, 5 January 1893, 7; 'Rev. A. D. Phillips', *Biblical Recorder,* 13 January 1869, 2; 'The Baptist Convention of South Carolina', *Biblical Recorder,* 4 August 1869, 2; 'Baptist School Convention', *The Friend of Temperance*, 16 June 1869, 3.

26. Leavell and Bailey, *A Complete History*, 859; 'Africa', *Republican Banner*, 1 November 1872, 4.

27. The federal government's failure to seize the *Clotilda* Africans or to meaningfully prosecute their kidnappers meant that the *Wanderer* was commonly held to be the last slave ship to traffic Africans to the United States. Second-hand reports of Phillips's meeting with the Africans not only reinforced his error but made additional mistakes about the circumstances and location of the group's kidnap. The *New York Daily Herald* reported in November 1870 – 19 months after Phillips's visit to Stone Street Baptist Church – that the Africans were not victims of an assault on their town, but, rather, were a trading party ambushed somewhere west of Abeokuta by the Dahomey army, which marched them to an unnamed town 'upon the coast near Porto Novo [sic], where the *Wanderer* was lying off the shore to receive them'. Subsequent American Colonization Society meeting reports were more specific about the location of the apparent ambush: a road 'between Abeokuta and Ikatu [Kétou]', which lies directly north of Porto-Novo in present-day Benin. There is no evidence that Phillips himself identified the group of mostly child and adolescent captives as adult traders or suggested that their place of kidnap was anywhere near Benin. 'Items of Intelligence'; 'Washington: Reminiscence of the Slave Trade – The Wanderer's Cargo', *New York Daily Herald*, 27 November 1870, 7; 'Fifty-Fourth Annual Report', 39.

28. Despite his generally sensitive account of Yoruba cultures and effort to help the Africans, Phillips's speech was marred by racism. He stressed

of the group that 'they have more intelligence than the colored people of this country.' Phillips probably knew he had to counter anti-Black prejudices to generate sympathy for the Africans in the post-war US South. The North Carolina-born, Mississippi-raised missionary may have been voicing his own prejudices, too; he was raised in a household that held a teenage girl enslaved. *Proceedings of the Fourteenth Meeting*, 25; 'Items of Intelligence'; 'Commencement', *Biblical Recorder,* 16 June 1869, 2; Phillips, 'Lecture on Africa'; John D. Phillips, 1850 US Slave Schedule, District 6, Itawamba, Mississippi.

29. Finlay was driven by a racist belief that free Black people were incapable of integrating into mainstream US society; he therefore saw emigration as a necessary component of emancipation. He also hoped that relocated Black Americans would help to Christianize Africans. The *Wanderer* survivor, whose identity is unknown, was a passenger on the ACS's ship the *Golconda*, which sailed from Charleston, South Carolina, in May 1867 and arrived in Liberia's capital Monrovia on 8 July, seven years to the day after the *Clotilda* sailed up Mobile Bay with its captives. The African travelled with two other unnamed Africans. Despite a huge volume of applicants, the ACS only managed to help 1,760 people to emigrate over the next 20 years. 'Religious Items', *Star Tribune*, 6 June 1869, 2; 'Our Charleston Letter', *Orangeburg News*, 25 May 1867, 2; *Fifty-First Annual Report*, 8; Barnes, *Journey of Hope*, 8–9.

30. 'Latest News by Mail', *Times-Picayune*, 4 December 1870, 16.

31. Unable to return to Yoruba territory, Phillips travelled instead to Liberia and Sierra Leone to survey the missionary work there. 'Colored People for Liberia', *Goldsboro Messenger*, 17 January 1878, 2; E. T. D., 'Meeting', 3; 'Fifty-Fourth Annual Report', 38; 'Pennsylvania Colonization Society Stated Board Meeting, 4 March 1871', in Pennsylvania Colonization Society Minute Book, 204; 'Missionary Exploration', 263; Martin, *Black Baptists*, 23; Agbeti, *West African Church History*, 122.

32. Land Sale, Thomas Buford to Jabez Chase, Horace Ely, Charley Lewis, Maggie Lewis, Matilda Ely, Lucy Wilson and Polly Shay. 5 April 1870. Deed Book 70, 242–4; Diouf, *Dreams*, 155.

33. 'News of the Churches', *Christian Intelligencer*, 10 October 1872, 2; Robert Jones, 1880 U.S. Census, Montgomery Ward 4, Montgomery, Alabama.

34. Phillips's letter, which caught the attention of the Pennsylvania Colonization Society, was reprinted anonymously. However, the

authorship of a follow-up letter was attributed to him. Andrew Dickerson Phillips, New York Passenger List, 22 June 1871; 'News of the Churches'.

35. Pennsylvania Colonization Society Stated Board Meeting, 12 November 1872, in Pennsylvania Colonization Society, 240; 'Colonization', *Philadelphia Inquirer*, 11 June 1873, 2; Pennsylvania Colonization Society Stated Board Meeting, 10 June 1873, in Pennsylvania Colonization Society, 253; 'Colonization', *Philadelphia Inquirer*, 11 September 1873, 2; 'Address of Rev. George W. Samson', 86; Tupper, *A Decade*, 877.

36. The African Colonization Society described Jackson as a 'fair scholar and mechanic'. 'The Wanderer', *Montgomery Advertiser*, 25 August 1875, 2; 'Liberia and the Congo', 29; 'The Columbus Enquirer . . .', *Montgomery Advertiser*, 27 August 1875, 3.

37. Jackson likely hid his literacy skills from the city's white authorities. Both censuses on which his name appeared classified him as illiterate. Jack Smith and Amanda Davis Marriage Record, Montgomery, Alabama, 1 January 1867; Bailey, *Neither Carpetbaggers*, 130; Hood, *One Hundred Years*, 372–3; John Smith, 1870 US Census, Montgomery Ward 2, Montgomery, Alabama; Jack Smith, 1880 US Census, Montgomery Ward 3, Montgomery, Alabama.

38. 'A Montgomery Negro . . .'.

39. 'A Few Days Ago . . .', *Weekly Advertiser,* 11 May 1880, 4.

40. 'Off to Africa', *Montgomery Advertiser*, 10 July 1883, 5.

41. 'The Monrovia', *African Repository*, 55.1 (January 1879), 27.

42. 'Liberia and the Congo', 31; 'Letter of a Native African', *Montgomery Advertiser*, 5 March 1884, 4.

43. Lorenzo Wilson's personal estate was valued at $20,000 (nearly $500,000 in 2023) in 1870. *Gone With the Wind* author Margaret Mitchell named *St. Elmo*'s eponymous hero as a model for Rhett Butler. Deed Book 30, 601; M. Lorenzo Wilson, 1870 US Census, Beat 2, Mobile, Alabama; Ayres, *The Life*, 1; Diane Roberts, 'Introduction', in Evans, *St. Elmo*, v; Amy Thompson McCandless, 'Augusta Jane Evans Wilson', in *The History of Southern Women's Literature*, 151; Young, *Disarming the Nation*, 258; Deed Book 30, 643, 655; Diouf, *Dreams*, 156; Hurston, *Barracoon*, 15 and 68.

44. Hoffman, *Back Home*, 187; Hurston, *Barracoon*, 69 and 74; 'Panic in a Negro Church', *Greenville Advocate*, 3 October 1867, 2.

45. Clara Aunspaugh and Samuel Turner Marriage Record, Mobile, Alabama, 8 March 1880; Cudgo and Cecilia Louis Marriage Record, Mobile, Alabama, 15 March 1880; Polle and Rosa Allen Marriage Record, Mobile, Alabama, 15 March 1880; Annie Kibbe and Arci Kibbe

Marriage Record, Mobile, Alabama, 15 March 1880; Zoma and John Livingston Marriage Record, Mobile, Alabama, 16 June 1887; Hurston, *Barracoon*, 72.

46. Another *Clotilda* conspiracist became a marksman's target. A few years before the trafficking plot began, John Dabney survived a gun and sword fight in the centre of Mobile. He instigated the reckless battle with lawyer Charles P. Robinson after Robinson criticized him for poor behaviour in court. The pair were arrested and fined $50 for affray, but the incident ended without injury. In March 1881, Dabney would not be so lucky. The 62-year-old was shot in mysterious circumstances by an assassin who lay in wait as he walked along a public road near Mount Vernon. Bullets entered the victim's left temple, shoulder and knee. No one was ever convicted of his killing. 'Capt. Tim Meaher's Sketch'; 'A Veteran Steamboat Man Dead', *Montgomery Advertiser*, 11 February 1885, 1; 'City Court of Mobile', *Mobile Daily Times*, 15 June 1867, 5; 'Meaher v. Tindal', *Montgomery Advertiser*, 11 August 1867, 4; 'James H. & Timothy Meaher . . .', *Montgomery Advertiser*, 13 February 1873, 1; 'Circuit Court', *Mobile Daily Tribune*, 23 February 1875, 3; 'City Court', *Mobile Daily Tribune*, 25 May 1876, 3; 'Mayor's Court', *Mobile Daily Tribune*, 28 December 1875, 3; 'Mayor's Court', *Mobile Daily Tribune*, 4 January 1876, 3; 'River', *Selma Morning Times*, 19 September 1869, 3; 'The Mobile Papers . . .', *Times-Picayune*, 14 April 1852, 1; 'Personal Rencontre in Mobile', *Montgomery Advertiser*, 27 April 1852, 1; 'Mobile, Ala.', *New Orleans Democrat*, 2 August 1881, 1; 'The Dabney Murder', *Clarke County Democrat,* 30 March 1881, 1; 'James C. Greer . . .', *Clarke County Democrat,* 26 October 1882, 4.

47. Ajanaku is a praise name for elephants that appears frequently in ijala, a poetic art form practiced mainly by traditional Oyo Yoruba hunters. 'Pa-Ajana-ku' means 'Killer of Ajana' and refers to a legendary hunter who sought to capture alive a specimen of every animal but ultimately was trampled to death by an elephant. Babalola, *The Content*, 3 and 93; Roche, *Historic Sketches*, 100; Simpich, 'Smoke', 740.

Chapter 10: Reunion

1. Report of Maj. J. P. Houston, in *Report on the Condition*, 71–2; Ovington, 'Slaves' Reminiscences', 1135.

2. Sworn Testimony of Judge William H. Smith in *Report of the Joint Committee*, 3, 11; Report of J. M. Phipps, in *Report on the Condition*, 71.

3. Bougier and Sarah were both recorded as 'Sarah Africa' on the 1870 census. Bougier's daughter was recorded across census data as Mary A. Brown, Sarah's son was called Samuel Jones (later Pettiway), and Unsey named her son John Henry. Bailey, *Neither Carpetbaggers*, 6−7 and 15−16; Sworn Testimony of Rev. Joseph E. Roy, in *Report of the Joint Committee*, 4, 68; Sworn Testimony of General A. L. Chetlain, in *Report of the Joint Committee*, 3, 150; Bettie and William Africa, 1870 US Census, Township 16, Range 19, Montgomery, Alabama; Sarah Africa and Sarah Africa, 1870 US Census, Township 16 Range 19, Montgomery, Alabama; Unsey Blair, 1870 US Census, Township 16 Range 19, Montgomery, Alabama; Nannie and D—Smith, 1880 US Census, Pike Road, Montgomery, Alabama.

4. Lucy Hunt, 1870 US Census, Prairie Bluff, Wilcox, Alabama; Lucy Hunt, 1870 US Census, McKinley, Marengo, Alabama.

5. Tilda Craigher, 1870 US Census, Athens, Dallas, Alabama.

6. Boynton Robinson, *Bridge Across Jordan*, 24; Mauldin, *Unredeemed Land*, 125−7; Silkenat, *Scars*, 169−70.

7. Fleming, *In the Shadow*, 26−7; Edwards, *Twenty-five Years*, 49.

8. The combined value of McDonald's real and personal estates in 1870 was $10,000 (equivalent to $230,000 today). James McDonald, 1870 US Census, Athens, Dallas, Alabama; Wynn, 'Woman Survivor'.

9. Boynton Robinson, *Bridge Across Jordan*, 23−4; Forner, *Why the Vote*, 20.

10. Cuffee Smith, 1880 Agricultural Schedule, Browns, Dallas, Alabama.

11. Boynton Robinson, *Bridge Across Jordan*, 33.

12. A farm valued at $300 in 1870 would be worth around $7,000 today. Dina Jenkins, 1870 US Census, Bonhams, Wilcox, Alabama; Sip Jenkins, 1870 Agricultural Schedule, Bonham, Wilcox, Alabama.

13. Their children were Minerva, Shad, Sally, John Henry and Jimmie. Dinah Jenkins and Gasoway Miller Marriage Record, Wilcox, Alabama, 6 January 1872; Gasoway Miller, 1880 Agricultural Schedule, Bonham, Wilcox, Alabama.

14. Given was conscripted into the 2nd Regiment, Alabama Volunteer Militia as a private in March 1862, but was ruled too old to fight. Vass, 'Montgomery Girl's Recollections'; 'Dr. B. R. Jones', *Montgomery Advertiser*, 15 September 1865, 3; 'Benjamin Rush Jones', in Owen and Owen, *History of Alabama*, 3, 925; du Mont, *du Mont de Soumagne*, 83; Alexander Given Confederate Military Record; Alexander F. Given, 1870 US Census, Montgomery Ward 5, Montgomery, Alabama; Blue, *A Brief History*, 26; Sulzby, *Historic Alabama Hotels*, 129.

Notes

15. DeLand and Smith, *Northern Alabama*, 657; 'Real Estate Agency', *Selma Morning Times*, 9 May 1866, 1; 'Col. W. M. Smith . . .', *Montgomery Advertiser*, 28 August 1867, 2; 'U.S. District Court', *Mobile Daily Times*, 25 December 1867, 2; 'Petitioners in Bankruptcy'; 'The Residence of M. W. Creagh . . .', *Livingston Journal*, 31 July 1868, 2; 'Southern Items', *New Orleans Crescent*, 2 August 1868, 3; M. W. Creagh, 1870 US Census, Demopolis, Marengo, Alabama.

16. 'Democratic and Conservative Club of Demopolis', *Southern Exponent*, 6 October 1870, 3.

17. 'Messrs. Creagh & Marschalk . . .', *Times-Argus*, 9 June 1870, 3; 'The Demopolis Exponent . . .', *Times-Argus*, 2 June 1870, 3; F. P. Ferris, 'Salutatory', *Exponent*, 4 August 1870, 2.

18. According to Davis, Clanton was part of the mob of up to one hundred and fifty Klansmen who surrounded a Republican voter rally in Huntsville on the eve of the 1868 presidential election and shot to death a Black man named Aleck Reed and a white Republican probate judge named Silas Thurlow. 'State Convention at Selma, Alabama', *Selma Times*, 26 July 1866, 1; 'Names of Delegates', *Selma Times and Messenger*, 15 July 1866, 2; 'Delegates to the National Democratic Convention', *Montgomery Advertiser*, 24 June 1868, 1; Davis, *Authentic History*, 45 and 70–1; Robb, 'Who Are These Masked Men?', 216–17.

19. The Klan was one of many named and nameless nocturnal white supremacist vigilante groups that emerged in the post-Civil War South, including the Knights of the White Camelia and blackface-wearing Black Horse Cavalry, both of which arose in Louisiana, and the Pale Faces, which emerged in Middle Tennessee. What set the Klan apart was its ability to present itself as a single coherent movement. As historian Elaine Parsons has noted, 'the many small groups that comprised the first Ku-Klux Klan would together become the most widely proliferated and deadly domestic terrorist movement in the history of the United States'. Parsons, *Ku-Klux*, 5–7; Feldman, *The Irony*, 8, 10 and 14–15; Bailey, *Neither Carpetbaggers*, 194.

20. Albert Pike, 'The Ku-Klux Klan', *Memphis Daily Appeal*, 16 April 1868, 2; Davis, *Authentic History*, 276–7; 'Vaudooism', *Memphis Daily Appeal*, 25 October 1868, 3.

21. Vass, 'Montgomery Girl's Recollections'; 'James H. Clanton', *Selma Morning Times,* 30 September 1871, 1; 'James H. Clanton', *Montgomery Advertiser*, 30 September 1871, 3; 'The Clanton Fund', *Montgomery Advertiser*, 10 April 1872, 2.

22. Arnett, 'Dinah', 93.

23. Ibid., 93.
24. As Charles S. Aiken notes, 'Wilcox County, Alabama, did not begin to assume responsibility for the education of black children until the 1930s. Even in 1965, more than 40 percent of Wilcox County's black students were taught in schools owned and operated by the United Presbyterian Church of North America.' Aiken, *The Cotton Plantation South*, 148–9; Fleming, *In the Shadow*, xvi and 37.
25. Arnett, 'Dinah', 94.
26. Memorable Creagh's gravestone lists his birth year as 1817, but that date is probably wrong as his mother Rebecca Walthall Creagh was born in 1765. The 1850 census, which records his age as 41, is more likely to be accurate. 'Death of Col. W. M. Smith', *Montgomery Advertiser*, 3 March 1869, 4; Forner, *Why the Vote*, 19; Dr. Memorable Walker Creagh, Findagrave.com. https://www.findagrave.com/memorial/103720953/memorable-walker-creagh; Rebecca Walthall Creagh, Findagrave.com. https://www.findagrave.com/memorial/113074880/rebecca-creagh; M. W. Creagh, 1850 US Census, Marengo, Alabama.
27. William Mays, 1870 US Census, Athens, Dallas, Alabama; John Mayes, 1850 US Census, Rascoes, Dallas, Alabama; J. S. Mayes, 1860 US Census, Athens, Dallas, Alabama; John S. Mayes, 1850 Slave Schedule, Athens, Dallas, Alabama; J. S. Mayes, 1860 Slave Schedule, Athens, Dallas, Alabama.
28. Susie also claimed that her father gifted Liza land, but the 1870 census recorded that Liza was a landless farm labourer. Hagedorn, 'Ole Bulja'; Joshua Ware and Crecy Casby Marriage Record, Montgomery, Alabama, 15 May 1871; Eliza Africa, 1870 US Census, Township 16 Range 19, Montgomery, Alabama.
29. Nolen, *African American Southerners*, 7; Olmsted, *A Journey*, 111; Egypt, *Unwritten History*, 54; *Remembering Slavery*, eds Berlin, Favreau, and Miller, 15.
30. Hagedorn, 'Ole Bulja'.
31. At least eight of Memorable Creagh's other former captives, Cransy Creagher, May Haywood, Peggy Crear, Mahala King, York Bryant, Pat Bradley, Pinkney Claiborne and Martha Martin, died – or at least disappeared from the historical record – in the 1870s and 1880s. Cransy died from pneumonia in Athens in May 1870; her death record gave her approximate age as 30. York's former housemate Pat was living in poor health in Limestone in the north of the state by the time he reached his mid-thirties. Guy is listed as 40 and Gracie as 38 on the

1870 census. Cransy Creagher, Federal Mortality Schedule, Athens, Dallas, Alabama, May 1870; Pat Bradley, 1880 US Census, Limestone, Alabama; Pinkney Claiborn, 1880 US Census, Demopolis, Marengo, Alabama; Gracie and Guy Craigher, 1870 US Census, Athens, Dallas, Alabama; Gracie Cragh, Federal Mortality Schedule, Liberty Hill, Dallas, Alabama, December 1879; Sallie Walker, 1870 US Census, Athens, Dallas, Alabama; Sally Walker, 1880 US Census, Liberty Hill, Dallas, Alabama.

32. Wynn, 'Woman Survivor'.

33. Boynton Robinson, *Bridge Across Jordan*, 30.

34. Martin enslaved 89 people in 1860. A. J. Martin, 1860 US Census, Orrville, Dallas, Alabama; A. J. Martin, 1870 Agricultural Schedule, Athens, Dallas, Alabama; Sally Walker and Matilda Creah, 1900 US Census, Martins, Dallas, Alabama; A. J. Martin, 1860 Slave Schedule, Orrville, Dallas, Alabama; Atlas J. Martin, Civil Appointments, Dallas, Alabama, 28 November 1868.

35. As Richard Bailey notes, 'the black vote carried the day for the Republican Party [in 1872] by providing the margin of victory. This fact was made clear as 55 percent of the 167,544 votes cast in the election came from the ballots of black counties.' Even into the late 1870s, Black voters in Wilcox County managed to return Republicans to office. Bailey, *Neither Carpetbaggers*, 204 and 219; Fleming, *In the Shadow*, 9–10 and 13.

36. The two Africans were Alex and Alice Burns, both apparently former captives of Memorable Creagh. Ossey Hunt, 1876 Voter List, Prairie Bluff, Wilcox, Alabama; Henry A. Woolf, 1870 US Census, Linden, Marengo, Alabama; *United States Congress Senate Committee*, 408 and 537.

37. 'The Registration of Voters', *Times-Argus*, 23 June 1876, 3; 'Testimony of Jeremiah Haralson, Washington, D.C., 13 February 1877', in *Senate of the United States for the Second Session of the Forty-Fourth Congress*, 151. Emphasis added.

38. The Republican Party abandoned the interests of freed people after Reconstruction, although Black voters remained loyal to the party as the party of Abraham Lincoln for decades. White Southern loyalty to the Democratic Party weakened when Democratic President Harry S. Truman desegregated the US military after the Second World War and weakened further when his fellow Democratic President Lyndon B. Johnson passed key civil rights legislation in the mid-1960s. Republican president Richard Nixon completed the South's transition from a Democratic to a Republican majority region in 1968 when he

adopted the so-called 'Southern Strategy', which sought to secure white Southern votes by playing up white Southern grievances.

39. Lynchings first began to be documented nationally in 1882.

40. 'Liberty Lodge No. 65', *Selma Times*, 10 June 1881, 4; 'Notice', *Daily Selma Reporter*, 6 April 1864, 2; 'Election Notice', *Times-Argus*, 7 July 1869, 2; Henry Ivey, 1880 US Census, Browns, Dallas, Alabama.

41. 'About the Release of Henry Ivy', *Selma Times*, 18 April 1882, 1; 'The Lynching', *Montgomery Advertiser*, 18 April 1882, 2; 'Lynching in Dallas County', *Eutaw Whig and Observer*, 20 April 1882, 3.

42. 'Lynch Law was Executed . . .', *Shelby Sentinel*, 20 April 1882, 2; 'The Lynching'.

43. 'Plantation Sold'.

44. Douglass, *Narrative*, 47.

45. Reuben Given, 1880 US Census, Montgomery Ward 4, Montgomery, Alabama; Silkenat, *Scars*, 114; Lucy Ann Lucas Estate and Case File, Montgomery, Alabama, 1895; 'Lucas Will Contest'; 'The Will of Lucy Ann Lucas', *Montgomery Advertiser*, 8 November 1895, 7; 'The Lucas Will Was Broken', *Montgomery Advertiser*, 20 December 1895, 7.

46. The 1910 census shows that Ossa's son Ossa, Jr. was Omolabi's nephew. 'Forty Years Ago in Selma', *Selma Times-Journal*, 28 August 1921, 4; 'Boarding', *Selma Times*, 28 August 1881, 4; 'The Funeral . . .', *Selma Times*, 9 December 1884, 4; 'Mrs. S. A. Z. Hunt', *Times-Argus*, 12 December 1884, 3; Katie Cooper and Archer [sic] Allen, 1910 US Census, Precinct 9, Mobile, Alabama.

47. The exact date of their journey is unclear, too, but writer Kirk Munroe recorded that the reunion occurred before December 1886. Munroe, 'The Industrial South', 503; Equiano, *The Interesting Narrative*, 59–60.

Chapter 11: Burials

1. 'The Harper Party', *Times-Picayune*, 29 November 1886, 1; 'Personal'; 'The New South'.

2. George and Juliet Craik are not identified in the *Harper's* edition of Munroe's article, but they are in its *Montgomery Advertiser* reprint. Munroe, 'Our Post-Office Box'; 'Kirk Munroe of the Harper Party', *Weekly Advertiser*, 27 January 1887, 3; Munroe, 'The Industrial South'.

3. An unreliable written account claimed the king killed himself; oral traditions suggest he was poisoned by his son and heir Kondo; historian Edna Bay suggests that old age was an equally likely cause of

Glele's death. 'A Veteran Steamboat Man Dead'; 'Mobile Matters', *Times-Democrat*, 8 November 1889, 4; Bay, *Wives of the Leopard*, 288–90.

4. Hines, 'Last Slave Cargo'.

5. O'Meagher, *Some Historical Notices*, 177; 'A Gentleman of Mobile . . .', *Clarke County Democrat*, 17 March 1892, 1.

6. Quiller Wheeler, 1910 US Census, Kosters, Mobile, Alabama; Ephraim Wheeler, 1908 City Directory, Mobile, Alabama.

7. Equilla Amy was born in August or September 1879. Kanko gave birth to Gerry in November 1865, but devastatingly the child did not survive infancy. Her oldest son Willie fled Mobile for New Orleans in 1874 at the age of 12 or 13. His parents would not see him again for decades. When he finally, briefly, returned home, he brought with him his 21-year-old son. Kattie Cooper and Oca Allen, 1900 US Census, Whistler, Mobile, Alabama; Amie Denis, 1880 US Census, Mobile Ward 5, Mobile, Alabama; Dennison, *Memoirs*, 29; Dennison, *A Memoir*, 35 and 46.

8. Ebeossi means 'no apology accepted' in Yoruba. Diouf, *Dreams*, 137; Celia Ebeossi Lewis, Findagrave.com. https://www.findagrave.com/memorial/116892860/celia-ebeossi-lewis; Hurston, *Barracoon*, 74.

9. Ibid., 34 and 74–5.

10. Approximately half the prisoners died. As Eugene Chihuahua, son of Chiricahua chief Chihuahua, remembered, 'We thought anything would be better than [Florida] with its rain, mosquitos, and malaria, but . . . We didn't know what misery was till they dumped us in those swamps.' Prisoners were forced to clear the forest and build their own accommodations. As survivor Sam Kenoi recalled, 'My own mother died working like a slave.' It's possible that Romeyn also made an earlier visit to African Town. He was stationed at Mount Vernon from May 1891, and he identified as one of his African interviewees a woman in her early fifties named 'Maum Polee'. There is no record of Rosallie Allen's death date, but her husband Polee married Abaché's daughter Lucy in December 1891. Romeyn, 'The Last Slaver'; 'Civilizing Apaches', *Montgomery Advertiser*, 14 December 1892, 2; Turner, *Wise Women*, 81; Conrad, *The Apache Diaspora*, 260; 'Captain Henry Romeyn, U.S.A.', in *Officers of the Army and Navy*, 353; Pole [sic] Allen and Lucy Turner Marriage Certificate, Mobile, Alabama, 17 December 1891.

11. The Dahomey Village imitated a similar human exhibition at the 1889 Exposition Universelle in Paris that was designed to justify France's war with – and ultimate conquest of – Dahomey. The Village was located at the foot of the Midway Plaisance, a mile-long display of ethnic groups ranked according to their perceived proximity

to Anglo-American 'civilization'. The formerly enslaved anti-racist activist Frederick Douglass despaired. '[T]he Dahomians are . . . here to exhibit the Negro as a repulsive savage', he concluded. Romeyn's visit to African Town and framing of most of the residents as Dahomeyan may have been rooted in voyeuristic interest in the kingdom stemming from the Chicago exhibition and its Parisian predecessor. Romeyn, 'The Last Slaver'; Frederick Douglass, 'Introduction', in Wells, *The Reason Why the Colored American*, 13.

12. The woman was very likely Abile given her frankness and fluency with English. Romeyn, 'The Last Slaver'; Wakeman, 'Simon-Pure Africans'.

13. For example, Ogun and Shango are associated with red and creator-God Olodumare is associated with white in present-day Yoruba culture. Pettaway, 'The Folklife', 80; Byers, 'The Last Slave-Ship', 742; Weir, 'The Last Slaver'; Blier, *Art and Risk*, 199–200.

14. Anon., Audio Interview with Clara Eva Bell Allen Jones; Berger, 'Cugo Lewis'.

15. Weir, 'The Last Slaver'; 'Finds Slave Ship Survivors', *Chicago Tribune*, 7 April 1902, 15; Jones, 'Editorial Correspondence', 54; Hurston, 'Cudjo's Own Story', 662; Imes, 'The Last Recruits', 359.

16. Toys thought to have been crafted by Gumpa for his grandchildren Josephine and Sidney were among the artifacts excavated from the remnants of his home in 2010. Diouf and Robertson both suggest that 'Jo-ko' was a diminutive of Bamijoko or Banjoko, a Yoruba name meaning 'sit/stay with me' given to babies whose older siblings may have died. Anon., Audio Interview with Clara Eva Bell Allen Jones; Roche, *Historic Sketches*, 125; Polle Allen, 1900 US Census, Whistler, Mobile, Alabama; Diouf, *Dreams*, 137; Robertson, *The Slave Ship Clotilda*, 158, 161 and 172; Pettaway, 'The Folklife', 68; Toulmin, 'The Family of Peter ("Gumpa") and Josephine Lee', 1–5.

17. Wakeman, 'Simon-Pure Africans'; Anon., Audio Interview with Clara Eva Bell Allen Jones.

18. Wakeman, 'Simon-Pure Africans'; Pettaway, 'The Folklife', 57; Robertson, *The Slave Ship Clotilda*, 163.

19. Ibid., 142; Jim Louis, 1900 US Census, Whistler, Mobile, Alabama; Imes, 'The Last Recruits', 358; 'Negroes of Plateau', *Southern Watchman*, 7 July 1900, 2; Hurston, *Barracoon*, 88.

20. 'Negro Community Attracts Attention', *New York Age*, 21 November 1912, 1; Tabor, *Africatown*, 162.

21. Jones, *Love and Loyalty*, 347; 'Brought the Last Slaves', *Shreveport Journal*, 12 February 1901, 1; 'Captain Wm. Foster'; Jones, 'Editorial Correspondence', 54.

Notes

22. As Wayne Flynt observes, 'A study by the Alabama Policy Conference based on the 1940 census estimated that in 1941 and 1942, various provisions of the state constitution disfranchised some 600,000 whites and 520,000 blacks directly and indirectly. Only 440,291 adults were registered to vote and in most counties, more whites than blacks fell victim to disfranchisement.' Flynt, 'Alabama's Shame', 69 and 75.

23. Feïchitan is a Yoruba name meaning 'born during troubles'. Diouf, *Dreams*, 137; Gilbert Thomas, 1880 US Census, Whistler, Mobile, Alabama; 'Mobile Matters', *Times-Democrat*, 12 August 1899, 7; 'Mobile Matters', *Times-Democrat*, 20 December 1898, 6; Hurston, *Barracoon*, 74–5.

24. Feldman, *The Irony*, 28–9.

25. Diouf, *Dreams*, 194–7.

26. The petition acknowledged that 'while the evidence did not show all the elements of technical self-defense, the jury and others familiar with the case believe that Lewis was not morally guilty.' The petition included a letter from Alabama's former Secretary of State Jabez J. Parker and future Mobile circuit judge Samuel Barnett Browne that described Gilbert as 'a *perambulating arsenal* of homicidal fury and destruction' who Cudjo was 'inexorably compelled to kill'. By contrast, Cudjo was 'a peaceable, quiet, well-behaved and industrious man, and extremely popular with the white people', and had provided great service to the sheriff and his deputies in 'ferreting out crime and arresting criminals of his own race'. The petition was co-signed by Timothy Meaher's son Augustine, as well as Sheriff Charles E. McLean, incoming Sheriff John F. Powers and the 10 jurors who could be located. Cudjo Lewis Pardon Materials. Emphasis in original.

27. 'News of the Gulf City', *Times-Democrat*, 31 January 1901, 8; 'News of the Gulf City', *Times-Democrat*, 6 August 1901, 14.

28. Alsobrook, 'Alabama's Port City', 157–8; 'Murder Near Mobile', *Montgomery Advertiser*, 19 November 1901, 3; Sledge, *The Mobile River*, 268; Bryant, *The Last Hero*, 32; Dennison, *Biographical Memoirs*, 52–3.

29. In May 1890, Gumpa married an African American woman named Clara Dozier. Peter Lee and Clara Dozier Marriage Certificate, Mobile, Alabama, 8 May 1890; Peter, Sidney and Feeny Lee, 1900 US Census, Whistler, Mobile, Alabama.

30. Peter Lee, Wills and Probate Records, Mobile, Alabama, 1902, Case No. 199.

31. Hurston, *Barracoon*, 77–8.

32. Ibid., 79 and 81.

33. Ibid., 80; 'Supreme Court Decisions', *Birmingham News*, 22 November 1904, 3.

34. Mobile's first two Black police officers were appointed in February 1954. They had no power to arrest white people. 'Mobile Citizens Becoming More Politically Active', *Pittsburgh Courier*, 27 February 1954, 19; 'In Mobile, Negro Policemen Succeed', *Birmingham News*, 18 September 1955, 32; 'Negroes to Preserve Order', *Montgomery Advertiser*, 18 November 1902, 10; Hurston, *Barracoon*, 75–6.

35. As Nick Tabor observes, Hurston told a slightly different story in *Dust Tracks*. In that text, Kossula initially refused to accept David's death because his head was still missing. It was Abile who 'persuaded him that the headless body on the window blind was their son'. Nor did Kossula run away from his wife's grief. Instead, he only 'cried hard for several minutes' before asking that a bell be rung for his child. Nevertheless, Hurston stressed in her memoir that David's brutal death was the African man's 'great sorrow in America'. Ibid., 83–6; Hurston, *Dust Tracks*, 168; Tabor, *Africatown*, 326.

36. Hurston, *Barracoon*, 87–8.

37. James's gravestone lists his birthdate as 15 December 1870, but he is likely the as yet unnamed baby boy born in December 1869 who appears alongside his parents on the 1870 census. 'The News of Mobile', *Montgomery Advertiser*, 20 February 1903, 2; 'The News of Mobile', *Montgomery Advertiser*, 4 March 1903, 8; James Lewis, State Convict Records; Cudgenle [sic], Phely [sic] and Unnamed Adams [sic], 1870 US Census, Beat 3, Mobile, Alabama; Hurston, *Barracoon*, 88; James Lewis, Findagrave.com. https://www.findagrave.com/memorial/116893475/james-ahnonotoe-lewis.

38. Robinson and Thompson's murders were not the first lynchings near African Town. Zachariah Graham was killed on 31 March 1891 by a mob of 'several hundred men' in the woods near Whistler station for allegedly running after the 12-year-old daughter of O. P. Page, section boss of the railway at Mauvilla. The mob surrounded Whistler station house, where the prisoner was being held, and fired shots through the windows and turned out the lights to terrorize Graham before storming the building. Graham was tied to a chair and had no hope of defending himself; prisoner and chair were carried away together. 'Mobile Mob Avenges The Assaults on White Children – Negro Rapists Are Hanged', *Montgomery Advertiser*, 7 October 1906, 1, 18; 'Swung Up High to a Limb of a Tree', *Montgomery Advertiser*, 1 April 1891, 2; 'Whistler, Ala.: A Negro Hanged To a Limb', *Times-Democrat*, 1 April 1891, 8.

39. 'Two Negroes Lynched By Citizens of Mobile', *Times-Democrat*, 7 October 1906, 7; 'Mobile Mob Avenges The Assaults', 18; Bryant, *The Last Hero*, 22.

40. 'Mob Lynches Negro', *Elba Clipper*, 27 September 1907, 5; 'Negro Lynched by Mob Near Mobile', *Birmingham News*, 23 September 1907, 2; 'Alabama Negro Lynched', *New York Times*, 23 September 1907, 3; 'Mobile and Vicinity', *Times-Democrat*, 28 September 1907, 3.

41. A 15-year-old boy accused of assaulting a white girl was also the target of an attempted lynching in Whistler in February 1910. The mob terrorized the community for six hours in its search for Houston Moseley 'despite considerable doubt as to [his] guilt' and the concurrent arrest of another suspect. Moseley survived the attack but was shot in the thigh and left permanently disabled; he had to be carried to court on a stretcher when he received a 20-year sentence for the assault in October that year. 'Militia Dispatched to Negro Village', *Los Angeles Express*, 27 September 1907, 4; 'Negro Uprising Near Mobile', *Daily Signal*, 27 September 1907, 1; 'Mobile and Vicinity'; 'Militia Called Out on False Alarm', *Birmingham News*, 27 September 1907, 1; 'Angry Mob Wanted to Lynch a Negro', *The Times* (Shreveport, Louisiana), 13 February 1910, 1; 'Convicted for Assault', *Montgomery Advertiser*, 27 October 1910, 6; 'Law is Unconstitutional', *Montgomery Advertiser*, 27 October 1910, 7; Moseley, State Convict Records'.

42. Two separate gravestones were erected for Innie in Plateau Cemetery. The second gravestone bears the name 'Annie Keeby' and the more succinct inscription 'gone but not forgotten'. Innie appeared as a 20-year-old on the 1870 census, although the gravestones position her as much older when she died. The first states that she was born on 23 April 1834 and the second gravestone simply states, 'age 70'. Anthony's personal property and real estate were collectively valued at up to $1,200 (equivalent to nearly $40,000 today). Sampson's life history prior to 1901 is unclear, although he may have been the Sampson Martin who was living in Conecuh in 1866, or the Sampson Martines who was living in Montgomery that year. Innie Keeby, Findagrave.com. https://www.findagrave.com/memorial/74875977/innie-keeby; Annie Keeby, Findagrave.com. https://www.findagrave.com/memorial/247397279/annie-keeby; Ernest [Inez] Auso, 1870 US Census, Beat 3, Mobile, Alabama; Ardisa Wiggfore and Sandy Brunson Marriage Record, Mobile, Alabama, 2 May 1880; Ardassa Bruntson, 1880 US Census, Mauvilla, Mobile, Alabama; Dissie Baun, 1900 US

Census, Whistler, Mobile, Alabama; Tony Thomas, Wills and Probate Record, Mobile, Alabama, 9 January 1911, Case No. 9; Napoleon Bonapart, Death Record, Baldwin, Alabama, 14 August 1918; Malinda Evans, 1910 US Census, Fairhope and Zundels, Baldwin, Alabama; Sampson Martin and Zuma Luviston, 1910 US Census, Precinct 9, Mobile, Alabama; Sampson Africa, City Directory, Mobile, Alabama, 1901; Sampson Mathews and Jane Levinson Marriage Record, Mobile, Alabama, October 1901; Sampson Martin, 1866 Alabama State Census, Conecuh; Sampson Martines, 1866 Alabama State Census, Montgomery, Alabama.

43. Hurston, *Barracoon*, 91−2; Celie Lewis Death Certificate, Plateau, Mobile, Alabama, 14 November 1908.

44. Roche, *Historic Sketches*, 122−3.

45. Eleck V. Lewis, Findagrave.com; Hurston, *Barracoon*, 92.

46. Roche, *Historic Sketches*, 121.

47. For an account of how Black radicalism shaped Park's scholarship, see Zine Magubane, 'Common Skies and Divided Horizons? Sociology, Race, and Postcolonial Studies', in *Postcolonial Sociologies*, 101−5. Park, 'The Conflict', 118; Washington, *The Story of the Negro*, 104.

48. Montgomery, 'Survivors', 621; Ward Lee, Mount Canaan Baptist Church Cemetery, Trenton, Edgefield, South Carolina. Findagrave. com. https://www.findagrave.com/memorial/110178730/ward-lee.

49. The Africans attended Stone Street Baptist Church in their youth alongside Reverend Henry Jefferson Europe, who became a Baptist church leader, and they probably encountered what one white newspaper termed his 'band of unearthly music'. Europe was the father of pioneering bandleader James Reese Europe. 'Alabama News', *Eufaula Weekly Times*, 5 September 1872, 1; Badger, *A Life in Ragtime*, 12; Dennison, *A Memoir*, 25, 38, 41 and 73−4.

50. Ibid., 35−6.

51. Roche, *Historic Sketches*, 126; Dennison, *A Memoir*, 25, 38 and 72.

52. Zuma's precise death date is unknown but was probably 1918 or 1919. John's 1923 obituary suggested he had been widowed for several years, and the 1920 census, which was taken in February of that year, shows that Abraham, Zuma's grandson and the youngest member of her household at the time of the 1910 census, had been adopted by Polee and Rosallie's daughter Mary. Klebsattel, 'Slaves Captured', 516 and 518; Imes, 'The Last Recruits', 358; '115-Year Old Negro Dies at Mobile', *Clarke County Democrat*, 22 November 1923, 1; Kattie Cooper

Deaths and Burials Index, Prichard, Mobile, Alabama, 10 October 1919; Clara Turner Deaths and Burials Index, Plateau, Mobile, Alabama, 23 October 1919; Mary Allen and Abraham Martin, 1920 US Census, Whistler, Mobile, Alabama.

53. 'The Funeral of Mr[s]. Quiller Wheeler . . .', *Press-Forum Weekly*', 15 July 1922, 2; Quiller Wheeler Death Record, Mobile, Alabama, 9 June 1922; 'Death of Mr. Holman', *Press-Forum Weekly*, 20 September 1930, 2; Ephriam Wheeler Death Record, Mobile, Alabama, 29 January 1923.

54. Amy Phillips Death Record, Daphne, Baldwin, Alabama, 2 May 1923; Lesley Farrey Pacey, 'Rubena Marino, 102-year-old, Granddaughter of Slave, Dies', *Mobile Register*, 4 April 1999, 2B. MPL. http://digital. mobilepubliclibrary.org/items/show/1860; Roche, 'Last Survivor'.

55. Berger, 'Cugo Lewis'; Robertson, *The Slave Ship Clotilda*, 170.

56. Neither Alice nor Quilla were among the eight *Clotilda* survivors that Emma Langdon Roche recorded as still living in 1914, although George Lake Imes and Christian Klebsettal both counted nine survivors three years later. Quilla lived outside the community, and Roche appears to have confused Alice with her shipmate Shamba, who died in May 1912. Given that she was perhaps as young as 5 years old when she was kidnapped, Alice is most likely the approximately 65-year-old *Clotilda* survivor identified by her African name 'Parloro' in a 1917 *Mobile Register* article. Osia Keeby's second wife was a 60-year-old widowed laundress named Ann Cannier. Kossula served as the couple's wedding witness. Ann died on 14 May 1920. Polee Allen Death Certificate, Plateau, Alabama, 19 August 1922; Alice Williams Death Record, Plateau, Mobile, Alabama, 19 November 1922; Roche, *Historic Sketches*, 120; 'Last Slave Ship Sunk'; Frank Sikora, 'Group Tracing History of Last Slaves to Arrive', *Birmingham News*, 16 March 1980, cited in Diouf, *Dreams*, 222; Anon., Audio Interview with Clara Eva Bell Allen Jones; Chamber Wigfall Death Record, Plateau, Alabama, 18 May 1912; Osia Keeby and Ann Cannier Marriage Record, Mobile, Alabama, 27 August 1913; Ann Keeby Death Record, Mobile, Alabama, 14 May 1920; Osia Keeby Death Certificate, Plateau, Alabama, 22 February 1923; 'Lonesome, But With Confidence'.

Chapter 12: Gee's Bend

1. Dinah's great-granddaughter Arlonzia understood that Dinah's daughter Sally, who was born on 10 July 1876, was about seventeen when Dinah left the region around Vredenburgh; Sally married Esau

Pettway in Camden in February 1898 before relocating to Gee's Bend. 'My Way', 93; Esi Pettway and Sallie Miller Marriage Index, Wilcox, Alabama, 19 February 1898; Kennedy, 'Life at Gee's Bend', 1072.

2. In 1971, local historian Elizabeth D'Autrey Riley recalled an isolated African woman named Dinah who lived close to her father William George Riley's Flat Creek plantation, just south of Bonham's Beat, when she was a child in the 1880s and 1890s. Riley described Dinah in a manner intended to deflect attention from the moral crime of slavery and the actual crime that brought the child to Alabama. According to Riley's dehumanizing account, the African woman was a 'grotesque looking human' and a 'truly a horrible old woman'. Riley and her friends were afraid of Dinah, believing a cruel rumour that she ate her meat raw, fears that were indulged by Riley's Klansman father William, who told her never to talk to the African woman. Riley's distorted account nevertheless conveyed Dinah's social isolation, as a single African woman, in the Black Belt. Dinah was so scared of her environment that she ran from place to place, never daring to look left or right, and muttering to herself, a sign of serious mental distress. She hid behind and peered out from trees and bushes whenever anyone passed close by her cabin. She refused to work for white people and did not associate with the local African American community.

   There was one other documented African woman living in Wilcox County south of the Alabama River at the turn of the twentieth century. Hester Thompson was estimated to be 70 years old on the 1900 census, which makes her a likely *Clotilda* survivor. Sarah McCants Death Record, Selma, Dallas, Alabama, 26 February 1930; 'The Situation', *Wilcox Progressive Era*, 14 November 1888, 2; Garroway [sic] Miller and Mary Washington Marriage Record, Wilcox, Alabama, 23 December 1888; Riley, *The Evergreen*, 61 and 80−1; Hester Thompson, 1880 Agricultural Schedule, Fox Mill Beat, Wilcox, Alabama; Hester Thompson, 1880 US Census, Fox's Mill, Wilcox, Alabama; Hester Thompson, 1900 US Census, Fox's Mill, Wilcox, Alabama.

3. Kennedy, 'Life at Gee's Bend', 1072−3.
4. Colleen E. Kriger concludes that workshops of women weavers were 'well established' in the Oyo Empire by the eighteenth century. Fry, *Stitched from the Soul*, 12−13; Jane Livingston, 'Reflections on the Art of Gee's Bend', in *The Quilts*, 53; Kriger, *Cloth*, 43; Gilfoy, *Patterns of Life*, 11; Johnson, *The History of the Yorubas*, 124.

Notes

5. Perceptions of the Gee's Benders' cultural exceptionalism in the reports of the Resettlement Administration, a US government agency that invested in Gee's Bend in the mid-1930s to combat its Depression-fuelled state of extreme poverty, were tied to racist assumptions about West African customs. Fixations on the community's apparent 'primitiveness' served the Resettlement Administration's agenda by underscoring the effectiveness of its efforts to improve the community's living conditions. In turn, efforts to promote the commercial value of Gee's Bend's quilts at the turn of the twenty-first century highlighted the apparent isolation of their makers and by implication the exceptional nature of their artistry. Yet an 1889 *Wilcox Progressive Era* article gave clues to the *Clotilda* Africans' presence around Gee's Bend when it noted of the community that 'A great many of them, are descendants of the real African and their lingo bears all the evidences of their ancestors' African language.' A period of feasting follows a person's interment in Yoruba communities. Sue F. Turner, 'Story Book Life in the Bend of a River', *Montgomery Advertiser*, 29 September 1940, 37; 'Arthur Rothstein: Tenant Farmers', in *Documenting America*, 147; 'Our County', *Wilcox Progressive Era*, 30 October 1889, 2; *Gee's Bend Project*, 1; Kennedy, 'Life at Gee's Bend', 1072–3; Adekemi Adegun Taiwo, 'Burial and Funeral', in *Encyclopedia of the Yoruba*, 53.

6. Joanne Cubbs, 'The Life and Art of Mary Lee Bendolph', in *Mary Lee Bendolph,* 14; Chave, 'Dis/Cover/ing', 225–6; Childers, 'From Jungle'.

7. For a history and critique of comparisons between the quilts and Abstract Expressionism, see Amelia Peck, 'Quilt/Art: Deconstructing the Gee's Bend Quilt Phenomenon', in *My Soul Has Grown Deep*, 53–91; Gilfoy, *Patterns of Life*, 17.

8. Shed Miller, 1910 US Census, Canton Bend, Wilcox, Alabama; William Arnett, 'Gee's Bend: The Architecture of the Quilt', in *Gee's Bend: The Architecture*, 30; Amei Wallach, 'The Living Legacy of Dinah the Slave', in ibid., 144.

9. Moseley's quilter descendants included his daughter Patsy, who was one of three women from the Gee's Bend community who wove cloth for curtains in Franklin Delano Roosevelt's White House; the women also created a blue and white striped cloth suit for the President. Dilys Blum, 'A Dirt Road in Rehoboth', in ibid., 125–6; William Arnett and Paul Arnett, 'On the Map', in *Gee's Bend: The Women*, 45; Callahan, *The Freedom Quilting Bee*, 147; Lucy [sic] Dansby, 1900 US Census, Rehoboth, Wilcox, Alabama; Peggy Crear, 1870 US Census, Camden,

Wilcox, Alabama; Ephriam Clanton, Richard Winters and Frederick Taylor, 1880 Agricultural Schedule, Boiling Springs, Wilcox, Alabama; Rachel Taylor, Caroline Perkins and Crecy Dansly [sic], 1880 US Census, Boiling Springs, Wilcox, Alabama.

10. Gaillard, Lindsay, and DeNeefe, *Alabama's Civil Rights Trail*, 153; Callahan, *The Freedom Quilting Bee*; Callahan, 'Freedom Quilting Bee'.

11. Cassandra Andrews, 'A Celebration of Heritage', *Mobile Press-Register*, 26 December 2006, 3D. http://digital.mobilepubliclibrary.org/items/show/1863; Anon., Audio Interview with Clara Eva Bell Allen Jones; Pettaway, 'The Folklife', 72–3.

12. Beardsley, 'Pettway', 218; Ogundiran, *The Yoruba*, 38.

13. Fleming, *In the Shadow*, 48; Williamson, *March On!*, 65; Cotton, *A Spark*, 205; McGranahan, *Historical Sketch*, 57.

14. Ibid., 51; Williamson, 67–8.

15. Carter, *The Politics of Rage*, 38–9.

16. Kolb had been a wealthy landowner and merchant before the Civil War, a Confederate war hero and a loyal Democrat until the early 1890s, and his commitment to Black civil rights proved fleeting. When his populist movement was defeated for a third time in the 1896 election, he sought to rejoin the Democrats. Strikingly, Sayre introduced the voting bill within weeks of becoming a father to a daughter named Clothilde. Clothilde's sister Zelda became famous in the 1920s as the wife of novelist F. Scott Fitzgerald. Boynton Robinson, *Bridge Across Jordan*, 29–30; William B. Bankhead, 'Impressions of Washington, 1893–94'. Unpublished manuscript, cited in Frederickson, *Deep South Dynasty*, 69; Forner, *Why the Vote*, 8; Carter, *The Politics of Rage*, 39; Aucoin, *Thomas Goode Jones*, 73–4.

17. Fleming, *In the Shadow*, 49–50; 'Judge Henderson Shot', *Selma Times*, 31 July 1895, 1; McGranahan, *Historical Sketch*, 52–6.

18. Ibid., 55. Emphasis in original.

19. The August 1893 lynching of 26-year-old Riley Gulley a few miles east of Dinah in Pine Apple may even have provoked her flight to Gee's Bend. Gulley's mother Caroline later married Nathanael Brown, the African man whose residence in Snow Hill and 1930 death suggest he probably arrived on the *Clotilda*. 'Israel and Billie', *Selma Times*, 2 August 1896, 2; 'Attempted Assassination', *Montgomery Advertiser*, 17 July 1896, 3; Reyley Gulley, 1870 US Census, Snow Hill, Wilcox, Alabama; 'A Would-Be Rapist', *Selma Times*, 19 September 1893, 1; 'A Brute's Fate', *Daily News*, 19 September 1893, 2; 'Getting Serious', *Montgomery Advertiser*, 2 September 1893, 1.

Notes

20. 'In Conversation with Mr. C. D. Hunter . . .', *Selma Times*, 23 February 1896, 2; 'C. D. Hunter's Farm', *Selma Times*, 10 June 1893, 1; 'To Import Germans', *Eufaula Daily Times*, 8 June 1893, 1.

21. Mauldin, *Unredeemed Land*, 3; Forner, *Why the Vote*, 19–20; Boynton Robinson, *Bridge Across Jordan*, 20–2.

22. 'A Gossipy Letter', *Selma Times*, 14 May 1893, 3; 'Atlas J. Martin is Dead in Selma', *Montgomery Advertiser*, 26 May 1908, 9; Forner, *Why the Vote*, 12–13; 'Hon. Victor B. Atkins', *Selma Mirror*, 28 June 1911, 77.

23. 'Entire Programme for Exhibition in Selma', *Selma Journal*, 15 June 1908, 7.

24. 'Tuberculosis and Servants – Col. W. W. Quarles', *Selma Journal*, 19 June 1908, 5.

25. Leon Lindsey, Findagrave.com. https://www.findagrave.com/memorial/118682754/leon-lindsey; 'Col. Quarles is Target For Rock of Negro', *Selma Journal*, 8 October 1908, 1.

26. Hunt Sims's child protagonist is named 'little Helen', and her mother is 'Mrs. Bradshaw', but the two characters are identifiable as Hunt Sims and her mother Siloma, the text presents its narrative as factual and a contemporaneous newspaper article acknowledged that the stories' setting was her mother's estate. 'Negro Mystic Lore', *Inter Ocean*, 25 January 1908, 5; Sims, *Negro Mystic Lore*, n.p., 31 and 34. Emphasis added; 'Selma Society', *Montgomery Advertiser*, 13 November 1910, 7; Fauset, 'Negro Folk Lore', in *The New Negro*, 445.

27. John Henry Miller Military Card Files, Primrose, Wilcox, Alabama, 1917; Wynn, 'Woman Survivor'; Thomas Crear Military Service Card, Martin Station, Alabama.

28. Bill Smith Death Record, Browns, Dallas, Alabama, 12 October 1918.

29. Before his death in the early twentieth century, Montgomery-based *Clotilda* captive Komo underscored the psychological significance of such grave decorations to a white journalist. Komo forced the journalist, who was otherwise disparaging of Black Southern cultural practices, to acknowledge that 'the various decorations which one sees in a country negro graveyard is *not a superstition* but a means of identification'. Komo pointedly characterized grave decorations as a West African survival. As the journalist noted, 'One often sees a wash bowl, a pitcher, a plate or a stone crock half buried on a grave[.] Komo says that in Africa various colored stones are used or the larger bones of animals.' When Jamaican traveller Robert Campbell witnessed a funeral in Oyo in 1860, he learned that a stone was sometimes placed on a person's burial site, 'on which offerings to his manes [soul] are

occasionally deposited'. Long, 'Folk Gravesites', 28; Boynton Robinson, *Bridge Across Jordan*, 30; Albert Dillard, 'Negro Clings to Ancient Superstitions Just As He Did Half a Century Ago', *Montgomery Advertiser*, 2 December 1917, 6. Emphasis added; Campbell, *A Pilgrimage*, 71.

Chapter 13: Cocolocco

1. 'The Weather', *Montgomery Advertiser*, 29 October 1895, 8; 'Schedule Changed', *Birmingham News*, 24 October 1895, 4.
2. At least two other shipmates were living in Elmore County in the 1880s and 1890s: a woman named Tamer, or Toma, and a man cruelly nicknamed 'Beast' by his enslavers, who was possibly Rush Jones's former plantation doctor given that an African man named 'Abdoul' does not appear on any census. Like Amanda, Mary's paternity is unknown.
3. Bay, *Traveling Black*, 31 and 68; Du Bois, *Darkwater*, 229.
4. 'The New Union Passenger Depot', *Montgomery Advertiser*, 14 February 1877, 3; 'Badly Wanted', *Montgomery Advertiser*, 17 October 1885, 5; Rabinowitz, 'From Exclusion', 335–6.
5. *Tenth Annual Report*, 25–6; John White, 'E. D. Nixon and the White Supremacists: Civil Rights in Montgomery', in *Before Brown*, 206; 'Negro is Fined', *Montgomery Advertiser*, 27 October 1918, 22; 'Recorder's Court', *Montgomery Advertiser*, 27 August 1919, 12; Hagedorn, 'Ole Bulja'.
6. Dr. Martin Luther King, Jr.'s wife Coretta Scott King later described having to 'back off the sidewalk if a white person approached us head-on' in Montgomery. Owen and Owen, *History of Alabama*, 2, 1037; King, *My Life*, 139.
7. Leading *Wanderer* conspiracist Charles Augustus Lafayette Lamar was killed in that battle. Hagedorn, 'Ole Bulja'; Campbell, *A Pilgrimage*, 54; Misulia, *Columbus*, 259–60; Causey, *Red Clay*, 126–8.
8. Sassafras, which the Choctaw knew as 'kombo', grew in abundance in the coastal regions of the US South. Ground sassafras leaves, known as filé powder, are commonly used to thicken the traditional creole stew gumbo. Enslaved people foraged the leaves to supplement their sparse diets, and enslaved doctors relied on the root as a medicine, believing that it cleansed the blood and alleviated high blood pressure, fevers, sexually transmitted diseases, rheumatism and a host of other ailments. As a formerly enslaved man from just outside Sparta, Tennessee, recalled in the 1930s, 'They would give you sassafras tea. Didn't get any medicine. You just had to keep going.' Sassafras may well have been the

main ingredient of the medicinal drink the Mobile Africans knew as 'life everlasting tea'. 'Bulger Loses Leg'; Covey, *African American Slave Medicine*, 111–12; Egypt, *Unwritten History*, 110.

9. Hoose, *Claudette Colvin*, 30–2.

10. Jones, *White Too Long*, 195.

11. 'Jim Crow Cars', *Montgomery Advertiser*, 24 July 1900, 4; Kelley, *Right to Ride*, 2; Meier and Rudwick, 'The Boycott Movement', 760 and 763–4; 'Editorial Notes', *Southwestern Christian Advocate*, 4 September 1902.

12. Robert Jones, 1883 Montgomery City Directory; Clara Cotes and Robert Jones Marriage Record, Montgomery, Alabama, 10 June 1904; Robert Jones, 1910 US Census, Montgomery, Alabama.

13. King, *My Life*, 48 and 63.

14. As the Jones's daughter Virginia 'Jennie' Jones Vass recalled, 'my mother and many others would go down to the hospital, take servants and do all we could for the sick'. Even the youngest captives in the Jones household were put to work. Jennie's enslaved playmate, a tiny dark-skinned girl ironically named 'Pink', was made to fan the patients. Enslaved workers in the Civil War-era South's hospitals were forced to perform menial roles, and their labours was carefully policed to ensure they could not rebel. Upper-class white women like Amelia managed their captives' labour as they were used to doing on their plantations. Amelia made bandages with her captives, but women enslavers did not perform strenuous labour themselves; instead, they sat at patients' bedsides and provided their patients with food prepared by their prisoners. The war was even brought to Ella's living quarters, as recovering soldiers were taken back to the family's home and nursed until they were well enough to return to their regiments. Vass, 'Montgomery Girl's Recollections', 4; Kate Hutcheson Morrissette, 'Social Life in the First Confederate Capital', *Selma Morning Times*, 13 March 1907, 12; Hilde, *Worth a Dozen Men*, 66, 135–6 and 142.

15. As Libra R. Hilde has observed, 'Dedicated matrons and nurses were frequently among the most vehement public defenders of Southern honor and most likely to call on women and men to carry on the "unfinished" work.' See also Janney, *Burying the Dead*. There was also a memorial window dedicated to John Whiting, who was a Ruling Elder of the church for 23 years, and whose son married Alex Given's daughter during the Civil War. 'Under the Spires', *Montgomery Advertiser*, 19 March 1893, 9; C. Claudia Moritz, 'Memorial Windows Tell Works Faithfully Done', *Montgomery Advertiser*, 4 April 1915, 6; Hilde, *Worth a Dozen Men*, 197; *The Confederate Monument*, 92–3.

16. Ibid., 3 and 4.
17. A question on the *Clotilda* formed part of at least one UDC chapter's historical programme. When the Headland chapter held its first meeting in 1925, the very week that Bougier's health was making the news in Montgomery, the group asked its members, 'What was the last slave ship sent to Alabama?' 'First Meeting of U.D.C. Occasion of Fine Program', *Wiregrass Farmer*, 17 September 1925, 1; Cox, *Dixie's Daughters*, 50−1 and 101−2.
18. Owen, *Our Women*, 2. Emphasis added.
19. Cozart, 'What the Women', 11; Hagedorn, 'Ole Bulja'.
20. Baker became the nation's first press secretary when, having supported and befriended Roosevelt's successor Woodrow Wilson, he joined the president in Paris at the end of the First World War, and he won a Pulitzer Prize for his biographical work on Wilson.
21. Over an 18-month period, Baker wrote twelve race-themed articles for the *American Magazine*. The series was so successful that it was published in book form as *Following the Color Line: An Account of Negro Citizenship in the American Democracy* (1908). The readership of the book, and many of the articles, exceeded 250,000, and Baker's opening piece on the aftermath of the Atlanta massacre prompted President Roosevelt to thank the journalist for giving him a 'clearer understanding' of the event. The *Montgomery Advertiser* reassured its readers of Baker that 'he sees everything and observes nothing. He will go back home more hopelessly, if not quite so densely, ignorant of the subject than when he started.' The *Birmingham News* was relieved to reprint an act of white charity that Baker witnessed. Godshalk, *Veiled Visions*, 197 and 203−4; 'Savoyard', 'LaFollette, Octopus Chaser', *Montgomery Advertiser*, 8 September 1907, 11; 'No Hash', *Birmingham News*, 3 May 1907, 3; Baker to Du Bois.
22. Baker, 'The Tragedy', 585. Emphasis added.
23. Dillard, 'Negro Clings'; Jarnagin, *A Confluence*, 187−90; King and Pell, *Montgomery's Historic Neighborhoods*, 31.
24. Nannie is listed in error as Sam's mother on the 1910 census. Sam's distinctive surname connects him to Gee's Bend; he grew up with his mother's enslaver's surname 'Jones', and so perhaps spent time as a farm labourer in the quilting community, whose inhabitants were required to take their landlord's Pettway surname. Sarah does not appear on the next census, but she may have been the Sarah Jones who died in Montgomery County on 3 October 1920. Four *Clotilda* Africans who would go on to become couples in Alabama after the

war, Dinah and William Seay, and Joseph and Martha Porter, also died around the start of the new century, as did Joseph and Martha's shipmate and housemate Isaac Porter and the man cruelly nicknamed 'Beast' Porter (likely Abdoul). The Porters' precise death dates are unclear, although the man who was probably Abdoul died sometime after his second marriage on Christmas Eve 1888, and only Martha lived to see in the new century. William Seay passed away on 29 June 1904. His widow Dinah died within two years of her husband's death. Bougier's Elmore County neighbour Tamer died sometime in the 1910s. Unsy Salary, 1900 US Census, Spring Hill, Barbour, Alabama; Sarah, Ben and Sam Jones, 1880 US Census, Walkers, Montgomery, Alabama; Nany Smith Death Record, Montgomery, Alabama, 22 April 1910; Nanie Smith, 1910 US Census, Precinct 17, Montgomery, Alabama; Sarah Jones Death Record, Montgomery, Alabama, 3 October 1920; Willie Quill Pettway, cited in *The Quilts of Gee's Bend*, 140; Martha Porter, 1900 US Census, Precinct 20 Walkers, Montgomery, Alabama; Beasly Porter and Caroline Nunn Marriage Record, Autauga, Alabama, 28 May 1871; Beasey Porter and Jane Brown Marriage Record, Autauga, Alabama, 24 December 1888; Jane Porter, 1900 US Census, Liberty, Autauga, Alabama; 'Vital Statistics', *Montgomery Times*, 2 July 1904, 1; William Seay, Petition for Probate of Will, Montgomery County, 8 December 1906; Tamer Rose, 1910 US Census, Edgewood, Elmore, Alabama.

25. Victoria Dunkin and Robert Avery Marriage Record, Autauga, Alabama, 6 December 1900; 'The Gillespie Auto Company . . .', *Prattville Progress*, 16 September 1920, 1.

26. Hagedorn, 'Ole Bulja'.

27. 'Wheel Chair Given "Old Bulja", Negro "Yerb" Seller, By Station Employees', *Montgomery Advertiser*, 20 September 1925, 22; Hagedorn, 'Ole Bulja'.

28. 'Bulger Loses Leg'.

29. 'Wheel Chair Given'.

30. E. D. Nixon lived at Robinson Springs as a baby. As a child, he lived at Precinct 5, Autauga; Ella lived at Precinct 1. He was a porter living at 6 Grady Street, Montgomery when Bougier's wheelchair was delivered. Edman [sic] Nixan [sic], 1900 US Census, Precincts 10, 17, Robinson Spring, Elmore, Alabama; Edmond [sic] Nixon, 1910 US Census, Precinct 5, Autauga, Alabama; Edward [sic] Nixon, 1925 City Directory, Montgomery Alabama.

31. 'Wheel Chair Given', 22.

32. Bougier died 43 years to the day after her former enslaver Rush Jones. Temperatures reached 94 degrees Fahrenheit (34 degrees Celsius) on the day of her death. P. M. Smyth, 'Weather Bulletin', *Montgomery Advertiser*, 28 June 1930, 13.

Chapter 14: The Courthouse

1. Tragically, Emmit's second daughter Para Lee, who was born a year to the day after her sister and 15 days after her father's death, died in May 1924 aged just 3 from tetanus after stepping on a rake. 'Million Spent on Mobile Equipment', *Montgomery Advertiser*, 7 June 1925, 12; David Holt, 'Oratory Flows After Gov. Brandon Leads State Docks Inspection', *Birmingham News*, 15 November 1925, 3; Cudjo Lewis deed to Eddy W. Cawthorn (cited in Diouf, *Dreams*, 218); Bertha May Lewis, Death Certificate, Plateau, Mobile, Alabama, 19 May 1920; Land Sale, Cujo Lewis to Thomas Dawson, 23 July 1920. Recorded 8 September 1920; Land Sale, Cujo Lewis to Thomas Dawson, 20 December 1920; Emmit Lewis, Death Certificate, Plateau, Mobile, Alabama, 9 April 1921; Para Lee Lewis, Death Certificate, Plateau, Mobile, Alabama, 28 May 1924; Land Sale, Cujo Lewis to Earl Amos Hill, 12 January 1922; Land Sale, Cudjo Lewis to Mobile County, 24 November 1926; David Holt, 'Mobile's $250,000,000 Bridge is Expected to be Completed on Schedule Time', *Birmingham News*, 18 July 1926, 12; Diouf, *Dreams*, 218 and 224.

2. For accounts of the industrialization of African Town and its environmental impact, see Raines, *The Last Slave Ship*, Ch. 9 and Tabor, *Africatown*, Pts 3 and 4. Hurston, 'Cudjo's Own Story', 661.

3. The parable was reprinted in the *Journal of American Folklore* and in both English and French translations in the short-lived francophone Caribbean journal *La Revue du Monde Noir*, whose celebration of African-derived cultural forms influenced the Négritude movement, an international Black liberation ideology that emerged in response to French colonial racism. Kossula provided both the Harlem Renaissance and the Négritude movement with a link to nineteenth-century West African oral culture. Arthur paired it with a B'rer Rabbit folktale that he also recorded in African Town to demonstrate continuities between African and African American folkloric traditions. Falola, *Counting*, 116–17; Arthur Huff Fauset, 'American Negro Folk Literature', 'T'appin (Terrapin)', and 'B'rer Rabbit Fools Buzzard', in *The New Negro*, 238–49; Arthur Huff Fauset, 'Negro Folk Tales'; Lewis, 'Molocoye T'appin (Terrapin)', 238–41.

Notes

4. Boas is celebrated as the 'father of American anthropology' for his professionalization of the discipline. He played a key role in developing the concept of cultural relativism, which challenged notions of fixed 'racial' identities by showing that a person's behaviour was shaped by their environment. Robert Hemenway calculated that only 18 of the essay's 67 paragraphs were Hurston's work and speculated that she plagiarized her text because she could not understand Kossula's accented English. Hurston's plagiarism was never identified in her lifetime. Hemenway, *Zora Neale Hurston*, 98. See also Hurston, 'Cudjo's Own Story', 648–63.

5. Hurston reported her travel plans to fellow writer Langston Hughes on 9 December 1927. She would visit the elderly man first in case he died soon. Hurston's posthumously published manuscript *Every Tongue Got to Confess* reveals that she was in Mobile from 16 December to 12 January and then again from 4 June to 3 September 1928. In her preface to *Barracoon*, Hurston stated that she interviewed Kossula in July and December 1927, and again at an unspecified time in 1928, although her narrative creates the impression that all her interviews took place in the summer. In fact, Hurston's patron Charlotte Osgood Mason noted that Hurston completed the bulk of her interviews with Kossula during that first visit. For a discussion of that film, see Durkin, 'Zora Neale Hurston's Visual and Textual Portrait'. Hemenway, *Zora Neale Hurston*, 110; Hurston, *Barracoon*, 6 and 89; Zora Neale Hurston to Langston Hughes, 9 December 1927, in *Zora Neale Hurston*, ed. Kaplan, 110; Hurston, *Every Tongue*, 257; Employment contract.

6. Kaplan, *Miss Anne*, 218; Hemenway, *Zora Neale Hurston*, 101–2 and 112–13; Zora Neale Hurston, 'How It Feels To Be Colored Me', *The World Tomorrow*, 11 (May 1928), in Hurston, *You Don't Know*, 187–8; Hurston, *Dust Tracks*, 168.

7. Zora Neale Hurston to Langston Hughes, 8 March 1928, and Zora Neale Hurston to Alain Locke, 10 May 1928, in *Zora Neale Hurston*, ed. Kaplan, 113 and 119.

8. Although archaeologist James Delgado recognizes the anchor as too big to be from the *Clotilda*, navigation lights recently uncovered by divers are believed to have been placed on the schooner around that time to warn other boats of a potential hazard in the water. In 1965, the Fort Gaines Museum on Dauphin Island, a barrier island at the entrance of Mobile Bay, was reported to have acquired the eye-bolt used for connecting the schooner's anchor to its anchor chain. In

February 1917, self-proclaimed Ugandan prince Umfraena Kaba Rega also claimed – falsely – to have raised the schooner with the aim of exhibiting its hull and its last remaining survivors to raise money for their welfare. When he returned to Mobile nearly fourteen years later, he claimed only to have found a piece of the schooner. 'Alabama State Docks Dedicated Monday', *Montgomery Advertiser*, 24 June 1928, 22; A. A. Calloway, 'State Docks Open to World', *Birmingham News*, 24 June 1928, 82; David Holt, 'Former Jungle Now Plant Site', *Birmingham News*, 28 October 1928, 6; 'Sudden Service' . . .', *Democrat-Reporter*, 3 August 1933, 4; James P. Delgado, email to the author, 19 April 2023; Specker, 'Biopsy'; 'Fort Gaines Museum Acquires "Anchor Eye"'; 'Last Slave Ship Sunk'; 'African Prince Visited City', *Press-Forum Weekly*, 4 October 1930, 1.

9. Three of the *Clotilda* Africans sent to Marengo County endured into the 1920s. Alice died in Jefferson, Marengo County, in June 1925, her husband Alex passed away in April 1927, and their shipmate Penelope died there sometime that decade. Alice Burns Death Record, Marengo, Alabama, 19 June 1925; Alex Burns Death Record, Jefferson, Marengo, Alabama, 29 April 1927; Penny Britton, 1920 US Census, Jefferson, Marengo, Alabama.

10. It is not clear if Hurston misreported or misremembered that Redoshi lived on the edge of the Alabama River, not the Tombigbee River. Hurston did mention Redoshi by her US name Sally Smith in an appendix to her posthumously published manuscript *Every Tongue Got to Confess*, which was an early version of her folkloric narrative *Mules and Men*, but she made no mention of the African woman in *Barracoon*, her memoir *Dust Tracks*, or her 1944 *American Mercury* article on the *Clotilda*. Given that she viewed Redoshi as more articulate than Kossula, Hurston may nevertheless have included her as an uncredited contributor to *Barracoon* in the same way that she drew on the uncredited work of Emma Langdon Roche to flesh out her narrative. Zora Neale Hurston to Langston Hughes, 10 July 1928, in *Zora Neale Hurston*, ed. Kaplan, 123; Hurston, *Every Tongue*, 263.

11. The 1910 census, in which Boynton Robinson appears as a 4-year-old, shows she was six years older than her obituaries reported. Her memoir records that she arrived in Dallas County in 1930, but the 1929 Selma City Directory and a 1929 newspaper article show she was working in Selma a year earlier. Boynton Robinson's son Bruce Carver Boynton was also a key figure in the civil rights movement. In December 1958, the 21-year-old Howard University student ordered a

cheeseburger at a whites-only section of a bus station restaurant in Richmond, Virginia. He challenged in court his subsequent arrest in the landmark civil rights case *Boynton v. Virginia* (1960), which led the US Supreme Court to affirm that racial segregation on public transportation was illegal and inspired the 1961 Freedom Rides movement, whose Black and white members rode interstate buses through the US South to protest segregated bus terminals. The violent backlash to that movement prompted President John F. Kennedy to order stricter enforcement of anti-segregation travel laws. Amelia Platt, 1910 US Census, Savannah Ward 1, Chatham, Georgia; 'Moton Delivers 216 Diplomas to Tuskegee Institute Graduates', *Montgomery Advertiser*, 26 May 1927, 20; Boynton Robinson, *Bridge Across Jordan*, 19; Amelia I. Platts, 1929 City Directory, Selma, Alabama; 'Fifty Negroes of County to Attend Tuskegee Sessions', *Selma Times-Journal*, 14 July 1929, 8.

12. Boynton Robinson, *Bridge Across Jordan*, 34.
13. LaFayette and Johnson, *In Peace*, 82.
14. Boynton Robinson, *Bridge Across Jordan*, 30.
15. Boynton Robinson knew Redoshi as 'Aunt Sally'. Photographs of Kossula and the Gee's Benders' homes by Erik Overbey and Arthur Rothstein show that their walls and window shutters were covered in newspaper. Kossula used sand and lime to fill the cracks in his walls and make his cabin wind-proof, and Addie Pettaway speculated that his newspaper wallpaper was for additional insulation. Ibid., 31; Pettaway, 'The Folklife', 110.
16. Redoshi's framing of the moon as a woman was likely a reference to Yemoja, water deity and mother spirit of the Yoruba people. Like the Mobile Africans, who continued to plea and make offerings to Yemoja for years after their enslavement, she showed that she had never abandoned her cultural beliefs and worldview, even after 70 years in the United States. Redoshi also insisted to Boynton Robinson that she never accepted her forced transplantation, asserting that 'Africa was my home'. Noah Hart understood of the Mobile Africans that 'At ebbery blessed new moon, dey all go out in de woods, an' git de leaves ob de bay tree, an' make crowns for deyselves. An' at night, when the little young moon is jes' tremblin' on de pine tree tops, dey digs a hole, an' all lays down an' whispers somethin' in it; den dey each puts one leaf in de hole an' kyvers it up, an' all jumps an' dances on top er it.' Boynton Robinson, *Bridge Across Jordan*, 31–2; Scott, 'Affika Town', 63.

17. Although Harpers & Brothers and Alfred A. Knopf demanded that Kossula's heavily accented English be made more accessible to general readers, a compromise Mason would not entertain, and Boni & Liveright also turned down the manuscript, Hurston removed *Barracoon* from consideration by Viking Press in June 1931 on the basis that 'considerable revisions' needed to be made. Mason did not realize until spring 1932 that Hurston stopped working on the manuscript after retrieving it from Viking. For discussions of Hurston's reluctance to publish *Barracoon*, see Panovka, 'A Different Backstory' and Tabor, *Africatown*, 152–6. Mason, note entitled 'Zora'; Block to Mason; Mason to Locke [draft]; Locke to Mason, 15 June 1931; Mason, note entitled 'Alain Leroy Locke'; Locke to 'Godmother', 14 March 1932; Hurston, *Dust Tracks*, 165. Emphasis in original.

18. Alain Locke, 'The New Negro', in *The New Negro*, 5; Deborah E. McDowell, 'Telling Slavery in 'Freedom's' Time: Post-Reconstruction and the Harlem Renaissance', in *The Cambridge Companion*, 163–5; Taylor, *Zora and Langston*, 67–9.

19. Susan Millar Williams has identified the photograph, which appears as the frontispiece to Ulmann and Peterkin's 1933 book *Roll, Jordan, Roll*, as a portrait of Kossula. For her discussion of the image, see Williams, 'Something to Feel About', 291–8. For a comprehensive list of Ulmann's photographic subjects, see Jacobs, *The Life*, 251–63. Following the pair's visit, Peterkin also fictionalized Kossula's story for her 1932 novel *Bright Skin*, in which a character named Big Pa, who was known in his homeland as Kazoola, was kidnapped and sold across the Atlantic by Dahomi, the head of a nearby village, after his king, Taki, refused to share his crops. Peterkin, *Bright Skin*, 133–8.

20. Diouf, *Dreams*, 228; Roche, *Historic Sketches*, 124.

21. Although Mason believed only an African American amanuensis could properly document Kossula's story, anti-Semitism also drove her to conspire with Alain Locke to prevent Jewish researcher Paul Radin from locating and interviewing Kossula weeks after Hurston interviewed him for *Barracoon*. Mason and Ulmann, who was also Jewish, both lived on Manhattan's Park Avenue and the pair had mutual acquaintances. Ulmann had even lately photographed Harlem Renaissance patron Carl Van Vechten and writer James Weldon Johnson. See Mason and Locke's letters between 6 February and 14 March 1928 in Box 164–68 of the Alain Locke Papers; Lewis to Mason, 4 September 1930.

Notes

22. Kato graduated with a BS degree in agriculture in May that year. Although many became disillusioned with their vocational focus, African independence leaders turned to all-Black US colleges such as Tuskegee because they viewed them as key symbols of Black power and pride. Mrs V. A. Robertson, 'Society News and Activities of Selma, Alabama', *Birmingham Reporter*, 17 January 1931, 7; 'Huge Class Gets Tuskegee Degrees', *Montgomery Advertiser*, 29 May 1931, 18; King, 'African Students', 26; Gershoni, *Africans on African-Americans*, 8; Harper, *Western-Educated Elites*, 56.

23. Robinson, *Bridge Across Jordan*, 33–4.

24. Daniel M. Kato, Calcutta to New York Passenger List, 23 March 1920; Owen and Mitchell, *Our Home Land*, 77.

25. The *National Geographic* did not address race relations in the South until a 1968 article on Mobile. When Black people appeared in the magazine before that date, they 'simply provide[d] a backdrop for the actions of southern whites, taking their places with the magnolias and cotton fields', according to one critical analysis. Childers, 'From Jungle'; Judy Brown, 'Alabama Is Given Wide Publicity By Magazine', *Birmingham News*, 6 December 1931, 34; Jansson, 'American National Identity', 362; 'National Recognition For State', *Birmingham News*, 25 March 1931, 8.

26. Simpich, 'Smoke', 740.

27. 'Celebration For a Former Slave', *Press-Forum Weekly*, 17 September 1931, 1; 'Cudjoe's Celebration Attracts Large Crowd', *Press-Forum Weekly*, 24 October 1931, 3.

28. David Schwartz, 'By the Way', *Wisconsin Jewish Chronicle*, 14 August 1931, 4; Sumner, *The Magazine Century*, 91; *Recent Social Trends*, 3859; Roche, 'Last Survivor'.

29. One possibility is that Amelia Boynton Robinson facilitated the *Clotilda* survivors' reunion and accidentally conflated it with Redoshi's meeting with Danieri Kato, which occurred earlier that year, when recalling the event decades later. That would explain why she remembered the pair discussing the same hometown and conversing in Yoruba. Prior to Matilda and Redoshi's trip, Kossula's communication with his lost shipmates extended to receiving occasional news of Redoshi and Yawith, who were the only shipmates outside Mobile he knew were still alive in 1914. Roche, *Historic Sketches*, 100.

30. Wynn, 'Woman Survivor'.

31. Yoruban historian Samuel Johnson recorded of nineteenth-century Oyo society that 'the hair is the glory of the woman', and that 'Women have

their hair done up in all sorts of ways dictated by their usual vanity; the unmarried ones are distinguished by their hair being plaited into small strips (from 8 to 14) from the right to the left ear, the smaller and more numerous the plaited strips the more admired. Married women on the other hand adopt other forms of plaiting; usually they commence on both sides and finish up in the middle in a sort of network running from the forehead to the occiput.' Ibid.; Johnson, *The History of the Yorubas*, 101.

32. Matilda's trauma was heightened by the many devastating losses she had endured over the past decade. Her sister Sally and her daughters Susie (probably the child named 'Winny' at birth), Eliza and Mae (probably the child named 'Matilda' on the 1900 census), and her son Frederick died in the 1920s. Devastatingly, her first-born Eliza and Mae died in the space of just two months in the autumn of 1928. Eliza was 56 when she died, but her siblings barely made it past 40. When the ageing African woman arrived in Mobile to confront the horrors of her past, only six of her fourteen children were still alive. The father of most of her children, a German-born man named Jacob Schuler, also died sometime in the 1920s. Frederick's precise death date is unknown, but his wife Annie was a widow by 1930. Sally's death date is also unknown. Wynn noted only that she 'died in Dallas County several years ago', but Llewellyn Toulmin concludes she was probably the widowed domestic servant living at 403 Sylvan Street in Selma according to that city's 1920 directory. Wynn, 'Woman Survivor'; Susie Kennedy Death Record, Mobile, Mobile County, Alabama, 3 March 1920; Mae Mason Death Record, Catherine, Wilcox, Alabama, 21 September 1928; Lizie Jackson Death Record, Eleanor, Dallas, Alabama, 26 November 1928; Annie Crear, 1930 US Census, Sumterville, Sumter, Alabama; Toulmin, 'The Crear/McCrear Lines?', 10.

33. The courthouse was rebuilt and redesigned following the clocktower's collapse in 1957. In 1924, Congress ruled that all First World War veterans should receive bonuses at a rate of $1.25 for every day served overseas and $1 for every day served within the United States. The bonus was initially not deemed payable until 1945, but the depression created such financial hardship that a lawmaker tried to pass a bill in spring 1932 releasing the money immediately. President Herbert Hoover threatened to veto the bill, and the failure to release the bonus prompted thousands of veterans and their families to camp outside the White House for weeks in the summer of 1932 before the US military launched a murderous assault that forced them to disperse. 'Wreckers

Tackle Job of Clearing Collapse Debris', *Selma Times-Journal*, 9 July 1957, 10; Laurie and Cole, *The Role*, 368; Tuccille, *The War*, 6–8.

34. Wynn, 'Woman Survivor'.

35. 'Sturdivant's Guardian Angel, Octavia Wynn, is Dead at 95', *Selma Times-Journal*, 23 July 1986, 5; Wynn, 'Woman Survivor'.

36. For a discussion of Matilda's courthouse visit, see Durkin, 'Uncovering the Hidden Lives'.

37. The number of voters increased to 11 during the 1936 election, when Martin's Station aimed to be the first precinct in the country to tally up its votes, although it was ultimately beaten by New England precincts that conducted their counts earlier in the day. Only 156 Black people in Dallas County had the right to vote in April 1961, and only 14 of them had been added to voter rolls since 1954. Atkins joined the registration board in 1961 after the Justice Department charged his predecessor John Pope Majors with racial discrimination. Atkins oversaw a much higher rate of voter approval, which allowed US district judge Daniel Holcombe Thomas to rule that exclusionary racist policies were no longer practised by the board. But the number of successful registrations was still tiny. And Atkins mocked an elderly Black man who demanded to be registered to vote in February 1965. O. S. Wynn, 'Up and Down The Town', *Selma Times-Journal*, 27 November 1932, 10; 'Martin Station First To Report In South', *Clarke County Democrat,* 5 November 1936, 1; Rex Thomas, 'Dallas County Registrars Promise To Comply With Voting Rights Law', *Alabama Journal*, 16 August 1965, 17; Garrow, *Protest at Selma*, 31; Fager, *Selma*, 65.

38. Sidney Flock, 1930 US Census, Selma, Dallas, Alabama; Flock, 'Survivor'.

39. Ibid.

40. Kossula dictated a letter to Mason the next day asking if she was still alive as he had not heard from her. Pettaway, 'The Folklife', 146; 'Cudjoe (Kazoola) Lewis', *Press-Forum Weekly*, 23 April 1932, 1; Lewis to Mason, 12 May 1932.

41. 'Nigeria' was a name imposed by the British Empire in the early twentieth century after it colonized Kossula's homeland and other kingdoms in the Niger River area of West Africa. Caver, 'A Lone Survivor', 3; Charles Leanman, 'Ex-Slave's Prayer Answered As News of Homeland Bared', *Mobile Register*, 21 March 1933, 1.

42. Caver, 'A Lone Survivor', 3 and 6; Percy Taylor, 'What's Happening in Alabama', *Birmingham News,* 24 March 1933, 3.

43. Beardsley, 'Pettway', 218; Arnett, 'Dinah', 92.

44. Kelley, *Hammer and Hoe*, 34; 'New Red Cross Code Used In State Flood', *Evergreen Courant*, 21 March 1929, 8.

45. Callahan, *The Freedom Quilting Bee*, 36; Gaillard, Lindsay and DeNeefe, *Alabama's Civil Rights Trail*, 151–2.

46. Hurston, *Barracoon*, 25; Robertson, *The Slave Ship Clotilda*, 159, 160 and 174; '"Uncle" Cujo Lewis, Last Imported Slave, Dies in Mobile at 105', *Pensacola News Journal*, 27 July 1935, 1; 'Local Residents Saw Old Negro in Mobile', *Stillwater Gazette*, 27 September 1935, 3; 'The Last Slave'; Dennison, *A Memoir*, 41.

47. Childers, 'From Jungle'.

48. 'Unusual Opportunity to See The Green Pastures', *Fairhope Courier*, 24 January 1935, 4; J. E. Crown, 'Waterfront Epic of John Henry Will Be Immortalized in Opera', *Anniston Star*, 25 October 1934, 6.

49. A local woman named Mrs. Singleton provided the details for Kossula's death certificate. Although she placed his age at 105, she was able to correctly identify his birthplace as Nigeria thanks to Mary Ellen Caver's visit two years earlier. Only five white people attended Kossula's funeral, including former *Mobile Register* journalist Merlin Nixon Hanson, who criticized Mobile's white community for losing interest in the African man in death. 'As soon as Cudjo died he lost his commercial worth', Hanson fumed. Roche, 'Last Survivor'; Cudjo Lewis Death Certificate, Mobile, Alabama, 26 July 1935; Merlin N. Hanson, 'Burial of the Last Slave', *Globe*, 1935, 58, cited in Pettaway, 'The Folklife', 219; Hoffman, *Back Home*, 187.

50. Hurston's footage of Kossula and the film of Redoshi may have been the only known cinematic document of a Middle Passage survivor, but Polee and Zuma were also interviewed by a Northern white film director in 1917. George Frederic Wheeler was researching material for *The Birth of a Race* (1918), a production that was radically revised at the production stage, but which was initially conceived to counter *The Birth of a Nation* (1915), whose portrait of freedmen as rapists and veneration of the Ku Klux Klan as saintly heroes sought to justify the South's lynching epidemic to Northern audiences and reignited the Klan as a terrorist organization. For a discussion of *The Negro Farmer*, see Durkin, 'Finding Last Middle Passage Survivor Sally "Redoshi" Smith'. 'Extension Work of Negroes Recorded by Gov't Cameras', *Selma Times-Journal*, 25 September 1936, 3; 'Booker T. Washington Book'; 'Birth of a Race to Be Filmed in this City and Vicinity', *Montgomery Advertiser*, 19 July 1917, 2.

51. Redoshi appears never to have owned the land on which she was enslaved. Her name does not appear on the 1920 census and the 1930 census does not record land ownership information, but the 1910 census shows that she and Yawith were still renting that year. Boynton Robinson, *Bridge Across Jordan*, 32; William and Sallie Smith, 1910 US Census, Mitchell, Dallas, Alabama.

52. 'Native African Slave and Oldest Resident of County Passes at 115', *Selma Times-Journal*, 15 December 1936, 8; 'Plantation Sold'.

53. John Bankhead's son John, Jr. admitted in the US Senate in 1944 that his father had been a Klansman. Marie Owen and fellow Alabamian historian Walter Mahan Jackson sought to justify the Klan's racist violence in *Our Home Land*'s companion school book *History of Alabama for Junior High Schools* by framing the terrorist organization as part of 'a movement which was started by the native whites to try to get some consideration for themselves . . . These men knew the negroes well enough to know how to frighten them.' 90 Cong. Rec. S4304 (1944). Frederickson, *Deep South Dynasty*, 3, 34–41 and 340, n. 81; Jackson and Owen, *History of Alabama*, 99–100.

54. The UDC's influence on the region's schoolchildren endured until the NAACP and Urban League took charge of cleaning up racist schoolbooks by establishing their own textbook committees in the 1960s. *History of the Sophie Bibb Chapter*, 6; DuRocher, *Raising Racists*, 42–3; Zimmerman, *Whose America?*, 111–15.

55. Owen and Mitchell, *Our Home Land*, 76.

56. Ibid., 75–7. Emphases added.

57. *Our Home Land* does not name Washington Smith, but it asserts that Redoshi was sent first to New Orleans before her enslaver bought her. Ibid., 75 and 77–8; 'Owens School', *Mobile Weekly Advocate*, 19 April 1952, 3.

58. By 1935, Atkins was claiming to breed 'some of the best blood lines' of cattle in the country on his land. He reported the loss of up to 25 'fine Hereford' cows from his plantation in a 1938 flood. Forner, *Why the Vote*, 68 and 72; 'New Levels Reached by Price for Cattle', *Alexander City Outlook*, 10 October 1935, 2; 'Alabama Heading for Record Crest', *Selma Times-Journal*, 8 April 1938, 3; Matilda Crear Death Certificate.

59. Matilda McCrear, Findagrave.com. https://www.findagrave.com/memorial/208830115/matilda-creagh-mccrear; Matilda Crear, Alabama Deaths and Burials Index, Martin Station, Dallas, Alabama, 16 January 1940.

Epilogue

1. 'A Tornado Scars Selma'; Duggins, 'Damage and Miracles in Selma'; 'Bridge Crossing Jubilee'; QuickFacts, Selma City, Alabama; Semega and Kollar, 'Income in the United States'; Avant, 'Tornado Debris'; Johnny Crear, email to the author, 21 January 2023.

2. When Johnny appeared before the board, its chair was Colonel Joseph Bibb. Its other member was Aubrey Allen. 'New Arrivals', *Selma Times-Journal*, 22 March 1970, 22; Johnny Crear, email to the author, 23 March 2023.

3. 'Four More Held in Selma Protests', *Birmingham News*, 19 September 1963, 6; 'Ala. White Tries Stuffing Snake'; email to the author, 23 March 2023; Przygoda, 'The Faces of Selma'.

4. Brown-Nagin, *Civil Rights Queen*, 178; Jones, *Bending Toward Justice*, 10–11.

5. Boynton Robinson, *Bridge Across Jordan*, 35.

6. Members of the Gee's Bend community were among the founders of the Wilcox County Civic and Progressive League, and they liaised with both Dr. King's Southern Christian Leadership Conference and the Student Nonviolent Coordinating Committee. Gee's Benders were also harassed, tear-gassed, fired from their jobs, evicted and jailed for their efforts to vote. Jack Nelson, 'Education Still Key to Negro Barriers in South', *Los Angeles Times*, 21 February 1965, 87; Gitin, *This Bright Light*, 197; Gaillard, Lindsay and DeNeefe, *Alabama's Civil Rights Trail*, 153 and 155; Turner, *Crafted Lives*, 170; J. R. Moehringer, 'Crossing Over', *Los Angeles Times*, 22 August 1999, 82.

7. Nelson, 'Education Still Key'; Callahan, *The Freedom Quilting Bee*, 18, 187, 193, 234 and 237; Gitin, *This Bright Light*, 197.

8. Sharp, 'Clotilda, Meaher Families'.

9. The bust was later stolen and dumped in Daphne, Baldwin County, and then retained for a time by Williams. The community's false belief about their ancestral origins likely stemmed from Ghana's symbolic status as the first West African nation to gain its independence from European colonizers (in that case, from Britain) four years earlier. John H. Smith, *Africatown, U.S.A.: A Pictorial History of Plateau and Magazine Point, Alabama* ([Mobile, AL?]: American Ethnic Science Society, 1981), 48 (cited in Diouf, *Dreams*, 234); 'Centennial Celebration Planned for Plateau', *Alabama Citizen*, 4 July 1959, 4; Diouf, *Dreams*, 233–7; Tabor, *Africatown*, 194; Charles W. Porter, 'From Africa to AfricaTown', *Inner City News*, 11.9, 1 March 1986. MPL. https://digital. mobilepubliclibrary.org/items/show/1781; 'Benin Official Apologizes

for Slavery', *Clarion-Ledger*, 19 February 2004, 13; Andrews, 'A Celebration of Heritage'; 'Africatown, Direct Descendants of Africa (Clotilda)', *Mobile Register*, 16 May 1984, 2D. MPL. http://digital. mobilepubliclibrary.org/items/show/1907.

10. As Nick Tabor notes, 15 or 16 homes was Henry C. Williams' estimate. Tabor, *Africatown*, 188–90, 207–8 and 270.

11. Amy Phillips Deaths and Burials Index, Daphne, Baldwin, Alabama, 3 May 1923; Marquis Watkins, conversations with the author, October 2022 to February 2023.

12. In 2015, a federal investigation found in Alabama a widespread failure to add new driving licence applicants to the voter registration system, which is a requirement in US law. According to the Southern Poverty Law Center, 'the state remains one of the most difficult places in the nation for an eligible voter to register and successfully cast a ballot'. Heavey and Adams, 'Alabama to Change Voter Registration System'; 'Alive and Well'; Sam Levine, 'Alabama Discriminated Against Black voters, US Supreme Court Rules', *Guardian*, 8 June 2023. https://www.theguardian.com/law/2023/jun/08/supreme-court-voting-rights-decision-allen-milligan; Walker, 'Alabama Again at Center of Challenges'; Liptak and Fossum, 'Biden Renews Call'.

13. The Black Belt counties, as identified in the study, are Barbour, Bullock, Butler, Choctaw, Crenshaw, Dallas, Greene, Hale, Lowndes, Macon, Marengo, Montgomery, Perry, Pike, Russell, Sumter and Wilcox counties. An additional eight of the 'failing' schools – another 10 per cent – are in Mobile County. Mann and Rogers, 'Segregation Now', 524–5, 529, 539 and 547; Bagley, *The Politics of White Rights*, 2; 'Lowest 6% of Schools'.

14. 'Nostalgia Rides the Rails with Amtrak', *Alabama Journal*, 16 February 1979, 14; 'Union Station, Montgomery'; Matt Smith, 'End of the Line: Gulf Breeze Bids State Farewell', *Montgomery Advertiser*, 1 April 1995, 1; Mia Bay, *Traveling Black*, 307–9; Albrecht, 'Study'; 'Car Access'.

15. Sheets, 'UN Poverty Official'; Alston, 'Report of the Special Rapporteur 13–14'.

16. Raines, *The Last Slave Ship*, 179–80; Tabor, *Africatown*, 168, 172–5, 214–15 and 217.

17. The legitimization of the *Clotilda* story owes a great deal to the 2007 and 2008 book-length histories by Sylviane A. Diouf and Natalie S. Robertson, although even as late as 2016, a major history website claimed that the *Wanderer* 'made the last documented voyage of an

American slave ship'. HB 7: Alabama House Bill; 'Education Gag Orders'; Dennison, *A Memoir*, 12; Klein, 'The Last American Slave Ship'.

18. Barbara Drummond, '"Mama Eva" a Treasure', *Mobile Press Register*, 16 February 1992, 21.

Bibliography

ADAH   Alabama Department of Archives and History
ALP   Alain Locke Papers, Moorland-Spingarn Research
            Center, Howard University
MPL   Mobile Public Library, Local History and Genealogy
NARA   National Archives and Records Administration,
            Atlanta, Georgia

NEWSPAPERS

Aiken Standard (South Carolina)

Alabama Citizen (Tuscaloosa, Alabama)

Alabama Journal (Montgomery)

Alabama State Sentinel (Selma)

Alexander City Outlook (Alabama)

Alexandria Gazette (Virginia)

Altoona Tribune (Pennsylvania)

Andalusia Star (Alabama)

Anniston Star (Alabama)

Atlanta Constitution (Georgia)

Azalea City News & Review (Mobile)

Baldwin Times (Alabama)

Baltimore Sun (Maryland)

Baltimore Wecker (Maryland)

Bangor Daily Whig and Courier (Maine)

Baptist and Reflector (Nashville, Tennessee)

Biblical Recorder (Raleigh, North Carolina)

Birmingham News (Alabama)

Birmingham Reporter (Alabama)

Boston Evening Transcript (Massachusetts)

Brooklyn Evening Star (New York)

Buffalo Commercial (New York)

Buffalo Daily Republic (New York)

Buffalo Morning Express (New York)

Burlington Times (Virginia)

Cahaba Gazette (Alabama)

Charleston Daily News (South Carolina)

Chicago Tribune (Illinois)

Christian Intelligencer (New York)

Cincinnati Enquirer (Ohio)

Clarke County Democrat (Alabama)

Clarion-Ledger (Jackson, Mississippi)

Cleveland Daily Leader (Ohio)

Courier-Journal (Louisville, Kentucky)

Daily Commonwealth (Topeka, Kansas)

Daily Constitutionalist (Augusta, Georgia)

Daily Delta (New Orleans, Louisiana)

Daily Empire (Dayton, Ohio)

Daily Exchange (Baltimore, Maryland)

Daily Milwaukee News (Wisconsin)

Daily News (Birmingham, Alabama)

Daily Selma Reporter (Alabama)

Daily Signal (Crowley, Louisiana)

Daily State Sentinel (Montgomery/Selma, Alabama)

Democrat-Reporter (Linden, Alabama)

Detroit Free Press (Michigan)

Dothan Eagle (Alabama)

Elba Clipper (Alabama)

Eufaula Daily Times (Alabama)

Eufaula Weekly Times (Alabama)

Eutaw Whig and Observer (Alabama)

Evening Star (Washington DC)

Evening Sun (Baltimore, Maryland)

Evergreen Courant (Alabama)

Fairhope Courier (Alabama)

Fall River Daily News (Massachusetts)

The Friend of Temperance (Raleigh, North Carolina)

Goldsboro Messenger (North Carolina)

Greenville Advocate (Alabama)

Guardian (Manchester/London, UK)

Hartford Courant (Connecticut)

Huddersfield Chronicle (Yorkshire, UK)

Independent American (Troy, Alabama)

Inner City News (Alabama)

Bibliography

Inter Ocean (Chicago, Illinois)

Janesville Daily Gazette
(Janesville, Wisconsin)

*Kirkcudbrightshire Advertiser and
Galloway News* (Scotland, UK)

Knoxville Daily Tribune
(Tennessee)

Lancaster News (South Carolina)

Leeds Mercury (Leeds, UK)

Liverpool Mercury (Liverpool,
UK)

Livingston Journal (Alabama)

Los Angeles Express (California)

Los Angeles Times (California)

Louisville Daily Journal
(Kentucky)

Luverne Democrat (Alabama)

Lynchburg Daily Virginian
(Virginia)

Macon Daily Telegraph
(Georgia)

Memphis Daily Appeal
(Tennessee)

Mobile Daily News (Alabama)

Mobile Daily Times (Alabama)

Mobile Daily Tribune (Alabama)

Mobile Mercury (Alabama)

Mobile Press (Alabama)

Mobile Register / Press-Register
(Alabama)

Montgomery Advertiser (Alabama)

Montgomery Mail (Alabama)

Montgomery Times (Alabama)

Montgomery Weekly Mail
(Alabama)

Montgomery Weekly Post
(Alabama)

Morning Democrat (Davenport,
Iowa)

Muscatine Evening Journal
(Iowa)

Nashville Banner (Tennessee)

Nashville Union and American
(Tennessee)

National Era (Washington DC)

New Orleans Crescent (Louisiana)

New Orleans Democrat
(Louisiana)

New York Age

New York Daily Herald

New York Times

Orangeburg News (South
Carolina)

Orlando Sentinel (Florida)

Oxford Intelligencer
(Mississippi)

Paxton Record (Illinois)

Pensacola News Journal (Florida)

Philadelphia Inquirer
(Pennsylvania)

Pittsburgh Courier (Pennsylvania)

Pittsburgh Dispatch
(Pennsylvania)

Prattville Progress (Alabama)

Prichard Herald (Mobile,
Alabama)

Progressive Age (Scottsboro,
Alabama)

Quad-City Times (Davenport,
Iowa)

Republican Banner (Nashville, Tennessee)

Richmond Daily Whig (Virginia)

Richmond Dispatch (Virginia)

Rock Island Argus (Illinois)

Selma Daily Reporter (Alabama)

Selma Journal (Alabama)

Selma Mirror (Alabama)

Selma Morning Times (Alabama)

Selma Times/Times and Messenger (Alabama)

Selma Times-Journal (Alabama)

Shelby Sentinel (Columbiana, Alabama)

Shreveport Journal (Louisiana)

Southern Champion (Claiborne, Alabama)

Southern Exponent (Demopolis, Alabama)

Southwestern Christian Advocate (New Orleans, Louisiana)

The Standard (London, UK)

Star Tribune (Minneapolis, Minnesota)

The State (Columbia, South Carolina)

Stillwater Gazette (Oklahoma)

Sumter County Whig (Livingstone, Alabama)

Syracuse Daily Courier and Union (New York)

The Tennessean (Nashville, Tennessee)

The Times (London, UK)

The Times (Shreveport, Louisiana)

Times-Argus (Selma, Alabama)

Times-Democrat (New Orleans, Louisiana)

Times-Picayune (New Orleans, Louisiana)

Troy Messenger (Alabama)

Tuskegee Republican (Alabama)

Vicksburg Daily Whig (Mississippi)

Watchman (Hayneville, Alabama)

Weekly Advertiser (Montgomery, Alabama)

Wheeling Daily Intelligencer (West Virginia)

Wilcox Progressive Era (Alabama)

Wiregrass Farmer (Headland, Alabama)

Wisconsin Jewish Chronicle (Milwaukee, Wisconsin)

Wisconsin State Journal (Madison, Wisconsin)

PRIMARY SOURCES

'Address of Rev. George W. Samson, D. D.', *African Repository*, 50.3 (March 1874): 71–86.

Agricultural Experiment Station of the Agricultural and Mechanical College, Auburn Alabama, Bulletin 18. Montgomery, AL: The Brown Printing Co., 1890.

'Ala. White Tries Stuffing Snake in Negro's Mouth', *Jet*, 3 October 1963, 55.

Anon. Audio Interview with Clara Eva Bell Allen Jones, Plateau, Alabama. *c.*1980. MPL.

Anon. 'Origin of Slaving by the Clotilda', n.p. MPL. http://digital.mobilepubliclibrary.org/items/show/1836.

Anon. Percy Phillip Mareno Interview Transcript. 22 May 1984.

The Anti-Slavery History of the John-Brown Year; Being the Twenty-Seventh Annual Report of the American Anti-Slavery Society. New York: American Anti-Slavery Society, 1861.

Ayer, Frederick. *The Reminiscences of Frederick Ayer*. Boston, MA: privately printed, 1923.

Ayer's American Almanac: For the Use of Farmers, Planters, Mechanics, and All Families. Lowell, MA: Dr. J. C. Ayer & Co., 1857.

Baker, Ray Stannard. 'The Tragedy of the Mulatto', *American Magazine*, 65.6 (1908): 582–98.

———, to W. E. B. Du Bois, 2 February 1907. W. E. B. Du Bois Papers. Special Collections and University Archives, University of Massachusetts Amherst Libraries.

Banks, Jourden H., and J. W. C. Pennington. *A Narrative of Events of the Life of J. H. Banks, an Escaped Slave, from the Cotton State, Alabama, in America*. Liverpool: M. Rourke, 1861.

Baquaqua, Mahommah Gardo, and Samuel Moore. *Biography of Mahommah G. Baquaqua, a Native of Zoogoo, in the Interior of Africa*. Detroit, MI: Geo. E. Pomeroy & Co., 1854.

Berger, Emma V. 'Cugo Lewis, "Freeborn ex-Slave"', *The Continent*, 26 January 1922, 93.

Blue, Matthew Powers. *A Brief History of Montgomery*. 1878; Birmingham, AL: Works Progress Administration, 1937.

Block, Harry, to Charlotte Osgood Mason, 10 March 1931, Box 164–99, ALP.

Boynton Robinson, Amelia (as Amelia Platts Boynton). *Bridge Across Jordan: The Story of the Struggle for Civil Rights in Selma, Alabama*. New York: Carlton Press, 1979.

Brannon, Peter A. 'A Study in Folk Lore – Notes on Visit to Jake Vanju at Seale, Ala.', *Arrow Points: Monthly Bulletin of the Alabama Anthropological Society*, 10.5 (May 1925): 69.

Bunch, Robert, to Lord John Russell, 21 March 1861, Russell Papers, FO5/750, Public Record Office, The National Archives, UK.

Burton, Sir Richard Francis. *Abeokuta and the Camaroons Mountains: an Exploration*, Vol. 1. London: Tinsley Brothers, 1863.

———. *A Mission to Gelele, King of Dahome*, Vol. 2. London: Tinsley Brothers, 1864.

Byers, S. H. M. 'The Last Slave-Ship', *Harper's Monthly Magazine*, 113 (October 1906): 742–6.

Campbell, Robert. *A Pilgrimage to My Motherland: An Account of a Journey Among the Egbas and Yorubas of Central Africa, in 1859–60*. New York: T. Hamilton, 1861.

'Captain Foster Sold the Clotilda . . .', n.d. MPL. https://digital. mobilepubliclibrary.org/items/show/1837.

Caver, Mary Ellen. 'A Lone Survivor', *Home and Foreign Fields*, 17.9 (September 1933): 3, 6.

Clarke, Lewis, and Milton Clarke. *Narratives of the Sufferings of Lewis and Milton Clarke*. Boston, MA: Bela Marsh, 1846.

'Clotilda – Sailed from Mobile . . .', n.d. MPL. https://digital. mobilepubliclibrary.org/items/show/1819.

Clotilda's Original Certificate of Registry, US Customs Service Coasting Licenses, 1855, NARA.

Cobbett, William, and Thomas Curson Hansard. *Hansard's Parliamentary Debates*, 3rd Series. London: Wyman, 1872.

Cotton, Ella Earls. *A Spark for My People: The Sociological Autobiography of a Negro Teacher*. New York: Exposition Press, 1954.

Cotton Sold to the Confederate States: Letter from the Secretary of the Treasury Transmitting, in Accordance with a Resolution of the Senate of April 22, 1912, a Report of Sales of Cotton to the Confederate States. Washington DC: Government Printing Office, 1913.

Cox, Benjamin B. 'Mobile in the War Between the States', *Confederate Veteran*, 24.5 (1916): 209–13.

Craighead, Erwin. *Mobile: Fact and Tradition.* Mobile: The Powers Printing Co., 1930.

Crew List for the *Clotilda*'s Final Voyage. US Customs Service Cargo Manifests, Mobile, Alabama, 1860. NARA.

Cugoano, Ottobah. *Thoughts and Sentiments on the Evil and Wicked Traffic of the Slavery and Commerce of the Human Species.* 1787; New York: Cambridge University Press, 2013.

Dalzel, Archibald. *The History of Dahomy: An Inland Kingdom of Africa.* London: T. Spilsbury & Son, 1793.

Delany, Martin Robison. *Official Report of the Niger Valley Exploring Party.* New York: Thomas Hamilton, 1861.

DeLeon, T. C. *Four Years in Rebel Capitals.* Mobile, AL: The Gossip Printing Company, 1890.

Dennison, Mable. *Biographical Memoirs of James Dennison.* Boynton Beach, FL.: Futura Printing, 1985.

—. *A Memoir of Lottie Dennison.* Boynton Beach, FL: Futura Printing, 1985.

'Despatches from Commodore Wilmot respecting his Visit to the King of Dahomey, in December 1862 and January 1863 (Presented to the House of Commons)', *The Athenaeum* (27 June 1863): 833–5.

Douglass, Frederick. *Narrative of the Life of Frederick Douglass, An American Slave.* Boston, MA: Anti-Slavery Office, 1845.

Drew, Benjamin. *The Refugee: Or The Narratives of Fugitive Slaves in Canada, Related by Themselves.* Boston: John P. Jewett, 1856.

Du Bois, W. E. Burghardt. *Darkwater: Voices from Within the Veil.* New York: Harcourt, Brace and Howe, 1920.

E. T. D., 'Meeting of the New York Colonization Society (19 December 1870)', *African Repository*, 47.1 (February 1871): 2–6.

Edwards, William J. *Twenty-Five Years in the Black Belt*. Boston, MA: The Cornhill Company, 1918.

Election in Alabama: Letter from the Secretary of War, House of Representatives, 40th Congress, 2nd Session, Ex. Doc., No. 303.

Egypt, Ophelia Settle. *Unwritten History of Slavery: Autobiographical Accounts of Negro Ex-Slaves*. 1945; Washington DC.: Microcard Editions, 1968.

Employment contract between Charlotte Osgood Mason and Zora Neale Hurston, 8 December 1927, Box 164—99, Folder 5, ALP.

Equiano, Olaudah. *The Interesting Narrative of the Life of Olaudah Equiano, or Gustavus Vassa, The African, Written by Himself*, Vol. 1. London: Author, 1789.

Farrior, Mabel. 'Interview with Martha Bradley', *Federal Writers' Project: Slave Narrative Project, 1, Alabama, Aarons-Young* (1936). https://www.loc.gov/resource/mesn.010/?sp=52.

——. 'Interview with Caroline Holland', *Federal Writers' Project: Slave Narrative Project, 1, Alabama, Aarons-Young* (1936). https://www.loc.gov/resource/mesn.010/?sp=191.

Fauset, Arthur Huff. 'Negro Folk Tales from the South (Alabama, Mississippi, Louisiana)', *Journal of American Folklore*, 40.157 (1927): 213—303.

Fifty-First Annual Report of the American Colonization Society. Washington DC: Colonization Society Building, 1868.

'Fifty-Fourth Annual Report of the American Colonization Society (17 January 1871)', in 'Receipts of the American Colonization Society', *African Repository*, 47.2 (February 1871): 33—47.

Final Outbound Manifest for the *Clotilda*, Cargo Manifests, Mobile, Alabama, 1860. NARA.

Forbes, Frederick E. *Dahomey and the Dahomans*, Vol. 1. London: Longman, Brown, Green, and Longmans, 1851.

'Fort Gaines Museum Acquires "Anchor Eye" of Last Slave Schooner', *Alabama on the Go*, June 1965, 29. MPL. http://digital.mobilepubliclibrary.org/items/show/1795.

Forty-Fourth Annual Report of the American Colonization Society. Washington DC: C. Alexander, 1861.

Bibliography

Foster, William. 'Last Slaver from U.S. to Africa. A.D. 1860'.
MPL. https://digital.mobilepubliclibrary.org/items/
show/1802.

Fox, William. *A Brief History of the Wesleyan Missions on the West
Coast of Africa: Including Biographical Sketches of All the
Missionaries who Have Died in that Important Field of Labour. With
Some Account of the European Settlements and of the Slave-Trade.*
1841; London: Aylott and Jones, 1851.

Franco, José Luciano. *Comercio clandestino de esclavos.* Havana,
Cuba: Editorial de Ciencias Sociales, 1985.

Fremantle, Sir Arthur James Lyon. *The Fremantle Diary: Being the
Journal of Lieutenant Colonel James Arthur Lyon Fremantle,
Coldstream Guards, on His Three Months in the Southern States.*
Boston, MA: Little, Brown, 1954.

Gee's Bend Project of the Farm Security Administration. Washington
DC: Farm Security Administration, 1939.

Georgia Writers' Project. *Drums and Shadows: Survival Studies among
the Georgia Coastal Negroes.* 1940; Athens: University of Georgia
Press, 1986.

Gosse, Philip Henry. *Letters from Alabama: Chiefly Relating to Natural
History.* London: Morgan and Chase, 1859.

Gronniosaw, Ukawsaw. *A Narrative of the Most Remarkable Particulars
in the Life of James Albert Ukawsaw Gronniosaw, an African Prince, as
Related by Himself.* Bath: W. Gye, 1770.

Halstead, Murat. *Caucuses of 1860: A History of the National Political
Conventions of the Current Presidential Campaign: Being a Complete
Record of the Business of All the Conventions,* etc. Columbus, SC:
Follet, Foster and Company, 1860.

Hamilton, Peter J. *Mobile of the Five Flags: The Story of the River Basin
and Coast about Mobile from the Earliest Times to the Present.*
Mobile: Gill Printing Co., 1913.

Hines, Jr., Richard. 'Annotated as Told . . .', March 1890. MPL.
https://digital.mobilepubliclibrary.org/items/show/1838.

Hoose, Phillip. *Claudette Colvin: Twice Toward Justice.* New York:
Melanie Kroupa Books, 2009.

Horton, James Africanus Beale. *Physical and Medical Climate and Meteorology of the West Coast of Africa: With Valuable Hints to Europeans for the Preservation of Health in the Tropics.* London: John Churchill & Sons, 1867.

Huntley, Sir Henry. *Seven Years' Service on the Slave Coast of Western Africa*, Vol. 1. London: Thomas Cautley Newby, 1850.

Hurston, Zora Neale. *Barracoon: The Story of the Last Slave*, Revd. & Updated. 2018; London: HQ, 2019.

———. 'Cudjo's Own Story of the Last African Slaver', *Journal of Negro History*, 12.4 (Oct. 1927): 648–63.

———. *Dust Tracks on a Road.* 1942; New York: Harper Perennial, 1995.

———. *Every Tongue Got to Confess: Negro Folk-Tales from the Gulf States.* New York: Amistad, 2001.

———. 'The Last Slave Ship', *American Mercury*, March 1944, 351–8.

———. *You Don't Know Us Negroes and Other Essays*, eds Henry Louis Gates, Jr., and Genevieve West. New York: Amistad, 2022.

Imes, G. Lake. 'The Last Recruits of Slavery', *The Southern Workman*, 46.6 (1917), 355–60.

'Items of Intelligence', *African Repository*, 45.11 (November 1869), 351.

Jackson, Walter M., and Marie Bankhead Owen. *History of Alabama for Junior High Schools.* Montgomery, AL: Dixie Book Company, 1938.

Johnson, Rev. Samuel. *The History of the Yorubas: From the Earliest Times to the Beginning of the British Protectorate.* 1921; Lagos, Nigeria: C.M.S. Bookshops, 1976.

Jones, Jenkin Lloyd. 'Editorial Correspondence', *Unity*, 27 March 1902, 53–5.

———. *Love and Loyalty.* Chicago: University of Chicago press, 1907.

Jones, Virginia K., ed., 'The Journal of Sarah G. Follansbee', *Alabama Historical Quarterly*, 27.3–4 (1965): 213–58.

Kennedy, Renwick C. 'Life at Gee's Bend', *Christian Century*, 1 September 1937, 1072–5.

King, Coretta Scott, with Dr. Barbara Reynolds. *My Life, My Love, My Legacy.* New York: Henry Holt & Co., 2017.

Klebsattel, Christian F. 'Slaves Captured in Africa in 1859 and Brought to Mobile and Sold the Same Year', *The American Missionary*, 71 (January 1917): 516–18.

Lewis, Cudjo, to Charlotte Osgood Mason, 4 September 1930, Box 164–99, Folder 15, ALP.

——, to Charlotte Osgood Mason, 12 May 1932, Box 164–99, Folder 15, ALP.

——. 'Molocoye T'appin (Terrapin)', *La Revue du Monde Noir*, 4 (1932), 238–41.

Lewis, Jr., Cudjo. Pardon Materials. July–August 1900, ADAH. https://cdm17217.contentdm.oclc.org/digital/collection/voices/id/4485.

Lewis, James. State Convict Records, Vol. 5: 1889–1903. ADAH.

'Liberia and the Congo', *African Repository*, 60.1 (January 1884): 29–32.

Locke, Alain, to Charlotte Osgood Mason, 15 June 1931, Box 164–69, Folder 5, ALP.

——, to 'Godmother', 14 March 1932, Box 164–69, Folder 14, ALP.

——, ed. *The New Negro: Voices of the Harlem Renaissance*. 1925; New York: Touchstone, 1997.

'Loss of Life by Steamboats in 1860', *Scientific American*, 3.24 (December 1860), 371.

Mason, Charlotte Osgood, to Alain Locke [draft], 7 June 1931, 164–100, ALP.

——. Note entitled 'Alain Leroy Locke', 6 December 1931, Box 164–100, Folder 8, ALP.

——. Note entitled 'Zora', 15 January 1931, 164–100, ALP.

McGranahan, Ralph W. *Historical Sketch of the Freedmen's Missions of the United Presbyterian Church, 1862–1904*. Knoxville, TN: Printing Dept., Knoxville College, 1904.

Meaher, A., to G. Donaldson, 10 November 1890. MPL. http://digital.mobilepubliclibrary.org/items/show/1827.

Mears & Turnbull, *City Directory of Montgomery, Alabama, 1859 to 1860*. Montgomery, AL: Advertiser Book & Job Printing Office, 1859.

'Missionary Exploration of Liberia', *African Repository*, 47.9 (September 1871): 262–5.

'The Monrovia', *African Repository*, 55.1 (January 1879), 27–8.

Montejo, Esteban. *The Autobiography of a Runaway Slave*. 1968; London: Macmillan Press, 1993.

Montgomery, Charles J. 'Survivors from the Cargo of the Negro Slave Yacht *Wanderer*', *American Anthropologist*, 10.4 (1908): 611–23.

Moore, Frank, ed. *The Rebellion Record: A Diary of American Events*, Vol. 11. New York: D. Van Nostrand, 1868.

Moseley, Houston. State Convict Records, Vol. 7: 1908–1913. ADAH.

Munroe, Kirk. 'The Industrial South', *Harper's Weekly*, 31.1595, 16 July 1887, 503.

—. 'Our Post-Office Box', *Harper's Young People*, 8.377, 18 January 1887, 194.

'Native Africans Enlisting', *Douglass Monthly*, 5.6 (April 1863), 829.

'The New South', *Harper's Weekly*, 30.1566 (25 December 1886), 838.

Nichols, Thomas Low. *Forty Years of American Life*, Vol. 1. London: J. Maxwell, 1864.

Olmsted, Frederick Law. *A Journey in the Seaboard Slave States, With Remarks on Their Economy*. 1856; New York: Mason Brothers, 1861.

'Our Serials and our Circulation', *Harper's Weekly*, 3.144 (22 October 1859): 673.

Ovington, Mary White. 'Slaves' Reminiscences of Slavery', *The Independent*, 68 (26 May 1910): 1131–6.

Owen, H. Burnard. 'Missionary Successes and Negro Converts', *Journal of the Anthropological Society*, 3 (1865): 184–246.

Owen, Marie Bankhead, and Mary Edward Mitchell. *Our Home Land*. Montgomery, AL: Dixie Book Company, 1936.

Owen, Thomas McAdory. *Our Women in the War: Memorial to the Women of the Confederacy*. Montgomery, AL: The Women's Memorial Committee of the United Sons of Confederate Veterans and the Committee of Co-operation of the United Confederate Veterans, 1905.

Park, Robert E. 'The Conflict and Fusion of Cultures with Special Reference to the Negro', *Journal of Negro History*, 4.2 (1919): 111–33.

Pennsylvania Colonization Society Minute Book, 1864–1877, Langston Hughes Memorial Library, Lincoln University. https://www.lincoln.edu/_files/langston-hughes-memorial-library/minute-books/1864-1877.pdf.

'Personal', *Harper's Weekly*, 30.1561 (20 November 1886): 743.

Peterkin, Julia Mood. *Bright Skin: A Novel*. 1932; Athens: University of Georgia Press, 1998.

——, and Doris Ulmann. *Roll, Jordan, Roll*. New York: Robert O. Ballou, 1933.

'Petitioners in Bankruptcy', *Weekly Bankrupt Register*, 1.1, 6 January 1868.

Price, Thomas W. *The Life of T. W. Price, Now of Rehobath [sic], Wilcox Co., Ala*. Selma, AL: Daily Times Job Printing Office, 1877.

Proceedings of the Fourteenth Meeting of the Southern Baptist Convention, Held in the First Baptist Church, Macon, Georgia, May 6th–11th, 1869. Baltimore, MD: John F. Weishampel, Jr., 1869.

Report of the Joint Committee on Reconstruction, at the First Session, Thirty-Ninth Congress, Pts 3 and 4. Washington DC: Government Printing Office, 1866.

Riley, Elizabeth d'Autrey. *The Evergreen Old Historical Cemetery in Evergreen, Alabama, Conecuh County*. Brewton, AL: Escambia Ptg. and Office Supplies, 1971.

Roche, Emma Langdon. *Historic Sketches of the South*. New York: The Knickerbocker Press, 1914.

Russell, Sir William Howard. *My Diary, North and South*. Boston, MA: T.O.H.P. Burnham, 1863.

——. *Pictures of Southern Life, Social, Political, and Military*. New York: J. G. Gregory, 1861.

'Sailed 4 Mar 1859 . . .', n.d. MPL. https://digital.mobilepubliclibrary.org/items/show/1840.

Schurz, Carl, ed. *Report on the Condition of the South*. 1865; New York: Arno Press and the New York Times, 1969.

Scott, Mary McNeil. 'Affika Town', *The Southern Magazine: A Popular Journal of Literature, Poetry, Romance, Art*, 3 (August 1893—January 1894): 59—65.

Senate of the United States for the Second Session of the Forty-Fourth Congress, 1876—1877. Washington DC: Government Printing Office, 1877.

Simpich, Frederick. 'Smoke over Alabama', *National Geographic*, 60.6 (December 1931): 703—58.

Sims, J. Marion. *The Story of My Life*. New York: D. Appleton, 1888.

———. 'The Treatment of Syphilis', *British Medical Journal* (10 March 1883): 448—50.

Sims, Mamie Hunt. *Negro Mystic Lore*. Chicago: To-morrow Press, 1907.

Skertchly, J. Alfred. *Dahomey as It Is: Being a Narrative of Eight Months' Residence in that Country*. London: Chapman and Hall, 1874.

'Slave Trade', in *Annals of British Legislation*, 8. London: Smith, Elder & Co., 1861, 107.

Sonkin, Robert. Audio Interview with Isom Moseley, Gee's Bend, Alabama. 1941.

'The Southern Convention at Knoxville', *De Bow's Review*, 23.3 (September 1857): 298—320.

Stone, R. H. *In Afric's Forest and Jungle; or, Six Years among the Yorubans*. New York: Fleming H. Revell, 1899.

Tenth Annual Report of the Rail Road Commissioners of Alabama, for the Year Ending June 30th, 1890. Montgomery, AL: The Brown Printing Co., 1890.

Thomas, Rex. 'Dallas County Registrars Promise To Comply With Voting Rights Law', *Alabama Journal*, 16 August 1965, 17.

'The Trade of Yoruba', *The Friend: A Religious and Literary Journal*, 32.8 (7 October 1858): 59—60.

United States Congress Senate Committee on Privileges and Elections, Report . . . to Inquire . . . Whether in and of the Elections in the State of Alabama in the Elections of 1874, 1875, and 1876 the Right of Male Inhabitants . . . to Vote Had

Been Denied Or Abridged. Washington, DC: US Government
Printing Office, 1877.

United States v. Burns Meaher, Writ of Seizure and Summons, n.
2620, US District Court, Mobile, Alabama, NARA.

United States v. Jno. M. Dabney, Writ of Seizure and Summons, n.
2619, US District Court, Mobile, Alabama, NARA.

United States v. William Foster, Summons, n. 2621, U.S. District
Court, Mobile, Alabama, NARA.

United States v. William Foster and Richard Sheridan, Summons and
Complaint, n. 3516, US Circuit Court, Mobile, Alabama,
NARA.

'The United States vs. Horatio N. Gould', *American Law Register*, 8.9
(July 1860): 531, 536–7.

Washington, Booker T. *The Story of the Negro*. 1909; Philadelphia:
University of Pennsylvania Press, 2005.

Walker, William. 'General Walker's Policy in Central America', *De
Bow's Review*, 28.3 (February 1860): 154–72.

Wells, Ida B. et al. *The Reason Why the Colored American Is Not in the
World's Columbian Exposition*, ed. Robert W. Rydell. 1893;
Urbana: University of Illinois Press, 1999.

SECONDARY SOURCES

Agbeti, Rev. Dr. J. Kofi. *West African Church History – Christian
Missions and Church Foundations: 1482-1919*, Vol. 1. Leiden: E. J.
Brill, 1986.

Aiken, Charles S. *The Cotton Plantation South Since the Civil War*.
1998; Baltimore MD: JHU Press, 2003.

*Alabama: A Guide to the Deep South, compiled by workers of the Writers'
Program of the Work Project Administration in the State of Alabama*.
c.1941; New York: Hastings House, 1949.

Albrecht, Peter. 'Study: Alabama Most Car Dependent State',
WKRG, 4 May 2021. https://www.wkrg.com/local-news/
study-alabama-most-car-dependent-state/#:~:text=

(WKRG)%20%E2%80%94%20Alabama%20is%20the,
miles%20traveled%2C%20and%20vehicle%20ownership.

'Alive and Well: Voter Suppression and Mismanagement in Alabama',
Southern Poverty Law Center, 10 February 2020. https://www.
splcenter.org/20200210/alive-and-well-voter-suppression-and-
election-mismanagement-alabama.

Allman, Jean, ed. *Fashioning Africa: Power and the Politics of Dress.*
Bloomington: Indiana University Press, 2004.

Alpern, Stanley Bernard. *Amazons of Black Sparta: The Women
Warriors of Dahomey*. London: C. Hurst & Co., 1998.

Alsobrook, David Ernest. 'Alabama's Port City: Mobile during the
Progressive Era, 1896–1917'. 1983. Auburn University, PhD.

Alston, Philip. 'Report of the Special Rapporteur on Extreme
Poverty and Human Rights on His Mission to the United States
of America', *United Nations*, 4 May 2018. https://
socialprotection-humanrights.org/wp-content/uploads/
2018/06/G1812530.pdf.

Andrews, Christopher Columbus. *History of the Campaign of Mobile.*
1867; New York: Van Nostrand Co., 1889.

Archaeological Investigations of 1Ba704, a Nineteenth Century
Shipwreck Site in the Mobile River, Baldwin and Mobile
Counties, Alabama, Final Report, Search Inc, May 2019.

Arnett, Paul, Joanne Cubbs and Eugene W. Metcalf, Jr., eds. *Gee's Bend:
The Architecture of the Quilt*. Atlanta, GA: Tinwood Books, 2006.

——, and Eugene W. Metcalf, Jr., eds. *Mary Lee Bendolph, Gee's
Bend Quilts, and Beyond*. Atlanta, GA: Tinwood Books, 2006.

Arnesen, Eric. *Brotherhoods of Color: Black Railroad Workers and the Struggle
for Equality*. Cambridge, MA: Harvard University Press, 2009.

Aucoin, Brent J. *Thomas Goode Jones: Race, Politics, and Justice in the
New South*. Tuscaloosa: University of Alabama Press, 2016.

Avant, Julia. 'Tornado Debris Still Remains in Selma', *WSFA News*, 7
February 2023. https://www.wsfa.com/2023/02/07/
tornado-debris-still-remains-selma/.

Ayres, Brenda. *The Life and Works of Augusta Jane Evans Wilson,
1835–1909*. New York: Taylor & Francis, 2016.

Bibliography

Babalola, S. A. *The Content and Form of Yoruba Ijala*. London: Oxford University Press, 1966.

Badger, Reid. *A Life in Ragtime: A Biography of James Reese Europe*. New York: Oxford University Press, 1995.

Bagley, Joseph. *The Politics of White Rights: Race, Justice, and Integrating Alabama's Schools*. Athens: University of Georgia Press, 2018.

Bailey, Richard. *Neither Carpetbaggers Nor Scalawags: Black Officeholders During the Reconstruction of Alabama, 1867–1878*, rev. 5th edn. Montgomery, AL: NewSouth Books, 2010.

Baldwin, Cinda K. *Great & Noble Jar: Traditional Stoneware of South Carolina*. 1993; Athens: University of Georgia Press, 2014.

Barnes, Kenneth C. *Journey of Hope: The Back-to-Africa Movement in Arkansas in the Late 1800s*. Chapel Hill: University of North Carolina Press, 2005.

Bay, Edna G. *Wives of the Leopard: Gender, Politics, and Culture in the Kingdom of Dahomey*. 1998; Charlottesville: University of Virginia Press, 2012.

Bay, Mia. *Traveling Black: A Story of Race and Resistance*. Cambridge, MA: Harvard University Press, 2021.

Beardsley, John, et al. *Gee's Bend: The Women and Their Quilts*. Atlanta, GA: Tinwood Books, 2002.

——, et al. *The Quilts of Gee's Bend*. Atlanta, GA: Tinwood Books, 2002.

Beckert, Sven. *Empire of Cotton: A Global History*. New York: Knopf, 2014.

Bellware, Daniel A. 'Africans in Columbus: Frank Bambush and His Contemporaries', *Muscogiana*, 30.2 (2019): 13–23.

Berlin, Ira, Marc Favreau and Steven F. Miller, eds. *Remembering Slavery: African Americans Talk about their Personal Experiences of Slavery and Emancipation*. New York: New Press, 1998.

Blier, Susan Preston. *Art and Risk in Ancient Yoruba: Ife History, Power, and Identity, c. 1300*. Cambridge: Cambridge University Press, 2013.

Bordewich, Fergus M. *Bound for Canaan: The Underground Railroad and the War for the Soul of America*. New York: Amistad, 2005.

Brewer, Willis. *Alabama, Her History, Resources, War Record, and Public Men: From 1540 to 1872.* Montgomery, AL: Barrett & Brown, 1872.

'Bridge Crossing Jubilee "Needed Now More Than Ever" in Tornado-damaged Selma', *AL.com*, 21 January 2023. https://www.al.com/news/2023/01/bridge-crossing-jubilee-needed-now-more-than-ever-in-tornado-damaged-selma.html.

Brown, William Garrott. 'The Orator of Secession: A Study of an Agitator', *Atlantic Monthly*, 83 (May 1899): 605–17.

Brown-Nagin, Tomiko. *Civil Rights Queen: Constance Baker Motley and the Struggle for Equality.* New York: Vintage, 2022.

Bryant, Howard. *The Last Hero: A Life of Henry Aaron.* New York: Pantheon Books, 2010.

Buchanan, Thomas C. *Black Life on the Mississippi: Slaves, Free Blacks, and the Western Steamboat World.* Chapel Hill: University of North Carolina Press, 2004.

Burnett, Lonnie A. *The Pen Makes a Good Sword: John Forsyth of the Mobile Register.* Tuscaloosa: University of Alabama Press, 2006.

Callahan, Nancy. 'Freedom Quilting Bee'. *Encyclopedia of Alabama* (2020). http://encyclopediaofalabama.org/article/h-1628.

———. *The Freedom Quilting Bee: Folk Art and the Civil Rights Movement.* 1987; Tuscaloosa: University of Alabama Press, 2005.

Calonius, Erik. *The Wanderer: The Last American Slave Ship and the Conspiracy That Set Its Sails.* New York: St. Martin's Press, 2006.

'Car Access', *National Equity Access*, 2020. https://nationalequityatlas.org/indicators/Car_access?geo=02000000000001000.

Carter, Dan T. *The Politics of Rage: George Wallace, The Origins of the New Conservatism, and the Transformation of American Politics.* New York: Simon & Schuster, 1995.

Cate, Margaret Davis. *Our Todays and Yesterdays: A Story of Brunswick and the Coastal Islands.* Brunswick, GA: Glover Bros, 1930.

Causey, Virginia E. *Red Clay, White Water, and Blues: A History of Columbus, Georgia.* Athens: University of Georgia Press, 2019.

———. 'Sleuthing through Columbus History', *Muscogiana*, 20.2 (2006): 28–36.

Bibliography

Chave, Anna C. 'Dis/Cover/ing the Quilts of Gee's Bend, Alabama', *Journal of Modern Craft*, 1.2 (2008), 221–53.

Coker, William S. 'The Moreno Family of Pensacola and the Civil War', *Gulf Coast Historical Review*, 4.2 (1989): 100–25.

Colcord, Bradford C. *The History of Pig Iron Manufacture in Alabama*. Woodword, AL: Woodword Iron Company, 1950.

Conrad, Paul. *The Apache Diaspora: Four Centuries of Displacement and Survival*. Philadelphia: University of Pennsylvania Press, 2021.

Covey, Herbert C. *African American Slave Medicine: Herbal and Non-herbal Treatments*. Lanham, MD: Lexington Books, 2007.

——, and Dwight Eisnach. *What the Slaves Ate: Recollections of African American Foods and Foodways from the Slave Narratives*. Santa Barbara, CA: Greenwood Press/ABC-CLIO, 2009.

Cox, Karen L. *Dixie's Daughters: The United Daughters of the Confederacy and the Preservation of Confederate Culture*. 2003; Gainesville: University Press of Florida, 2019.

Davis, Susan Lawrence. *Authentic History, Ku Klux Klan, 1865–1877*. New York: S. L. Davis, 1924.

DeLand, T. A., and A. Davis Smith. *Northern Alabama: Historical and Biographical*. Chicago: Donohue & Henneberry, 1888.

de la Riva, Juan Pérez. *El monto de la immigración forzada en el siglo XIX*. Havana: Editorial de las Ciencias Sociales, 1979.

Delgado, James P., et al. *Clotilda: The History and Archaeology of the Last Slave Ship*. Tuscaloosa: University of Alabama Press, 2023.

——, 'Diving for the Clotilda: The Archaeology, History, and Legacy of the Last Known Slave Ship', Archaeological Institute of America, 15 October 2022.

Diouf, Sylviane A. *Dreams of Africa in Alabama: The Slave Ship Clotilda and the Story of the Last Africans Brought to America*. New York: Oxford University Press, 2007.

Du Bois, W. E. B. *The Suppression of the African Slave Trade to the United States of America, 1638–1870*, Vol. 1. New York: Longmans, Green & Co., 1896.

DuBose, Joel Campbell. *Notable Men of Alabama: Personal and Genealogical*, Vol. 1. 1904; Spartanburg, SC: Reprint Company, 1976.

Du Bose, John Witherspoon. *The Life and Times of William Lowndes Yancey*. Birmingham, AL: Roberts & Son, 1892.

Duggins, Pat. 'Damage and Miracles in Selma after Killer Tornado', *Alabama Public Radio*, 13 January 2023. https://www.apr.org/news/2023-01-13/damage-and-miracles-in-selma-after-killer-tornado.

du Mont, John Sanderson. *du Mont de Soumagne and Allied Families*. Greenfield, MA: John S. Du Mont, 1960.

Durkin, Hannah. 'Finding Last Middle Passage Survivor Sally "Redoshi" Smith on the Page and Screen', *Slavery & Abolition: A Journal of Slave and Post-Slave Studies*, 40.4 (2019): 631–58.

———. 'Uncovering the Hidden Lives of Last *Clotilda* Survivor Matilda McCrear and Her Family', *Slavery & Abolition: A Journal of Slave and Post-Slave Studies*, 41.3 (2020): 431–57.

———. 'Zora Neale Hurston's Visual and Textual Portrait of Middle Passage Survivor Oluale Kossola/Cudjo Lewis', *Slavery & Abolition: A Journal of Slave and Post-Slave Studies*, 38.3 (2017): 601–19.

DuRocher, Kristina. *Raising Racists: The Socialization of White Children in the Jim Crow South*. Lexington: University Press of Kentucky, 2011.

'Education Gag Orders Seek to Enforce Compulsory Patriotism', *PEN America*, 30 March 2022. https://pen.org/update-educational-gag-orders-seek-to-enforce-compulsory-patriotism/.

Eiland, Sarah. 'The Unspoken Demands of Slavery: The Exploitation of Female Slaves in the Memphis Slave Trade', *Rhodes Historical Review*, 20 (2018): 43–62.

English, Bertis D. *Civil Wars, Civil Beings, and Civil Rights in Alabama's Black Belt: A History of Perry County*. Tuscaloosa: University of Alabama Press, 2020.

Evans, Augusta Jane. *St. Elmo; Or, Saved at Last*. 1866; Tuscaloosa: University of Alabama Press, 1992.

Fager, Charles Eugene. *Selma, 1965*. New York: Scribner, 1974.

Bibliography

Falola, Toyin. *Counting the Tiger's Teeth: An African Teenager's Story*. Ann Arbor: University of Michigan Press, 2014.

——, and Akintunde Akinyemi, eds. *Encyclopedia of the Yoruba*. Bloomington: Indiana University Press, 2016.

Feldman, Glen, ed. *Before Brown: Civil Rights and White Backlash in the Modern South*. Tuscaloosa: University of Alabama Press, 2004.

——. *The Irony of the Solid South: Democrats, Republicans, and Race, 1865–1944*. Tuscaloosa, AL: University of Alabama Press, 2013.

Ferrer, Ada. *Cuba: An American History*. New York: Scribner, 2022.

Fett, Sharla M. *Recaptured Africans: Surviving Slave Ships, Detention, and Dislocation in the Final Years of the Slave Trade*. Chapel Hill: University of North Carolina Press, 2016.

——. *Working Cures: Healing, Health, and Power on Southern Slave Plantations*. Chapel Hill: University of North Carolina Press, 2002.

Finley, Cheryl, Randall R. Griffey, Amelia Peck and Darryl Pinckney, eds. *My Soul Has Grown Deep: Black Art from the American South*. New York: Metropolitan Museum of Art, 2018.

Fisch, Audrey A., ed. *The Cambridge Companion to the African American Slave Narrative*. Cambridge: Cambridge University Press, 2007.

Fitts III, Alston. *Selma: A Bicentennial History*. Tuscaloosa: University of Alabama Press, 2017.

——. *Selma: Queen City of the Blackbelt*. Selma, AL: Clairmont Press, 1989.

Fleischhauer, Carl, and Beverly W. Brannan, eds. *Documenting America, 1935–1943*. Berkeley: University of California Press, 1988.

Fleming, Cynthia Griggs. *In the Shadow of Selma: The Continuing Struggle for Civil Rights in the Rural South*. Lanham, MD: Rowman & Littlefield, 2004.

Fleming, Lynwood. *Civil War and Reconstruction in Alabama*. New York: Columbia University Press, 1905.

Flynt, Wayne. 'Alabama's Shame: The Historical Origins of the 1901 Constitution', *Alabama Law Review*, 53.1 (2001): 67–76.

Forner, Karlyn. *Why the Vote Wasn't Enough for Selma*. Durham, NC: Duke University Press, 2017.

Frederickson, Kari. *Deep South Dynasty: The Bankheads of Alabama*. Tuscaloosa: University of Alabama Press, 2021.

French, Howard W. *Born in Blackness: Africa, Africans, and the Making of the Modern World, 1471 to the Second World War*. New York: W. W. Norton, 2021.

Frost, Diane. *Work and Community among West African Migrant Workers since the Nineteenth Century*. Liverpool: Liverpool University Press, 1997.

Fry, Gladys-Marie. *Stitched from the Soul: Slave Quilts from the Antebellum South*. 1990; Chapel Hill: UNC Press, 2002.

Gaillard, Frye, with Jennifer Lindsay and Jane DeNeefe. *Alabama's Civil Rights Trail: An Illustrated Guide to the Cradle of Freedom*. Tuscaloosa: University of Alabama Press, 2010.

Garrow, David J. *Protest at Selma: Martin Luther King, Jr., and the Voting Rights Act of 1965*. New Haven, CT: Yale University Press, 1978.

Gershoni, Yekutiel. *Africans on African-Americans: The Creation and Uses of an African-American Myth*. London: Macmillan, 1997.

Gilfoy, Peggy Stoltz. *Patterns of Life: West African Strip-Weaving Traditions*. Washington DC: National Museum of African Art by the Smithsonian Institution Press, 1987.

Gitin, Maria. *This Bright Light of Ours: Stories from the Voting Rights Fight*. Tuscaloosa: University of Alabama Press, 2014.

Go, Julian, ed. *Postcolonial Sociologies: A Reader*, Vol. 31. Bingley, UK: Emerald Group Publishing, 2016.

Godshalk, David Fort. *Veiled Visions: The 1906 Atlanta Race Riot and the Reshaping of American Race Relations*. Chapel Hill: University of North Carolina Press, 2005.

Green, Toby. *A Fistful of Shells: West Africa from the Rise of the Slave Trade to the Age of Revolution*. London: Penguin, 2019.

Grinker, Roy Richard, Stephen C. Lubkemann, and Christopher B. Steiner, eds. *Perspectives on Africa: A Reader in Culture, History and Representation*, 2nd edn. Malden, MA: Wiley-Blackwell, 2010.

Gunn, Jeffrey. *Outsourcing African Labor: Kru Migratory Workers in Global Ports, Estates and Battlefields Until the End of the 19th Century*. Boston, MA: De Gruyter, 2021.

Harper, Jim C. *Western-Educated Elites in Kenya, 1900–1963: The African American Factor*. 2006; London: Routledge, 2016.

Harris, John. *The Last Slave Ships: New York and the End of the Middle Passage*. New Haven, CT: Yale University Press, 2020.

HB 7: Alabama House Bill, *FastDemocracy*, n.d. https://fastde mocracy.com/bill-search/al/2023rs/bills/ALB00014834/.

Heavey, Susan, and David Adams. 'Alabama to Change Voter Registration System after Federal Probe', *Reuters.com*, 13 November 2015. https://www.reuters.com/article/ alabama-election-idUSL1N1381W120151113.

Hemenway, Robert E. *Zora Neale Hurston: A Literary Biography*. 1977; Urbana: University of Illinois Press, 1980.

Herskovits, Melville J., and Frances S. Herskovits. *Dahomean Narrative: A Cross-cultural Analysis*. 1958; Evanston, IL: Northwestern University Press, 1998.

Hilde, Libra R. *Worth a Dozen Men: Women and Nursing in the Civil War South*. Charlottesville: University of Virginia Press, 2012.

History and Directory of the First Presbyterian Church: Adams Avenue, between Court and Perry Streets, Montgomery, Alabama, 1824–1914. Montgomery, AL: The Church, 1914.

History of the Sophie Bibb Chapter: Daughters of the Confederacy. Montgomery, AL: Brown Printing Co., 1911.

Hoffman, Roy. *Back Home: Journeys Through Mobile*. Tuscaloosa: University of Alabama Press, 2007.

Hood, James Walker. *One Hundred Years of the African Methodist Episcopal Zion Church Or, The Centennial of African Methodism*. Fairfield, NC: J. W. Hood, 1895.

Inikori, Joseph E., and Stanley L. Engerman, eds. *The Atlantic Slave Trade: Effects on Economies, Societies and Peoples in Africa, the*

Americas, and Europe. Durham, NC: Duke University Press, 1992.

Jacobs, Philip Walker. *The Life and Photography of Doris Ulmann*. Lexington: University Press of Kentucky, 2001.

Jackson III, Harvey H. *Rivers of History: Life on the Coosa, Tallapoosa, Cahaba, and Alabama*. Tuscaloosa: University of Alabama Press, 1995.

Janney, Caroline E. *Burying the Dead but Not the Past: Ladies' Memorial Associations and the Lost Cause*. Chapel Hill: University of North Carolina Press, 2008.

Jansson, David R. 'American National Identity and the Progress of the New South in *National Geographic Magazine*', *Geographical Review*, 93.3 (2003): 350–69.

Jarnagin, Laura. *A Confluence of Transatlantic Networks: Elites, Capitalism, and Confederate Migration to Brazil*. Tuscaloosa: University of Alabama Press, 2014.

John, Philip Hayab. 'Narratives of Identity and Sociocultural Worldview in Song Texts of the Ham of Nigeria: A Discourse Analysis Investigation'. March 2017. Stellenbosch University, PhD.

Johnson, Malcolm Lee. *Texas Tales and Tall Ships: Texas History from 1548–1945 The End of WW2, Vol. 2*, 2nd edn. Pittsburgh, PA: Dorrance Publishing Co., 2021.

Johnson, Walter. *River of Dark Dreams: Slavery and Empire in the Cotton Kingdom*. Cambridge, MA: Harvard University Press, 2013.

Jones, Doug. *Bending Toward Justice: The Birmingham Church Bombing that Changed the Course of Civil Rights*. New York: St. Martin's Press, 2019.

Jones, James Pickett. *Yankee Blitzkrieg: Wilson's Raid Through Alabama and Georgia*. Athens: University of Georgia Press, 1976.

Jones, Robert P. *White Too Long: The Legacy of White Supremacy in American Christianity*. New York: Simon & Schuster, 2021.

Josephides, Lisette, and Alexandra Hall, eds. *We the Cosmopolitans: Moral and Existential Conditions of Being Human*. New York: Berghahn Books, 2014.

Bibliography

Kaplan, Carla. *Miss Anne in Harlem: The White Women of the Black Renaissance*. New York: HarperCollins, 2013.

——, ed. *Zora Neale Hurston: A Life in Letters*. New York: Anchor Books, 2003.

Kelley, Blair Murphy. *Right to Ride: Streetcar Boycotts and African American Citizenship in the Era of Plessy v. Ferguson*. Chapel Hill: University of North Carolina Press, 2010.

Kelley, Robin D. G. *Hammer and Hoe: Alabama Communists during the Great Depression*. Chapel Hill: UNC Press, 2015.

Keenan, Jerry. *Wilson's Cavalry Corps: Union Campaigns in the Western Theatre, October 1864 Through Spring 1865*. 1998; Jefferson, NC: McFarland, 2006.

King, Carole A., and Karren I. Pell. *Montgomery's Historic Neighborhoods*. Charleston, SC: Arcadia Publishing, 2010.

King, Kenneth J. 'African Students in Negro American Colleges: Notes on the Good African', *Phylon*, 31.1 (1970): 16–30.

Klein, Christopher. 'The Last American Slave Ship', *History*, 15 May 2016 (updated 20 November 2019). https://www.history.com/news/the-last-american-slave-ship.

Kotar, S. L., and J. E. Gessler. *The Steamboat Era: A History of Fulton's Folly on American Rivers, 1807–1860*. Jefferson, NC: McFarland: 2009.

Kriger, Colleen E. *Cloth in West African History*. Lanham, MD: AltaMira Press, 2006.

LaFayette, Jr., Bernard, and Kathryn Lee Johnson. *In Peace and Freedom: My Journey in Selma*. Lexington: University Press of Kentucky, 2013.

Laurie, Clayton D., and Ronald H. Cole. *The Role of Federal Military Forces in Domestic Disorders, 1877–1945*. Washington DC: Center of Military History, US Army, 1997.

Law, Robin. 'Commémoration de la Traite Atlantique à Ouidah', *Gradhiva: Revue d'anthropologie et d'histoire des arts*, 8 (2008):10–27.

——. *Ouidah: The Social History of a West African Slaving 'Port', 1727–1892*. Athens, OH: Ohio University Press, 2004.

—. *The Oyo Empire, c.1600–c.1836: A West African Imperialism in the Era of the Atlantic Slave Trade*. 1977; Aldershot, UK: Ashgate, 1991.

Leavell, Zachary Taylor, and Thomas Jefferson Bailey. *A Complete History of Mississippi Baptists: From the Earliest Times*, Vol. 2. Jackson, MS: Mississippi Baptist Publishing Co., 1904.

Liptak, Kevin, and Sam Fossum. 'Biden Renews Call for New Voting Protections in Visit to Selma', *CNN*, 5 March 2023. https://edition.cnn.com/2023/03/05/politics/joe-biden-selma-bloody-sunday/index.html.

Lloyd, Christopher. *The Navy and the Slave Trade: The Suppression of the African Slave Trade in the Nineteenth Century*. 1949; London: Cass, 1968.

Long, Carolyn Morrow. 'Folk Gravesites in New Orleans: Arthur Smith Honors the Ancestors', *Folklore Forum*, 29.1 (1998): 23–50.

Lovejoy, Henry B. 'Mapping Uncertainty: The Collapse of Oyo and the Transatlantic Slave Trade, 1816–1836', *Journal of Global Slavery*, 4.2 (2019): 127–61.

'Lowest 6% of Schools Identified for the Alabama Accountability Act of 2015', *Alabama State Department of Education*, November 2022. https://www.alabamaachieves.org/wp-content/uploads/2022/11/RD_20221110_November-2022-Failing-School-List_V1.0.pdf.

Mann, Bryan, and Annah Rogers. 'Segregation Now, Segregation Tomorrow, Segregation Forever? Racial and Economic Isolation and Dissimilarity in Rural Black Belt Schools in Alabama', *Rural Sociology*, 86.3 (2021): 523–58.

Mann, Kristin, *Slavery and the Birth of an African City: Lagos, 1760–1900*. Bloomington: Indiana University Press, 2007.

Martin, Sandy Dwayne. *Black Baptists and African Missions: The Origins of a Movement, 1880–1915*. Macon, GA: Mercer University Press, 1989.

Mauldin, Erin Stewart. *Unredeemed Land: An Environmental History of Civil War and Emancipation in the Cotton South*. New York: Oxford University Press, 2019.

Bibliography

McCarty, Clinton. *The Reins of Power: Racial Change and Challenge in a Southern County*. Tallahassee, FL: Sentry Press, 1999.

McCash, June Hall. *Jekyll Island's Early Years: From Prehistory Through Reconstruction*. Athens: University of Georgia Press, 2014.

McIlwain, Christopher Lyle. *Civil War Alabama*. Tuscaloosa: University of Alabama Press, 2016.

Meier, August, and Elliott Rudwick. 'The Boycott Movement Against Jim Crow Streetcars in the South, 1900−1906', *Journal of American History*, 55.4 (1969): 765−75.

Merritt, Keri Leigh. *Masterless Men: Poor Whites and Slavery in the Antebellum South*. Cambridge: Cambridge University Press, 2017.

Miller, Rex. *Croxton's Raid*. Fort Collins, CO: Old Army Press, 1979.

Misulia, Charles A. *Columbus, Georgia, 1865: The Last True Battle of the Civil War*. Tuscaloosa: University of Alabama Press, 2016.

Mitchell, Betty L. *Edmund Ruffin, a Biography*. Bloomington: Indiana University Press, 1981.

Moffat, Charles H. 'Charles Tait, Planter, Politician, and Scientist of the Old South', *Journal of Southern History*, 14.2 (1948): 206−33.

Noe, Kenneth W. ed. *The Yellowhammer War: The Civil War and Reconstruction in Alabama*. Tuscaloosa: University of Alabama Press, 2013.

Nolen, Claude H. *African American Southerners in Slavery, Civil War and Reconstruction*. Jefferson, NC: McFarland, 2005.

Ockenden, I. M. Porter, ed. *The Confederate Monument on Capitol Hill, Montgomery, Alabama, 1861−1900*. Montgomery, AL: Ladies Memorial Association, 1900.

Ogundiran, Akinwumi, and Paula Saunders, eds. *Materialities of Ritual in the Black Atlantic*. Bloomington: Indiana University Press, 2014.

———. *The Yoruba: A New History*. Bloomington: Indiana University Press, 2020.

O'Meagher, Joseph Casimir. *Some Historical Notices of the O'Meaghers of Ikerrin*. London: Elliot Stock, 1887.

Owen, Thomas McAdory, and Marie Bankhead Owen. *History of Alabama and Dictionary of Alabama Biography*, Vols 2 and 3. Chicago: S. J. Clarke, 1921.

Oyeniyi, Bukola Adeyemi. *Dress in the Making of African Identity: A Social and Cultural History of the Yoruba People*. New York: Cambria Press, 2015.

Panovka, Rebecca. 'A Different Backstory for Zora Neale Hurston's "Barracoon"', *Los Angeles Review of Books*, 7 July 2018. https:// lareviewofbooks.org/article/different-backstory-for-zora-neale-hurstons-barracoon/#!.

Pargas, Damian Alan. *Slavery and Forced Migration in the Antebellum South*. Cambridge: Cambridge University Press, 2014.

Parsons, Elaine Frantz. *Ku-Klux: The Birth of the Klan during Reconstruction*. Chapel Hill: University of North Carolina Press, 2015.

Perry, Carolyn, and Mary Weaks-Baxter, eds. *The History of Southern Women's Literature*. Baton Rouge: Louisiana State University Press, 2002.

Pettaway, Addie E. 'The Folklife and Material Culture of a Historic Landscape: Africatown U.S.A.' 1983. University of Wisconsin-Madison, MA thesis.

Piersen, William Dillon. *Black Legacy: America's Hidden Heritage*. Amherst: University of Massachusetts Press, 1993.

Przygoda, Dan. 'The Faces of Selma, 50 Years Later', *Bloomberg*, 6 March 2015. https://www.bloomberg.com/news/features/2015-03-06/the-faces-of-selma-50-years-later.

Powell, William H., and Edward Shippen, eds. *Officers of the Army and Navy (regular) who Served in the Civil War*. Philadelphia, PA: L. R. Hamersly & Co., 1892.

QuickFacts, Selma City, Alabama. United States Census. https:// www.census.gov/quickfacts/selmacityalabama.

Rabinowitz, Howard N. 'From Exclusion to Segregation: Southern Race Relations, 1865–1890', *Journal of American History*, 63.2 (1976): 325–50.

Raines, Ben. *The Last Slave Ship: The True Story of How Clotilda was Found, Her Descendants, and an Extraordinary Reckoning*. New York: Simon & Schuster, 2022.

Recent Social Trends in the United States: Report of the President's Research Committee on Social Trends, Vol. 1. New York: McGraw-Hill, 1933.

Rediker, Marcus. *The Amistad Rebellion*. New York: Viking, 2012.

———. *The Slave Ship: A Human History*. London: John Murray, 2008.

Riggins, Roosevelt. *Riggins Family Ancestry Book*. Privately printed, n.d.

Robertson, Natalie S. *The Slave Ship Clotilda and the Making of AfricaTown, USA: Spirit of Our Ancestors*. Westport, CT: Praeger, 2008.

Robb, Frances Osborn. 'Who Are These Masked Men? The Early Ku Klux Klan, a Photograph, and a North Alabama Family', *The Princeton University Library Chronicle*, 75.2 (2014): 201–24.

Rogers, William Warren. *Confederate Home Front: Montgomery During the Civil War*. Tuscaloosa: University of Alabama Press, 1999.

Roland, Charles P. *An American Iliad: The Story of the Civil War*, 2nd edn. Lexington: University Press of Kentucky, 2004.

Scott, Florence Dolive. *Daphne: A History of Its People and Their Pursuits, as Some Saw It and Others Remember It*. Mobile, AL: Jordan Publishing, 1965.

Scott, Lieut. Col. Robert N. *The War of the Rebellion: A Compilation of the Official Records of the Union and Confederate Armies*, Series I – Vol. 35, Pt I. Washington DC: US Government Printing Office, 1891.

Scroggs, William O. *Filibusters and Financiers: The Story of William Walker and His Associates*. New York: The Macmillan Company, 1916.

Sellers, James Benson. *Slavery in Alabama*. 1950; Tuscaloosa: University of Alabama Press, 1994.

Semega, Jessica, and Melissa Kollar. 'Income in the United States: 2021', *United States Census Bureau*, 13 September 2022. https://

www.census.gov/library/publications/2022/demo/p60-276.
html#:~:text=Real%20median%20household%20income%20
was,and%20Table%20A%2D1.

Severance, Ben H. *Portraits of Conflict: A Photographic History of Alabama in the Civil War*. Fayetteville: University of Arkansas Press, 2012.

Sharp, John. 'Clotilda, Meaher Families have Historic First Meeting 162 years after Nation's Last Slave Voyage', *AL.com*, 12 December 2022 (updated 13 December 2022). https://www.al.com/news/2022/12/clotilda-meaher-families-have-historic-first-meeting-162-years-after-nations-last-slave-voyage.html.

Sheets, Connor. 'UN Poverty Official Touring Alabama's Black Belt: "I Haven't Seen This" in the First World', *AL.com*, 8 December 2017. https://www.al.com/news/2017/12/un_poverty_official_touring_al.html.

Silkenat, David. *Scars on the Land: An Environmental History of Slavery in the American South*. New York: Oxford University Press, 2022.

Sinha, Manisha. *The Counterrevolution of Slavery: Politics and Ideology in Antebellum South Carolina*. Chapel Hill: University of North Carolina Press, 2000.

Sledge, John S. *The Mobile River*. Columbia: University of South Carolina Press, 2015.

Specker, Lawrence. '"Biopsy" of Clotilda Site Yields Wealth of Data for Study', *AL.com*, 12 May 2022. https://www.al.com/news/mobile/2022/05/biopsy-of-clotilda-site-yields-wealth-of-data-for-study.html.

Sulzby, James Frederick. *Historic Alabama Hotels and Resorts*. Tuscaloosa: University of Alabama Press, 1960.

Sumner, David E. *The Magazine Century: American Magazines Since 1900*. New York: Peter Lang, 2010.

Swift, Charles Jewett. *The Last Battle of the Civil War*. Columbus, GA: Gilbert Printing Co., 1915.

Tabor, Nick. *Africatown: America's Last Slave Ship and the Community It Created*. New York: St. Martin's Press, 2023.

Bibliography

Taylor, Maureen A. *Rhode Island Passenger Lists*. Baltimore, MD: Genealogical Publishing Co., 1995.

Taylor, Michael. *The Interest: How the British Establishment Resisted the Abolition of Slavery*. London: Bodley Head, 2020.

Taylor, Yuval. *Zora and Langston: A Story of Friendship and Betrayal*. New York: W. W. Norton, 2019.

Thomas, Hugh. *The Slave Trade: The History of the Atlantic Slave Trade, 1440–1870*. London: Picador, 1997.

'A Tornado Scars Selma'. *Earth Observatory* (2023). https://earthobservatory.nasa.gov/images/150857/a-tornado-scars-selma#:~:text=According%20to%20the%20National%20Weather,Selma%2C%20and%20ended%20near%20Burnsville.

Toulmin, Llewellyn. 'The Crear/McCrear Lines? Genealogical Descents from Africa and the Slave Ship *Clotilda* to the Present' (unpublished pdf).

———. 'The Family of Peter ("Gumpa") and Josephine Lee of the Slave Ship *Clotilda* and Africatown, Alabama' (unpublished pdf).

Trans-Atlantic Slave Trade Database. Slave Voyages v2.2.13 (2021). The Slave Voyages Consortium. Rice University. https://www.slavevoyages.org/.

Tuccille, Jerome. *The War Against the Vets: The World War I Bonus Army During the Great Depression*. Lincoln, NE: Potomac Books, 2018.

Tupper, Henry Allen. *A Decade of Foreign Missions, 1880–1890*. Princeton, NJ: Foreign Mission Board of the Southern Baptist Association, 1891.

Turner, Erin H., ed. *Wise Women: From Pocahontas to Sarah Winnemucca, Remarkable Stories of Native American Trailblazers*. Gulford, CT/Helena, MN: TwoDot, 2009.

Turner, Patricia A. *Crafted Lives: Stories and Studies of African American Quilters*. Jackson: University Press of Mississippi, 2009.

'Union Station, Montgomery.' *Encyclopedia of Alabama*, n.d. http://
encyclopediaofalabama.org/article/m-8996#:~:text=
Until%201979%2C%20it%20hosted%20trains,the%20
Landmarks%20Foundation%20of%20Montgomery.

Usman, Aribidesi, and Toyin Falola. *The Yoruba from Prehistory
to the Present*. Cambridge: Cambridge University Press,
2019.

Wall, Austin. 'Direct from Congo: Nathan Bedford Forrest's
Involvement in the Illegal African Slave Trade', *Rhodes Historical
Review*, 20 (2018): 63−81.

Walker, DeArbea. 'Alabama Again at Center of Challenges to
Voting Rights Act', *The Center for Public Integrity*, 6 October
2022. https://publicintegrity.org/politics/elections/who-
counts/alabama-again-at-center-of-challenges-to-voting-
rights-act/.

Walther, Eric H. *William Lowndes Yancey and the Coming of the
Civil War*. Chapel Hill: University of North Carolina Press,
2006.

Wells, Tom Henderson. *The Slave Ship Wanderer*. 1967; Athens:
University of Georgia Press, 2009.

Williams, Susan Millar. '"Something to Feel About": Zora Neale
Hurston and Julia Peterkin in African Town', *Mississippi
Quarterly*, 63.1−2 (2010): 291−8.

Williamson, C. J. *March On! with the United Presbyterian Church of
North America*. Pittsburgh, PA: Board of Administration, United
Presbyterian Church, 1933.

Wills, Mary. *Envoys of Abolition: British Naval Officers and the
Campaign Against the Slave Trade in West Africa*. Liverpool:
Liverpool University Press, 2019.

Young, Elizabeth. *Disarming the Nation: Women's Writing and the
American Civil War*. Chicago: University of Chicago Press, 1999.

Zimmerman, Jonathan. *Whose America? Culture Wars in the Public
Schools*. Cambridge, MA: Harvard University Press, 2002.

List of Illustrations

FIRST PLATE SECTION

Kossula *(Emma Langdon Roche, photographer)*

Portraits of Abaché and Polee *(Emma Langdon Roche)*

Daily life nineteenth-century Oyo *(Courtesy of TuckDB)*

A map drawn by Kossula *(Emma Langdon Roche, co-author)*

Chief *Clotilda* conspiracist Timothy Meaher *(Courtesy of Mobile Public Library, Local History & Genealogy Division. A. Sandoz, photographer)*

Clotilda captain William Foster *(Courtesy of Mobile Public Library, Local History & Genealogy Division. A. Sandoz, photographer)*

The wreck of the *Clotilda (Courtesy of Mobile Public Library, Local History & Genealogy Division. Emma Langdon Roche, photographer)*

Matilda *(Courtesy of the Crear family)*

Jefferson Davis being sworn in *(Archibald Crossland McIntyre, photographer)*

Gumpa *(Courtesy of Delisha Marshall)*

Portrait of Osia Keeby *(Emma Langdon Roche)*

African Town judge Charlie *(Courtesy of Mobile Public Library, Local History & Genealogy Division. Emma Langdon Roche, photographer)*

SECOND PLATE SECTION

A view up Market Street *(Courtesy of the Alabama Department of Archives and History)*

Boudousquie's 1889 reference map *(Courtesy of the Alabama Department of Archives and History)*

Group sketch of African Town residents (Times-Democrat, *New Orleans, Louisiana, 1 April 1894)*

Sketch of Shamba (Times-Democrat, *New Orleans, Louisiana, 1 April 1894)*

Sketch of Zuma (Times-Democrat, *New Orleans, Louisiana, 1 April 1894)*

Sketch of Osia and Innie Keeby's home *(Courier-Journal, Louisville, Kentucky, 18 April 1897)*

Zuma on her porch *(Courtesy of the Amistad Research Center, Tulane University, New Orleans)*

The cable ferry *(Courtesy of the Library of Congress, Prints & Photographs Division. Marion Post Wolcott, photographer)*

Gee's Bend quilters *(Courtesy of the Library of Congress, Prints & Photographs Division. Arthur Rothstein, photographer)*

'Zigzags' *(Courtesy of Loretta Pettway Bennett and the Souls Grown Deep Foundation)*

Dinah's daughter Sally *(Courtesy of the Library of Congress, Prints & Photographs Division. Marion Post Wolcott, photographer)*

Ray Stannard Baker's 1907 photographs of Bougier and her daughter Amanda (American Magazine, *65.6, 1908)*

An anchor (Democrat-Reporter, *Linden, Alabama, 3 August 1933)*

Kossula in his cabin *(Courtesy of the Doy Leale McCall Rare Book and Manuscript Library, Mobile, Alabama. Erik Overbey, photographer)*

Doris Ulmann's 1930 photograph of Kossula *(Courtesy of the Library of Congress, Prints & Photographs Division)*

The old Gothic-style Dallas Country Courthouse *(Courtesy of the Alabama Department of Archives and History)*

Redoshi *(Courtesy of the National Archives and Records Administration)*

Index

Survivors

Index

Index

hold on, 48, 50–1; slave voyage as national/international news, 67–9; voyage east across Atlantic (1860), 29–30; voyage west across Atlantic (1860), 46, 47–60; wreck of discovered (2019), 264, 269

Clotilda African slaves: and the ACS, 150–2; adoption of anglicized names, 140–1, 143; arrival in Alabama, 58, 60, 61–5; Black Belt survivors, 101–16, 160–1, 162–6, 170–80, 205–15; boarding of ship, 43–6; bondage names, 74; bought as arbitrary 'married' couples, 73, 74, 100, 107–8, 160, 258; centenary of arrival in Mobile, 265; clothing of in America, 76, 80–1, 207–8; confused with *Wanderer* survivors, 93, 149, 150, 151, 229, 232; conversions to Christianity, 148, 156–7, 170, 173, 272; Dahomeyan army's assault on Tarkar, 1–3, 8, 11, 13, 186; death of final survivor (Matilda), 259, 261; deaths of in America, 172, 173–4, 183–4, 198–204, 217, 230–1, 234, 235, 241, 252–6, 259, 261; deaths on board *Clotida*, 57–9; destruction of graves of, 266; dispersal of in Alabama River area, 72–6, 78, 79–88, 99–102, 117; enslaved by Rush Jones, 120–1, 122, 132, 133; entrapped in former prisons after liberation, 134, 160–3, 170–80, 205–15, 217, 238–9, 240–1, 255–6; erasure of heritage of, 270; failure to board last 15 prisoners, 46, 50; federal officers search for, 71, 72, 77; first sight of ship, 42; Foster's inspection/selection of in Ouidah, 38–40; at funeral of Meaher (1892), 182–3; held captive at Ouidah, 31–6, 37–41; hidden in swamps near Mount Vernon, 58, 66–7, 69–70, 71, 184–5, 258; hopes for return home, 136–8, 148–52, 185–6, 200–1, 204; immediate post-liberation period, 134–5, 136–44, 145–7, 160–2; importance of in historical record, 270–1; Lewis Quarters in Mobile, 151, 159, 265; liberation of (1865), 96–7, 114–15, 116, 132–3, 134–5, 136, 160–2, 221–2; and local African American communities, 147, 156, 170, 190, 194–5; march of to the sea, 13–15, 257–8; 'Middle Passage' across Atlantic, 40–6, 47–60, 258, 270–1; newspaper used as wallpaper, 241; Phillip's efforts to repatriate, 149–50, 151–2, 200; property/land owned by in Alabama, 142–3, 151, 156, 165–6, 224; psychological links to Yoruba culture/identity, 3–4, 52–3, 174–5, 184, 186, 236, 238, 240–1, 244–6, 255–6, 272; rage and anger of, 76–7, 81–2, 171, 250, 251–2; reunion of survivors at African Town, 179–80, 183; skeletal physique of on arrival in USA, 69–70, 76; solidarity/protective actions on plantations, 81–2, 128–9; stripping of Yoruba identity from, 43–4, 48, 52; taken to Burns Meaher's plantation, 71–2, 117; time spent on deck during voyage, 54–5, 56, 59; transferred to *Czar* (steamboat), 65, 66, 67; undermining of legacies of, 266; and US citizenship, 147, 169; and violence at plantations, 80, 81–2, 102, 107, 110, 128–9; visibility of during Civil War, 92–3; white reporting distorts/misrepresents stories of, 216–17, 227–8, 232–3, 249–50, 256–8; working on Alabama River steamboats, 83–94

Clotilda conspiracy, 22–4, 26, 62–9, 89, 120, 139; deaths of conspiracists, 112–13, 171–2, 182–3; dismissing of as a hoax, 270; Hurston's abandonment of *Barracoon*, 241–2; Montgomery participants, 121–2; publication of *Barracoon* (2018), 242, 264, 269; scholarly documentation of, 236–7

Index

Index

Survivors

Kanko – *cont.*
Kossula visits family of, 253; liberation of (1865), 96, 136; memories of childhood in Tarkar, 4, 6, 7–8, 52, 201–2; owned by Burns Meaher, 75–6, 79–80, 83, 94–6, 182; psychological links to Yoruba culture/identity, 52, 201, 202

Kato, Danieri (Daniel), 244–5

Katrina, Hurricane, 264

Kelley, William Darrah, 145

Kennedy, Renwick Carlisle, 206, 207

King, Coretta Scott, 225

King Jr, Dr. Martin Luther, 223, 225, 233, 239–40, 261–2, 263, 264

Klebsattel, Christian Frederick, 202

Knight, Eulean Marino, 203

Knoxville College (Tennessee), 210

Kolb, Reuben, 212, 214

Komo/Robert Jones, xviii, 135, 145, 146, 151, 224–5, 230

Kossula/Cudjo Lewis, xvii; adopts surname Lewis, 140–1; and African Town, 140–1, 143, 156, 188, 235, 245, 253; arrival in Alabama, 60, 64, 65, 66, 67; becomes US citizen, 147; boarding of the *Clotilda*, 43–4, 46; bronze bust of, 265; Caver talks of Yorubaland with (1933), 250–1; children of, 143–4, 184, 188, 190–2, 194–6, 200, 208, 217, 237; on circus elephants, 159; confronts Meaher, 138–40; conversion to Christianity, 148, 170; death of (26 July 1935), 254; death of wife Abile, 199–200, 208, 235; deaths of children, 184, 194–6, 200, 208, 217; disabled by train accident, 193–4; enslaved to James Meaher, 75, 79–80, 81, 83; finally gives up hope of going home, 253–4; first sight of the *Clotilda*, 42; friendship with Osia Keeby, 46, 58, 137, 204; grandchildren of, 202, 235, 253, 254; grief for parents, 34, 39–40; held captive at Ouidah, 33–4, 35–6, 38–9; hidden in swamps near Mount Vernon,

66; Hurston records story of, 11, 236–8, 241–2; interviewed by Moncur (1886), 182; and Kanko, 8, 202; learns the secret of the Oro, 12, 49; liberation of (1865), 96–7, 136; lifelong memories of homeland, 1, 2, 3, 5, 6, 12–15, 238, 251, 253–4; marries Abile, 143, 157; memories of his kidnapping in West Africa, 1, 2, 11, 13–15, 35, 38–9, 40, 41–2, 186, 258; 'Middle Passage' across Atlantic, 48–9, 51, 54, 55, 56, 57, 58–60; military training, 7; ninetieth birthday celebration and fundraiser, 246, 248, 250; parting from *Clotilda* shipmates, 75; psychological links to Yoruba culture/identity, 52, 184, 186, 202, 236, 238, 245–6; registers to vote, 145; reunion with Redoshi and Matilda (1931), 246–7; second benefit for (1932), 250; as sexton at Mobile Africans' church, 193, 202, 203, 253; as shingle maker, 137; and spiritual songs, 203, 254; three-minute film of, 237, 255; Ulmann photographs, 243; visibility/fame in last decade of life, 236–8, 241–3, 245–6, 253; works on Alabama River steamboats, 83–94

Kpengla (Dahomey's king), 10–11

Kru oarsmen, 41–2, 43, 46

Ku Klux Klan, 115, 118, 153, 168–9, 175, 240, 256; 16th Street Baptist Church bombing, 263; connections with the *Clotilda* captors, 169–70

LaFayette, Jr., Bernard, 240

Lagos, 15, 45, 251

Lanier, Sidney, 166

Lapsley, John Whitfield, 104

Lehman Brothers, 104

Leonidas William Spratt, 24–5, 26–7

Lethe (daughter of Redoshi), 107, 175, 238–9

Liberia, 41, 51, 82, 150–1, 154–6

Liberty Hill (Athens), 162–3, 172, 175, 176

Index

Index

Index

Index

Survivors